THE
SILK
ROAD:
A HISTORY

THE SILK ROAD: A HISTORY

by Irene M. Franck and
David M. Brownstone

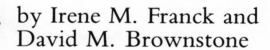

Facts On File Publications
New York, New York ● Oxford, England

THE SILK ROAD: A HISTORY

Library of Congress Cataloging-in-Publication Data

Franck, Irene M.
    The silk road: a history
    1. Silk Road—Description and travel. 2. Franck,
Irene M. I. Brownstone, David M. II. Title.
DS786.F73 1986   951'.5   84-10144

ISBN 0-8160-1122-2 (hardcover)
ISBN 0-948894-19-9 (UK paperback)

Printed in the United States of America

10 9 8 7 6 5 4 3 2

Composition by Maxwell Photographics/Facts On File

CONTENTS

MAPS

I sometimes think of the saga of East and West as if it were music—an orchestrated symphony with solos, mostly sad, here and there, flashes and discords: and ever in the background heard in its quieter moments, moving in a rough repeated harmony, the padded footsteps of the caravans.

—Freya Stark,
Rome on the Euphrates

PREFACE

Often the best book to write is the one you have long sought and never found. This is one such. We have for 20 years lamented the absence of a comprehensive history of the Silk Road—one that ties together the threads of Asian history that link the Mediterranean and China—and have for most of that time been determined ultimately to write one. Our determination has taken a long time to bear fruit. Perhaps this has become a better book for its long period of gestation.

Throughout THE SILK ROAD we have used a great many quotations and excerpts; most of those from the Chinese are drawn from pre-Pinyin translations. Since the book is aimed primarily at a general readership, we have chosen to retain the older style of representing Chinese names, on the theory that a general audience may be unnecessarily confused by the juxtaposition of Pinyin and pre-Pinyin names, and quite put off by the technique of using both, with one in brackets, every time a name is used. In addition, for people and places throughout Eurasia, we have used the form of name that seemed most likely to be familiar to a general English-speaking readership.

We thank the following for allowing us to quote from their copyrighted works:

Excerpts on pp. vi and 7 are from *Rome on the Euphrates*, by Freya Stark, published by John Murray (Publishers) Ltd., London.

Excerpts on pp. 8-9 and 50 are from "Caravan Routes of Inner Asia," by Owen Lattimore, published by the Royal Geographical Society in its *Geographical Journal*, Volume 72, December 1928.

Excerpts on pp. 53, 89 (bottom), 146 (bottom) to 147, 160 (top), 169 (bottom) to 170 (top), and 205 are from *The Rise and Splendour of the Chinese Empire*, by René Grousset, translated from the French by Anthony Watson-Gaudy and Terence Gordon, published by the University of California Press.

Excerpts on pp. 34–36 are from "Travels of the Emperor Mu," by Chêng Tê-K'un, published in the *Journal of the Royal Asiatic Society, North China Branch*, in 1933 and 1934.

Excerpts on pp. 31 and 233–234 are from *The Mongol Mission*, edited by Christopher Dawson, published by Sheed and Ward in 1955, by permission of Eastview Editions of Westfield, New Jersey.

Excerpts on pp. 170 (bottom) to 172, 174–175, 181, and 186–187 are from *In the Footsteps of Buddha*, by René Grousset, translated from the French by J.A. Underwood, by permission of Librairie Plon, Paris.

Excerpt on p. 49 is from *Memories and Adventures*, by Arthur Conan Doyle, published by Little, Brown in 1924.

Excerpt on p. 56–57 is from *The Heartland*, by Stuart Legg, published in the United States by Farrar, Straus & Giroux and in Britain by Secker and Warburg.

The excerpt on p. 80 is from *The Traditional Trade of Asia*, by C.G.F. Simkin, published by the Oxford University Press in 1968.

Excerpts on pp. 40–41 (top) are from *Foreign Trade in the Old Babylonian Period*, by W.F. Leemans, published by E.J. Brill of Leiden in 1960.

Excerpts on p. 91 are from "The Heavenly Horses of Ferghana: A New View," by Arthur Waley, published in *History Today*, May 1955.

Excerpts on pp. 185, 196–197, and 207 are from *The Golden Peaches of Samarkand*, by Edward H. Schafer, published in 1963 by the University of California Press.

Excerpts on pp. 256–258 are from *Medieval Trade in the Mediterranean World*, translated and edited by Robert S. Lopez and Irving W. Raymond, and published by W.W. Norton as part of the Records of Civilization series.

The excerpt on p. 279 is from "Explorations in the Gobi Desert," by Roy Chapman Andrews, published in the *National Geographic Magazine*, Volume 63, June 1933.

Our warmest appreciation goes to the Chappaqua Library and the Westchester Library System, whose people have been so helpful throughout the entire preparation of the work. Thanks to the ever-ready assistance of library director Mark Hasskarl, and his predecessor, Doris Lowenfels; to the library's superb reference staff, including Mary Platt, Paula Peyraud, Helen Barolini, Terry Cullen, and, formerly, Linda Goldstein and Karen Baker; and to Jane McKean and to Marcia Van Fleet and her circulation staff, who handled the steady stream of books from all over the Northeast. Our thanks also to the many people—to us nameless—who staff the Interlibrary Loan system; without their help, independent scholars like ourselves would quail at attempting a history such as this.

Our thanks, too, for the fine work of Mary Racette, who helped with bibliographic research and typed early portions, and to Mary Bunch, who typed the balance of the work on her computer; to our publisher, Edward Knappman, our editor, Kate Kelly, and her assistant, Claire Johnston, who have been most encouraging during the whole course of the book's writing; to book designer Ed Smith, cover designer Duane Stapp, and cartographer Dale Adams, for their unique contributions to the look of the book; and finally to Gene Hawes, Jacques Sartisky, and Ruth Siegel, who gave us very special support and listened to all our Silk Road stories along the way. Few writers have been as fortunate in their friends and professional colleagues as we have been in this work.

Irene M. Franck
David M. Brownstone
Chappaqua, New York

THE SILKEN THREAD

So Marco Polo bade the world listen to his tale of the wonders he had seen on the fabled Silk Road to the East. Writing at the very end of the 13th century, Polo found few to appreciate, much less believe his stories; crude, untutored, and insular, Europeans of late medieval times were incredulous at his tales of ancient cities in the sand, of nomad kings in silken robes on gold-encrusted thrones, of Eastern cities far greater and more magnificent than the finest European cities.

But what neither Polo nor his contemporaries fully realized was that he was a latecomer to this great trans-Asian highway, that he was being granted a precious glimpse of the Silk Road in its last great flowering. For this was the greatest road of the ancient world, the road of Alexander, Darius, Ch'ang Ch'ien, and Genghis Khan.

Traders, pilgrims, fortune hunters, soldiers, adventurers, emigrants, wandering players, and refugees had been traveling the Silk Road for thousands of years before Marco Polo's time. The traditional date for the opening of the Silk Road is 105 or 115 B.C., when the Chinese drove halfway across Asia to link up with a like route running from the Mediterranean to Central Asia. But the Silk Road is actually far older than this, perhaps by 2,000 years or more. It was, for at least 4,000 years, the main avenue of communication between the Mediterranean and China.

Great Princes, Emperors, and Kings, Dukes and Marquises, Counts, Knights, and Burgesses! and People of all degrees who desire to get knowledge of the various races of mankind and of the diversities of the sundry regions of the World, take this Book and cause it to be read to you. For ye shall find therein all kinds of wonderful things, and the divers histories of the Great Armenia, and of Persia, and of the Land of the Tartars, and of India, and of many another country.

—The Book of Ser
Marco Polo, *1298*

The trans-Asian highway was christened *die Seidenstrasse*, the Silk Road, by 19th-century German explorer Baron Ferdinand von Richthofen, although the people of the Byzantine Empire had apparently had a similar name for it, and silk, above all, captured the fancy of these observers, for China kept the secrets of sericulture for at least 2,000 years, and until the sixth century A.D. was the West's sole provider of the luxurious gossamer fabric. The Chinese themselves desired other rare items from the West—sacred green and white jade, twilight-blue lapis lazuli, delicately colored glass, and powerful Central Asian horses, among them—and pushed their imperial borders halfway to the Mediterranean in search of them. But it was silk that most attracted the people of the West, and caused empire after empire to push eastward along the Silk Road.

Though the Silk Road was one of the greatest trading routes in the world, it was also perhaps more significantly an avenue for the exchange of ideas. Some of the most fundamental ideas and technologies in the world—writing, the wheel, weaving, agriculture, riding, among many others—made their way across Asia via this highway. Religion, too, played a key role on the Silk Road. Buddhism and Islam were perhaps most important in shaping the character of the route in their time, but many other religions—Christianity, Zoroastrianism, Manichaeism, Judaism, Mazdaism, Confucianism, Taoism, among them—passed across the face of Asia along this highway.

The Silk Road also provided for exchanges of a rather different sort. Many of the flowers and vegetables that we take so much for granted in the West originated in China or Central Asia and traveled toward Europe along the Silk Road—including roses, azaleas, chrysanthemums, peonies, and camellias; and oranges, peaches, and pears. From the same route, China gained as much as it gave: grapes and grape wine, alfalfa, cucumbers, figs, and pomegranates, along with sesame, chives, coriander, and safflower. Horses and two-humped camels, the mainstays of civilization and trade in Asia, were first domesticated in Central Asia, and came to both East and West Asia along the Silk Road and its northerly cousin, the Eurasian Steppe Route.

In medieval times, while Europe languished, thriving China sent westward, albeit inadvertently, some of the most massive contributions of all: paper and printing (what Michael Edwardes has called the "scaffolding of the modern world"), new thinking and practical developments in medicine, astronomy, and engineering, and weapons, including the crossbow, siege engines, gunpowder, armor, and war chariots.

It is no wonder that this lifeline of Asia, the Silk Road, attracted the attention of some of the world's greatest figures. From the earliest times, the highway held prizes worth the attention of the most ambitious conquerors.

But for all the importance of the Silk Road, it was very far from a natural route. To a geographer, its course lies through what seems an extension of the Sahara Desert into Asia.

From the Mediterranean to the heartland of China is all desert; some parts are more arid than others, it is true, but the whole swath is largely wasteland. Along the way the Earth's crust is, on occasion, crumpled up into lofty plateaus and mountains. Although these too are rather dry, they provide some relief, for moisture gathers and falls on the heights, then forms rivulets, streams, and rivers running down into the desert basins, where the waters often terminate in oases surrounded by sand. The path taken by the Silk Road is, in truth, one of the most inhospitable on this Earth, passing over scorched and waterless land as it links one oasis to the next. Only the importance of this avenue of communication to both East and West kept it open as a major highway for thousands of years.

Not everyone was enamored of the trans-Asian contact, however. The centuries echo with complaints about Eastern luxuries corrupting Westerners and turning them from purer ways. The sixth-century Byzantine Christian Cosmas Indicopleustes was typical in his complaint about "men who cannot be put off from going to the ends of the earth to fetch silk just for greed of money." But still they came. Persians, Greeks, Romans, Arabs, Crusaders, each in turn were seduced from their simpler, more Spartan ways by Phoenician purples, Chinese silks, Arabian perfumes, Indian spices, Central Asian gems. Not only Westerners but also wave after wave of fiercely proud and sometimes ferocious Central Asian nomads were somewhat tamed by silks and other finery.

Yet, in the whole course of its history, few people ever completed a round trip on the Silk Road. The highway, nearly 5,000 miles long, passed through many nations, each jealous of its own territory and of the middleman's profits to be made in trade. None was more jealous than Iran (Persia). And because the Silk Road is funneled through one easily blocked slot across the Iranian Plateau, the local rulers over the centuries were able to bar Easterners and Westerners from making direct contact with each other. Even in the greatest days of the Silk Road—in Han and Roman times, when China delighted in the West's fine colored glass and Rome swathed itself in silken robes—we know of no person who traveled the length of the Silk Road and back. In medieval times, too, when the Moslems ruled in the West and the T'ang dynasty shone in the East, few people could travel the whole route freely. Almost always one section or another of the tortuous route was beset by wars or revolutions.

Only in the late 13th and early 14th centuries, under the Mongols, whom Europeans have generally seen as merely destructive wasters, was most of Asia united under one power, and made safe and secure enough for east-west travel to become almost routine. During this brief *Pax Mongolica*, European traders set out for China with such regularity that some even wrote guidebooks telling what kinds of goods to bring and where to stop along the way to find the best markets—all the way to China. It was Marco Polo who, with his father and uncle, opened the way for these long-distance traders. Within decades, the Silk Road was so frequented that, for one of the few times in its history, some travelers journeyed East and West for the sheer pleasure of it.

Marco Polo's early biographer, John Baptist Ramusio, writing in the mid–16th century, gave some sense of how the Polo family's pioneering efforts were seen by their fellow Italians (as compared with Christopher Columbus's first voyage to the New World):

> . . . if patriotic prejudice delude me not, methinks good reason might be adduced for setting the land journey above the sea voyage [of Columbus]. Consider only what a height of courage was needed to undertake and carry through so difficult an enterprise, over a route of such desperate length and hardship, whereon it was sometimes necessary to carry food for the supply of man and beast, not for days only but for months together. Columbus, on the other hand, going by sea, readily carried with him all necessary provision; and after a voyage of some 30 or 40 days was conveyed by the wind whither he desired to go, whilst the Venetians again took a whole year's time to pass all those great deserts and mighty rivers.

With the Mongols passed the last of the great days of the Silk Road. The nations of Asia fragmented once more, and East and West again held only fanciful, romantic, sometimes utterly outlandish notions of each other. With the fall of Constantinople in the mid–15th century, the Silk Road was decisively cut for a time. Though trans-Asian trade and travel would resume, the Silk Road would never recover. For in that great Age of Discovery, Western Europeans were opening up new sea routes, not only to the New World, but also around Africa and Asia to China. No matter that the voyage took over a year and, especially before mariners learned how to prevent scurvy, cost many lives. The sea route passed through no one's territory, and the profits were shared with no middlemen. So, despite its difficulties, the sea route finally eclipsed the overland highway that had dominated Asia for thousands of years. The silken thread was cut.

In the gray times that followed, even the peoples who lived along the Silk Road seem to have forgotten what greatness their forebears had witnessed. Cities built by great conquerors, nourished by colonists and refugees, enriched by traders, edified by priests and pilgrims, shrank and were often abandoned to the sands.

Then began the long, slow process of rediscovery. Explorers, adventurers, scholars, archaeologists, traders, travelers, gradually uncovered for the world the story of the great highway. The names of the cities they found ring with all the romance of the East: in Western Asia: Antioch, Aleppo, Petra, Palmyra, Tyre, Sidon, Babylon, Baghdad, Ctesiphon; on the high Iranian Plateau: Ecbatana and Rayy; out on the arid steppe of Turkestan: Merv, Samarkand, Bukhara, Bactra, Tashkent; in the mountain spine of the Pamirs: Kashgar and Yarkand; in the dreary desert of the Tarim Basin: Khotan, Shan-shan, Kucha, Karashahr, Loulan, Turfan, Hami; and finally, in China itself: Tunhuang, the Caves of the Thousand Buddhas, and the ancient capitals, Ch'ang-an and Loyang.

The fortunes of these and more cities rose and fell with the Silk Road. Though the highway's great days are long gone, its grandeur is witnessed all along the route, from the ruined, colonnaded avenues of Palmyra, where a merchant queen drank from Cleopatra's cup, to the abandoned ramparts of Bactra, where an army of statues buried in a royal tomb hints at the magnificence of the early Chinese civilization.

The story of the Silk Road is a long, deep look into human history. It is the story of all the peoples of Asia's deserts, steppes, and mountains, and most of all of the caravans that opened and kept alive this great highway across the heart of the continent.

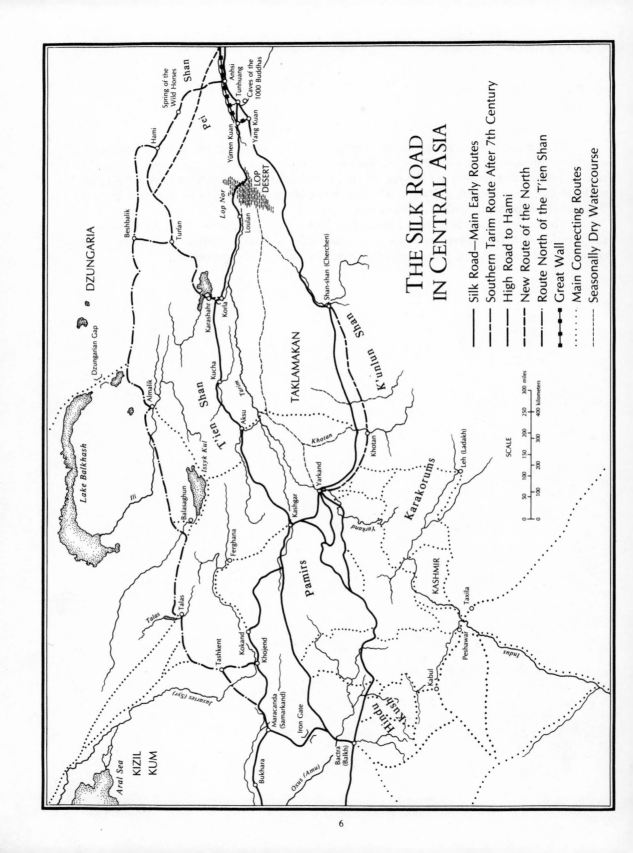

The Silk Road in Central Asia

Silk Road—Main Early Routes
Southern Tarim Route After 7th Century
High Road to Hami
New Route of the North
Route North of the T'ien Shan
Great Wall
Main Connecting Routes
Seasonally Dry Watercourse

SCALE

0   50   100   150   200   250   300 miles
0   100   200   300   400 kilometers

DZUNGARIA

Lake Balkhash

Dzungarian Gap

Ili

Almalik

Issyk Kul

T'ien Shan

Beshbalik

Turfan

Karashahr

Korla

Kucha

Aksu

Tarim

Spring of the Wild Horses

Pei

Shan

Hami

Yümen Kuan

Anhsi
Tunhuang
Caves of the 1000 Buddhas

Yang Kuan

Lop Nor

LOP DESERT

Loulan

TAKLAMAKAN

Shan-shan (Cherchen)

K'unlun Shan

Khotan

Khotan

Yarkand

Kashgar

Ferghana

Balasaghun

Talas

Talas

Tashkent

Kokand

Khojend

Jaxartes (Syr)

Maracanda (Samarkand)

Iron Gate

Bukhara

Oxus (Amu)

Bactra (Balkh)

Pamirs

Yarkand

Karakorums

Leh (Ladakh)

KASHMIR

Taxila

Peshawar

Kabul

Hindu Kush

Indus

KIZIL KUM

Aral Sea

6

CHAPTER TWO

ON THE ROAD

The Silk Road is history now. A sufficiently in-trepid or foolhardy traveler might, of course, attempt to traverse the route today, passing from China through the Soviet Union, Iran, Iraq, and Syria, and possibly through Afghanistan, Turkey, Pakistan, India, Lebanon, Israel, Jordan, and Egypt as well. But even if one were able to steal across closed, hostile borders and pass unscathed through life-threatening war zones, such a traveler would see little of the Silk Road as it was in its great days. Today railroads and motor highways, albeit rough and often treacherous ones, snake across Asia, where once only narrow caravan trails existed. Gone, too, are the continent-wide string of *caravanserais* (palaces of the caravans) that once provided sheltered resting spots for travelers and their animals. Only their ruins remain to mark the line of the old Silk Road.

The once-great caravan cities have changed, too, and not simply because of centuries of obscurity and the uneven penetration of modern technology. The very face of the land is different. Cities along the Silk Road sometimes lie 10 or even 20 miles away from their earlier sites. They shifted to escape the encroaching sands and to follow the receding water supply: exhausted, glacier-fed streams that sank ever-faster into the parched earth. Many of the oasis-cities that once marked the route, especially on the southern rim of the arid Tarim Basin, now lie under tens or even hundreds of feet of sand, buried by the dunes that have been pushing relentlessly over the land. The city of Bactra in northern

. . . no mere river of water can be compared to this perennial stream of the caravans, that has carried a half of human history from stage to stage, from wasteland to wasteland and climate to climate, on the puny strength of men.

—Freya Stark

Afghanistan, where Alexander the Great married the princess Roxane, was once called a paradise on earth, for its fertile site beside a flowing river, fed by glacier run-off from the nearby peaks. Today the river has dried up and the site has been abandoned. In Western Asia, the lower reaches of the Tigris and Euphrates Rivers, toward which the Silk Road pointed from the East, have shifted their courses many times over the centuries. The exact locations of some early cities are unknown; some may lie under today's swamps.

The way of life has changed, too. Stretches that once took days, weeks, or months to traverse are now crossed in hours or days by motor, rail, or air. And peoples who were, in recent centuries, cut off by distance and superstition following the earlier days of continent-wide travel, are once more linked with the world, as even television reaches into remote yurts on the far steppe.

There is only one way to travel the Silk Road today—via imagination. If the present masks the past, we can in our own minds still try to recreate the life of the Silk Road, as it was experienced by the hundreds of thousands of travelers who for many centuries made it one of the world's greatest travel routes—so great that, even today, it is the most glamorous and best-known of all human highways. To help us recreate the feel, sights, sounds, and smells of the Silk Road in history, there remain the words of many extraordinary travelers who have been drawn to this road and moved to write about it.

World travelers like Marco Polo left incomparable records of life along the road during the astonishing and unique age of peace under the Mongols, the *Pax Mongolica*. Chinese annals over the centuries detailed contacts with foreign lands, mixing fact with fancy, as did chronicles from the West. Envoys from all across Eurasia wrote of their attempts to forge alliances over the vast expanse of desert, mountain, and steppe. Pilgrims and religious refugees—Buddhists, Christians, Zoroastrians, Jews, Moslems, among others—left accounts of their tortuous journeys in search of enlightenment. Merchants over the millennia wrote guidebooks, based on their experiences, as they tried to maintain tenuous trade routes across Asia in the face of enormous odds. And, after a hiatus of centuries, explorers like Marc Aurel Stein, Sven Hedin, Baron Ferdinand von Richthofen, and Owen Lattimore rediscovered the historic east-west trail, publishing their finds in a remarkable series of works in the late 19th and early 20th centuries.

The experiences of these rediscoverers are invaluable, for they confirm much of what we have learned from earlier travelers about the pattern of life on the Silk Road. As late as 1928, before the changes of the 20th century had penetrated into innermost Asia, Owen Lattimore was able to write:

If there is any value in the work I was able to do, it is chiefly because what I learned was learned while travelling the ancient routes of Inner Asia with caravans practically the same as those which tramped the same routes hundreds, in fact thousands, of years ago.

The conditions were the same. The dangers of thirst, cold, sand-storm, snow-blizzard and attack by robbers were the same. The caravan men and traders were not different in any important respect. Everything that I saw, felt and heard would have been seen, felt and heard, with little exception by a stranger travelling two hundred or two thousand years ago. I had not even any maps that were of any use in illustrating the daily march. [He noted in passing: "Sketching would have aroused the most awkward suspicions; and both my compasses went out of order."] The problems of direction and distance over which I puzzled every day would have appeared in the same light to Marco Polo, say, or William of Rubruck. I had only one advantage over them—in knowing the language of the people with whom I lived.

Luckily, we, too, are not barred by language, for these works have all been made available to us in English by the incomparable Asian scholars of this and the last century. With their help we can begin to reconstruct, in our imaginations, the life of the Silk Road. Politics and even geography may have changed over this long time, but for much of its history the life experienced by travelers on the Silk Road was remarkably similar. We should perhaps start by following in the footsteps of those travelers who linked East and West with a steady stream of caravans through the ages.

★   ★   ★

From China, travelers would set out from the great walled city of Ch'ang-an, for many centuries China's first or second city, often its capital. Westerners today know the city best for the remarkable army of full-sized terra-cotta statues discovered in 1974 in the tomb of Ch'in Shih Huang Ti, first unifier of China. Already, by 210 B.C., Ch'ang-an was a large capital city; by the seventh century A.D. it would have an estimated 2,000,000 people, as the modern city nearby, Xi'an, does today. Even in those periods when the capital was shifted eastward to Loyang or elsewhere, Ch'ang-an remained the main market city for the Western trade, bridgehead for the Silk Road, a true cosmopolitan city where Westerners and Easterners came together to sell the silks, muslins, gems, fine glass, metalwork, perfumes, spices, tea, and other desirables that were their stock in trade. And Ch'ang-an was long the entry point for new ideas, religions, and peoples from the West.

The city itself lay in the Wei River valley, in the heartland of early China. Spread out over the gentle southern slope of the valley, it exhibited "its walls and palaces at one view like the interior of an amphitheatre," according to one modern observer. Graced by several palaces, theaters, and parks, and by a network of lakes and canals, Ch'ang-an was an attractive and bustling city, a center of trade and industry. Goods were collected there from around the country, often to be refined and processed before being sent in caravans to the West. And from there exotic items imported from Central and Western Asia were distributed on imperial highways to provinces throughout the land.

Through gates like this one in turn-of-the-20th-century Xi'an travelers passed from the sheltered inner city to the open road beyond. (By Sven Hedin, from his *Through Asia*, 1899)

Leaving Ch'ang-an by the west gate, Silk Road travelers would find themselves in the wide and fertile Wei River valley. Here the dominant colors are yellow and green. Green, for the prosperous fields and orchards of the region; Marco Polo would mention the "fine plains planted with mulberries," the trees on whose leaves the precious silkworms feed. Yellow, for loess, the fine dust that for millennia has blown in from the northern steppes and lies packed many feet thick on the ground.

This is the same dust that makes up the red-gold dunes on the lifeless deserts through which the Silk Road passes, but here abundant water turns the loess into some of the most productive farmland in the world. The yellow is so prominent, in both the earth and the air, that the earliest Chinese emperors styled themselves Huang Ti, meaning "Lord of the Earth" or "Lord of the Yellow Loess." The dust was less attractive to travelers, for it constantly blew into eyes, nose, and mouth, and covered them and their gear.

Heading toward inner Asia, travelers would follow the Wei River westward out of Ch'ang-an for some 250 to 300 miles. Here, in about 300 B.C., the Chinese built an early earthworks version of their Great Wall, at what was then the outer limits of their dominion. This part of the westward route, which the Chinese called the Imperial Highway, was well maintained for travelers. The route was sufficiently hard or well-paved in most places to be usable by wheeled vehicles, and it was well patrolled by Chinese officials, seeking to protect travelers and collect whatever taxes were due the emperor. Caravaneers here did not have to carry all their food, for it was gathered from surrounding farms and sold at regular stages along the way. Shelters were also provided, so they were not obliged to sleep out in the open or under tents.

From the valley of the upper Wei, travelers cut slightly northwest, through more forested, hilly terrain, to the upper reaches of the Huang (Yellow) River, just before it begins its great top-hat-shaped loop to the north. Travelers crossed the river at various points during the centuries, in most times near modern Langchow.

The Huang River itself springs from the range of mountains known as the K'unlun, the northern fringe of the great massif made up of the lofty Tibetan Plateau and, farther south, the skyscraping Himalayas. Arcing northwest toward inner Asia, the Silk Road followed the northern outposts of the Kunlun, a range called the Nan Shan (Southern Mountains), for over 200 miles. On this passage travelers moved beyond the moisture-laden winds from the Pacific Ocean. From here westward, virtually the only water to be found was in streams and wells fed by glacier and snowmelt from Central Asia's lofty mountain barriers.

The route along the foothills of the Nan Shan traversed what was, in effect, an elongated oasis, watered by a small river, the Sulo, beyond which lay a great expanse of desert, the outer reaches of the infamous Gobi. With plentiful grazing lands and fertile fields, this strip of land, a panhandle known as the Kansu Corridor, was the natural thoroughfare to the West. So vital was this region that China extended the Great Wall to enclose it as soon as direct relations were opened with the West, about a century before the time of Christ. From the top of the Huang River's northern loop, the Great Wall ran down to and along the Kansu Corridor. Watchtowers and lookouts were stationed all along the way, and troops were generally on call in case of trouble.

At the end of the Kansu Corridor, between civilization and wilderness, stood the frontier outpost of Tunhuang. Long a center of Buddhist culture, Tunhuang was often known as the City of the Sands, for here travelers faced the great dunes of drifting sand that would characterize much of the landscape for over 1,500 miles. Nearby were the famous Caves of the Thousand Buddhas, a great loess cliff honeycombed with monks' cells. Here, in 1907, Marc Aurel Stein found a treasure-house full of manuscripts, including the Diamond Sutra, the world's oldest dated printed book (actually a scroll), from about 868 A.D. (Printed fragments from a century earlier have been found elsewhere.)

At the last major stop within China's fortified barrier, Tunhuang, travelers prepared for a very different kind of travel. Now they were on the edge of the desert—the Flowing Sands, as the Chinese called it. Oasis farmers in these parched lands were incredulous that anyone could farm *without* irrigation, relying on rain alone to water their crops. Once beyond Tunhuang, travelers would have to carry all their food and enough water to get them from well to well, sometimes days apart.

Animals, too, had to be provided with food and water, for little grazing was to be found in the wasteland ahead. Here camels proved their value; their prodigious stamina allowed them to travel vast distances on very little food or water. Horses and donkeys were also used on the Silk Road, partly because they could carry heavier loads.

But camels were the mainstay for Silk Road travelers. In Central Asia these were two-humped Bactrian camels (not the one-humped Arabian ones) that were able to stand not only the heat of the desert day but also the bitter-cold nights and freezing winters. Pack animals often could scent water from great distances, and could warn of the treacherous sandstorms that might suffocate or bury the unwary traveler. As the Chinese chronicle *Pei Shih* described:

> *When such a wind is about to arrive, only the old camels have advance knowledge of it, and they immediately stand snarling together, and bury their mouths in the sand. The men always take this as a sign, and they too immediately cover their noses and mouths by wrapping them in felt. This wind moves swiftly, and passes in a moment, and is gone, but if they did not so protect themselves, they would be in danger of sudden death.*

In sandstorms on the Taklamakan, travelers often had to cover their faces to prevent suffocation. (By Sven Hedin, from his *Through Asia*, 1899)

Water, food, and sandstorms were not the only problems that travelers faced on the Silk Road. Once beyond China's Great Wall, they were exposed to rapacious marauders. Though the land was too desolate to support a large population of either nomads or bandits, small raiding parties could exist very well, drawing water from isolated waterholes and garnering necessities and luxuries from passing caravans. As a result, only rare travelers, mostly pilgrims or royal messengers traveling fast on urgent business, ventured alone into the lands of inner Asia. Most joined together in large caravans, often with hundreds of camels and with armed escorts. Though numbers gave some protection, the size of the party and their loads also made the caravan more vulnerable, for it moved slowly. Once into the Flowing Sands, wheeled vehicles were left behind and everyone, not just the pack animals, walked.

Throughout history, most travelers, including modern ones like Stein and Lattimore, have traversed the Silk Road on foot. Beasts of burden—variously camels, donkeys, asses, yaks, or horses, depending on the climate and terrain—were far too precious to spare for the comfort of travelers. They were required to carry vital supplies, especially food and water, and trade goods or tribute. They were ridden only in extremis, for on their health depended the safety and survival of the caravan. Even in modern times, when explorers first began to take an occasional motorized vehicle into Central Asia, the vehicles were often reserved for essential equipment, rather than passengers, while camels carried the all-important supply of gasoline, to fuel the machines in the wasteland. So the whole party walked. The pace was excruciatingly slow, not a brisk trot but a crawl set by the load-bearing animals—quite different from the speed of mounted, lightly geared nomadic raiding parties.

★   ★   ★

Beyond Tunhuang, westbound travelers faced the deserts of the Tarim Basin. Largely enclosed by icy, barren mountain ranges—the K'unlun range in the south, the Pamirs in the west, the T'ien Shan (Celestial Mountains) in the north, the low Pei Shan (Northern Mountains) in the northeast—the Tarim is cut off from the life-giving rains of the oceans and seas around Asia. It is one of the driest, most desolate lands in the world. The deserts here are not "tame" deserts, such as those of Western Asia, in which the peoples of the Bible wandered, in which whole tribes of nomads and their herds can live out their lives on the move. The deserts that form the heart of the Tarim Basin are true home to no man, and to precious few plants and animals.

The largest of the basin's deserts is the dreaded Taklamakan, a region 600 miles across, east to west, by 250 miles, north to south, formed of shifting red-gold dunes—some over 300 feet high—that dwarf and suffocate all life. Occasional stunted vegetation—tamarisks, wild poplars, or reeds—live along the edges of old watercourses. But dead stumps are a more common feature of the landscape, often packed around by drifted sands into what are called tamarisk cones, some over 50 feet high. In the eastern portion of the Tarim Basin is a smaller, even more hostile wasteland, the Lop (Salt) Desert, made up of hard-packed clay and salt-encrusted plains, the remains of a once-great inland salt sea.

The little moisture to be found in the Tarim Basin comes from streams of snowmelt that rush down the mountains through glacier-carved, water-scoured gorges to disappear in the desert below. Along the southern rim of the Tarim, these mountain streams terminate in a series of widely spaced oases. Waters from the western and northern mountains combine to form a slightly more substantial river, the Tarim, along the northern arc of the oval basin. This is sometimes swelled by the Khotan River, whose seasonally dry watercourse cuts north through the Taklamakan. It was the Tarim River that once filled the ancient sea called the Lop Nor (Salt Sea), in historic times largely a salt marsh. The Lop Nor's remnant today is so shrunken that a change of season will sometimes change the course of the streams that feed it and, therefore, its location. For this reason modern archaeologists dubbed Lop Nor the "Wandering Lake."

The difficulties of crossing this desert region are well described by Marco Polo:

> [This desert is] all composed of hills and valleys of sand, and not a thing to eat is to be found on it. But after riding for a day and a night you find fresh water, enough mayhap for some 50 or 100 persons with their beasts, but not for more. And all across the Desert you will find water in like manner, that is to say, in some 28 places altogether you will find good water, but in no great quantity; and in four places also you find brackish water. Beasts there are none; for there is nought for them to eat. But there is a marvelous thing related of this Desert, which is that when travelers are on the move by night, and one of them chances to lag behind or to fall asleep or the like, when he tries to gain his company again he will hear spirits talking, and will suppose them to be his comrades. Sometimes the spirits will call him by name; and thus shall a traveler ofttimes be led astray so that he never finds his party. And in this way many have perished. Sometimes the stray traveler will hear as it were the tramp and hum of a great cavalcade of people away from the real line of road, and taking this to be their own company they will follow the sound; and when day breaks they find that a cheat has been put on them and that they are in an ill plight. Even in the daytime one hears those spirits talking. And sometimes you shall hear the sound of a variety of musical instruments, and still more commonly the sound of drums. Hence in making this journey 'tis customary for travelers to keep close together. All the animals too have bells at their necks, so that they cannot easily get astray. And at sleeping-time a signal is put up to show the direction of the next march.
> So thus it is that the Desert is crossed.

Desert travelers around the world have described the illusory sounds and mirages that can lure the unwary to their deaths. Many desert peoples have labeled these illusions as the work of evil spirits, but modern scientists think the desert sounds are caused by sharp temperature changes in the almost cloudless climate which set off avalanches from the towering dunes. Whatever the reason, these sounds and mirages posed both the image and reality of danger to travelers in Central Asia.

By rights, such a region, so hostile to life, so cut off from the outside world, should have had no claim to the attention of the world. Yet, because it lay on the main road across Asia, the Tarim Basin was a key section of the Silk Road. Over the centuries, travelers opened a route across it as fragile as a silken thread, inching from oasis to oasis on the hostile pathway between East and West.

★   ★   ★

Travelers who decided to make the journey regardless chose at Tunhuang whether to follow the southern or northern route around the rim of the Tarim. The southern route was much the more difficult because its oases were widely spaced, but it was often preferred because the very depth of its desolation discouraged roving parties from attempting to attack or settle in the region. Nor were travelers much exposed to marauders from the K'unlun, for there were few natural routes through the mountains, most stream gorges being so precipitous as to be impassable. Leaving the protection of the Great Wall through the Yang Kuan gate, travelers would arc slightly southwestward, following the Tarim Basin's oval curve. This route the Chinese called the Nan Shan Pei Lu (the Road North of the Southern Mountains).

The journey on this portion of the Silk Road consisted of a series of short, but often extremely hazardous passages from one walled oasis-city to the next. Out on the road, travelers were forced to camp in the open, on bedrolls and under light tents. Between cities, the caravan often traveled as quickly as possible, for the survival of both humans and animals depended on arriving at the next well and finding sufficient water. Water being so vital and in such short supply, travelers—among them modern explorers like Stein and Hedin—sometimes preferred to travel this route in winter, when they could carry ready supplies of water in the form of blocks of ice. In warmer seasons they often traveled during the cool night, setting their course by the stars. Some caravan masters and guides even studied in nautical schools in India, for the techniques of stellar navigation were the same for sailor and caravaneer. During the day, then, the party could use their tents for shelter from the most direct rays of the sun. Once at an oasis, behind protective walls again, the party would rest, sometimes for a week or two, recuperate from the strain of forced marches, repair their gear, replenish their supplies, and prepare to set out again.

The first major rest and reprovisioning city on the southern route was Shan-shan (Cherchen). Marco Polo noted that the "whole of the province is sandy, and so is the road all the way . . . and much of the water that you find is bitter and bad," though he noted that some is fresh and sweet. An index of the desolation surrounding Shan-shan is given in a tale he related:

> *When an army passes through the land, the people escape with their wives, children, and cattle a distance of two or three days' journey into the sandy waste; and knowing the spots*

*where water is to be had, they are able to live there, and to keep their cattle alive, whilst
it is impossible to discover them; for the wind immediately blows the sand over their track.*

Clearly this was not a land to be entered lightly by the uninitiated. Experienced caravan masters and guides were always eagerly sought out and hired by Silk Road travelers.

Further along on the southern route travelers came to the great city of Khotan. More than a mere provisioning center, Khotan was a major cultural center in Central Asia, important not only because of its position on the Silk Road, but also because it lay near the head of a mountain route over the lofty Karakorum Mountains into Kashmir and India, roughly the route taken by the modern Karakorum Highway between China and Pakistan. High and cold—the Karakorum Pass itself is over 18,000 feet high—the region is also dry and bleak, as reflected by the name Karakorum (Black Gravel). Still this was an important route for many centuries, being the main pathway by which Buddhism reached the heart of Central Asia from its homeland in India. Well-watered by the Khotan River, the city was always pleasant and prosperous. Marco Polo found that: "Everything is to be had there in plenty."

What interested the Chinese especially was the green and white jade found in abundance in mountain riverbeds near Khotan. Long before silk was sent westward to the Mediterranean, jade was imported along the southern Tarim route to China. Travelers headed for India would sometimes go straight through the mountains just beyond Khotan. More often they would continue on the southern route to the cities of Yarkand or Kashgar into the less precipitous Pamirs, then cut back southeastward, once past the highest of the Hindu Kush, and follow the natural corridor through what is now Afghanistan and Pakistan onto the Indian plains, a route used by invaders through the ages.

★　　★　　★

Travelers taking a route from Tunhuang north of the Taklamakan followed a different course to the Pamirs. Leaving the Great Wall by the Yümen Kuan, widely known as the Jade Gate, for a time they followed a course roughly parallel with the southern route and across a like desert, but beyond lay the absolutely lifeless Lop Desert. Travelers crossing the salt bed had to carry all their water and food, for none would be found on the dead ground. On the far side of the desert, travelers in early times would find salt marshes, fringes of the receding Lop Nor, with at least some moisture and vegetation. On the shores of the marsh lay the oasis city of Loulan (dubbed City of the Dead), which gave shelter and succor to travelers. During the years when this was the main route westward, China extended its line of watchtowers, beacon stations, and forts from the Great Wall out past Loulan. These provided both protection and food, wrung out of the lightly watered ground.

Beyond Loulan travelers found yet more sandy desert until they reached Korla, where waters from the nearby T'ien Shan joined those from the more distant western mountains, providing an oasis valley with plentiful grazing and easy traveling. The Chinese called this route the T'ien Shan Nan Lu (the Road South of the Celestial Mountains) or the Route of the Center. Unfortunately, by the third century A.D., at the latest, the trickle of water that had given life to the Loulan region receded. The whole of inner Asia grew drier, and the city, no longer an oasis, had to be abandoned.

Travelers who wished to go north of the Taklamakan then had to search out other alternatives, circling north from the Kansu Corridor and then west to the few oases in the land, making a wide detour, before rejoining the old main route at Korla. The way was difficult, for beyond the Great Wall lay an arm of the vast Gobi Desert, which rims northern China. The Chinese historian Ma Twan-lin described the desert there:

> . . . you have to cross a plain of sand, extending for more than 100 leagues. You see nothing in any direction but the sky and the sands, without the slightest trace of a road; and travellers find nothing to guide them but the bones of men and beasts and the droppings of camels. During the passage of this wilderness you hear sounds, sometimes of singing, sometimes of wailing; and it has often happened that travellers going aside to see what these sounds might be have strayed from their course and been entirely lost; for they were voices of spirits and goblins.

Dangerous as this desert was, however, the distance to oases on its far side was shorter than on the desiccated Loulan route.

★   ★   ★

Travelers would leave the protection of the Kansu Corridor and the Great Wall about 90 miles short of Tunhuang, at the city of Anhsi, sometimes called the Melon City, for the fruit often grown in the oases of the region. Cutting northwest across the Gobi they found several well-watered oases near the low range of the Pei Shan. The first of these oases was a fertile basin variously called Hami, Kumul, and I-wu; and this northwest route was sometimes called the High Road to Hami. From Hami the route followed the line of hills north and then southwest to Turfan, a large basin that lies some 300 feet below sea level. Turfan is so favored by mountain run-off that it has over the centuries been both an agricultural center and a haven for dust-weary travelers. Their view of the region is reflected by an alternate Chinese name for the route, the Road Through the Willows. Similarly, the first main oasis in the Turfan Basin was early named the Dragon Spring. As Marc Aurel Stein commented:

> Its name [was] an appropriate Chinese designation for the life-giving fountain in the midst of a stony wilderness. Chinese fancy has always been . . . prone to associate striking natural features with the celestial monsters . . .

Turfan also occupies a strategic position, lying at the head of one of the main mountain passes by which travelers have often passed from the steppes beyond the T'ien Shan to the inner lands of the Tarim Basin. For nomadic raiders, Turfan was attractive in itself, but it was also an extremely useful base from which to attack the lucrative trade of the Silk Road or to invade China itself. In more peaceful times, migrant laborers have traveled from Turfan through the T'ien Shan's passes to pick crops in the cooler mountainside fields, in between the two growing seasons that are usual in warmer Turfan. (Turfan is, indeed, so hot in summer that the local nobility often moved to subterranean chambers to avoid the heat—as their nomadic counterparts would ascend the mountainside for the same purpose.)

Some travelers bound for Turfan from China chose a different path, leaving the Great Wall even further east at Yümen, cutting more sharply across the desert and bypassing the Hami oasis. This New Route of the North was especially useful when the oases of Hami or Turfan were in dispute or under direct attack. But the Hami route to Turfan was generally preferred, especially for large parties who had to be sure of plentiful water.

Whichever route they took to Turfan, travelers leaving it would angle southwest, follow the foothills of the T'ien Shan to the favored oasis of Karashahr, join the Loulan route at the crossroads city of Korla, and then pass westward to the large oasis centers of Kucha and Aksu. When no central power controlled inner Asia, these oasis centers—like Turfan and Hami—were often petty independent states, each with its own complement of walled cities. Travelers in those times moved at considerable difficulty and expense, for each city through which they passed collected taxes in cash or kind on all trade goods, generally at a specified rate per pack load. Travelers were obliged to pay, for they needed the shelter and supplies offered by these cities in an otherwise inhospitable land. Well-supplied travelers deliberately bypassed oasis centers like Hami, if they could, to avoid both duties and exorbitant charges for supplies. But when inner Asia was part of a larger empire, the central government usually rationalized the tax burden on merchants and offered protection, fresh animals, and plenty of food at reasonable prices along the way, often through colonists sent out as soldier-farmers.

Whoever was in power, Kucha and Aksu were important centers on the northern route through the Tarim Basin. Kucha was often an administrative center for the region, under the Chinese, the Turks, and other powers. Several passes through the T'ien Shan feed into the Kucha region. Aurel Stein noted that: "All of them, though closed by snow during part of winter and early spring, are practicable with laden animals during the rest of the year." Through these passes streamed traders from the northern steppes, come to share in the Silk Road trade, exchanging their gold, furs, hides, and horses for the fine works of the settled peoples.

Yet these passes, being both high and narrow, were easier to defend than those north of Turfan and Hami, making Kucha less vulnerable to wanton attack. The Kucha region itself was a kind of rampart, not against the northern nomads but against the desert to the south.

Occupying a wide plain along a slender river, Aurel Stein noted that it:

> . . . *acts as a natural fosse or fence against that advance of the drifting sand with which the proximity of the great dune-covered area of the Taklamakan threatens outlying cultivated areas . . . whenever the irrigation of these is reduced from physical or human causes.*

Travelers also found in Kucha a convenient rest and repair area. Whether they had started from Loulan or Turfan, it was roughly halfway across the basin on the way to the Pamirs. Even in modern times, which are much drier than in the early days of the Silk Road, travelers have noted with pleasure Kucha's pleasant orchards and fields, and its lively suburban bazaars.

The region of Aksu, the next main center westward on the route, was also a crossroads. Like Kucha, Aksu is situated on a tributary of the Tarim River, though today it is much drier and less irrigable than in the past. Some passes through the nearby T'ien Shan are so low and gentle that they could be traversed easily by carts. Perhaps more to the point, the seasonally dry Khotan River, the one main watered belt that crosses the central Taklamakan, directly connects Aksu with Khotan, linking the northern and southern routes across the desert.

Whichever road travelers took from China, whether the southern Tarim route or what Stein calls "the great Central Asian high road," they had to cross the Pamirs, the spine of Asia, to reach the West. The two roads that had divided around the Tarim came together in the foothills of the Pamirs, sometimes at Yarkand but more often at Kashgar. Kashgar's site is superb. The northerly T'ien Shan and the southerly K'unlun curve around and, with the Pamirs, form a continuous line of peaks, enclosing Kashgar in the westernmost point of the Tarim. Stein noted "the magnificent panorama of glittering snowy ranges" surrounding Kashgar on three sides.

Here Silk Road travelers faced the forbidding eastern rampart of the Pamirs. Caravaneers from Ch'ang-an had been climbing slowly but steadily toward the watershed of Asia, and by the time they reached Kashgar they were already about 5,000 feet above sea level. But some of the Pamirs shoot up over 25,000 feet, high and difficult enough to attract some of the world's most adventurous mountain climbers—and to cause the Persians to call this region "the Roof of the World." The Chinese named these mountains the Tsung-Ling (Onion Mountains), blaming that plant for the dizziness and nausea that were, in truth, induced by the thin air on the heights. Luckily for travelers who were not seeking the artificial frisson of scaling ice-covered peaks, the barren east face of the range is shot through with wide, accessible passes. "Pamirs," indeed, refers to these wide upland valleys that lie "at the foot of mountain peaks." Several were apparently used by Silk Road caravans, with no single one predominating.

The first part of the climb west from Kashgar or Yarkand was the steepest and most difficult. The road was sometimes extremely precipitous and difficult for laden animals. Here, as in other difficult mountain reaches, the pack animals might be unloaded and led across narrow passages, with the goods being carried in short stretches by human porters. In some places the track was artificially widened so as to accommodate more readily camels and other pack animals. On his first passage through the Pamirs from the east, Aurel Stein noted:

> *By the time we had reached easier ground on plateaus overlooking the snout of the large glacier at the valley bottom, I felt duly impressed with the fact that I had passed the great mountain barrier of ancient Imaos, which divided Ptolemy's "Inner" and "Outer Scythia."*

Once over the watershed of Asia, travelers had easier going, along more gently sloping plateaus and wide river plains. Some of these natural thoroughfares, 6 to 10 miles wide, could even be used by cart traffic. It was often bitter cold on the heights, however. On his trip through the Pamirs, Stein met with a late-July snowstorm and found that the temperature dropped below freezing overnight. Even so, the caravan trail was, he judged, usable for most or all of the year. The river valleys provided plentiful water and grazing for passing caravans. Permanent settlements of herders and farmers were to be found in the wide valleys up to 9,000

En route through the Pamirs in late winter, this party takes a sounding through ice of the depth of a lake they are crossing. (By Sven Hedin, from his *Through Asia*, 1899)

feet high, and in the warmest months nomads lived even higher. Travelers therefore could find shelter and supplies all along the route for eight to nine months a year; and even in winter they had only about 70 miles, or three easy marches, over the watershed to reach the first permanent settlement on the far side. Stein suggested that some routes now closed during the winter months could be crossed, as like passes are elsewhere, if there were "sufficient traffic to tread a track through the snow and keep it clear," as there would have been during the great days of the Silk Road.

After a long trek through the parched Tarim and the equally arid eastern Pamirs, travelers found on the far side of the mountains a land of rivers and gardens, which some have called the Babylonia of the East. In the cities of these well-watered foothills, inhabitants were not content simply to reside on the riverbanks. They built an elaborate system of canals to bring water into all parts of their cities—in a few cities to nearly every house. The river valleys travelers had followed through the Pamirs led them down into this favored land, their choice of valley varying with their choice of destination, and with political conditions at the time. The two main rivers—the Oxus (now called the Amu Darya) and the Jaxartes (Syr Darya)—drop out of the Pamirs and curve gradually northward to empty in the Aral Sea. (During some centuries water from the Oxus flowed partly westward into the Caspian Sea.) Along the way these waterways are joined by myriad smaller streams, some of which no longer reach the great rivers, but die in the sands of the surrounding dry lands.

Generally called Western or Russian Turkestan, because in modern times the Turkish language and culture became paramount, this region includes all or part of the Soviet republics of Turkmenia, Uzbekistan, and Kazakhstan and the northern strip of Afghanistan. (By contrast, the Tarim Basin is called Eastern or Chinese Turkestan, sometimes Kashgaria or Sinkiang, and is today Chinese territory.) That these lands are known to few travelers today is testimony to the modern political isolation of the region, for here was one of the great crossroads of Asia, where the Silk Road intersected with the main north-south route between the Eurasian Steppe in the north and the Indian plains in the south. The cities which dot the river valleys of this great meeting ground grew to prominence largely because traders from around the continent met there to exchange goods and, not so incidentally, ideas.

Silk Road travelers who wished to take advantage of the rich trade with India, would generally head through the Pamirs toward Bactra, often from Yarkand or Kashgar. Other mountain routes had earlier split off to head over the Karakorums or the high Hindu Kush to Kashmir and India. But Bactra was at the head of the Indian Grand Road, the main invasion route, trading route, and travel route across the northwest frontier onto the plains of the Punjab. The city of Bactra was roughly the midway point on the Silk Road, but it was also the bridgehead on the main road into India. Antioch, Damascus, Babylon, Baghdad, Rome, Byzantium, Ch'ang-an—all these names are more familiar to the modern ear than that of Bactra. Yet for well over 1,500 years, Bactra (later called Balkh) was the peer of all these great cities.

Its importance is reflected in its history. One tradition has it that Zoroaster was born in Bactria. Later Alexander the Great took a bride here, in one of the most famous marriages in history. Still later, it was a major center of Buddhism, receiving pilgrims from all across East Asia. Later yet, it became a jewel in the necklace of cities that was strung across Moslem Asia, its greatness finally destroyed by Genghis Khan. Even in its decline, it was visited by the great travelers of Mongol times, including Marco Polo and Ibn Battuta. Beautifully placed on the banks of a tributary to the upper Oxus, Bactra was capital of the "land of a thousand cities." Though the site is now abandoned, since the stream that once watered it runs there no longer, its present obscurity in northern Afghanistan belies its great importance in Eurasian history.

★   ★   ★

From Bactra, westbound travelers would head across the dusty steppe toward the key caravan city of Merv, in ancient times called Antiocheia Margiana—that is, Antioch in the Persian province of Margiana—one of the many cities founded or at least developed by Alexander the Great. Other Silk Road travelers reached Merv by a different route, some by the relatively short mountain crossing from Kashgar to the land of Ferghana, on the upper reaches of the Jaxartes River. Long a prime breeding ground for horses and camels—its fertile plains grew high, abundant crops of their favorite fodder, alfalfa—Ferghana played an important role in China's opening of the eastern half of the Silk Road. As westbound travelers emerged from Ferghana, an elongated strip of land surrounded on three sides by mountains, they found themselves on an open plain, a tongue of the great, wide steppeland of Eurasia. Here, in a line stretching westward toward the Iranian Plateau, were numerous caravan cities, among them Samarkand (earlier called Maracanda) and Bukhara.

Exposed to raids from both the steppelands of the north and the mountainous regions in all other directions, Samarkand and Bukhara, like Bactra and most other cities of any size in the region, were heavily fortified. Often they had a capacious outer wall, which included fields, villages, suburbs, gardens, and private castles, and then a smaller inner wall enclosing the heart of the city. Here were often found, in later times at least, a citadel and perhaps a palace with a moat and drawbridge, and a major temple, the religion varying over time. Canals, large and small, brought water directly into the heart of each city, and in later times a complex arrangement of dams, locks, and sluices allowed inhabitants to divert overflow away from the city during the flood season.

Bazaars were spread throughout the city environs, with the most important ones often placed near the gates that served the main roads, such as the Silk Road, and near the places of worship, where people always gathered. From very early times, special quarters were provided for itinerant merchants. Often merchants from other cities or countries would band together and set up a caravanserai, here sometimes called a *rabat*, providing shelter and warehousing for their common use. Similar arrangements were made for the armed escorts or residential regiments who were responsible for safety on the roads and who manned the watchtowers that were built every half-mile or so in the city's outer wall.

These cities were, in their day, settlements of considerable size. The ruins of Bactra are estimated to extend over some 16 miles. Samarkand may have had a population of over half a million at some points in its early history. Even a lesser-known early city, Paykand, in the region of Bukhara, is said to have had 3,000 rabats. Clearly there was an enormous amount of traffic in this region; the road between Samarkand and Bukhara was for good reason sometimes called the Royal Road or the Golden Road, skirting the arid steppe, the Kara Kum (Black Sands), and hemmed in by mountains and plateaus. Transoxiana, this favored land east of the Oxus River, was a proper meeting place of cultures.

One common alternative route across the Pamirs was from Yarkand to the upper reaches of the Oxus River. Indeed, in the first century A.D., the Greco-Roman writer Ptolemy wrote of a place perhaps in this region called the Stone Tower, where Western, Indian, and Chinese traders routinely met to exchange their wares. Where this Stone Tower was is unclear. Its Turkish translation, *Tashkurgan*, is the name of many cities in the region, and many other "Stone Towers" may have existed earlier. It may have been somewhere near the headwaters of the Yarkand River.

Travelers heading westward from China had still another alternative: They could avoid the Taklamakan and the Pamirs altogether by circling right around the enclosing ring of mountains. From eastern oasis centers like Hami and Turfan, they would cut through the low Pei Shan into the semi-arid Dzungarian Basin. Once there they could travel westward by crossing a relatively modest mountain spur or by arcing around it through the Dzungarian Gap, the ancient passageway between the Dzungarian Mountains and the Altai (Golden) Mountains to the north. They then found themselves on the north side of the T'ien Shan, from which flowed the many rivulets that gave the region its name: the Land of the Seven Streams.

The Ili River, which gathered these waters and carried them into Lake Balkhash to the north, provided a fine thoroughfare for Silk Road travelers. On the way they passed several small cities, notably Beshbalik, often administrative center for the region, and Almalik, a fertile town of prosperous fields and fruit orchards. Attacks from the steppe kept these cities from being too many or too large. Beyond these lay the Issyk Kul (Warm Lake), so named because it did not freeze, being high in salt content. This route, which the Chinese called the T'ien Shan Pei Lu (Road North of the Celestial Mountains), followed the curve of the T'ien Shan and then the adjoining Pamirs west and then south, carrying travelers to Western Turkestan's caravan cities of Samarkand and Bukhara.

If the world were a peaceful place, this would have been the main route of the Silk Road, for on it travelers met no fearsome deserts like the Taklamakan, no piercing heights like those in the Pamirs, and no necessity to walk the roads, for wagons could readily be used on the flat lands. True, there were desert stretches, such as those of the Kizil Kum (Red Sands) that lay between the Oxus and the Jaxartes and the Kara Kum (Black Sands) beyond, but these were far easier to manage than the wastelands of the Tarim. And the ability to use wagons meant that travelers could carry sufficient supplies of water, without hopelessly overburdening the caravan. In short, this was by far the most attractive route from China to Western Turkestan.

But, since peace is seldom found in this world, the Road north of the Celestial Mountains was favored for only a very few times in history, notably under China's T'ang dynasty and under the Mongols, when the great powers of Asia were sufficiently strong and determined to assure the safety of travelers beyond the natural defenses of the mountains. For the rest of the time—that is, for most of history—Silk Road travelers were forced to follow the tortuous route through the Tarim and the Pamirs, the very difficulty of the enclosing mountains and deserts ensuring a measure of safety from marauders that could rarely be found north of the T'ien Shan.

By whichever route westbound travelers reached the far side of the Pamirs—the traditional dividing line between East and West Asia—they headed toward Merv. In truth, these were seldom the same travelers who had departed from China, for people generally traveled only 1,000 to 2,000 miles, making their trades or visiting shrines or foreign palaces and then returning to their homelands. Many people may have wished to travel the full length of the Silk Road, but most were barred from doing so. Marco Polo was able to make the journey only because the Mongols in the 14th century controlled virtually the whole of the route. Oddly enough, China—at times in history so very xenophobic—sometimes opened the Silk Road to travelers of other nations. During the glittering T'ang dynasty, Westerners were welcome in Ch'ang-an, and their clothes, music, art, and religious beliefs sparked the most popular fashions of the time. The main barriers to travel on the Silk Road for many centuries lay on the Iranian Plateau. Cities like Bactra and Tashkurgan became international markets, not simply way stations, partly because the peoples of the West wanted to monopolize traffic on the route, to increase their profits. If they often succeeded handsomely, they also kept the full road closed to others.

The Iranian Plateau itself is roughly a raised triangle pointing southward toward Arabia, with mountain ranges along the three sides and an almost lifeless desert in the middle, the salty remains of a once vast sea. Caravans were forced to follow the mountain ranges, for only there would they find the necessary water. The Silk Road followed the east-west range, the Elburz Mountains, which runs along the southern coast of the Caspian Sea, forming the base of the upside-down triangle. In some eras travelers, especially merchants, tried to avoid the Iranian Plateau by swinging north to the eastern shore of the Caspian Sea, and then crossing the sea to the region of modern Baku. They followed the valley of the Araxes River to the southeast corner of the Black Sea, reaching their European destinations without passing through Persian territory. Others circled northwest around the Caspian and arrived on the north coast of the Black Sea. But often the peoples who ruled the Iranian Plateau were strong enough to force most traffic on the old Silk Road to cross their territory.

Persia had its own products to add to the mix of those that were passed along the Silk Road. The peoples of the plateau relied on the lowlanders of the Near East for finery; in return, they offered vital raw materials, for their otherwise desolate land was rich in natural resources, especially metals and gems. They were also prime breeders of horses, and long supplied the peoples of the West with steeds, as the breeders of Ferghana supplied the East. This single, main east-west route of the Silk Road was important to highlander and lowlander alike.

As a result, from very early times a string of walled cities lined this section of the Silk Road. Soldiers, foreign merchants, and artisans were among the prime inhabitants; many of the cities actually came into existence because of the trade. Crossing the Iranian Plateau from Merv, travelers came to Hecatompylos (the City of a Thousand Gates), once a capital of the region. As the route wound through the Elburz Mountains, travelers were funneled through a narrow pass called the Caspian Gates, before emerging at the city of Rhagae (later Rayy), near modern Teheran. Northwest of here (near modern Qazvin) lay Alamut, main fortress of the Assassins, where the "Old Man of the Mountain" led a cult that for over two centuries spread its power throughout the region by the use of murder and terror.

Caravanserais like this one in Persia offered shelter and provisions to Silk Road travelers for thousands of years. (By Engelbert Kaempfer, c. 1680, MS. Sloane 5232, British Library)

On the far western side of the Iranian Plateau was Ecbatana (modern Hamadan), yet another capital of one of the many kingdoms that contended for control of the western part of the Silk Road. From here, the main road wound down through the Zagros Mountains, the western fringe of the plateau, to the lowlands, where a tongue of the mountains forces the Tigris River close to the Euphrates. Here, at the "waist" of Mesopotamia (literally, "the Land Between the Rivers") were found a succession of great cities, among them Babylon, Seleucia, Ctesiphon, and Baghdad, each of which owed much of its power to its position astride the Silk Road. This region was like a catherine wheel, with subsidiary routes spinning off in all directions, depending on the climate and the times.

★   ★   ★

From the river crossroads, most travelers throughout history chose the Great Desert Route, which cut northwest to the prime caravan cities of Aleppo and Antioch in Syria—entries to the whole Mediterranean world. This route followed the inner curve of the Fertile Crescent, along the edge of the Syrian Desert that lies at the crescent's heart. Not a true desert, like the Taklamakan, this desert was an arid wasteland where nomads could exist comfortably with their herds in many periods—though drought could drive them into the wetter, more fertile lands outside. Nor was it a region of sand dunes. As 18th-century traveler Bartholomew Plaisted described:

> . . . this desert has generally been represented as a level sandy plain; whereas in reality the greatest part is a hard sandy gravel like some of our heaths in England. In some places it is full of large loose stones, and in others full of small hills, which are more barren than the valleys or plains.

Travelers here might be troubled by the heat, by scorpions, by lions and tigers, and by the flies that clustered about the mouth and eyes in search of moisture. But caravaneers on the Great Desert Route were unlikely to perish of thirst. Water was found rather readily all along the route, though it was often cloudy, brackish, or full of algae. As Plaisted noted:

> Even the very best is soon rendered unfit for present drinking; for when you come to a pool, everyone is for taking care of his own camels, and therefore as many of these plunge in at [a] time, that the water soon becomes muddy and unfit for use. I have been forced to take up with it, and have drank it as thick as Turks do their coffee, who always shake the pot before they pour it out . . .

On the Great Desert Route, travelers generally avoided any large settlements, instead camping out in the open. Though they lost the possiblility of trading in bazaars along the way, they also avoided paying the tolls, taxes, and bribes demanded by the many cities that lined the river valleys. Nor were the rivers themselves much used for transport. From the cities of the lower Tigris and Euphrates, travelers and traders sometimes shipped downriver to the ports of the Persian Gulf, there to embark on the great Spice Route that linked all of southern Asia by sea. But upstream the rivers were unfit for travel, what with spring floods and low, sluggish currents in the drier parts of the year, not to mention the Euphrates's whirlpools and the Tigris's wide loops. More serious, the riverbanks were haunts of pirates, always ready to prey on travelers. Even the downstream rafts, wood being scarce in the region, were generally supported on unsafe, inflated animal skins, which had an unfortunate tendency to burst.

The Great Desert Route also had its "pirates," but they were generally willing to change the role of brigand for that of protector, given sufficient payment. Like the mountain people who guarded strategic passes, these desert predators supported themselves, in part, with payments—a portion of the trade goods or a fee per pack load—meant to keep them from attacking travelers. Sometimes a "human passport" was sent along with a caravan, to indicate that the proper bribe had been paid to the dominant tribe in the region, which would then regard any attack on the caravan as an attack on itself. In many periods, when the desert tribes were sufficiently peaceful, this system operated rather well. Sometimes, notably during Greco-Roman times, the region was so peaceful that regular routes stretched across the desert itself toward the coastal lands. One much-frequented route in that period cut from the frontier city of Dura-Europos on the upper Euphrates across the desert to the oasis of Palmyra (City of Palms). Here in the cup of two hills, where life-giving, hot sulphur springs flowed, a great city sprang up, with long colonnaded avenues and numerous temples, banks, and mausoleums. So powerful were the Palmyrenes that for a time they operated as a semi-independent buffer state between the massive Roman Empire and its more easterly neighbors on the Silk Road.

Another cross-desert route cut from Babylon through even drier country to Petra, an astonishingly beautiful city cut out of solid rock, gold and pink and gray-green, a natural canyon-fortress where caravans found shelter after crossing the desert. In early centuries, Petra was one of the most important crossroads cities in Western Asia, the hub of routes in all directions. In addition to the cross-desert route, Petra was closely linked with the nearby port of Aela, at the head of the Gulf of Aqaba on the Red Sea, through which it was connected with the great Spice Route to the East. From Petra, caravans went on toward the coast, to Gaza, to Egypt (especially to Alexandria), and to the Phoenician cities of Tyre, Sidon, Byblos (Gebal), and Beirut that were both refining centers and distribution ports for the whole Mediterranean world. But, perhaps most important, Petra lay astride the Incense Road, the great inland caravan route that ran from southern Arabia all the way north through Damascus and along the inner western arc of the Fertile Crescent to Aleppo and Antioch.

Each of these two cities, in its time, formed the terminus not only of the Silk Road but also of the Incense Road. Aleppo was and is primarily an Arab city, known locally as Haleb. Built on a rocky elevation beside a small stream, Aleppo dominated the semiarid countryside around it. Its main ties were with the inland caravan routes, since it lay some 70 miles from the Mediterranean. Antioch, on the other hand, was a Greco-Roman city with strong Christian influences. Partly shielded by mountains, through which lay the pass for caravans from the East, Antioch benefited from the Mediterranean's sea breezes. Renowned for its healthfulness and beauty, it was a popular summer retreat for people fleeing either the damp, malarial coast or the parching inland heat. From its site on the Orontes River, goods were often shipped the 18 miles to the Mediterranean, where a succession of ports were located. During Greco-Roman times, Antioch was dominant, but Aleppo, far older, resumed its importance in Islamic times. The fame and fortunes of both cities were made by the junction there of the Silk Road's westernmost branch, the Great Desert Route, and the Incense Road, from Arabia.

But these desert routes to the Mediterranean required peace, a commodity often in short supply. When the tribes and clans of the desert warred among themselves, a bribe paid to one had little influence on the others. Then, even an army of archers was insufficient escort for a caravan. In such times, Silk Road travelers chose different courses. From Babylon, many travelers instead followed the inner curve of the Tigris River, where throughout history many cities rose and fell, most notably Ashur and Nineveh (Mosul), prime cities of the Assyrian Empire. Another spur of the Silk Road cut from Ecbatana on the Iranian Plateau directly to Nineveh; from there the route curved around the Fertile Crescent, following the hilly rim of the Anatolian Plateau to Aleppo and Antioch.

In many periods, travelers would completely bypass these cities, climb instead onto the Anatolian Plateau at some point on this more northerly curve, and head for the great port cities on the Aegean Sea: Miletus, Ephesus, Smyrna, Phocaea, or Troy—whose fame in the *Iliad* may have had more to do with trade routes than with the abduction of a queen. Later destinations were Byzantium (renamed Constantinople, now Istanbul) and the Black Sea ports of Sinope and Trapezus (later Trebizond, now Trabzon). Routes in this region are extremely old; in the region of the upper Tigris, archaeologists have found a 10,000-year-old city whose buildings include one-ton slabs of stone that must have been imported from outside the region. In early times, the Anatolian Plateau was a destination equal in importance to Mesopotamia. The Silk Road coursed through them both.

In certain periods, as in Marco Polo's day, when the lowlands were in sharp contention, the main route of the Silk Road stayed in the highlands altogether, curving from the crossroads of Ecbatana northwest around the Caspian Sea through the region now called Azerbaijan to the ancient city of Tabriz. From there it passed on through the highlands of Armenia, near Lakes Van and Urmiya and near Mt. Ararat (where tradition has it that Noah's ark came to rest), to Trebizond, connecting to Europe via the Black Sea and Mediterranean routes. Modern travelers sometimes called this the Golden Road to Samarkand.

The route is nowhere near as simple as it seems on paper, however, for the hills are precipitous and the weather severe, with snow making the route extremely dangerous much of the year. In his *Armenia* the early 19th-century English traveler Robert Curzon wrote of the

Fortresses like this one at Baiburt lined the hazardous route between Trebizond and Erzerum. (From *L'Armenie* by Texier, reprinted in Yule's *Marco Polo*)

difficulty of the route between Trebizond, perched high on a table of rock overlooking the Black Sea, and the city of Erzerum, the main caravan center on the mountain route from Iran or Persia (in Curzon's time, the only place to obtain fresh horses between Persia and Turkey). On one snow–covered hill, Curzon noted that:

> . . . the road consisted of a series of holes, about six inches deep, and about eighteen inches apart, the track being about sixteen inches wide.

Down this hill road, which the locals rightly called a ladder, they went, "plunging, sliding, scrambling in and out of the deep holes." Curzon's party was lucky; their horses were surefooted and arrived safely. But he described seeing on the road a woebegone group of Persian travelers:

> . . . they were seated in a row, on the ledge of the precipice, looking despairingly at a number of their baggage-horses which had tumbled over, and were wallowing in the snow many hundred feet below. They did not seem to be killed, as far as I could see, as the

snow had broken their fall . . . [but] it did not appear that there was any probability of their getting up [on the road] again . . . I presume their horses were frozen to death before we had left them very long.

Horses were not alone in facing such a fate, as Curzon continues:

Dead frozen bodies were frequently brought into the city; and it is common in the summer, on the melting of the snow, to find numerous corpses of men, and bodies of horses, who had perished in the preceding winter. So usual an event is this, that there is a custom, or law, in the mountains of Armenia, that every summer the villagers go out to the more dangerous passes, and bury the dead whom they are sure to find. They have a legal right to their clothes, arms, and the accouterments of the horses, on condition of forwarding all bales of merchandise, letters, and parcels to the places to which they are directed.

Not an easy route, by any means, and this accounts in part for the long predominance of the Syrian Desert routes to the Mediterranean, whatever the hazards they may have entailed.

By land or sea via Trebizond, travelers through Anatolia came finally to Constantinople, known to the Greeks as Byzantium and to the later Moslems as Istanbul or Stamboul. Though technically in Europe, being on the north side of the Bosporus, traditional dividing line between the two continents, Constantinople was long, and remains today, an Asian city in thrust and character. Lying on a readily defended peninsula and encurving its famous crescent harbor, the Golden Horn, the city extended its fortifications inland several times as it grew. In the end, this city of seven hills (like its counterpart, Rome) was virtually impregnable from land attack, being sheltered behind three major sets of walls. After the decline of Rome in the West, Constantinople was for many centuries the proper terminus of the Silk Road.

★   ★   ★

So the Silk Road arced across desert and mountain to link China with the Mediterranean world. But it was far from being the easiest route across Eurasia. That honor goes to the Eurasian Steppe Route. North of China, north of the T'ien Shan and Pei Shan, north of the Aral, Caspian, and Black Seas, north of the mountains of Central Europe, lies the Eurasian Steppe, a vast plain that stretches over 8,000 miles from Pacific to Atlantic.

So wide and flat is this steppeland that it seems made for wheeled vehicles. The nomads who lived there for millennia may have spent a good part of their lives in the saddle, but their homes and all their possessions were traditionally carried on great wagons, generally hauled by oxen. Writing in the 13th century, European friar William de Rubruck gave a striking account of life on wheels on the open steppe:

> One woman will drive twenty or thirty carts, for the country is flat. They tie together the carts, which are drawn by oxen or camels, one after the other, and the woman will sit on the front one driving the oxen while all the others follow in step. If they happen to come on a bad bit of track they loose them and lead them across it one by one. They go at a very slow pace, as a sheep or an ox might walk.

Travelers on the steppe could also be more comfortable. They did not have to trudge through drifting sands and across mountains, sometimes carrying part of the load themselves (or employing local porters to do so) in difficult passages. When the Eurasian Steppe Route was in active use, especially in Mongol times, travelers could obtain wagons and teams from local people who made it their business to hire them out—where they were not required by the government to provide them.

Describing the passage from Sarai, atop the Caspian Sea, to the caravan centers on the Oxus, 15th-century Moslem traveler Ibn Battuta shows that travel on the steppe, even passing through desert regions like the Kizil Kum, was not terribly arduous for travelers, however hard it might be on camels:

> From this place [Sarai] we went on for thirty days by forced marches, halting only for two hours each day, one in the forenoon and the other at sunset. The length of the halt was just as long as the time needed to cook and sup . . . everybody eats and sleeps in his wagon while it is actually on the move, and I had in my wagon three slave girls. It is the custom of travelers in this wilderness to use the utmost speed, because of the scarcity of herbage. Of the camels that cross it the majority perish and the remainder are of no use except a year later after they are fattened up. The water in this desert is at certain known waterpoints, separated by two or three days' march . . .

The Eurasian Steppe Route starts on the dry and stony flatlands north of China, a mixture of semi-arid steppe and inhospitable desert. From Peking (Beijing) travelers would head across the Gobi Desert, northwest to the Mongolian Steppe and then westward past the Altai Mountains and through the Dzungarian Gap to emerge north of Lake Balkhash on the wide and grassy Kirghiz Steppe. From here, the plains stretched out before them with scarcely any impediment clear across the continent to Europe. There, faced with the boomerang-shaped Carpathian Mountains, they could—without taking the trouble to thread the mountain passes—simply sweep to either side of them, north onto the plains of Poland and Germany or south into the Danube River valley, either way penetrating into the heart of Europe.

Northern Europe would be the main goal for modern travelers on the Eurasian Steppe Route. But in earlier times traffic more often angled toward the caravan cities of Western Turkestan or toward the Mediterranean world, then the center of Western civilization. From the north coast of the Black Sea, travelers could embark from one of the trading cities of the Crimea for the great city now known as Istanbul, the entryway into the Greek and the wider Mediterranean world. If they chose to stay on land, they simply arced between the Black and Caspian Seas through the narrow Derbend Pass in the Caucasus Mountains, that otherwise bar the way.

Slicing across Eurasia unhindered, as it does, the Eurasian Steppe Route should have been the natural route between East and West. It was surely the main route of nomad armies throughout the ages, as they swept across the plains in search of empire or perhaps, more modestly, better grazing lands. It was just as surely the favored route during those few periods in which it could be traveled safely, notably during Mongol times. But though it played a significant role in the history of Eurasia, perhaps as the avenue of communication for some of the main early contacts between East and West, its exposure to the ever-contending peoples of the steppe meant that it could rarely be the main route for vulnerable travelers.

It is astonishing that both these routes, the Silk Road and the Eurasian Steppe Route, were in use in a primitive form for thousands of years. We of the modern world may regard ourselves as nonpareil travelers, but the peoples who first opened the routes across the Eurasian landmass are the ones who truly deserve our awe. For they spent their lives on the move, traveling thousands of miles—in prehistory without either vehicles or animals to lighten their burdens—opening the routes that thread the land today. Theirs is a part of the story of the Silk Road that we are only beginning to learn about.

CHAPTER THREE

DAYS OF JADE AND BRONZE

When the Chinese first ventured west into the heart of Central Asia, we do not know, for Chinese tales of early travels are more romance than history. Among these annals is the *Travels of Emperor Mu*, which was included in a collection called the *Bamboo Annals*, edited in the third century B.C. Emperor Mu himself was supposed to have ruled during the Chou Dynasty around 1000 B.C. Since it was the practice in early China to ascribe honorable achievements—everything from the discovery of silk cultivation to the development of medicinal drugs—to the emperors, this tale may have been sparked by the actual travels of unknown and unnamed Chinese merchants and explorers, which were then attributed, with fanciful elaborations, to Emperor Mu. (In much the same way, and at roughly the same time, the energetic commercial activities of early Greek traders were being given mythical status as part of the legend of Hercules.)

Like most westbound travelers, Emperor Mu is said to have left through the Yü Pass, the famous Jade Gate that would mark China's main western frontier for thousands of years. On the plains beyond the frontier, he found people who were, like him, "descendants of Ho-tsung," the god of the Huang (Yellow) River, the fertile valley that formed the heartland of Chinese culture. Welcomed by local royalty, Mu was offered "ten leopards' skins and 26 good horses" as gifts. Finding other descendants of Ho-tsung farther west, Mu was offered further presents, including a *pi*, a round jade

Emperor Mu wished to satisfy his ambition by touring around the world and by marking the countries under the sky with the wheels of his chariots and the hoofs of his horses.
—From a commentary on
Classic of Spring and Autumn

ornament with a center hole, used as a symbol of civil office. The *pi* was ceremoniously submerged in the river, as was an offering to the God of the River, along with an ox, a horse, a pig, and a sheep, all of which were sacrificed for the purpose. In thanks, the tale proceeds, the God of the River appeared from the water and said:

> *Mu Man, be thou forever on the throne and may thy rule be wise and prosperous . . . let me show thee the precious articles of the Ch'un Mountain and the beautiful palaces of K'un-lun, where there are four plains from which flow seventy springs. Proceed, then, to the K'un-lun Mountain and behold the precious articles of the Ch'un Mountain.*

The K'unlun Mountain, in Chinese mythology, is the home of the gods, akin to Mount Olympus for the Greeks, and of the godlike people credited with founding the Chinese civilization. K'unlun is also the name (at least in modern times) of the high range of mountains that divides the lofty Tibetan Plateau from the Tarim Basin. The pathway between the K'unlun Range and the Taklamakan Desert was the southern Tarim route, later to be one of China's main routes to the West. Not the least of the route's attractions was the jade for which the region, especially around Khotan, was famous. Jade figured in Emperor Mu's adventures as well, as the story continues:

> *. . . the emperor ascended the K'un-lun Mountain and visited the palaces of Huang Ti [the Yellow Emperor, legendary founder of the Chinese people, who—say the Chinese annals—ruled the land from 2697-2597 B.C.]. And, in order to identify the burial place of the God of the Clouds for future generations, he heaped up earth upon his grave . . . in the last month of the summer, the emperor ascended the Ch'un Mountain on the north, from where he could see the wilderness stretching in four directions . . .*
>
> *It is said that the Ch'un Mountain was the richest mountain in the world, a store of precious stones and valuable jades. It was a place where the most flourishing crops grew and the trees were tall and the bushes beautiful. The emperor gathered some species so that he might cultivate them in the central kingdom [China] when he returned. It is also said that the emperor rested at the foot of the mountain for five days and amused himself with music . . . and [was presented with] many beautiful women. It is said that the country of the Red Bird was famous for its beautiful women and valuable jade.*

The story becomes even more interesting as Mu travels farther into what his chronicler calls the "Wild West," on the way installing rulers to rule over certain portions of the territory.

> *. . . the emperor rode westward arriving at Bitter Mountain. The name of the Wild West was Garden of Prosperity. The emperor stopped for hunting and here he tasted the bitter herb. [No other details help up guess what herb is meant.] They proceeded westward until . . . they arrived at the domain of the Royal Mother of the West.*

Many have been the attempts to link some figure in Western Asia with the "Royal Mother of the West," who is mentioned in many myths and legends, some referring to early in the second millennium B.C., or even earlier. Some scholars have gone so far as to suggest that she was the Queen of Sheba, who in the time of the Emperor Mu is thought to have ruled in southwestern Arabia, controlling trade on the Incense Road to Syria and Mesopotamia. Whether the Royal Mother was inspired by a real person, and real contact with the West, or was a wholly legendary divinity, we shall probably never know. But clearly, whoever chronicled Emperor Mu's travels thought the encounter an important one:

> . . . the emperor, carrying a white [stone] scepter and a black pi, paid a visit to the Royal Mother of the West. To her he offered as presents one hundred pieces of embroidered silk and three hundred pieces of [other] fabric. After bowing many times, the Royal Mother accepted the presents.

On the next day the emperor invited the Royal Mother to a banquet on Emerald Pond. During the occasion she sang extempore:

> "Hills and mountains come in view
> As fleecy clouds ascend the sky.
> Far and wide, divided by waters and
>   mountain ranges
> Our countries separately lie.
> Should long life preserve thee,
>   come again."

To this the emperor responded:

> "When I to east return
>   to millions bringing order and peace;
> When they enjoy prosperity and ease
> To thee shall I return;
> From this day count three years
> To this country again I shall come."

The emperor then rode on to the Hsi [Western] Mountains and on the rocks engraved a record of his visit. He planted a memorial tree . . . and named the place the Hsi-Wang-Mu-Shan [Mountain of the Royal Mother of the West].

On his return, the emperor would compose another poem, which began:

In the distant west she rules,
Happily on the wide, wide plain,
Accompanied by tigers and leopards,
Sleeping with crows and jackdaws.

On the way home, Emperor Mu visited numerous other princes, receiving lavish gifts and presenting equally lavish presents in return. The Chih family, for example, offered Emperor Mu:

. . . two teams of three white horses, forty wild horses and wild buffaloes, and seventy dogs. They presented in addition four hundred horses and three thousand cattle for food.

For his part the Emperor gave:

. . . a piece of fabric made of dog's fur, twenty-nine gold cups, forty shell girdles, three hundred red pearls, one hundred kang *[measures] of cassia and ginger.*

The Chih family, so the tale tells us, accepted the gifts with the "ceremony of prostration." This kind of lavish exchange of gifts would for much of history pass for "trade" among the Chinese, who preferred to keep up the fiction of "tribute" paid to them and "offerings" freely made by them, though the pattern was generally quite regularized into what we would call trade.

Continuing homeward with his six divisions of soldiers, Emperor Mu stopped on the way for a great hunting expedition, capturing "countless birds and animals." The "good furs and beautiful feathers" were shared out and carried home in carriages, the tale continues, and the emperor had for himself "100 carriages full." But even the emperor had no proof against crossing the desert:

. . . he was thirsty and water could not be obtained in the desert, so [a soldier] stabbed the left horse of his chariot in the neck and presented a drink of pure blood to his royal master. The emperor was very much pleased and gave him a piece of ornamental jade . .

At last the party reached "the end of the Piled Stone Mountain Range," which meant they were in their homeland once again.

Whatever proportion of fact and fiction we may assign to the tales of Emperor Mu's travels, they certainly indicate some knowledge of the peoples of Central Asia and considerable interest in their products and the possibility of continuing exchanges. Some of the gifts received, notably wheat, were previously unknown in China and were introduced only in this period. And Persian legends from this era also indicate some knowledge of China, though they, too, are far from being verifiable history. Whether or not Chinese adventurers and traders actually traveled into Central Asia in Emperor Mu's time—and, if so, how far west—a tribe-to-tribe relay trading network certainly existed and not just with China, but all across Asia.

This was nothing new. The peoples of the whole Eurasian landmass had been in motion and continual contact, like the atoms in a hot-air balloon, from long before the last ice age. The needles and ornaments of bone, teeth, shells, mother-of-pearl, and the like of the peoples of the ice-age Aurignacian cultures in Western Europe are nearly identical with those of northern China—so much so that, as some experts have commented, it is hard to tell the difference between them.

The contact continued in the shadowy millennia that followed, as the peoples of Eurasia were developing the skills and techniques we now call "civilization." Some 10,000 to 12,000 years ago, these peoples began to domesticate both plants and animals, laying the basis for the two great cultures into which the massive continent would be divided: nomadic herding and agriculture, what some have termed "the steppe and the sown." But if their patterns of life diverged, contact between the two groups continued, whether through war or primitive trade, and as new discoveries were made they passed from clan to clan across the expanse of Eurasia. As some of these peoples passed from making and using flint and stone implements to working with metals (gold, silver, copper, later bronze, and, still later, iron), so others soon would move along similar lines. Methods of making pottery, the remains of which have been so vital to modern archaeologists, the innovation of the wheel, techniques of domesticating animals, the idea of writing—all, in time, made their way across the face of Eurasia.

Traditionally, archaeologists have painted a picture of movement from West to East, with the high cultures of the Near East, of Mesopotamia and Egypt, passing innovations to China via the Iranian Plateau and the steppes and deserts of Central Asia. According to this view the inner Asian lands were mainly a conduit and China, in early millennia, primarily a passive receiver, only later developing its own distinctive civilization. Though the main outlines of this picture may be true, some archaeologists today argue that it is too simplistic and believe that some important innovations of early culture, perhaps even the wheel and agriculture, were developed in Central Asia. Whatever the direction of movement, however, it is clear that many of the basic aspects of civilization did diffuse across Asia, sometimes passed on one to another, sometimes carried by whole peoples on the move.

As Asia's inhabitants gradually divided into "the steppe and the sown," the interplay between the two began to result in the emergence of regular travel routes. Those who lived in

Nomads were among the earliest traders on the Silk Road; these in modern
Afghanistan continue the old tradition. (By Delia and Ferdinand Kuhn)

the well-watered river valleys and oases scattered across Asia came to lead more sedentary
lives, centered on agriculture. Secure behind the walls of their cities, they often developed
crafts like weaving, potterymaking, and metalworking to a higher degree than did the nomads
of the steppe. These wandered with their herds in search of pasture, for the growth on the
steppe was too thin to allow them to settle in one spot.

    But nomads did not wander aimlessly or without direction. Nomadic herders generally
followed a regular migration route, on the plains in winter and on the cooler, moister uplands
in summer. This pattern could easily be disrupted by changes in climate or population, spur-
ring groups to expand their territory at the expense of others. The effect was akin to a line of
falling dominoes, each one pushing the next, with nomad often pressing down into farmer
domains. But in stable times, the pattern of nomadic migration served the purposes of both
herders and farmers, for the nomads desired fine city goods, while the settled farmers required
raw materials for their crafts. On their seasonal migrations the nomads would pack these

goods on their herd animals. So, at a very early time, nomads were bringing to the cities copper, tin, and turquoise from Iran, gold from the Altai Mountains of Mongolia, lapis lazuli and rubies from Afghanistan, furs from Siberia, incense from Arabia, cottons from India, and their own products like wool, hides, and livestock. In the process, they carved out the main routes across Asia, among them the Silk Road.

We should not imagine that these contacts and exchanges were necessarily conducted in a rational or organized manner. A good deal of the trade carried on by ancient peoples could more accurately be called war and robbery, taking by force of arms or as the spoils of victory the things desired. Among some peoples robbery even became formalized as "pirate trade," in which a group broke in at night, took away food or other desirables, often destroyed some other items in the bargain, and left what they regarded as fair payment when they departed.

Another conventional, if primitive, form of trade, widespread not only in Eurasia but throughout the world, was silent trade, also called dumb barter. At some convenient, tacitly agreed-upon site, one trading party laid out the goods it wanted to exchange and left the scene; the other party appeared and laid down what it felt was an equivalent array of goods. The first party then returned and the two parties alternated appearances, adding or subtracting from their piles of goods until both were satisfied with the equivalent. Each then departed with the goods of the other. The whole process occurred without the two parties ever speaking or meeting face-to-face, though certainly the pattern implied a longstanding, if limited, trust. Only much later would the peoples of Eurasia develop more direct trading with traveling merchants and markets at a fixed time and place.

★   ★   ★

At some time around 3000 B.C. herders began the domestication of animals more directly suited for use as beasts of burden in long-distance trade. Donkeys were developed from the wild asses of Nubia, on the upper Nile, and soon became widely used all along the eastern Mediterranean coast, in the Fertile Crescent, on the Iranian Plateau, and later in northern China. They were the mainstay of caravans in Western Asia throughout these early centuries. In the same period, most likely in the Ukrainian steppes north of the Black and Caspian Seas, the horse was domesticated from wild stock. These were small horses, only about four feet high, apparently much like the wild Przewalski horses that survive today. They were at first intended mostly for food and other by-products, as were cattle, but as the nomads of Central Asia bred larger, stronger stock, their domestication would centuries later produce a revolution.

At the same time, the peoples along the western half of the Silk Road were developing much more sophisticated long-distance contacts. While empires and dynasties rose and fell, trade relations seem to have extended and continued, and a class of traders emerged where once trading had been only incidental. Precious metals, such as copper and tin—the vital constituents of the all-important bronze—had long been brought down into Mesopotamia from the Iranian Plateau. By 3000 B.C. gems, precious stones, and minerals such as alabaster, carnelian, mother-of-pearl and the volcanic glass, obsidian (used for making extremely sharp knives), were also arriving, joining the semi-precious stones like lapis lazuli that had long been carried by the same route. Timber from the then heavily forested mountains of Iran supplied Babylon and other Mesopotamian cities with building materials, while the very temples of Babylon and Sumer were built, in part, of marble and other stone from the high Iranian Plateau.

Even this early, Mesopotamian merchants seem to have established outposts in towns along the Iranian route, where they collected the products of the local herders, miners, and farmers, and transported them down into Western Asia for trade among the great cities of Egypt, the Levant, and Mesopotamia. While some merchants traveled back and forth between their home city and their places of supply, others settled in the distant cities, generally living in that quarter of the town set aside for foreigners. There they established permanent relationships with local suppliers, acting as intermediaries between them and itinerant merchants, who would otherwise have to reopen trade relations anew on each visit (the visits being spaced months or years apart). Some villages on the Iranian Plateau even seem to have turned into production centers of a sort. One such produced a kind of stone bowl that, because it is far more common in Mesopotamia than in Iran, seems to have been produced for export. Iranian bowls also traveled eastward, and have been found in the settled lands of Ferghana from about 2500 B.C. In these centuries, patterns were set that would be followed by generation after generation of traders on the Silk Road.

Merchants residing in distant trading outposts were, of course, vulnerable, as their kin are today. Many of the records that survive from the early civilizations of Mesopotamia are commercial documents, some of which speak poignantly across the millennia about the dangers of long-distance trade and travel. One trader wrote from a station on the Iranian Plateau:

> Since I arrived here I am in trouble and the whole land is in trouble. Do not come here this year . . . Till I send you a dispatch, do not come! Better return to Susa.

Another wrote:

> When I had entered [the distant city] . . . my apprentice took the donkeys and made off; furthermore I fell ill and almost lost my life. And as for the slave-girl who was to be sent to you, she died . . . You told me: "I will have Almanusv, your brother, bring to you about 12 minas of silver with an expedition after you." For heaven's sake, send him! Do

not keep him any longer. As soon as I finish here, I will be on my way to you. Do not worry, I am well. There is here a splendid slave-girl; I offered her to the travelers, but nobody accepted her from me. They say: "The journey is dangerous."

Extension of the trading network continued into the second millenium B.C.; in Babylonia, Hammurabi included merchants under his famous code of laws, and the documents of the time indicate a rather elaborate set of arrangements. In earlier times, much of this trade seems to have been on behalf of palaces and temples, those institutions which had the money and hired many of the artisans working in the state. But by Hammurabi's time (if not before) merchants seem to have been operating independently, some traveling the long, difficult roads themselves, others hiring agents to trade for them. So the long chains of donkeys wound with their precious goods—light, portable, and highly valuable items were most favored—along the deserts and valleys of the Near East, into the Anatolian, Armenian, and Iranian uplands, across the steppes into the Pamirs, and southeast into Afghanistan and India. There traders exchanged their goods not only for local items but also for goods from further afield.

The letters they sent back and forth along the route often indicated what goods were being sent and specified what should be done on their arrival. Commercial transactions in Mesopotamia were cleared through a merchant's organization called a *karum;* the merchants themselves were called *tamkarum.* In a typical "covering letter," one Mesopotamian merchant wrote of the 30 *minas* of silver he had sent:

This silver belongs to the trust of Kudatum . . . buy goods of the city—for half of our silver buy linen-cloths, and for half the silver, tin; carry out a fitting purchase, profitable for him. When you perform the buying, do not buy a brightly colored cloth . . . You are my brothers—as my hand has been laid in the silver here so must you there, when you entrust the goods, in the towngate lay your hands as my representatives, and if Dadaja [the agent appointed to bring back the goods] is delayed, send the goods with the first one who leaves to us.

The fiction "you are my brothers" or "you are my father" appears in many such letters. The reality is indicated by the many plaintive cries of "Why did you not do as I asked you?" Agents were generally paid with a piece of the goods, and the harnessers who handled the donkeys and cared for the trade goods en route usually received some bolts of cloth as their compensation.

Through a network of traders such as these, goods from as far afield as India, the Hindu Kush, and the Pamirs came in caravans on what we now call the Silk Road across the Iranian bridge, down to the all-important waist of Mesopotamia to the region of Babylon, and then along the Fertile Crescent, to the city of Aleppo near the Syrian coast and to other cities on the

Mediterranean. The trade was so favorable to all concerned that traders en route were sometimes housed as guests in the palaces of the lands they visited. Local princes often under-took to police the roads in their domains, and aided merchants by providing storehouses for them and helping them collect money owed by the state's inhabitants. The knife cut both ways, however, for these princes generally demanded payment, sometimes masked as tools, for providing such protection.

Where geography restricted travelers to a single route, or when a region had a monopo-ly on some vital or highly desirable product, such as tin or gold, local rulers had considerable power in their relations with the supposedly stronger and more sophisticated empires in the rich lowlands. That was true of the peoples of the Iranian Plateau, who would long use their position astride the Silk Road to gain extraordinary riches and influence.

But the trade, or rather the products it brought, was so important that many a lowland empire sent its armies into the hills to try to secure the trade routes and the flow of vital supplies. For example, Sargon, king of Akkad, in the region later known as Babylonia, reportedly sent an expedition at some time around 2300 B.C. to rescue a merchant colony established on the Anatolian Plateau.

★   ★   ★

We have followed the opening and early development of the western half of the Silk Road, up to the dividing line of the Pamirs. But what of the eastern half? There we know much less. Archaeology in China and the Tarim Basin has proceeded only fitfully in the last century, a period dominated there by civil war and world war. Written chronicles and more work-a-day accounts, such as those we see in Western Asia, have not so far been found in China from such an early period. The writings that have survived are from a relatively recent time, by Western standards—not surprisingly, since writing came to China centuries, perhaps even millennia, later than to Western Asia. The oldest Chinese writings, the famous oracle bones discovered in the 20th century, which apparently confirm some of the later chronicles of China's early dynasties, date only to about 1300 B.C. (Unconfirmed Chinese tradition places the development of writing over a thousand years earlier.) The problem is that during the great Ch'in dynasty in the third century B.C., a massive effort was made to collect and combine records of early China into coherent, continuous chronicles. Unfortunately, the rulers at the same time destroyed many of the records from which the chronicle editors worked. So we have relatively few works from before the Ch'in period; most of these were written from about the ninth to the sixth centuries B.C., based on earlier writings and oral traditions now lost. These are hardly firm bases on which to construct a picture of the eastern half of the Silk Road. But they are not without considerable interest, if we consider that the myths and legends may have a substratum of reality, as did Homer's story of Troy.

Many of these tales, like that of Emperor Mu, told of Hsi Wang Mu, the Royal Mother of the West. Always she was seen as having special knowledge or powers and living in a garden-like place, sometimes called the Flowery Land. Select mortals, as well as immortals, were invited to eat at her banquet table. The mythical early Chinese hero Hou I—half god, half man, as Hercules was for the Greeks—sought out the Royal Mother of the West for pills to make him immortal. In another tale Hsi Wang Mu gave Chinese envoys some white jade rings, some thimbles of green jade, and topographical maps. Another legendary hero was supposed to have studied with her. And at least one representative of the Royal Mother of the West is said to have visited the Chinese court, bringing with him objects of white jade.

These mythical romances are, of course, shot through with fanciful descriptions of such prodigies as donkeys that can be "folded up" when not in use, or a woman who conceived a child by stepping into the tracks of a giant. But the many references to goods and knowledge from the West make it likely that the Chinese had contacts out through the Kansu Corridor and at least some distance along the northern and southern Tarim routes at a very early time. Probably, few Chinese citizens actually traveled westward (as would be true in historical times as well), and that would give tales of these rare journeys a fantastic quality, to be inflated in the

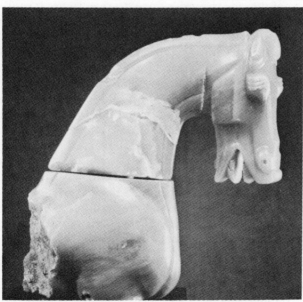

Heavenly horses like this one carved in jade enticed the Chinese halfway across Asia to Ferghana. (Han period, from Victoria and Albert Museum)

retelling over many generations. If later experience provides any pattern, it seems more likely that there developed very early a group of Central Asian merchants who operated the trade on the east-west route that later became known as the Silk Road. In these early times, the route might better be called the Jade Road for, as the Chinese romances indicate, jade was highly prized and was described as coming from the West.

Here we need not rely wholly on the oft-retold myths of the Chinese past, for the jade itself is a witness to the traffic. Jade is the common name for two types of gemstone, each of various colors. Jadeite, which occurs in most colors of the rainbow, including white and black, is an exceedingly rare stone found primarily in Burma and apparently unknown in China until the 18th century A.D. Nephrite, the "Jewel of Heaven" to the Chinese, ranged from a highly prized deep spinach-colored green through lighter greens (depending on the iron content of the stone) to a translucent, but not transparent, white sometimes called mutton-fat.

These were the jades so desired by the early Chinese, and they began to appear in China by about 2000 B.C., perhaps even earlier. But nephrite jade does not appear naturally in China proper, certainly not in any significant amounts mined in such early times. These jades are thought, instead, to have come from the mountains near Khotan and Yarkand, 1,500 miles away across the Tarim Basin. (Sources of jade cannot be determined with certitude chemically because the composition of the jade changes somewhat over time.) It seems likely, then, that the eastern half of the Silk Road, which historians have traditionally described as being "opened" in the second century B.C., was, in fact, a trading route as much as 2,000 years earlier.

That jade was important in Chinese civilization from very early times is made clear in the land's legends and myths. It was, as the story of Emperor Mu's travels indicated, widely used for ceremonial purposes. The different levels of imperial officials were distinguished by the grade of jade used in carving their symbols of office. Rich people ate from jade bowls and wore amulets of the gemstone, believing that it would enhance their chances of immortality. Jade objects were buried with the dead—those whose families could afford it—for it was thought to help prevent decay of the body. Beyond these uses, of course, jade was used as a beautiful ornament in everything from jewelry and fine sculptures to vases and carved screens.

Jade was not, however, simply ornamental. An extremely hard stone that holds a good cutting edge, jade was also used for tools; apparently, it could even cut through some metals, such as iron. Axheads called *celts*, made of jade, have been found from prehistoric times not only along the Tarim routes to China but also along the Jaxartes and Oxus Rivers, south of the Caspian Sea, and in Mesopotamia, where jade was also prized as a gem, though not so highly as by the Chinese.

In truth, the distribution of jade tools and ornaments seems to mark out a route clear across Asia: the route of the Silk Road. We have seen that Western Asian traders were, in the third millennium B.C., trading up onto the Iranian Plateau, and that trade from there had reached across to Ferghana, where Iranian export pottery has been found. The jade finds seem to indicate that, by the opening of the second millennium B.C., a trading route stretched clear across Asia; not a continuous road, to be traversed by any one person, but a chain of many trading links, connecting Western Asia and China over a distance of almost 5,000 miles.

★　　★　　★

The Silk Road was the path also by which ideas and techniques might travel across the continent, as some clearly did. Tradition has it for example, that writing was developed in China in this period. It was said to be inspired by bird tracks in the sand, a description that, as many have pointed out, aptly describes the Mesopotamian cuneiform writing of the time. The innovation of writing in China is linked to the reign of the legendary Huang Ti, the Yellow Emperor, traditionally dated at 2697-2597 B.C. Huang Ti is, in the Chinese way of attributing discoveries to the emperor, also credited with introducing mathematical calculations, the 60-year cycle of the Chinese calendar, money, building blocks, the compass, bamboo, certain musical instruments, boats, carts with oxen, and medicine.

Looking at the astonishing burst of activity under Huang Ti, some Western scholars have been tempted to ascribe a Western origin to virtually all of early Chinese civilization. Some have gone so far as to suggest that Huang Ti himself was not only a historical figure but also a conqueror from the jade country of the Pamirs, a Central Asian potentate, the leader of an elite band of blue-eyed, fair-skinned followers, whose empire stretched not only eastward to China but also westward to Mesopotamia, and who passed on to China great chunks of Near Eastern culture. That seems an excessively chauvinistic view, based on far too much supposition. Many modern scholars have gone to the other extreme and look at China as if it had developed in total isolation from the rest of the world. They largely ignore the probable existence of transcontinental connections, albeit through innumerable middlemen, from very early historical times.

Both views may underestimate the role played by the peoples of Central Asia, partly because we know so little about them directly. But the pattern of later history indicates that they are likely to have had a considerable impact, both in blood and ideas, on the more settled peoples at either end of the Silk Road. China's own legends, as the tale of Emperor Mu attests, indicate that Huang Ti and his kin were "foreigners," born outside the small Chinese heartland of the time, which lay along the Huang (Yellow) River, and that they came from the lands west of the Kansu Corridor. Whatever the truth of Huang Ti's background, contributions, or even his very existence, it seems fair to say that, through the medium of the early jade trade, some new techniques and practices entered China from the West, helping to spark a remarkable flowering in the land.

One other discovery of Huang Ti's time, a most important one for our story, was that of silk. Tradition credits it to the emperor's chief wife, Lei-tzu, revered by the Chinese into this century as Si Ling-chi, the "Lady of the Silkworm." According to tradition she was walking under a mulberry tree in her garden and happened to pick up a white cocoon from the leaves.

Playing with it idly, she accidentally dropped it into her tea, and found that she could pull from it a long white filament. In truth, we do not know how or when sericulture began, but certainly by the mid-second millennium B.C., when China was beginning to emerge into recorded history, silk cultivation was well established.

The techniques of sericulture are essentially simple, though the West was kept in the dark about them for many centuries. Silk thread is a fiber produced by certain species of caterpillars as they form cocoons, really protective shelters, in which the caterpillars transform themselves into moths. For some days, the caterpillar, or silkworm, produces a double-stranded fiber which it winds around itself in a figure-eight pattern. After another 10 to 15 days, if the process is not disturbed, the silkworm will burst out of the cocoon in its new form as a moth, breaking the filaments as it does so. Such broken filaments have been used by many cultures to form wild silk thread. But the Chinese found a way to keep the filaments whole. Dropping the cocoons into boiling water and stirring the water with branched sticks, they softened the gummy protein called *sericin* that holds the fibers together. That allowed them to unwind the strands into continuous filaments that can stretch to over half a mile.

But the loosened filaments were too thin and delicate for use singly, so the strands from several cocoons would be unwound at the same time and joined to make a single thread. This process, called *reeling,* was delicate and time-consuming because the threads are always thinner and weaker at the ends and need to be carefully spliced together. Most silk threads were still so fragile that they were twisted together in yet another process, called *throwing,* with the style and amount of twist varying with the type of yarn desired. The resulting thrown silk was then looped into skeins. (In modern times, cocoons are often killed by exposure to steam or hot air, and the sericin is often retained until a later stage, since the raw silk therefore has greater strength during the reeling and throwing processes. Sericin is then generally removed by boiling the yarn or the woven fabric—or by dyeing it, which has the same effect.)

Waste silk, especially from damaged cocoons or broken filaments, was combed and spun as well, though the resulting yarn had (like wild silk) considerably less transparency and sheen than the finest silks. Floss silk, unsuitable even for spinning, was used as an insulating material in winter clothes, something like down in our modern jackets. Often even the dead chrysalis, the stage between caterpillar and moth, was not wasted but was roasted and eaten. But it was the soft, lustrous silk produced by the continuous filaments that brought merchants halfway across the world.

Sericulture requires great skill, knowledge, timing, patience, and delicacy, for the silkworm is a demanding creature. The *Bombyx mori,* by far the most popular species, which produces the finest and whitest Chinese silk, subsists on white mulberry leaves. It gorges on these for over a month, eating roughly its own weight each day and shedding its skin four times, before moving into the cocoon stage. Some species produce colored silk, the hue varying with the caterpillar's diet. Silkworms are also very sensitive to extremes of temperature, noise, or even smells. The people who tended the silkworms had to provide just the right

For over 2,000 years, the Chinese kept the secrets of sericulture, from feeding the silkworms on mulberry leaves (1), to throwing, twisting together strands into threads (2), to weaving the silk fabric (3), often in imperial workshops. (From *T'ien-kung k'ai-wu*, by Sung Ying-sing, 1637)

environment and know just when to kill the incipient moth inside the cocoon, as well as have the gentle touch required for unwinding the delicate strands.

So important was sericulture to the Chinese that the women of every family, including empresses and princesses, were made responsible for producing silk. A certain section of every farm or garden, though not more than a prescribed proportion, was set aside as "mulberry land," in which mulberry trees were carefully tended and the young, tender leaves picked and fed to the silkworms. During many periods in China's history, taxes were payable in silk, so the family's fortunes could rest upon the women's skill and industry at sericulture. Skeins of silk were collected at state-controlled workshops, where they were woven into bolts of fabric of a set width and style, dictated by Chinese fashion and, later, by the desires of foreign markets. Si Ling-chi is also credited by tradition with the invention of weaving, and certainly Chinese weavers produced some extraordinarily fine fabrics from these delicate silken filaments. But though the practice of sericulture spread through virtually every household in China, the secret did not pass the Great Wall for many centuries, and did not reach the West until about the sixth century A.D.—so important was China's monopoly.

★   ★   ★

In the third and second millennia, when the peoples of China, India, and Western Asia were developing a new, more sedentary way of life, they were diverging ever more sharply from the nomadic peoples of Central Asia. The tension between steppe and sown, herder and farmer, lowland and upland, city and country was, in these early times, sharpened by a tension between the literate and the illiterate. Literacy was still largely a thing of city life. To the people of Babylon and Sumer, who seem to have first developed writing in the fourth millennium B.C., civilization ended at the Zagros Mountains. (Though, interestingly, the Sumerians may originally have been immigrants from Central Asia.) The Chinese, too, often saw the people beyond their borders as barbarians, and compared them to dogs or insects. Early archaeologists were not immune to this view, especially since what little they knew of the nomads in this misty era came primarily from the surviving fragmentary writings of the settled lowland cultures.

But the despised herders were making their own contributions to civilization, and to our story of the Silk Road, in the early second millennium B.C. Most important for long-distance travelers on the Silk Road was the domestication of the camel. An ungainly looking animal, the camel has the extraordinary capability, vital for desert travel, of going for days without water. Camels also need very little food, subsisting for long periods on only the sparsest and roughest desert scrub, for they can draw on the reserves of fat which are stored in their distinctive humps. It is the humps that most clearly distinguish the two main species of camel: the Arabian camel has one, and the Bactrian two. Chinese writer Kuo P'u, in the third century A.D., wrote an admirable description that might fit both the Arabian and the Bactrian camel:

> The camel is an unusual domestic animal; it carries a saddle of flesh on its back; swiftly it dashes over the shifting sands; it manifests its merit in dangerous places; it has secret understanding of springs and sources; subtle indeed is its knowledge!

Precisely when camels were tamed for human use, and which species was domesticated first, is unclear. From its homeland around Bactra or on the Iranian Plateau, the Bactrian camel may have been brought into Mesopotamia first; but, if so, its use did not survive there. The Bactrian camel is extraordinarily well adapted to both the sandy and hard gravel terrains of Central Asia, and to the extremes of temperature found there. Shorter and stockier than the Arabian camel, it has a heavy winter coat that it sheds in great clumps each spring. The Arabian camel, domesticated around 1800 B.C., is far better suited to the conditions of the Near East and North Africa. So the two species have roughly divided the world, or at least the Silk Road, between them. Both species have extraordinary speed and endurance. Camels are also graced with some protective features especially useful in the desert, where sandstorms are an everyday occurrence. Their eyes are doubly lidded, they can close their nostrils against penetration by dust, and even their ears have hairy screens over the openings. And their extraordinary senses of sight and smell have often saved the lives of themselves and parched caravaneers by allowing them to locate water through faint whiffs of greenery on the wind.

By well over three thousand years ago, the camel driver had become an important figure on the Silk Road. (T'ang period, from Chicago Natural History Museum)

Camels have, indeed, been so useful that Asian travelers have been willing to overlook their undeniably difficult personalities. When not properly handled or trained, or when angered or in the mating season, camels can be extremely dangerous, kicking, biting, or spitting at those unfortunate enough to arouse their ire. Their looks can be deceptive to the unwary, as Arthur Conan Doyle found when he prepared to take a camel journey in the Near East around the turn of the 20th century:

> [The camel] is the strangest and most deceptive animal in the world. Its appearance is so staid and respectable that you cannot give it credit for the black villainy that lurks within. It approaches you with a mildly interested and superior expression, like a patrician lady in a Sunday school. You feel that a pair of glasses at the end of a fan is the one thing lacking. Then it puts its lips gently forward, with a far-away look in its eyes, and you have just time to say, "The pretty dear is going to kiss me," when two rows of frightful green teeth clash in front of you, and you give such a backward jump as you could never have hoped at your age to accomplish. When once the veil is dropped, anything more demoniacal than the face of a camel cannot be conceived. No kindness and no length of ownership seem to make them friendly. And yet you must make allowances for a creature which can carry 600 lb. for 20 miles a day, and ask for no water and little food at the end of it.

And allowances *were* made by travelers throughout the Old World. Camel-drivers who were experienced at handling the recalcitrant creatures were regarded with some considerable awe and respect. Like the camels they managed, they were a breed apart, passing their expertise down through the generations. The camels themselves were so highly prized that, among some peoples, injuring them came to be taboo. Traveling on the Mongolian steppes in the early 20th century, Owen Lattimore found:

> *A caravan man may not slaughter a camel, nor eat camel flesh, nor sell the hide of a camel. If a camel becomes too weak to follow the caravan, it is left by the trail to die. The owner will not kill it, for fear that its soul might follow the caravan, haunting the other camels.*

Whether that taboo is of ancient vintage, we do not know. No such prohibition seems to have applied in Western Asia, nor was it universal in Central Asia, for in extremity caravaneers sometimes drank the blood or even urine of a camel, and ate the meat of a camel that died en route—or gave a weakened camel to a local tax or toll collector as a bribe.

★   ★   ★

But if the camel, once domesticated, was destined to be the mainstay of Asian travel, it was the horse that helped produce a revolution in Eurasia. The horse was the special property of Central Asia's nomads. Throughout the whole of the third millennium B.C., these herders had been gentling the horse, and breeding larger, stronger animals. At some point after 2000 B.C., these more powerful breeds were hitched to a new type of cart called a chariot. Other beasts had been used with varied success to pull heavy, awkward, solid-wheeled carts in Mesopotamia since about 3500 B.C.; by around 3000 B.C., such four-wheeled carts were joined by two-wheeled chariots. The cumbersome vehicles were designed to carry a charioteer, who did the driving, and a warrior, who fought with javelin, axe, or spear. But in the early second millennium B.C., the peoples of Central Asia harnessed the horse to a new, much more maneuverable type of chariot, soon made even lighter by the use of spoked wheels. More than that, the Central Asian nomads developed a compound bow, designed to be shot accurately and powerfully from a fast-moving vehicle, and far superior to an ordinary bow and arrow. The combination made these nomads, for a time, almost unstoppable.

The relative calm of the third millennium B.C., with its long-distance trade so characteristic of the early Bronze Age, was shattered by wave after wave of invaders from inner Asia. When they first appeared in Western Asia, horses were so unfamiliar that the unfortunate victims of these attacks called them "asses from the mountains." Memories of devastation from raiding charioteers echo through the Old Testament, and through many other records of the second and first millennia B.C. These are only two of the many lamentations:

> *. . . and behold they shall come with speed swiftly . . . whose arrows are sharp, and all their bows bent, their horses' hoofs shall be counted like flint, and their wheels like a whirlwind.*
> *Isaiah 5: 26, 28*

> *. . . the destroyer of the Gentiles is on his way; he is gone forth from his place to make thy land desolate; and the cities shall be laid waste, without an inhabitant . . . Behold, he shall come up as clouds, and his chariots shall be as a whirlwind: his horses are swifter than eagles. Woe unto us! for we are spoiled.*
> *Jeremiah 4: 7, 13*

The chariot and the compound bow were wielded with the most devastating effect by the nomads loosely called the Indo-Europeans. A multi-racial people sharing language and a good deal of culture, the Indo-Europeans in this period burst out in all directions from the Russian steppes north of the Black Sea. Diverging in language, culture, and racial stock as they conquered and merged with other peoples, the Indo-Europeans were the scourge of Eurasia in these dark times. Their success over the following millennium is attested to by the fact that most of the present inhabitants of Europe, Iran, and India speak related languages derived from these people—hence their name, "Indo-European." In the second and first millennia B.C. they came to control much of Asia as well, including most of the Eurasian Steppe and the Tarim Basin. The Hittites, the Greeks, the Scythians, the Slavs, the Balts, the Germans, the Celts, and the Armenians are just some of the Indo-Europeans who pushed into Europe and Western Asia. The Scythians also moved eastward, as did the Iranians, the Indians (Aryans), and countless other tribes.

The Indo-Europeans were far from being a united people. Following the ancient pattern of steppe nomads, they were like quarreling cousins in a great mixed clan. The strongest would hold the most prime land and—in times of over-population, drought, technological advantage, or pure expansionism—would push the weaker ones to less favored territories. The result was wave upon wave of migrations in all directions from the prime steppeland north of the Black and Caspian Seas, with lesser migrations occurring like shockwaves throughout Eurasia, as the same pattern repeated itself all across the landmass. This is the story of much of the Asian heartland in the second and first millennia B.C. Since the nomads were pre-literate, we know the story largely through the effects of waves of migrants on the more settled and literate shores of China, India, Iran, Mesopotamia, Syria, and Anatolia, as well as Europe. That story begins to take us across the shadowy border between prehistory and history.

In about 1600 B.C. the western half of the Silk Road was feeling the full brunt of the Iranian thrust toward the rich, settled lands of Mesopotamia and India. The heirs to the ancient kingdoms of Sumer and Babylon fell before the Iranian charioteers and their distant kin, the Hittites, who swept down from the Anatolian Plateau. Aleppo, then the strongest city on the Mediterranean end of the Silk Road, was taken, and Babylon was sacked. In this dark age many people migrated from the Fertile Crescent into Egypt. (Immigrant nomads were known to the Egyptians as "Apiru," a name later transformed into "Hebrew" and applied solely to one of these groups, the Jews.) Egypt itself was not proof against the devastating attacks, though it soon recovered its independence. India was less fortunate. Its great river-based civilization, centered on the Indus Valley, which had traded with Sumer overland and by sea, was effectively destroyed, and would not revive for centuries.

Through the rest of the second millennium B.C., the map of the western half of the Silk Road resembles an ever-shifting kaleidoscope. The advantage did not long remain with the Indo-Europeans. The high cultures of Mesopotamia quickly adopted the chariot style of warfare. In truth, they had larger numbers of skilled artisans—chariot-makers, wheelwrights, leather-workers, and metalsmiths—than did the steppe nomads. They set about breeding their own horses—the so-called Arabian horse was developed from Central Asian stock—and securing both the wood and metals needed for chariot construction. Since both were found in abundance on the Iranian Plateau, or in lands farther to the east, the lowland peoples made continual efforts to secure the routes into the hills of Iran to supply their vital needs.

The language of trade on this western end of the Silk Road was, and would long continue to be, Akkadian, the language of old Babylonia. And the long-distance commercial arrangements, though often interrupted in these turbulent times, generally followed their old patterns. Prime among the desired resources was tin, needed to alloy with copper to make bronze, still the pre-eminent metal of the time. (Tin was so important in this Late Bronze Age that Near Eastern sailors were pushing all the way across the Mediterranean and out into the Atlantic to Cornwall, in the British Isles, to supplement Iran's limited supply of the metal.) Artisan-traders worked along the western half of the Silk Road and on nearby branch routes, buying up scrap metal, working it into usable implements and ornaments, and then selling them.

★   ★   ★

Throughout the second millennium, when Western Asia was emerging into historical times, we have only occasional flickering images of what might have been happening on the eastern half of the Silk Road. China certainly shows modern archaeologists evidence of contacts with the people of the West. In the mid-second millennium B.C., China—meaning the heartland centered on the Wei and lower Huang Rivers—was under the Hsia and Shang dynasties, the first of the legendary dynasties about which archaeology has given us some knowledge, though few firm dates. In this period China's comb-decorated pottery was very similar to that of Siberia and European Russia; the Chinese apparently started using chariots; and, most striking, they seem to have rather suddenly begun to use bronze. Bronze-working may well have been learned from the peoples of Central Asia, especially those on the Eurasian Steppe. Noted sinologist René Grousset explains why:

> . . . several very early bronze arrow heads discovered in China . . . indicate a Siberian origin. Moreover, several early bronze vases of the Shang period betray a naive imitation of woodwork, the bronzeworker having copied his model faithfully, even to imitating the notches and knife-marks. The Chinese, suddenly encountering the Siberian techniques of metal working, seem as it were to have taken their ancient earthenware and wooden ritual vases and converted them into bronze overnight.

Whatever the beginnings of Chinese bronze-working, the Shang workers created a fine art out of their metal statues and ritual vessels, one which has seldom been equalled, in China or anywhere else in the world—and one increasingly characterized by stylized animal figures, a theme perhaps also adopted from the Central Asian peoples, but soon made China's own. These skilled Chinese artisans also continued to work in jade, which was apparently still arriving via the routes of the Tarim Basin.

Under the Shang dynasty, China was an expansionist nation. The people did not call their country "China"; that was apparently a later, Western name. Rather, they were the "Middle Kingdom," the only inhabitable land in the midst of a barbarian wilderness. The Shang people set out to change all that. They spread out in all directions from their Chinese heartland to conquer and absorb the strikingly diverse tribes of the region, over the long centuries welding them into the people and nation we today know as China. René Grousset commented of early China:

> . . . if one is to compare the history of China with that of any other great human society it is to Canada or to the United States that one should look. In both China and America the fundamental and essential concern, far beyond the vicissitudes of politics, was the conquest of immense stretches of virgin territory by a labouring people who found only seminomadic populations in their path.

The process was not swift, like the Americans', which was accomplished in only 300 years; in China the integration of the land into one large cultural unit occupied the better part of 4,000 years.

The Shang expansion was also rather selective, taking place first along the main trade routes; it is no coincidence that "shang" means "merchant". One of the hardiest and most

Elaborate figured and patterned silk weaving required large, complicated looms like this Chinese one. (From *Encyclopaedia Britannica*, 11th edition)

powerful of the pioneer families of this time was the Chou clan, who headed toward what was then the Chinese frontier along the Wei River; there, legend has it, they set the hunting and gathering tribes "to till and sow." Their way was not easy, and more than once they had to retreat from their prized farmlands, near where Ch'ang-an would later stand, back toward the Huang River.

But the Chou became so strong through three centuries of struggle against the "barbarians," that when the Shang dynasty produced an intolerable tyrant in the mid–11th century B.C., the Chou led a successful revolt, ending the Shang and initiating the Chou dynasty. For three centuries, the Chou kept their capital in the Wei Valley, until in 771 B.C. they were driven out by "barbarians of the West," and forced to a more easterly capital near Loyang, in the ancient heartland of the Huang Valley. Certainly they always had to keep a watchful eye on potential raiders from the west.

Indeed, so tradition has it, the Chou dynasty might have survived longer had the emperor not "cried wolf" too many times. Signal fires intended to alert the army were lighted once too often for the amusement of the royal mistress. When an attack actually threatened, the army failed to respond and, so the story is told, the Chou capital fell to the invaders.

Under the Chou, roads were given considerable attention, as avenues for tribute and trade and as highways for administration and control. A poem from the ninth century B.C. indicates the care taken with these vital arteries:

> The roads of Chou are [smooth] as a whetstone,
> Straight as an arrow:
> Ways where the lords and officials pass,
> Ways where the common people look on.

Lords, officials, and soldiers all relied on chariots to speed them around the land. Open at the rear, these vehicles each carried a driver, a lancer, and an archer, all with brightly painted shields and colorful flags flying. Drawing the chariot were generally four horses, of a short, though muscular, breed, each with bits decorated by tiny bells. Such bells would later decorate camels as well; even gentlemen at court wore jade ornaments on their belts, to give a "harmonious, tinkling sound." Two-humped camels, which the Chinese called "mountain camels" or "sack-carriers," came into use in China in the early first millennium B.C. as well.

By this time, silk so dominated China's internal trade that it was used as a common medium of exchange. But whether the silk was yet being traded to the Central Asian nomads—in exchange for jade, horses, camels, or gold, all of which were supplied from outside China—we cannot say for sure, though it seems highly probable.

Under the Chou dynasty, "China" was simply a small, primarily rural country, surrounded by numerous petty principalities, each with its own ruler, roads, and practices—though sharing something of language and culture. But the Chou ruled the main westward route and, though they were sometimes open to attack from that region, seem to have kept open lines of contact with the countries of Central Asia. The legendary Emperor Mu was a member of the Chou clan, and historical romances of early times contain many tantalizing references to visitors from the West bringing new gifts, possibly including asbestos cloth, made from mineral fibers found in the mountains of northeastern Afghanistan, in the region called Badakshan, where lapis lazuli was also mined. An early Chinese "book of marvels," possibly from Chou times, describes a certain mountain that "lacks vegetation, but has abundant white and green jade, and as for its fauna, it has abundant camels," noting also that the jade appears on the "sunny side" of a nearby mountain, while on the "dark side [is] an abundance of iron." The description is strongly suggestive of Chinese Turkestan, especially the region around Khotan. But beyond that, in these centuries when the Indo-Europeans from the West were moving across the continent to the borders of China, we have little idea of the routes across the Tarim Basin.

Legends from the Iranian Plateau suggest contacts with China in this period. Around 1000 B.C. a new wave of Iranians began to head over the crest of the Iranian Plateau, at about the time when China's Emperor Mu was supposed to have visited the Royal Mother of the

West. Their legends, though of no more value as historical records than the early Chinese travel tales, indicate some knowledge of China from very early times, and suggest a good deal more than that. The ancient Iranian king Jamshid is said to have married the daughter of the king of Machin (Great China); the king himself is said to have been pursued by his enemies through China and India. Another Iranian king reportedly willed to his second son parts of Central Asia and China; another son was, so the legends go, given part of China and Khotan at his marriage; another royal hero of the Iranians supposedly captured the Emperor of China on his white elephant; another exacted homage from the rulers of China and Central Asia; yet another pursued a Central Asian ruler to his capital and slew him there.

It is possible that in referring to the eastern lands the Iranians were speaking of regions far to the west of China proper in Central Asia (as would happen in later times), even though such territories were not under direct Chinese control. But the proliferation of these legends and the occurrence of travel tales regarding Central Asia at both ends of the Tarim Basin, make it likely that, at the least, trading and perhaps political contacts continued along the eastern half of the Silk Road. If so, these were soon disrupted, for 3,000 years ago, at the beginning of the first millennium B.C., the nomads of Central Asia were on the move again.

★　　★　　★

Once more the horse was at center stage in a new revolution. Through the whole of the second millennium B.C., the nomadic herders of Central Asia had experimented with riding horses. The task was not an easy one, for these powerful, high-spirited, independent-minded creatures strongly resisted the process. The nomads were not alone in their efforts; others in the Near East had also tried riding horses in battle or during hunts. But the practice was not widespread, if only because of the difficulty of doing anything other than simply riding, given the absence of either saddle or stirrups to aid the rider in staying mounted. Only the beautifully ornamental bridle bits, probably developed for use with chariots, allowed the rider some control. But by 900 B.C., the nomads of the west-central Asian steppes had learned how to control and direct their horses with the lower half of the body, leaving their arms free for shooting with bow and arrow. The chariot, with its costly and elaborate workmanship and its driver and spearman, would gradually become obsolete. The mounted archer had both speed and power. Since no special equipment was required, every male—among some nomadic groups, every female as well—was a potential soldier, in a land where horses were plentiful.

So the cavalry was born, and with it new techniques of warfare, which could carry invaders over vast expanses at astonishing speed. Stuart Legg, in his book, *The Heartland,* describes the changes:

> *Unencumbered by chariots and their trappings, bands of horsemen could now move swiftly*
> *from the steppes into the cultivated zones. They could spread panic and scatter local*

resistance with their volleys of arrows launched at full gallop. They could ransack villages in a few hours, gather up the spoil, vanish before organized defence could be brought to bear. They could operate in hostile territory for almost indefinite periods wherever there was open country and grass or captured fodder for their horses. If they met with serious opposition they could withdraw and strike elsewhere. Where defence was weak or non-existent they could penetrate deeper, summon larger numbers of their kind, and turn a tip-and-run raid into an expedition in force. In this way probing taps quickly became hammer blows. Before long, the beating hooves and whistling arrows of the mounted archer from the Heartland were making their presence felt all round its south-western fringes.

This pattern of warfare gradually spread across Asia, not only to those Indo-Europeans who had headed eastward toward China, but also to the other peoples of the Eurasian Steppe, ancestors of peoples like the Mongols and the Manchus. Throughout the steppe, the mounted warrior or rider became the most characteristic feature on the landscape. Wagons continued to be important on the flat plains, but largely for transport of goods; great wide trailers, pulled by many teams of oxen, were used to haul the nomads' "mobile homes," felt-covered, semi-permanent *yurts*. In time—and in pure self-defense—some of the citified nations gradually adopted the cavalry, too; but they were rarely a match for these people who rode the wind, people for whom the horse was the center of life. Swift-riding nomads continued to rule much of the steppes, or at least to bedevil the settled lands around them, until modern times.

Not all of these new cavalry were solely raiders, however. The Iranians did continue their assault on the plateau that would later bear their name. But it was not a sudden invasion. Theirs was a slow, inexorable migration, complete with whole families and herds, over a period of three or four centuries. Often the newcomers signed on as cavalry in the service of local princes, gradually taking over, one by one, the series of small city-states that lined the main route of the Silk Road. In the process, they learned much about the importance of trade and of the trade route that snaked through their new land. Earlier Indo-European invaders to the region had largely been absorbed by the local population, and the peoples of the hinterlands were little affected by the massive changes along the Silk Road, but these new Iranians kept their own distinct culture, while drawing on that of the older cultures along the way.

Their migration was not without resistance, however. The peoples of Mesopotamia had also continued to send traders and armies onto the plateau in attempts to control the trade route. They fought even more strongly for the route with the coming of iron.

Iron had been known in Western Asia and Egypt since the fourth millennium B.C., as a by-product of metalworking, especially of gold. But iron produced in this way was rare and inferior to bronze, so it had been largely for ceremonial use, sometimes even being set in gold, as a decorative ornament. It was not until shortly after 1500 B.C. that techniques were developed to produce stronger iron, and in sufficient quantity to be a force in society, especial-ly in weaponry. Such iron seems to have been produced first on the Anatolian Plateau, in the iron-rich region of Armenia. The people there kept their ironworking techniques as a monopoly for a considerable time; local rulers controlled large-scale export to potential enemies, while loudly lamenting their inability to send their "friends" more than a single dagger blade of the precious metal. But as these Armenian ironworkers battled with their southern neighbors, the secret gradually got out, if only in the warlike way of captured artisans being set to work their skills for new masters. By 1000 B.C., knowledge of ironworking had spread from Armenia to Greece in the west, to the Caucasus in the north, across the Iranian Plateau in the east, and throughout the Fertile Crescent.

The main beneficiaries of this iron technology were the Assyrians, a Semitic or Arab people, like many of the inhabitants of the Near East. By 900 B.C. they had an iron-equipped army that was the terror of the region. From their capital of Nineveh, on the northern curve of the Tigris River, the Assyrians tyrannized their neighbors, from Babylonia to Syria, and guarded the vital route across the Iranian Plateau. Iron also being more readily available and cheaper than bronze, more weapons could be provided for more soldiers, so the infantry once again became important as a military arm. The power and ferocity of Assyria's iron-equipped army for a time held off further nomadic incursions from the east.

More than that, the Assyrians strongly contended with the Iranians for control of the western half of the Silk Road, especially after they were cut off from Armenia's iron and forced to depend on supplies from Iran and further east. Though they had iron weapons, the Assyrians still fought from war chariots, a poor choice on caravan tracks not designed for wheeled vehicles. Chariots were also no match for the Iranian mounted archers, who could literally run circles around them. As a result, the Assyrians soon adopted the cavalry form themselves. Indeed, many of their forays were, in essence, rustling raids—some of which reached as far as the region of modern Teheran—designed to gather horses for the Assyrian army.

In response the various Iranian tribes formed an alliance against the Assyrians. And it was this alliance that would—after a time—unite the western half of the Silk Road for the first time.

CHAPTER FOUR

THE ROYAL ROAD

So far the Silk Road seems to have been primarily for traders and invaders. But in the early centuries of the first millennium B.C., changes were put in motion that would transform the western half of the highway for a time into a road for all, a road by which physicians, musicians, metalsmiths, acrobats, writers, farmers, sculptors, prostitutes, and just plain adventurers—in short, the whole range of people who make up a culture—could travel, see the world, find a new home, win fame, make a fortune, or have the hope of doing all these things. Two peoples would be responsible for this transformation: the Persians and the Greeks.

At the beginning of this period, the Persians were simply one of many Iranian tribes who had established themselves on the Iranian Plateau. Their base was in the southern Zagros Mountains, and they did not even live on the Silk Road. That part of the plateau was controlled by the Medes, the other main tribe in this loose Iranian confederation. The Median capital, Ecbatana (Place of Assembly), today called Hamadan, was squarely on the Silk Road. And it was from here that the Medes based their campaigns against the Assyrians for control of the great route. For their part, the Assyrians often drove deep onto the plateau, and attempted to hold temporary gains along the Silk Road by settling Jewish colonies as far east as Rhagae (near modern Teheran), following the common imperial practice of colonizing frontier lands with dissidents.

Now the truth about this road is as follows. All along it are royal post-stations and very good inns, and it goes all the way through country that is inhabited and safe . . . This country is crossed by four navigable rivers, which you must pass over by ferry-boat . . . There are a hundred and eleven stages in all, and as many inns, on the way from Sardes to Susa . . .

—Herodotus

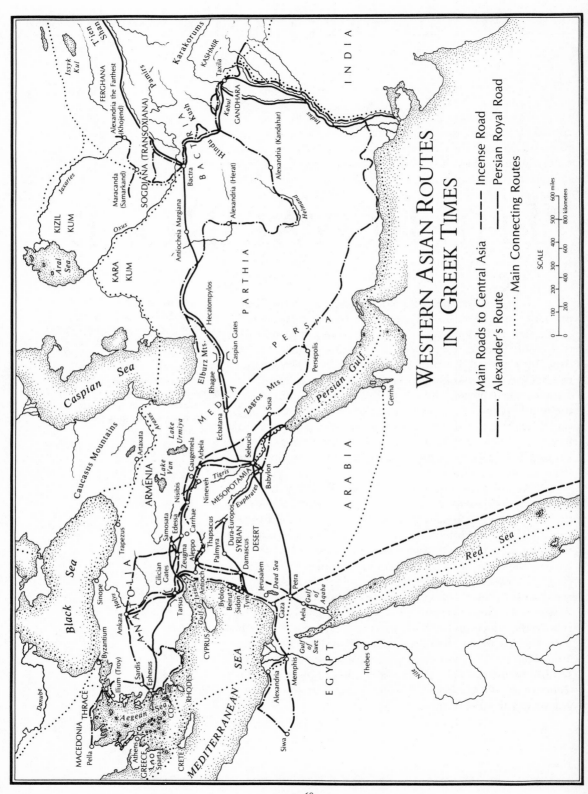

WESTERN ASIAN ROUTES
IN GREEK TIMES

Main Roads to Central Asia — — — Incense Road
Alexander's Route — — — Persian Royal Road
Main Connecting Routes

SCALE

0   100   200   300   400   500   600 miles
0   200   400   600   800 kilometers

INDIA

KARAKORUMS

KASHMIR

Taxila

GANDHARA

Kabul

Alexandria the Farthest
(Khojend)

FERGHANA

Pamirs

Hindu Kush

Indus

Tien Shan

Issyk Kul

Jaxartes

Maracanda
(Samarkand)

SOGDIANA (TRANSOXIANA)

BACTRIA

Bactra

Antiocheia Margiana

Alexandria (Kandahar)

Alexandria (Herat)

Helmand

Oxus

KIZIL KUM

KARA KUM

Aral Sea

PARTHIA

Hecatompylos

PERSIA

Caspian Gates

Rhagae

Elburz Mts.

Ecbatana

MEDIA

Zagros Mts.

Susa

Persepolis

Persian Gulf

Gerrha

ARABIA

Caspian Sea

Caucasus Mountains

Artaxata

Araxes

Lake Urmiya

Lake Van

ARMENIA

Gaugemela

Arbela

Nineveh

Nisibis

Edessa

Samosata

Carrhae

Tigris

MESOPOTAMIA

Euphrates

Seleucia

Babylon

Thapsacus

Dura-Europos

Palmyra

SYRIAN DESERT

Damascus

Aleppo

Zeugma

Antioch

Issus

Tarsus

Cilician Gates

ANATOLIA

Halys

Ankara

Sinope

Trapezus

Byzantium

Ilium (Troy)

Sardis

Ephesus

MACEDONIA

Pella

THRACE

Danube

Black Sea

Athens

Sparta

GREECE

Aegean Sea

CRETE

RHODES

COS

CYPRUS

MEDITERRANEAN SEA

Byblos

Beirut

Sidon

Tyre

Jerusalem

Dead Sea

Gaza

Petra

Aela

Gulf of Aqaba

Gulf of Suez

Alexandria

Memphis

EGYPT

Siwa

Thebes

Nile

Red Sea

But around the end of the eighth century B.C. the Median–Assyrian struggle was interrupted by invaders from the north. Hordes of mounted archers, Scythians and Cimmerians, funneled through the narrow passes of the Caucasus into the Near East. Their onslaught was quite unlike the slow, insinuating arrival of the Iranian tribes, but it was hardly a ragtag band of nomads that had emerged to terrorize the Near East. The Greek historian Herodotus, writing in the fifth century B.C., tells how the event was remembered. After relating how the Median king had conquered the Persians and was making war on the Assyrians, he continues:

> He won a battle against the Assyrians, but as he was besieging the city a great host of
> Scythians came into his kingdom . . . They had entered Asia in the course of driving the
> Cimmerians from Europe, and it was in pursuit of them that they came into the land of
> the Medes.

They swept before them the peoples of the land, devastating much of the Near East, as Herodotus describes:

> For 28 years the Scythians held sway in Asia, and by their unruliness and disregard
> brought it to ruin; for besides exacting from every man the tribute that was laid upon him
> they rode about the country and carried off anything that a man had left.

But the Medes survived their encounter with the Scythians. The Median leader, Cyaxares, during this period reorganized his army, as Herodotus explains:

> [Cyaxares] is said to have been a far greater man of war than his forefathers; he was the
> first to group the fighting-men of Asia by regiments and to give each a separate task,
> some to be spearmen, some bowmen, some to fight on horseback; whereas until then all
> alike were put together without distinction.

In time, the Medes were able to force the main body of Scythians and Cimmerians back north of the Zagros, into the Armenian hills. But many of these wandering warriors stayed in Media and formed the core of the new, more effective army that now ruled the Iranian Plateau. The Medes allied themselves with rebellious Babylonia against the Assyrians, and in 612 B.C. they took and razed Nineveh, the capital of the kingdom that had often boasted of its terrorist rule. The Medes and the Babylonians then divided much of Western Asia between them, with the Medes ruling the Silk Road from the Oxus to the Tigris, as well as much of the Anatolian connection, and the Babylonians ruling the Great Desert Route from the Mesopotamian rivers across to the Mediterranean.

But another power was eyeing the great trade route through Ecbatana: the Persians, who were ready to make a move against their distant kin, the Medes. Recognizing a threat from the Medes, and fully aware of the Hebrew prophecies of the fall of Babylon, the Babylonians allied themselves with the Persians, then led by Cyrus II. Though now a semi-sedentary people, the Persians had remained close to their roots. One of Cyrus's predecessors even had engraved on a gold tablet: "This land of the Persians, which I possess, [is] provided with fine horses and good men." The Medes attempted to weaken the Babylonians by cutting the Silk Road, but the Persians eventually succeeded in their imperial aims, taking Ecbatana and making it the summer capital of their own empire.

But Cyrus was not done. He had in mind nothing less than control of the whole western half of the great trans-Asian route. For him, this meant first of all Asia Minor, where the wealthy King Croesus still ruled beyond the old Median territory, and where Greek port cities collected the riches of the East to be passed on to European Greece. Cyrus captured Croesus's seemingly impregnable capital of Sardis, and then forced his way into the coastal Greek cities one by one, starting centuries of battle between Persians and Greeks. He then turned his atten-

Way stations like this modern one on the route to India dotted the Silk Road and its tributaries. (By Delia and Ferdinand Kuhn)

tion to the East, where still other nomadic raiders were pressing toward the Iranian Plateau. Cyrus drove through the Elburz Mountains, out onto the steppe and across the Oxus, and set his eastern border at the Jaxartes River, building a series of fortified towns to defend his empire from the depredations of steppe nomads.

It was in this region—some say around Rhagae, others near Bactra—that a prophet named Zoroaster had shortly before laid the foundations of the Zoroastrian religion. A reform offshoot of the older Magian religion of the Iranian tribes, Zoroastrianism spread widely throughout Central Asia, especially along the Silk Road. It came to share a number of ideas with Judaism, which was developing a cohesive form in the same period. Among these ideas were belief in a savior or messiah, in resurrection, in a last judgment and a heavenly book in which human actions are recorded, and in a heavenly paradise. It is tempting to wonder if the Jewish trader–colonists, settled by the Assyrians at Rhagae and perhaps even farther east, were the conduits of religious exchange between the main bodies of these two religions. Certainly the Zoroastrian religion, with its emphasis on contending forces of good and evil in the world, would much influence Christianity, especially the latter's Near Eastern forms which some have deemed heretical. Zoroastrianism later became the official religion of the Persian Empire, but in these early times the Persians were tolerant not only of many religions but also of many peoples, projecting the comforting illusion of independence within a paternalistic empire.

Turning back toward Mesopotamia, Cyrus then ended the long rule of the Babylonian kings, taking over the lands of the Fertile Crescent and the great chain of caravan cities and seaports that linked Persia with Arabia, Egypt, and the Mediterranean world. Cyrus was hailed as a liberator by many, especially by the Jews, for whom his triumph meant the end of their "Babylonian captivity" and whom he allowed to return to Jerusalem, there to rebuild their temple. The Bible tells the tale, in Ezra 1: 2-3:

> *Thus saith Cyrus king of Persia, The Lord God of heaven hath given me all the*
> *kingdoms of the earth; and he hath charged me to build him an house at Jerusalem . . .*
> *go up to Jerusalem . . . and build the house of the Lord God of Israel . . .*

Cyrus's successors expanded the borders of the Persian Empire even farther: in the west to Egypt and North Africa, in the north to Thrace, and in the east even across the Afghan Mountains into India, to create by far the largest empire the world had yet seen. One of his successors, the great Darius, at the turn of the fifth century B.C. united his vast territory with an unparalleled network of roads. The most famous of these roads, the Persian Royal Road, linked the old Persian capital at Susa with Croesus's old city, Sardis, in Anatolia. A spur fed from Susa through the Zagros Mountains to Ecbatana on the Silk Road.

Like modern expressways, these roads were built for speed, bypassing major cities, both because travelers might be slowed by city street traffic and because highways might too easily lead enemies up to the city gates. Using fast horses, messengers could travel the over-1,600-mile route between Susa and Sardis in nine days, ten to the port cities of Smyrna or Ephesus. So famous was this messenger service that, well into the Middle Ages, its name—*angareion*—was a symbol for speed. Herodotus tells how it worked:

> *Now there is nothing mortal that accomplishes a course more swiftly than do these messengers, by the Persians' skillful contrivance. It is said that as many days as there are in the whole journey, so many are the men and horses that stand along the road, each horse and man at the interval of a day's journey; and these are stayed neither by snow nor rain nor heat nor darkness from accomplishing their appointed course with all speed. The first rider delivers his charge to the second, the second to the third, and then it passes on from hand to hand, even as in the Greek torch-bearer's race in honor of Hephaestus.*

This is the ancestor not only of the Pony Express but also of virtually all post services in the world. The U.S. Postal Service even adopted a version of Herodotus's commentary as their motto:

> *Neither snow nor rain nor heat nor gloom of night stays these couriers from the swift completion of their appointed rounds.*

$\star$ $\star$ $\star$

The western end of the Silk Road in this period, as in the past, headed toward Babylon, still the crossroads of Mesopotamia, with many caravans then passing on via the Great Desert Route to Aleppo or Damascus. Travelers generally crossed the Tigris near the old Assyrian capital of Nineveh (today Mosul) and the Euphrates at Zeugma, whose very name means "bridge" or "crossing." But with the empire's orientation toward the northwest, toward Anatolia and the Greek cities on the Aegean and Black Seas, the Persian Royal Road took a great many travelers and traders farther across the empire. Though the land routes through Anatolia were long and arduous, they were often preferable for people heading toward Greece, for pirates made sea travel on the Mediterranean a dangerous business. From Aleppo, a different leg of the Persian Royal Road—by Herodotus's time the preferred route—led around the finger-shaped Gulf of Issus to Tarsus, through the narrow Cilician Gates, and then onto the Anatolian Plateau, joining the old main route at Ankara (Ancyra). Caravans would, of course, travel much more slowly than the post messengers described by Herodotus. He estimated that a traveler on foot or a caravan at its normal slow pace would take about 90 days to complete the whole journey along the Persian Royal Road.

And travelers' needs were well-provided for, in all likelihood following the models developed over the previous two millennia for long-distance traders on the Iranian Plateau. Shelter and supply stations were established at reasonable intervals: close together, sometimes only 12 miles apart, in rugged mountain country, where the route was sometimes hewn out of solid rock; farther apart in easier lowland terrain, where travelers could expect to cover more ground in a day. Ferries, and later seasonally permanent boat-bridges, were generally used at river crossings where fording was impractical. Aside from the paucity of wood and building-stone in the lowlands, permanent bridges were seldom used because the Mesopotamian rivers tended to flood badly.

Although the Royal Road is the best known of the Persian routes of this period, it was by no means unique. The same attention to security and comfort for travelers was paid on main roads throughout the empire, including, of course, the Silk Road. Indeed, the relative peace prevailing in the vast Persian territories allowed travel and trade to proceed more easily and more profitably to all concerned than ever before.

It was in this period that the great caravan cities of Syria—Aleppo, Hama, Homs (Emesa), and Damascus, in particular—truly came into their own, receiving goods from the Silk Road as well as spices and perfumes from Arabia's Incense Road and other luxuries brought by sea from India. Aramaeans (one of many Semitic groups living in and around the Syrian Desert) were such active traders in these caravan cities that their speech became the common commercial language, the *lingua franca*, on the western third of the Silk Road. The Persians actively encouraged trade throughout the empire, introducing standard weights and measures, as well as minted coins to replace the old systems of bartering or paying by weight in kind. Given the greater security and the resultant drop in transport expenses and risk, the Silk Road began to carry not just luxury goods or vital metals but also large quantities of everyday items, such as household wares, cheap clothing, and grain.

In this trade, the camel reigned supreme. The horse may have been the mount of royal messengers and swift invaders, and the donkey may have been used for humble trade, but the camel had by this time established itself as the mainstay of the Silk Road trade. While the Arabian camel was generally confined to the hot lowlands, the two-humped Bactrian camel dominated the highlands and was often a part of the tribute sent to mountain rulers. Bactrian camels were even represented in sculpture on the walls of the Persian palace at Persepolis, wearing bells around their necks and led by halters. Professional camel-pullers and camel-drivers were important figures on the Silk Road; it is no accident that Zoroaster's name in Iranian was Zara-ushtra or Zarathustra, meaning "camel-driver." Beasts of burden who had to travel the rough roads were aided in the fourth century B.C. by the development of shoes, made of copper, leather, or horsehair.

The breadth and richness of the Persians' empire is indicated by the inscription Darius had written on his palace at Susa in about 521 B.C.:

> *This is the palace which I built at Susa. From afar its ornamentation was brought . . .*
> *the earth was dug downward, and . . . the rubble was packed down, and . . . the sun*

dried brick was molded, [by] the Babylonian people . . . The cedar timber . . . [is] from a mountain named [Lebanon] . . . the Assyrian people brought it to Babylon; from Babylon the Carians and the Ionians brought it to Susa. The yaku timber was brought from Gandara [in India] and from Carmania. The gold was brought from Sardis and from Bactria, which here was wrought. The precious stone lapis-lazuli and carnelian, which was wrought here, was brought from Sogdiana. The precious stone turquoise was brought from Chorasmia, which was wrought here. The silver and the ebony were brought from Egypt. The ornamentation with which the wall was adorned was brought from Ionia. The ivory, which was wrought here, was brought from Ethiopia and from Sind and from Arachosia. The stone columns, which here were wrought, were brought from Elam. The stone-cutters who wrought the stone were Ionians and Sardians. The goldsmiths who wrought the gold were Medes and Egyptians. The men who wrought the baked brick were Babylonians. The men who adorned the well were Medes and Egyptians.

Regardless of their prodigious stamina, many camels would die on an especially difficult journey. (By Sven Hedin, from his *Through Asia*, 1899)

To this palace came princes, foreign envoys, physicians, writers, artists, all of the political and cultural elite of the mid–first millennium B.C.

Persian rule brought other changes to the Silk Road. Massive public works were undertaken, such as the building of many underground canals called *qanats* to provide water for irrigation in the dry plateau, where water was precious and liable to evaporation in open canals or ditches. In the wetter lowlands, conversely, marshes were drained, all to bring more land under active cultivation. Darius, in particular, strongly encouraged the transplantation of new plant species throughout his empire. It was in this period that alfalfa, the favorite fodder of horses, spread from the Iranian Plateau across Asia Minor to Greece. In a letter to one of his governors, Darius wrote: "I commend your plan for improving my country by the transplantation of fruit trees." In this period, too, pistachios first arrived in Aleppo, sesame in Egypt, and rice in Mesopotamia.

★　　★　　★

During this time, the eastern half of the Silk Road was still in shadow. Some foreign envoys and traders apparently made their way eastward across part of the route. But the road, like China itself, seems to have been divided among numerous petty states and clans. There was, however, one long-distance route across the landmass in this period: the Eurasian Steppe Route, running between the northern borders of China and the European steppes north of the Black Sea. There, in the presumed ancient homeland of the Indo-Europeans, the powerful Scythians ruled.

The Scythians are perhaps best remembered today for their nobility's extraordinary array of gold ornaments and implements. Everything from their riding gear and armor to their plates and personal ornaments was either made of solid gold or gold-encrusted, much of the work done by fine artisans in the new Greek colonies on the shores of the Black Sea. There the Greeks traded for the grain produced by those Scythians who were agriculturally inclined; but an equal attraction was the gold which, along with furs, Scythian traders brought across the steppes from the East.

A Greek adventurer named Aristeas claimed that he had followed the Scythian caravans eastward from the marts north of the Black Sea to get gold, in the sixth or seventh century B.C. Aristeas's fanciful poem relating his experiences is now lost, but Herodotus summarized how Aristeas declared that he:

> . . . *journeyed to the Issedones by the inspiration of Apollo; that beyond the Issedones dwell the Arimaspi, a one-eyed people, beyond them are griffins that guard gold, and beyond them the Hyperboreans who reach to the sea; that each of these nations except the Hyperboreans pressed upon its neighbors, starting with the Arimaspi . . .*

Because of the obvious imaginary elements and the confusing, unfamiliar names in the story, it was for a long time discounted. But, following the masterful analyses of people like G.F. Hudson, many now believe that the story described an actual route across Eurasia.

Herodotus continues about the supposed route:

> *As far as the bald people [perhaps Mongolian peoples, who lack the abundant body hair of Caucasians], the country and the nations that inhabit it are well known, for there are Scythians who journey to them, and it is not difficult to obtain information from these or from Greeks of the mart on the Borysthenes [Dnieper] and the other Pontic [Black Sea] marts. The Scythians who make the journey do business through seven interpreters in seven languages . . . The country to the east of the bald men is known for certain to be inhabited by the Issedones, but the region beyond towards the north both of the bald men and of the Issedones is unknown, except for such stories as these people tell of it . . . There is a report from the Issedones that in the land beyond them are the one-eyed men and the gold-guarding griffins; the Scythians have passed on this tale . . . As for the Hyperboreans, neither the Scythians nor any other people in that quarter give any account of them, unless it be the Issedones. For my part I do not believe that even the Issedones tell of them, for if they did, the Scythians would speak of them as they do of the one-eyed men.*

Here is a more practical approach to the situation, including some frank scepticism. Drawing on Herodotus's further descriptions, Hudson believed that the Scythian gold caravans started from a city at the mouth of the Don River, probably Tanais (later Tana), in a territory "destitute both of wild and of cultivated trees for a 15 days' journey to the north." Beyond them lay a lightly wooded country, where the people sold furs, and then a desert of seven days' journey. Herodotus goes on:

> *. . . as far as the country of these Scythians the whole land is level and deep-soiled, but henceforth it is stony and rugged; when one has passed over a long stretch of the rugged ground, one comes to a people living at the foot of lofty mountains.*

For Hudson, this corresponds to a route from the Don River across the steppe to the Volga, on whose east bank timber growth begins, and beyond which there lies a salty barren waste. The "high impassable" mountains he takes to be the Altai (Golden) Mountains, reached after passage through rough and broken foothills.

The Altai's snow-covered peaks would indeed be striking to steppe people used to featureless plains, and the hills in that region might seem to constitute a barrier to easy travel for those unaware of the Dzungarian Gap by which the Eurasian Steppe Route funnels easily onto the Mongolian Steppe. It is here, in the Altai, that the great Siberian gold mines are found, the mines that provided most of the gold for Scythia—gold that also found its way around the Aral Sea into Russian Turkestan and then, via the Silk Road, into Western Asia. Hudson then places the Issedones in the region of the Lop Nor (where the second century A.D. Greco-Roman geographer Ptolemy also placed them).

Having reached so far across the continent, to beyond the Altai and the Lop Nor, Hudson suggests that the Hyperboreans "who reach to the sea" were, in fact, the Chinese. The name, which means "beyond the north wind," he explains by the fact that China's climate is temperate. By contrast, in Scythia, as Herodotus says: "The winter continues eight months and during the other four it is cold there." Herodotus also noted that the Hyperboreans were vegetarians—and certainly the Chinese were, at least by contrast with the Central Asian nomads, whom they derided as meat-eaters.

This hypothesis of a trans-Asian overland route is supported by modern finds of Chinese silk dating from this period in graves from the Altai Mountains through Scythia and even into Central Europe. By now, if not well before, the Chinese were trading their peerless silk for the furs, jade, camels, and horses that only the steppe nomads could supply, and hoping, in the process, to secure some semblance of peace on their borders.

If Hudson is right, Aristeas is the first person we know by name who traveled from Europe across Asia to the outskirts of China, and gave us a glimpse of a long-distance caravan trade that stretched across some thousands of miles of unsettled land. Did a similar trading network stretch the length of the Silk Road? We do not know for sure. Certainly jade was, for the Chinese, as powerful a lure as gold was for Europeans. But we have no record of a Tarim traveler of the same period to match with that of Aristeas. And, indeed, by the time Herodotus was writing—at least one, perhaps two centuries after Aristeas—the trade route across the Eurasian Steppe had apparently been broken. For Herodotus was passing on hearsay information, which he acknowledges he could not confirm from any current reports. The Eurasian Steppe Route, always the easiest in terrain, had presumably fallen prey to its fatal defect—its exposure to the ever-contending nomads of the plains.

★   ★   ★

The Greeks, who gave us this fragmentary picture of a trans-Asian route, were soon to further develop the western half of the Silk Road, in the centuries just before its emergence as a through road from Syria to China. The Persians may have brought the road and the region under one ruler, but it would be the Greeks who gave it a semblance of cultural unity, if only for a brief time. The man responsible for this transformation was none other than Alexander the Great.

When Alexander arrived on the scene, the great days of Classical Greece were over. Though educated by Aristotle, Alexander was not truly a product of Greece's Golden Age, for he came from the rougher northern lands of Macedonia. But he set himself the task of avenging

Greece's defeat at the hands of the Persians—and of winning for himself the glory of not only duplicating Darius's empire but also conquering all of the known world and carrying Hellenistic culture throughout Western Asia.

He began, quite naturally, by crossing the Hellespont (the Dardanelles), the narrow channel between the Balkans and Anatolia, more specifically between the peninsula of Gallipoli and the region once ruled by Greece's ancient rival, Troy. This had long been the main crossing between Europe and Asia; the Bosporus channel to the northeast, guarded today by Istanbul, came into prominence only later. Troy and all the other cities facing the Aegean Sea had long vied for the trade that flowed from Western Asia across the Anatolian Plateau. Alexander was mindful of this rich commerce, and of its importance in Greek history. On arriving in Asia, in the spring of 334 B.C., his chroniclers tell us, Alexander stopped first at the site of Troy to pay homage to Achilles, hero of the Trojan War. As historian Margaret Bryant described it:

> . . . *[he] there went through those dramatic acts of sacrifice to the Ilian Athena, assumption of the shield believed to be that of Achilles and offerings to the great Homeric dead, which are significant of the poetic glamour shed, in the young king's mind, over the whole enterprise, and which men will estimate differently according to the part they assign to imagination in human affairs.*

After winning a brief skirmish with the Persians, Alexander went on to regain the Greek cities that lined the west coast of Anatolia. Heading inland, he detoured from the general line of the Persian Royal Road eastward to subjugate local princes who had continued to enjoy great autonomy under the Persians. At the city of Gordium, he was unable to untie the famous Gordian knot, so with characteristic impatience cut it instead, to signify that he would one day "rule all Asia."

On his way to meet the main Persian army, Alexander took the route southward from Ankara to Tarsus on the Mediterranean. This was the main route of the Persian Royal Road in the fourth century, as it had been a century before when Herodotus praised the great highway. But it was a dangerous choice, for Alexander to thread his army through the tight pass called the Cilician Gates, in places only wide enough for four soldiers abreast and, so the fourth-century military chronicler Xenophon had reported, "impassable if obstructed by the enemy," who generally threw boulders down the cliffs at invaders attempting to breach the gates. But Alexander forced through with a daring night attack and emerged on the humid, unhealthy plains of Tarsus.

So far Alexander had met no major opposition; the main Persian army lay ahead. The two forces finally met in the spring of 333 B.C., on the plains east of the Gulf of Issus, the bay forming the corner between Anatolia and Syria. The clash turned into a rout, and Darius was forced to flee on horseback into the Persian hills. Alexander did not pursue him, but began to put into effect plans of his own.

The Greeks had long had cities along the coasts of Anatolia; that these had been under Persian rule was, in part, what had prompted Alexander's invasion. South of the Gulf of Issus, too, the Greeks had long traded, through port cities such as Al Mina and Ugarit. But once beyond them, in Syria, the Greeks were in territory that had, for thousands of years, been in the hands of the Semitic peoples of the region.

There, along an inland route, was a string of caravan cities, among them Aleppo, Damascus, Amman, in the land of Jordan, and Petra, in a rockbound desert fastness just north of the Gulf of Aqaba. In the hands of various Arab tribes, these cities and the road linking them formed the northern extension of the fabled Incense Road, which began at southwestern Arabia's crossroads city of Arabia Eudaemon (Arabia the Blessed, now called Aden). As Alexander well knew, into Arabia Eudaemon and up along the Incense Road flowed all the riches of the East. Arabia's own spices—like frankincense and myrrh—were joined on this route by gems and spices from India and farther east, which had long been brought by sea on the Spice Route. Many centuries before Alexander, in about the 10th century B.C., the queen of this south Arabian land had made a visit to the Jewish king of Israel. The splendor of her caravan from Saba (Sheba) is recorded in Kings 1:10:

> And when the queen of Sheba heard of the fame of Solomon . . . she came to Jerusalem
> with a very great train, with camels that bore spices, and very much gold, and precious
> stones . . . And she gave the king a hundred and twenty talents of gold, and of spices a
> very great store, and precious stones . . .

The trade on this Incense Road had continued and expanded in the intervening centuries. Even when seagoing traders were able to bypass inland Arabia by sailing up the Red Sea to the port of Aela (Aqaba), the inland caravans still took the rich stuffs northward from there to Petra, Damascus, and Aleppo.

★   ★   ★

Of equal, if not greater, interest to Alexander were the cities along the Mediterranean coast, held by the Phoenicians, for many centuries the Greeks' rivals in the Mediterranean and Atlantic sea trade. Chief among the cities of Phoenicia (roughly the region of modern Lebanon) were Byblos, Sidon, and Tyre. Byblos was the ancient center of the Egyptian papyrus trade, and would give its name to the Bible—literally, "The Book." In Sidon and Tyre were the Phoenician dye factories where, in secrecy nearly as total as that of the Chinese

Incense gathered in Arabia was shipped north to Aleppo and
then east on the Silk Road. (From an engraving from
Cosmographie Universelle, by Thevet, 1575, reprinted in Yule's
Marco Polo)

regarding silk manufacture, the famed "royal purple" so highly prized by the aristocrats of the
Mediterranean world was produced.

The dye itself plays an important role in our story, for one of silk's greatest attractions is
its receptiveness to dyes, especially purple. And for some centuries, until the secret of
manufacturing this especially high-quality purple dye passed beyond Phoenicia, the course of
the Silk Road would be bent toward these cities, so the imported silk could receive the finish-
ing of fine dyeing.

Phoenician purple was made from molluscs found on the Mediterranean seashore.
Local legend told of how the god Melgarth discovered the dye when his dog bit into a shellfish
and was stained red about the mouth; myth credits Melgarth with first using the stain to dye a
tunic for his mistress. The purple produced was not simply the modern color we know by that

name, but a whole array of hues ranging from a deep reddish–purple "the color of congealed blood" to an inky blue-black. The glandular liquid of the *murex*, the most favored of the shellfish, is yellow at first, but is changed by the action of the sun to the whole range of colors at the dyers' command.

Dyeing could only take place in the autumn and winter, when the molluscs were available; and since the stain had to be collected and used immediately after the molluscs were killed, the dye factories were confined to the seashore (until many centuries later, when people learned how to keep the molluscs alive inland). The precious glandular fluid could be extracted directly from larger molluscs; but smaller ones had to be crushed together into a mass, then soaked in salt, washed, and boiled to extract the dye from the shells, meat, and dirt. All in all, it was a laborious, costly process. Even today, the sites of old dye factories near Tyre are marked by ancient mounds of broken and discarded shells.

The color of the dye depended on the mollusc used, the amount of exposure to sunlight, the method of preparation, and the amount of concentration achieved by boiling. One of the rarest and most expensive of the shades was a flaming red, produced by double dyeing, in which a fabric was dipped the second time in a dye from a different shellfish. Such costly production made purple dye extremely expensive to use on any fabric. Only the richest and most powerful people—such as Darius or the high priest of the Hebrews—could afford a whole robe of purple.

The purple dye was certainly important to the history of the Phoenicians; their very name comes from the Greek word for purple, *poeni*. (This would, in Roman times, be transformed to Punic; the Phoenicians called themselves Canaanites, and are known by that name in the Bible.) The Phoenicians had many more strings to their bow, however. They were skilled artisans and manufacturers, especially in making colored glass. As long-time sea traders, they also handled much of the exchange between Asia and the Mediterranean world. That the Phoenician cities, especially Tyre, were active trading centers is described fulsomely in the book of Ezekiel 27:

> . . . *say unto Tyrus, O thou that art situate at the entry of the sea, which art a merchant of the people for many isles . . . Syria was thy merchant by reason of the multitude of the wares of thy making: they occupied in thy fairs with emeralds, purple, and broidered work, and fine linen, and coral, and agate. Judah, and the land of Israel, they were thy merchants: they traded in thy market wheat . . . and honey, and oil, and balm. Damascus was thy merchant in the multitude of the wares of thy making for the multitude of all riches; in the wine of Helbon, and white wool . . . The merchants of Sheba . . . they were thy merchants: they occupied in thy fairs with chief of all spices, and with all precious stones, and gold . . . These were thy merchants in all sorts of things, in blue clothes, and broidered work, and in chests of rich apparel, bound with cords, and made of cedar . . . When thy wares went forth out of the seas, thou filledst many people; thou didst enrich the kings of the earth with the multitude of thy riches and of thy merchandise.*

With their combination of skilled manufacturers, long-established crossroads fairs, and seaports to take wares throughout the Mediterranean world, the Phoenician cities were attractive prizes to be won.

On shore or inland, these were all cities worthy of Alexander's attention. The Greeks were, after all, pre-eminently a trading people. In the past their commercial activities had largely focused on the sea. For centuries colonists from the overpopulated, hardscrabble land of Greece had been streaming across the seas, from Gibraltar to the Crimea, to establish trading posts from which they funneled the resources of these more bountiful countries to their homelands. Now Alexander and his successors were to apply the same approach to the lands of Western Asia. They took the existing cities; they would add to them cities of their own.

★   ★   ★

Temporarily ignoring the disordered Persian army on which he had sworn revenge, Alexander chose instead to spend the next two years taking the prime caravan centers and ports of Western Asia, from Syria to Palestine and Egypt. Darius had, indeed, been so badly beaten that he offered to give Alexander all the lands west of the Euphrates, in exchange for peace. Perhaps he was swayed in part by the fact that Alexander had captured the women of the Persian royal family after the debacle at Issus. But Alexander refused the bargain, signaling his intention to take it all.

Alexander did not capture these prosperous, well-fortified cities without a fight. The strongest opposition, not surprisingly, came from Tyre, once the island stronghold of the Phoenicians. Though the Tyrenes had long since fallen under the domination of the Persians, they balked at coming under the yoke of their ancient rivals, the Greeks. For seven months they held out behind the walls of their fortress; only when Alexander built a half-mile-wide causeway (the remains of which still exist) to the island and mounted a joint sea and land attack, did the city fall. The Philistine stronghold of Gaza, farther south along the coast, also withstood a siege for two months. In the end, the two cities were sacked, though not destroyed, and the inhabitants dispersed into slavery; the cities themselves were soon repopulated by Greek colonists and other settlers from nearby cities.

After that, Alexander's way was easier. He passed along the Gaza Strip into the delta and desert lands of Egypt. There his most famous action was probably the founding of a Greek port at the mouth of a western arm of the Nile—Alexandria. Destined to be one of the world's great cities, Alexandria came to be the main outlet for marine traders on the Spice Route. As a major refining and distribution center for the Mediterranean world, it sometimes even acted as a terminus for the Silk Road, rivaling the more logical terminus in northwestern Syria.

Returning from Egypt, Alexander now progressed up the inland caravan road through Damascus, finally turning toward the East in the spring of 331 B.C. The winter rains had swollen the rivers of Mesopotamia, but the Greek army crossed the upper Euphrates River on a specially constructed pontoon bridge. The Tigris was shallow enough near the site of the ancient Assyrian town of Nineveh so Alexander could plant the cavalry in two rows, blunting the force of the current enough to allow the infantry to cross on foot. It was on the plains of Gaugamela (literally, "pasture of camels") east of the upper Tigris that the Greek and Persian armies resumed battle. Once again, the superior numbers of Darius should have had the advantage, especially on the open plains, but Alexander's strategy carried the day, and the Persians were routed, with Darius seeking refuge on the Iranian Plateau.

And once again, Alexander declined to pursue him immediately, choosing instead to proceed southward toward Babylon, richest city of Mesopotamia. All along the way, cities opened their doors to their new ruler, their old one having fled to the hills. At Babylon, which Alexander naturally made his capital in Western Asia, he ordered that Greek flora be planted in the famous Hanging Gardens. Then, still heading southward, he added to the riches of Babylon those of Susa, the Persians' spring capital. Then, in a stunning winter campaign, Alexander forced his way through the Zagros Mountains and onto the Iranian Plateau to the old Persian summer capital at Persepolis. The extraordinary palace at Persepolis, product of fine artists and artisans from as far away as India and Anatolia, was burnt in a night—whether as part of a drunken revel or because of a conscious decision to destroy a possible rallying ground for the Persians, we shall probably never know. That deed done, Alexander moved along the Iranian Plateau, aiming for the strategic site of Ecbatana, the old Median capital on the Silk Road, to which Darius had fled. No longer was Alexander facing the open doors of lowland cities; here he met with rough mountain tribes. But he gave better than he got, as Margaret Bryant noted:

> The mountain tribes on the road . . . accustomed to exact blackmail even from the king's train, learnt by a bitter lesson that a stronger hand had come to wield the empire.

Fleeing before Alexander, Darius retreated along the Silk Road from Ecbatana through Rhagae and beyond the Caspian Gates, with much of his army dispersing and melting away into the hills. In the end, the Persian army's tattered remnants, seeing Alexander's stalwarts come into sight one morning, killed Darius before he could be captured by the Greeks. In the summer of 330 B.C., only a little over four years after he had arrived in Asia, Alexander had avenged the past defeat of the Greeks. He now assumed the Persian mantle as ruler of the western half of Asia. Defeat of Darius did not give him automatic control over the mountain peoples to the east, however; that he would have to win. And for that the Greeks would need help.

★   ★   ★

All along the route from Macedonia to the Caspian Gates, Alexander had moved to bring into the Greek orbit the newly conquered peoples. Alexander's own army was not simply a spare, tightly honed Macedonian force. Rather it by this time included Thracians, Illyrians, Iranians, Anatolians, Semites, and Indians, among many others. Some had regarded the Greek victory as a liberation from Persian domination; others were drawn by the promise of adventure and profit. Though each military division had a Macedonian core, non-Greeks made up at least half the army. Supporting and holding together this polyglot army was a whole array of specialists, including military engineers and mechanics, interpreters and guides, doctors for the wounded soldiers, and veterinarians for the all-important horses. And beyond these were the camp followers, the wives, mistresses, children, servants, slaves, and prostitutes, as well as the merchants and moneylenders, who handled the large sums of money won, saved, and circulated by the enriched soldiery. The result was, as historian Mikhail Rostovtzev put it, that the "Hellenistic army of this period was an enormous moving city, comparable to the moving cities of the Oriental nomads in eastern Europe and in Asia," or more precisely, "a moving capital, containing a population larger than that of many Greek capitals"—and a wealthy one, at that.

The composition of Alexander's "moving capital" changed as it moved across the face of Asia. All along the way, at each new city added to the Greek domain, Hellene governors, administrators, soldiers, artisans, and merchants were left behind to bind the city into the Hellenistic Empire. At the same time, many of the conquered inhabitants joined the great wandering train, of their own free will or as slaves, in the process taking on Hellenistic ways. Alexander himself was changed in the process, adopting the more opulent Asian style of dress, incurring the criticism of his own people but winning further support from those who had joined him on the way. In particular, Alexander's wearing of the Persian-style all-purple robe angered many of his fellow Macedonians, for whom it symbolized his sharp divergence from the army's original, rougher, more egalitarian camaraderie. That division between Alexander and his countrymen would later cause him considerable difficulty. But for now, the policy of attempting to fuse Hellenistic and Asian ways strengthened the army more than weakened it.

So the Greeks were able to leave behind them relatively secure territories, and still head in strength eastward along the Silk Road. Such strength was necessary in eastern Persia, for here the Greeks encountered a proud Iranian population that resisted outside domination. As Alexander's army passed through this region, there were frequent revolts in the regions behind them. Progress was slow, and took the Greeks on a slow curve southeastward toward India, as far as the Kabul River valley. But finally Alexander was ready to face the major power in the region—Bactria—important not only because of its position on the Silk Road but also because Darius's murderers had brought the Persian crown there, to the king of Bactria.

In the spring of 328 B.C., Alexander came down from the Afghan highlands to the plains of Bactria, pursuing the remnant of Persian opposition all the way through Maracanda (Samarkand) to Bukhara, pushing his frontier out beyond the Jaxartes River, roughly the limit of cultivable land, and finally securing his hold on the region by taking the remaining

Itinerant merchants like this Persian peddler
traveled the Silk Road for many centuries.
(Pennsylvania Museum)

mountain strongholds of the local princes. The easternmost city he founded was named
Alexandria the Farthest, near the site of modern Khojent.

Though he continued to draw criticism from his European followers for his adopted
Asian ways—and to deal with such attacks harshly—Alexander still tried to unite the diverse
lands under his command into one Hellenistic Empire. In token of this, he took as his wife a
Bactrian princess, Roxane. Alexander's chronicler, Arrian, notes that Roxane was one of the
most beautiful women in all Asia; perhaps more to the point, he points out that Alexander "did
not think it derogatory to his dignity to marry her." Clearly the Bactrian princess was considered someone worth a marital alliance, quite aside from any personal charms she might have
possessed. Changing the name of the capital city from Zariaspa to Bactra, he made this his
eastern capital, at the crux of Asia. As had been his pattern elsewhere, he established a Greek

city alongside the older Persian one, peopling it not only with soldiers but also with artisans, skilled workers, and, of course, merchants.

★   ★   ★

So Alexander had reached halfway across Asia, halfway across what would soon become the Silk Road. Did he know about China, roughly an equal distance to the East across the mountains and deserts? We cannot tell. The Greeks apparently knew of China's precious commodity—silk. By the fifth century B.C. some silk had, as we have seen, worked its way across the expanse of Asia into Eastern Europe, though we cannot be sure that any reached the Mediterranean world. Aristotle, Alexander's old tutor, seems to have mentioned silk in his scientific writings, speaking of a:

> . . . great worm which has horns and so differs from others. At its first metamorphosis it produces a caterpillar, then a bombylius and lastly a chrysalis—all these changes taking place within six months. From this animal women separate and reel off the cocoons and afterwards spin them. It is said that this was first spun in the island of Cos by Pamphile, daughter of Plates.

Many people feel that Aristotle was speaking of an inferior wild-silk fabric, much like what is now called bombazine, made from the cocoon of a caterpillar native to the Greek island of Cos. Whether he was speaking of Cos or Chinese silk, it is notable that many later Classical writers came to believe that the thread was of vegetable origin.

"Silk" was, indeed, the Western name for the gossamer fabric. The Chinese knew it as something approximating see or szu; the various nomads of Central Asia generally called it sir, sirghe, or sirkek. (Some have hypothesized that this derives from ser, the Central Asian root-word for "yellow," which is the color most closely associated with Chinese civilization.) The Jews may have known the fabric as sherikoth; the Arabs apparently called it saraqai; and the Greeks knew it as serica, which by a transmutation of r to l, later became our modern silk. As far as we can tell, the people of Alexander's age did not know of China as such. Naming the people after the product, they called the silk-producers Seres; the northern Chinese would be known to the West by the name for centuries.

How small amounts of silk reached Western Asia from China is unclear. Some may have come westward along the Eurasian Steppe, following the route described by Herodotus, or cutting down through Russian Turkestan to meet the Silk Road. Or silk may have been passed along the Silk Road itself, by the old relay trade. A semi-nomadic people called the Yüeh-chih, who occupied the Kansu Corridor in this period, were middlemen in supplying jade from the Pamirs to China; silk might well have passed in the opposite direction, especially since it would be such a unique and valuable item in trading with the West. These routes are the most likely at this time, for the Greeks and the Romans who succeeded them knew the Seres as a northern people, reached by an overland route, occupying the lands between Scythia and India.

Some silk may have reached Western Asia via India in this period. Two centuries later we learn that some Chinese fabric (possibly silk) is found in Bactria, having been brought there from southern China through Burma, across the Bay of Bengal (or, less likely, overland through Southeast Asia) to India and on to Bactria. This was an old route and may have been operating at this time; if so it could have been the source of the rumor that the Indians had discovered how to make silk. Similarly, some silk may have reached the West, especially Egypt, via the Spice Route, which was long established by this time. But the southern Chinese, in touch with the West by these routes, were called *Sinae* or *Thinae*. Not until some centuries later did Westerners generally realize that the Seres and the Sinae were inhabitants of the same country. So, because the persistent view in Classical times is that the Seres were a northern people, the overland Asian routes are more likely avenues for the small amounts of silk to reach the West.

Actually, Greeks seem to have taken Central Asian middlemen for the secretive silk-producers. (In a similar way, some of the peoples of Mesopotamia knew silk as *medic*, the Medes being the last link in their chain of supply.) And what little the Greeks knew about the Seres was more fantasy than fact. A Greek physician at a Persian court—a man named Ctesias—for example, said in about 400 B.C.:

> It is said that the Seres and the Northern Indians are so tall, that one meets men 13 cubits high; they live more than 200 years.

Certainly the silk-producers were far off, both their product and information about them passing through many hands. One need only play the old parlor game of Gossip to understand how some of the outlandish tales of distant peoples, like Ctesias's and for that matter Herodotus's, could have come about. It was also common for early traders to deliberately spread false information and thus guard their sources of supply.

Of course, it is not universally accepted that silk did, in fact, reach the West in these centuries. Some would count the admittedly small evidences of silk or knowledge of the fabric at naught, believing them to be misinterpretations or later interpolations. (Some have even argued that we cannot be sure that silk arrived in Western Asia until nearly 100 B.C., when the first known Chinese envoys crossed the Pamirs.) But that seems an extreme view. Apart from anything else, the extraordinary welcome accorded those first Chinese envoys when they reached the Iranian Plateau (as we shall see) makes little sense unless we assume some longer knowledge of and eagerness for China's unique offerings.

Beyond that, it is hard to credit that the transcontinental trading chains that had already existed for thousands of years were not still operating, even if occasionally constricted or interrupted by nomadic upheavals in Central Asia. Indeed, it seems to be in these centuries that wheat was first introduced to China from the West, implying the continuance of some contact, no matter how tenuous, between East and West. In *The Traditional Trade of Asia*, C.G.F. Simkin notes that from the eighth century B.C., China had experienced rapid economic progress:

> *Iron replaced bronze for even ordinary tools . . . large-scale irrigation developed . . . silk became so abundant as to replace, together with metal ingots, cowrie shells as a medium of exchange, trade grew rapidly, and towns became commercial centres. These developments were partly the result of contacts with India or Iran, and occurred, significantly enough, after Darius had unified West Asia and part of North India.*

Though the detailed proof is not available, the strong inference is that relay trading continued to link China with the West.

Whether Alexander knew anything of truth and substance about the Chinese is unclear. Nor do we know whether he ever considered striking through the Pamirs and across the desert, or following the steppe beyond the Jaxartes River, to the land of the fabled Seres. Had he wished to so so, however, he might not have carried his army with him, for they were becoming increasingly disaffected by his Asian ways.

In any case, India was closer and seemed richer. Alexander (like Darius before him) pushed to the southeast, through the Kabul valley and on into northern India. It was thought at the time that the Indian rivers might be the headwaters of the Nile, so Alexander hoped to fulfill his dream of encompassing the "known world." But the army refused to proceed and forced him to turn back before he had passed beyond the five rivers of the Punjab. Leaving Greek governors behind in northwest India, as elsewhere, he took the desert route along the coast of the Persian Gulf to Susa. There he took another wife—Darius's daughter, Statira—as part of a great five-day-long marriage festival in which as many as 10,000 of his soldiers and dozens of his generals also took Asiatic wives. From there Alexander rejoined the Silk Road at Ecbatana, where his great friend Hephaestion died, occasioning a massive funeral ceremony. Alexander himself returned to Babylon, and there died of a sudden and severe fever in the spring of 323, only 11 years from the time he had arrived in Asia.

Though Alexander ruled the land for less than a decade, and in some parts of Western Asia the Greeks would rule for only 50 years beyond his death, tales of his exploits would circulate around Asia for centuries. (Some have even alleged that his empire inspired the first unification of China's disparate states.) Be that as it may, the Hellenistic influences he brought to the region survived for many centuries and would later spread the length of the Silk Road, the great thoroughfare that was soon to open fully to the East.

★   ★   ★

But at first, the tenuous unity Alexander had imposed on the region was shattered by civil wars among his would-be successors. These rivals roughly partitioned the territory won by Alexander, and, by 300 B.C., the western half of the Silk Road was in the hands of one man: Seleucus Nicator. His was by far the largest share, including Afghanistan, Bactria, Persia, Mesopotamia, Armenia, Syria, and parts of Anatolia. His chief rival in Western Asia was Ptolemy, whose pearl was Alexandria, but who also took control of the valuable Phoenician cities along the coast. In addition, Ptolemy controlled the western end of the Spice Route from India, which would grow in importance.

The Seleucid and Ptolemaic empires were often sharp competitors in commerce, a contest quickened by occasional monopolies. In particular, before the Spice Route was fully opened to Greek sailors from Egypt, the Seleucids controlled the very small supply of precious silk from the East. On the other hand, the Ptolemies held the famed purple dye factories of Phoenicia. The Seleucids would try hard to eliminate dependence on the Ptolemaic cities, but despite their best efforts goods from the Silk Road often found their way to the Phoenician towns for refining and distribution.

Others of Alexander's successors held the western end of Anatolia, including the old Greek trading ports on the Aegean, as well as Thrace and Greece. But the Seleucids were not about to share trade with them either, if they did not have to. As a result the old main roads across Anatolia atrophied. Though they retained local importance, they were no longer the termini of the great long-distance caravan routes. Instead the Seleucids made Syria the western focal point of the Silk Road.

In token of this, Seleucus built the great city that would mark the western end of the transcontinental highway for centuries to come: Antioch. Founded in 300 B.C., the city is well situated by any standards. Twenty miles from the Mediterranean, where it has been served by various ports on the Gulf of Issus over the centuries, Antioch lies on the Orontes River, whose gorge forms a natural thoroughfare to the sea. The Anatolian route from Tarsus also emerges on the plains near Antioch via the Beilan Pass; and the roads from the various Euphrates crossings—especially those at Zeugma, Samosata, and Thapsacus—all readily converge here through valleys in the region. Alexander is said to have camped on the site of Antioch; and the site is even associated with some of the Greek mythical heroes of earlier times, when Greeks were trading in the region.

Antioch itself was laid out on a grid, with two great avenues, lined with colonnades, crossing in the center; this city and its citadel hugged the shore of the river. Soon a second walled city was added to this, and later two other walled quarters were attached. By the second century B.C., the city was commonly known as *Tetrapolis* (Four Cities). The old Incense Road that had long borne caravans from southern Arabia to Aleppo now shifted its northern terminus to Antioch, which was, for much of the Hellenistic period, the western capital of the Seleucids.

In the same period Seleucus built another city of equal importance—Seleucia on the Tigris. Although he had first made Babylon his residence, following Alexander's model, he soon decided to build a truly Greek city nearby, to replace the old, decadent city of Babel. The new eastern capital of Seleucia was sited at the mouth of the royal canal which, at the time, linked the Tigris and Euphrates Rivers, where they draw near each other. About 50 miles north of Babylon and 15 miles south of modern Baghdad, the new city became the main Mesopotamian crossroads city for the Silk Road trade, much of which was funneled from Ecbatana down through the hills to Seleucia, and only then along the desert northwest to Antioch. From Seleucia, some smallish caravans cut straight across to Damascus via the oasis

From Aleppo, travelers had to thread their way through coastal mountains to reach Antioch, in the distance. (From *The Desert Route to India*, ed. Douglas Carruthers)

city of Palmyra (also called Tadmor) or across even more arid terrain to the rock-bound city of Petra, feeding their wares into the Ptolemaic empire. Others followed the rivers down to the Persian Gulf; a southern route from India also converged on Seleucia. But the Seleucids tried, as much as possible, to retain control of the whole trade, directing it toward the seaport of Antioch.

Antioch and Seleucia were two of the most important cities in the Near East, but they were not unique. Many like them were being founded, rebuilt, or expanded and renamed throughout Seleucid lands—indeed, throughout the Hellenistic Empire. At least 16 Antiochs were founded, and a dozen other cities given the name. There were, perhaps, even more Alexandrias, some founded by Alexander himself, others named after him. And there were at least eight Seleucias. As they had been doing by sea for centuries, the Greeks poured out of the Aegean region to colonize the territory won by Alexander. Soldiers, farmers, artisans, administrators, physicians, all were drawn out of their impoverished homelands by the promise of a new, richer life. The colonists themselves were—like many settlers of the American West after the Civil War—often given farmland, a house, seed, and cattle. Such inducements were made especially to encourage soldier-colonists to settle the wilder, more dangerous parts of the empire, including the Persian and Bactrian portions of the Silk Road. Greek colonists were joined by other peoples from Thrace and Anatolia, Syria and Mesopotamia, all of them threading their way along the Silk Road to Bactria and beyond.

A citadel manned by a garrison was a fixture in the Hellenized cities, whether they were newly founded, or built alongside older Asian towns. Ecbatana was rebuilt as a Greek city. Farther east, the city of Europos temporarily eclipsed nearby Rhagae; and even farther east was founded the many-gated walled city called Hecatompylos (literally, a "hundred gates"). On the less dangerous route between Seleucia and Antioch, other walled cities were established on the edge of the desert, the most famous being Dura-Europos, on the middle Euphrates, destined for later importance as a border clearinghouse. All of these cities provided not only security along the trade route but also places of shelter and supply for traveling caravans. Some of them became free cities, with their own constitutions, in which citizenship was not limited to Greeks; for example, the free city of Seleucia included among its inhabitants numerous Syrian and Jewish citizens.

With such a mixture of peoples, these new cities were not completely Greek, of course. For a long time, especially in the lowlands, the everyday, common language continued to be Aramaic, as in the highlands it would be Persian. But Greek was the language of power—the language of the administration and the courts, the language of the ambitious, the language of the dominant literature, philosophy, and science. As a result, in the cities along the main routes at least, Greek gradually became the common working language, used by travelers and merchants throughout Hellenistic lands. Cutting across the dialects spoken by Greeks and Macedonians from different parts of Hellas, a new, somewhat streamlined standard version of the language emerged—the *koine dialektos* (common language), or simply the *Koine*. This language cut across political boundaries, as well. It could be found in a Bactrian bazaar, a Persian court, an Alexandrian library, or a Jewish synagogue (being the language of the Septuagint, the Greek version of the Old Testament, translated in around 250 B.C.). The *Koine* gradually replaced Aramaic as the lingua franca of the Silk Road.

Along with Greek language came Greek art and culture. Inhabitants of the Hellenistic Empire were under no compulsion to speak the *Koine*; still less were they obligated to adopt Greek artistic styles. But with the Greeks dominant, with the Greek culture offering the only hope of advancement, and indeed permeating the region, the Hellenistic styles were widely adopted. The caravan cities of Palmyra and Petra are striking examples of the Greek influence in architecture. At Palmyra a modern traveler can still see the ruins of great avenues lined with pillars and great stone edifices, all executed in Greek style, as are those at Petra, where the city was largely carved out of the region's sandstone.

Greek artistic styles were also transmitted through the Hellenistic coinage. Alexander replaced old, local coins with standard coins for the empire, adorned with his profile. These were so well-controlled as to weight and quality of the precious metals that they were much admired by the Central Asian peoples. In particular the Indians—who were in this period becoming a substantial trading power themselves, partly because the Greeks had brought both peace and trading acumen to the region—were so much impressed that they made the Greek coins their standard commercial currency. These were, at first, generally of gold; but later, when the flow of Siberian gold was pinched off, the Seleucids more often used silver and copper coins. The head of Alexander on these coins was so well known that it helped spread the Greek art style deep into India. In time, Greek art would influence the Buddhists, who would carry Indo-Greek styles of representation and architecture clear across Asia, even into Japan. The mints themselves were, not surprisingly, established on the main roads, at places like Seleucia, Ecbatana, and Bactra.

★   ★   ★

The eastern part of Alexander's conquests did not remain long under Seleucid rule. Before Alexander's successors had concluded their struggle for power, in 321 B.C., the Indians under Chandragupta had regained their northern lands. Nor did Seleucus campaign actively to reconquer these territories. Certainly he was occupied with the other Greek rivals, but, as much to the point, he seems to have preferred a peaceful and profitable commercial relationship with a strong and vital India. And so India was, for the first time in many centuries. The petty states into which northern India had been fragmented since the arrival of the Aryan invaders over 1,000 years before, had coalesced into the powerful Mauryan empire. And through it ran a major road, which now emerged as a full partner to the Silk Road. From the Bay of Bengal in the east the Indian Grand Road ran along the valley of the Ganges River across to the plains of the Punjab—literally, the "five rivers" that join to form the Indus

River—and on up into the Afghan hills, through the Khyber Pass and the Kabul River valley to Bactria.

The Indians had gained from their contact with both the Persians and the Greeks, and it showed in the management of their 2,600-mile Grand Road. A state official was charged with maintaining the highway in good order, supplying causeways and ferries where needed. Signposts and milestones were set up to guide travelers, and wells were dug and trees planted to provide them with refreshing water and shade. Road crews worked to keep the highway clear of obstacles like trees and rocks. Shelters and itineraries were provided for travelers, whether traders, pilgrims, or adventurers. And staging posts and guardhouses were set up for the imperial messenger service, modeled on Persia's royal post. Even Greek diplomats resident at the Indian court praised the Mauryans' handling of the Grand Road.

The Greeks in their own territories made many improvements, supplying more shelters for travelers, with soldier-farmer garrisons providing protection and supplies en route. Itineraries were drawn up describing the route and the stations along the way, for the benefit of merchants, government officials, and other travelers. The Greek merchants who helped to colonize the Silk Road brought other improvements as well. Greek accounting and business methods proved more efficient than those of the Persians, and—with centuries of

What looks in the distance like an "undulating thread" is transformed into a camel caravan as it comes closer. (By Delia and Ferdinand Kuhn, taken in Western Turkestan)

sea-trading experience on the Mediterranean—the Greeks were better geared to establish a long-distance international trade, not only with Syria, but also with Europe.

Of all the Greek territories, perhaps none benefited so much from these improvements as Bactria, at the head of the Indian Grand Road. In 250 B.C., feeling their own power, and feeling that the Seleucids were very far away, with their capitals in Mesopotamia and Syria, the Bactrians seceded and set up their own independent kingdom. Still flourishing with the canals and lush gardens built by the Persians, Bactria in this period earned its names: "land of a thousand cities" and "paradise on earth."

But the effect of Bactria's secession was not quite what had been expected, for on the Iranian Plateau, the Iranian tribes continued their reaction against Greek rule. Just after 250 B.C. one of them—the Parthians—led a successful rebellion, establishing an independent kingdom astride the Silk Road. It was in this period that the Seleucid supply of Siberian gold was cut off. In the coming decades, the Parthians would expand their holdings along the plateau portion of the Silk Road, making the former Greek city of Hecatompylos their capital. The Seleucids tried, with only temporary success, to win back the crucial portion of road that ran below the Caspian Sea, but they were hard-pressed elsewhere by the Ptolemies, who in this period were attempting to take the Syrian ports.

Despite this struggle, however, trade not only continued but also swelled, for both the Seleucids and the Parthians realized the great profits to be gained. As always, the plateau peoples supplied the lowlands with horses and with metals and gems. But now added to these were beautifully woven wool, textiles and carpets, fine metalware, drugs, seed corn, and even pedigreed dogs. More than this, there were the silks, cottons, and muslins, the spices, drugs, and dyes that were from now on to characterize the traffic between Syria, India, and Central Asia, and later China directly. Far from rejecting the improvements brought by the Greeks, the Parthians chose to take advantage of them. The Parthian leaders even labeled themselves *Philhellenes* (lovers of Hellas), and much of the administrative, commercial, and literary writing of the empire continued to be done in Greek. For centuries non-Greeks in Parthia would even take honorary Greek names in addition to their own ethnic names.

★　　★　　★

Other influences were also at work in the region. Asoka, grandson of Chandragupta, and last ruler of the Mauryan dynasty in India, converted to Buddhism shortly after 261 B.C. With his encouragement, the new religion—in truth, a reformed version of Hinduism, as Zoroastrianism was a reformed version of the old Persian religion—quickly spread throughout India and farther east by sea. So zealous was Asoka in proselytizing for his new faith that he sent missionaries up along the Indian Grand Road, over the mountains and along the Silk Road to try to make new converts. Buddhist missionaries not only reached courts in Syria and Egypt, but also went farther afield in the Hellenistic world, to Macedonia, Crete, even to Epirus, on the Adriatic Sea. Chinese annals record the arrival of Buddhist missionaries around 220 B.C., possibly by way of the bleak and lofty Tibetan Plateau, over which a trail leads down past the Koko Nor (Blue Lake) into the Kansu Corridor. None of these missions seems to have had a lasting effect.

One Tibetan legend does suggest that Asoka himself visited the Tarim Basin city of Khotan; another that the city itself was founded by Asoka's son. Archaeologist Marc Aurel Stein's work in oasis cities near Khotan yielded some tablets written in an early Indian script that may support the idea that Buddhists settled in the Tarim during Asoka's time. Documents in a similar script are found as far east as Loulan, along with some wooden carvings in the Greco–Buddhist style that would later be so common. Khotan would certainly be a center for Indianized Buddhist culture for many centuries. These early Buddhist missionaries, in any case, foreshadowed the real and very great influence their successors would have in centuries to come.

What happened to the Bactrian kingdom in this intervening period is not entirely clear. Reaching a stalemate with the Parthians at the Iranian Plateau, the Bactrians turned their attentions south and east. In the south, the Mauryan Empire swiftly collapsed with Asoka's death in 232 B.C., an event that the Bactrian Greeks turned to their advantage. Writing two centuries later, around the time of Christ, Greek geographer and historian Strabo reviewed their career:

> . . . the Greeks who occasioned [Bactria's] revolt became so powerful by means of its fertility and the advantages of the country that they became masters of Ariana [near modern Herat] and India . . . They extended their empire also as far as the Seres and the Phauni.

The latter is an intriguing reference, for it has suggested to some observers that the Bactrians extended their domain over the Pamirs into the Tarim Basin, where they met the people they knew as the silk-providers, thinking them also the silk-producers, or Seres. And the Phauni may be a Western version of Hsiung-nu (Terrible Slaves), the name by which the Chinese knew the fierce nomadic warriors to their north and west.

In this period the Hsiung-nu—a people of mixed Indo-European and Mongol stock, and probable ancestors of the Huns who would later bedevil Europe—were expanding rapidly, setting into motion virtually all of Asia's steppe nomads, who were sent hurtling in every direction. Many peoples of the Tarim Basin and the Kansu Corridor were either submerged by them or sent careening westward, as the Hsiung-nu took the most favored grazing lands. Under these conditions, the tenuous trading chain that had stretched across the eastern Silk Road was either broken or at least badly disrupted. In the late third century B.C., at least one of the Bactrian kings, Euthydemus, attempted to reach the Seres directly, mounting an expedition that followed the steppe around the Pamirs and north of the T'ien Shan. But to no avail. There, too, they were stopped by the Hsiung-nu.

The Bactrian Greeks themselves came under heavy pressure from the steppe nomads. Acting incidentally as a buffer for both the Parthians and the Indians, they held off the invaders for some decades, before losing their independence in the late second century B.C. to a group of Indo-European nomads called the Sakae (who would themselves soon fall to other migrant nomads from Central Asia). The remnants of the Bactrian Greeks moved south into the Kabul River valley, notably to the trading city of Taxila—at the head of one of the mountain trading paths from the Tarim Basin via Kashmir—and survived there to play another role in the history of the region. It was left to the Chinese to open the eastern half of the Silk Road.

★   ★   ★

In the centuries when the Persians, the Greeks, and the Indians were building centralized empires and grand roads, the Chinese were largely a feudal people, broken up into many small principalities. The era following the decline of the Chou dynasty in the late eighth century B.C. is, in fact, called the period of the Warring States. Like many turbulent periods in history, this one produced some people of extraordinary influence and energy. Among them was the preeminent philosopher K'ung Fu-tzu (K'ung the Master), better known to the West as Confucius. Confucian teaching emphasized reverence for the past, for the ancient ways of government, for the ancestors, for a certain kind of cosmic order in which the emperor is the "Son of Heaven." On a personal level, this often expressed itself in a kind of courtesy and chivalry that Westerners might associate with the European feudal ideal. It was in this period, and largely by the Confucians, that some of the main patterns of Chinese culture were set; but the temper of the time differed radically from Confucius's ideal.

The period of the Warring States was noted for astonishing brutality. In the centuries immediately after the fall of the Chou, codes of chivalric warfare were widespread, though the massed battles of chariots and spears were bloody affairs. But as the centuries wore on, the rather ritualized forms of warfare gave way to wholesale slaughter, in which tens of thousands of people—men, women, and children—in a captured city might be decapitated. In this era of full-scale warfare, the Chinese developed the techniques of siegecraft, inventing the siege machines, mobile towers, and catapults that allowed them to attack the walled cities of the land.

The Chinese were not only fighting each other, however. The Hsiung-nu were attacking on China's northern border and, with their fast-riding cavalry, were able to surprise and encircle the cumbersome Chinese chariot troops seemingly at will. In self-defense, the Chinese quickly began to create troops of mounted archers, especially in those states in the north and west. At the same time, they adopted from the steppe peoples the trousers and tunic suited to riding, though they continued to wear long, flowing gowns for ceremonial purposes.

Equally to the point, the various Chinese states began to build walls, some as early as the fourth century B.C., against the nomadic raiders, who did not have the siegecraft to breach them. In addition, the Chinese continued their attempts to buy peace with the nomads on their borders by lavish gifts and marital alliances—practices of long standing. One Chinese official, escorting a Chinese princess to her Hsiung-nu fiance in about 170 B.C., apparently had some question about this policy, and tried to warn the Hsiung-nu to keep their freedom, advising:

> Your whole horde scarcely equals the population of a couple of Chinese prefectures, but the secret of your strength lies in your independence of China for all your real necessities. I notice an increasing fondness for Chinese luxuries. Reflect that one-fifth of the Chinese wealth would suffice to buy your people completely. Silks and satins are not half so well suited as felts to the rough life you lead, nor are the perishable delicacies of China so handy as your kumiss [fermented mare's milk] and cheese.

These were home truths, but the Hsiung-nu were hardly softened by the contact. Indeed, much of the silk apparently made its way westward in the ancient tribe-to-tribe trade along the Eurasian Steppe Route and perhaps along the Silk Road as well.

Within China's walls, meanwhile, as the contenders among the warring states resolved themselves into a few key kingdoms, one emerged as the most powerful: the northern state of Ch'in. Most powerful, and perhaps most bloody. Prisoners once held for ransom would now be summarily executed; some were reportedly thrown into cauldrons of boiling water, forming a soup that the leaders drank to "increase their prestige." Ch'in soldiers were paid only on delivering the heads of the losers, who were decapitated en masse. Yet out of this horror was to come the strength to unite China for the first time. It was partly a matter of geography, as a later Chinese historian, Ssuma-Ch'ien, would write:

> The country of Ch'in was a state whose position alone predestined its victory. Rendered difficult of access by the girdle formed around it by the Yellow River and the mountains, it was suspended [high] . . . above the rest of the empire. With twenty thousand men it could hold back a million spearmen. [The position of its territory was so advantageous, René Grousset commented, that when it poured out its soldiers] . . . it was like a man emptying a jug of water from the top of a high house.

In 246 B.C., in the years when Bactria and Parthia were declaring their independence in the west, the kingdom of Ch'in came into the hands of a new ruler, King Cheng. In the next 25 years, he annexed all the other Chinese kingdoms centered on the Wei and Huang Rivers and, in 221 B.C., adopted the name by which he is known to history—Ch'in Shih Huang Ti (first emperor of the Ch'in dynasty). In what would continue to be the Chinese style, emperors gave up their personal names—it was a crime for anyone to speak them—and were given general dynasty names, often after they died.

Ch'in Shih Huang Ti was a ruler of extraordinary ability. It was he who united the fragmentary system of defensive walls into one Great Wall, which he extended to shield China north and west from the Pacific to the Nan Shan. Dissidents, criminals, troublemakers of any sort were sent to build the Great Wall, along with soldiers to guard and protect them from nomadic raiders while the wall was being put up. Generally the garrison towers were built first so both soldiers and workers could take shelter there, if necessary; then the wall was extended between the outposts. It was he also who moved the Chinese capital westward to Ch'ang-an, at the strategic site where the Wei River valley opens out onto the wide north Chinese plains.

Ch'in Shih Huang Ti also improved the roads in China, building embankments to protect the highways from floods, planting trees to provide shade (and perhaps to hold the earth, as well), setting standard widths for axles of wheeled vehicles (no small question when dealing with dirt roads that were readily chewed up by wheels), and standardizing weights, measures, and laws, among them those relating to commerce and travel. Unfortunately, his urge for standardization also turned toward literature, with an order that all works not approved by him should be burnt. Though some survived, among them Confucian documents, it is to this one powerful ruler that we owe the loss of most of the early records of the Chinese people.

Nevertheless, Ch'in Shih Huang Ti created the first unified China, for which he is still honored in his homeland, and set the conditions for China's expansion beyond its ancient boundaries, not least into the desert lands of Central Asia. But the Ch'in dynasty had troubles with the succession—ever a problem with absolute rulers—and in 202 B.C. it was replaced by the Han dynasty. The Han were destined to rule for over four centuries, during one of China's greatest periods in history. Even today many northern Chinese describe themselves as "Sons of Han." It was under the Han that the eastern half of the Silk Road was finally and fully opened.

CHAPTER FIVE

THE HEAVENLY HORSES OF FERGHANA

The Heavenly Horses celebrated in this Chinese hymn from about 101 B.C. are a particularly magnificent breed of horses found in the heart of Central Asia, in the region of Ferghana, near the farthest eastern reaches of Alexander's conquests. From India to China to Mongolia were found legends of dragon-horses, sacred horses supposedly born in water, which carried semi-mythical rulers to immortality in heaven. The horses of Ferghana, dun-colored but sometimes marked with two or three dark stripes on their backs, were said to have been "issued from the waters of a pool" and so were second in their powers only to full-fledged dragons, offering the hope of heaven to Chinese emperors. The hymn continued:

The Heavenly Horses are coming,
Coming from the Far West
They crossed the Flowing Sands
For the barbarians are conquered.
The Heavenly Horses are coming
That issued from the waters of a
* pool.*
Two of them have tiger backs;
They can transform themselves like
* spirits.*
The Heavenly Horses are coming
Across the pastureless wilds
A thousand leagues at a stretch,
Following the eastern road
The Heavenly Horses are coming...

Open the gates while there is time.
They will draw me [presumably Emperor Wu] up and
* carry me*
To the Holy Mountain of K'un-lun.
The Heavenly Horses have come
And the Dragon will follow in their wake.
I shall reach the Gates of Heaven.
I shall see the Palace of God.

To gain some of these Heavenly Horses, the Han Emperor Wu, late in the second century B.C., sent a great army of tens of thousands of soldiers across 2,500 miles of desert against the hostile ruler of Ferghana, in the process opening up Central Asia directly to Chinese power for the first time. Astonishingly, the distant land that the Chinese emperor so boldly attacked had been quite unknown to China only a generation before. How the Chinese opened the way to the heart of Asia is a story in itself.

During the early decades of the Han dynasty, "China" still extended only as far west as roughly the headwaters of the Wei River, that fertile valley sheltering the early empire. There its western boundary was delineated by the earthen Great Wall, which protected China's industrious farmers and city-dwellers from the depredations of raiders from the Central Asian steppe.

Beyond the wall, in the hospitable Kansu Corridor, the Chinese panhandle that lay between the craggy Nan Shan and the fearsome Gobi Desert, there had lived for some time a rather pacific people the Chinese called the Yüeh-chih ("meat-eaters"). One of the many Indo-European nomadic groups of Central Asia—some even had flaming red hair and piercing blue eyes—the Yüeh-chih had for some time acted as a buffer against attack on China's western border. They had also operated as middlemen for the tribe-to-tribe trade by which valuables like jade reached China and finely worked metals and silks reached the West.

★   ★   ★

In the middle of the second century B.C., the most powerful of the Central Asian steppe peoples, the Hsiung-nu, were expanding from their traditional territories into those of others, incidentally breaking the trading chain that had long stretched across Central Asia. The Chinese themselves felt the pressure, and held the Hsiung-nu beyond the Great Wall only with some difficulty. The Yüeh-chih were less fortunate. Unprotected by earthworks, they felt the brunt of the Hsiung-nu's attacks. The writings of Ssǔ-ma Ch'ien, sometimes called the Herodotus of China, one of a long line of chroniclers who recorded China's history and its contacts with the West, tell the fate of the Yüeh-chih:

> . . . the Son of Heaven [at that time, the Emperor Wu] made inquiries among those of the Hsiung-nu who had surrendered and been made prisoners, and they all reported that the Hsiung-nu had overcome the king of the Yüeh-chih and made a drinking vessel out of his skull [a practice reported among Central Asian nomads for centuries]. The Yüeh-chih had decamped and were hiding somewhere, constantly scheming how to revenge themselves on the Hsiung-nu; but they had no ally to join with them in striking a blow.
>   The Chinese, wishing to declare war on the Hsiung-nu to wipe them out, when they learned this, desired to establish contact with the Yüeh-chih; but the road to them led through the territory of the Hsiung-nu. The emperor called for volunteers.

Answering the call was the first of the great Chinese travelers in historical times, Chang Ch'ien, then a young officer in the imperial household. Whatever direct contacts with inner Asia may have been intimated by the earlier legendary travels of Emperor Mu or by the reports of Herodotus, Central Asia was to the Chinese of this period an unknown land filled with danger. But in 138 B.C., Chang Ch'ien started westward with a caravan of over 100 men, as Ssu-ma Ch'ien related:

> Chang Ch'ien . . . enlisted in a mission to seek out the Yüeh-chih. He took with him Kan Fu, a Tartar who had been a slave . . . and set out from Kansu to cross the Hsiung-nu territory. Almost immediately he was caught, taken prisoner, and sent to the Great Khan, who detained him, saying, "The Yüeh-chih are to the north of us. How can China send ambassadors to them? If I wanted to send ambassadors to [eastern China] . . . would China be willing to submit to us?" He held Chang Ch'ien for more than ten years; he gave him a wife by whom he had a son. All this time Chang Ch'ien kept possession of the emperor's token of authority, and when in the course of time he was permitted greater freedom, he watched his opportunity and succeeded in making his escape with his men.

He at first intended to seek the Yüeh-chih in the Ili River valley, north of the T'ien Shan, but he found they had moved on from there. Then, after marching "several tens of days to the West," along the rim of the Tarim Basin and into the rugged Pamirs, Chang Ch'ien arrived at the land of Ferghana (which the Chinese called Ta-yüan). He was much impressed by the fertile land with its prosperous fields and its wine, made of grapes (probably introduced to the region by Alexander's Greeks and, until then, unknown to the Chinese). He estimated that Ferghana's 70 or so walled cities held a population of several hundreds of thousands. The warriors of the land were well equipped in Central Asian style, Ssu-ma-Ch'ien recorded: "Their arms consist of bows and halberds [a battle-axe combined with a long spear] and they can shoot arrows while on horseback."

There was much in Ferghana to interest Chang Ch'ien and his emperor, not the least of which were the horses that "come from the stock of the Heavenly Horse." The people of Ferghana were equally pleased with the contact. They had "heard of the wealth and fertility of China" and "had vainly tried to communicate with it." (This may refer to the abortive attempts by the Bactrian King Euthydemus or others to reach the Chinese in the previous century.) Chang Ch'ien explained that he had a mission to complete:

> I have now escaped the Hsiung-nu and would ask your king to have someone guide me to the country of the Yüeh-chih. If I succeed in reaching that country, on my return my king will reward you with untold treasures.

The people of Ferghana offered "joyful assistance," providing him with safe conduct, interpreters, and guides, to the smaller kingdom of Sogdiana to the west and then, curving around a mountain spur, southeast to the Yüeh-chih. These weary migrants had come to rest in Bactria, where they took over the remnants of the Hellenistic kingdoms founded by Alexander and his heirs. (Some of the Greeks had moved on to found a short-lived kingdom in northwest India.) From their prime positions at the crossroads of Asia, the Yüeh-chih seemed to be perfectly placed for an alliance with the Chinese; the two could press on the Hsiung-nu from both east and west.

But the result of Chang Ch'ien's visit to Bactria was not all he might have wished. Sšu-ma Ch'ien relates:

> *After the king of the Yüeh-chih had been killed by the Hsiung-nu, the people set up his heir as king (though one authority says it was the queen who named the successor). Since that time they had conquered Bactria [in Chinese, Ta-Hsia] and occupied the country. It was a rich and fertile land, seldom harassed by robbers, and the people decided to enjoy this life of peace. Moreover, since they considered themselves too far away from China, they no longer wanted to revenge themselves on the Hsiung-nu. After having made his*

An arrow is being removed from the chest of this powerful horse, descendant of the Heavenly Horses of Ferghana. (T'ang period, from University Museum, University of Pennsylvania)

way through so many tribes to find Bactria, Chang Ch'ien was unable to persuade the Yüeh-chih to move against their former enemy. He remained there for a year and then started for home.

The Yüeh-chih were later to play an important role on the Silk Road, being known to the West as the Kushans, but for now Chinese attention was turned elsewhere.

Hoping to avoid the Hsiung-nu on his homeward journey, Chang Ch'ien returned on the southern Tarim route, seeking shelter in the difficult Nan Shan. But in vain. He was once again caught and was imprisoned by the Hsiung-nu for a year. Only when the old khan died and the nomads became involved in a dispute over the succession was Chang Ch'ien able to escape, along with his wife and Kan Fu, his original companion. Luckily Kan Fu "was an excellent bowman and, when supplies were exhausted, provided food by hunting game." This was no small contribution, for they were traveling through hostile and inhospitable territory. In the end, 13 years after setting out, only two of the original caravan returned to China.

★　　★　　★

If Chang Ch'ien failed in his given mission, his journey was nevertheless a success. He had opened contact with the friendly people of Ferghana, and had learned of many other new peoples and places. Given the Chinese passion for the gemstone, his report that Khotan was a "country that contains much jade" certainly sparked interest. And the tales of the Heavenly Horses of Ferghana held particular appeal for the emperor—and for the army that now relied on its cavalry, whose horses were inferior to those of the Hsiung-nu.

Chang Ch'ien also brought back tales of areas even farther distant, all unknown to the Chinese. West of Bactria lay the land the Chinese called An-hsi. This was the land of Parthia, on the broad and vital Iranian Plateau. Sšu-ma Ch'ien recorded:

The people live in fixed abodes and are given to agriculture; their fields yield rice and wheat; and they make wine of grapes. Several hundred small and large cities belong to it . . . .it is a very large country and close to the Oxus. Their traders and merchants travel in carts and boats to the neighboring countries, perhaps several thousand li distant. [One li = approximately 1/3 of a mile.] They make coins of silver; the coins resemble their king's face. Upon the death of a king the coins are changed for others on which the new king's face is represented. They paint rows of characters running sideways on . . . leather to serve them as records.

The practice of striking coins with the ruler's image, introduced centuries earlier by the Persians and Greeks, much impressed the peoples of Asia. Because these coins were of uniform size, weight, and quality, they acted as the general coin of exchange in much Asian trading,

including that on the Silk Road and the Indian Grand Road. Some have suggested that the
Parthian parchment, specially treated leather, later inspired the Chinese to develop paper for
writing, to replace the previously used silk and bamboo.

Chang Ch'ien even brought home the first word of the Near Eastern countries, noting
that Syria and Babylonia (which is "hot and damp") were several thousand *li* west of Parthia
and close to the "Western Sea," which seemed variously to refer to either the Persian Gulf or
the Red Sea, on either side of the Arabian Peninsula. The geography is somewhat confused,
and the rest of the commentary shows its origin in hearsay descriptions:

> *The inhabitants plow their fields in which they grow rice. There is a big bird with eggs
> the size of jars [probably a reference to the ostrich]. The number of its inhabitants is very
> large, and they have in many places their own petty chiefs; but Parthia, while having
> added it to its dependencies, considers it a foreign country.*

This reflects the fact that Parthia had steadily increased its territory and had now reached the
shores of the Tigris River. Chang Ch'ien also noted that the Syrian people there "have clever
jugglers." These jugglers would prove most attractive to the Chinese and would later be specially imported—giving rise to the acrobatics tradition that is still so popular in modern China.
Most intriguing of all the references to this region is the brief comment that: "Although the old
people in Parthia maintain the tradition that ...Hsi-wang-mu [is] in Babylonia, [she has] not
been seen there." The suggestion is that the peoples of Western Asia knew of the Royal Mother
of the West and of the legendary east-west contacts of almost a millennium earlier. But, alas,
no more is said about it.

Of more practical interest was the account of what the party saw while in Bactria.
Chang Ch'ien did not yet fully understand that he had linked up with an ancient trade route
between the Pamirs and the Mediterranean—what we call the western half of the Silk Road. He
did note that the now-subject peoples of Bactria were shrewd traders (as, indeed, the Greeks
were); that the population of the land was more than a million; and that their capital "has
markets for the sale of all kinds of merchandise," especially products from another country
previously unknown, at least to the northern Chinese. The report was so astonishing that
Chang Ch'ien's own words were given in the Chinese annals:

> *When I was in Bactria, I saw there a stick of bamboo . . . and some cloth [possibly silk]
> from Szechuan [a province of Southwest China]. When I asked the inhabitants how they
> obtained possession of these they replied, "The inhabitants of our country buy them in
> India." India may be several thousand li to the southeast of Bactria.*

This was his, and his emperor's, first word of the great land of India.

It may seem surprising that Chang Ch'ien and his emperor had no knowledge of India—or of its receiving products from southwestern China. But the distances were great and the terrain difficult, even within the wide empire of China itself. Northern China, the heartland, was separated from southwest China—only recently added to the empire and by no means fully ingested—by the Chin Ling Mountains. And it was divided from India even more definitively, by the vast barrier of the high Tibetan Plateau and the whole range of the Himalayas. Southwestern China was itself divided from India by steaming, disease-ridden jungles. Trade between the two was, in any case, carried on by a chain of middlemen, some of whom transported goods part of the way by sea from Burma to Bengal. A few Buddhist missionaries, the annals record, had reached Chinese territories in decades past; since the Chinese knew nothing about India, however, it is possible that they came not from India itself but from the fledgling Buddhist centers around Khotan.

In any case the reports of India were most interesting, and, keeping in mind the difficulty of his westward passage and the attractiveness of the products of the West, Chang Ch'ien made a most reasonable proposal:

> *According to my calculation, Bactria must be 12,000* li *distant from China and to the southwest of it. Now the country of India, being several thousand* li *to the southeast of Bactria, and the produce of Szechuan being found there, that country cannot be far from Szechuan. If we send ambassadors to Bactria through [the Nan Shan] the people there . . . will object; and if we send them farther north, they will be captured by the Hsiungnu. But going by way of Szechuan they may proceed directly and will be unmolested by robbers.*

Emperor Wu saw the sense of Chang Ch'ien's proposal for an alternate way of reaching Ferghana, Bactria, and Parthia, which he thought were "large countries, full of rare things," though with "weak armies" and considerable interest in Chinese goods. (Did this, perhaps, refer to the Greek preference for trading rather than fighting on the Bactrian portion of the Silk Road?) In the end, Chang Ch'ien's attempt to reach India from the south failed dismally, however. The mountain jungles southwest of China were ruled by fierce tribes, who preferred robbery or trade with border smugglers to any contact with official Chinese emissaries.

So the Chinese were forced once more to turn their attention to Central Asia, both for opening possible trade routes and for securing their borders against the marauding Hsiung-nu. In these endeavors, Chang Ch'ien's experience was most helpful. Ssŭ-ma Ch'ien noted that when Chang Ch'ien served as advisor to the chief commander in a campaign against the Hsiung-nu, his "knowledge of their pasturelands" kept the army from falling short of provisions. Chang Ch'ien himself later fell from grace, losing all his favored titles but, thanks to his distinguished career as "opener of roads," not losing his head as well. (He was lucky; his chronicler, Ssŭ-ma Ch'ien, would be castrated when he fell from favor.) Over the next two

years the Chinese armies attacked the Hsiung-nu to the north and west, until in 121 B.C. they
drove the Hsiung-nu from the Kansu Corridor. Then, Sšu-ma Ch'ien reported:

> . . . to the west and all along the Nan Shan as far as the Lop Nor [Salt Lake], no
> Hsiung-nu remained. Occasionally Hsiung-nu would raid caravans, but such harassment
> was rare, and two years later the Chinese forced the khan of the Hsiung-nu to retreat to
> north of the desert.

The way was now open for a full-scale attempt to establish contact with the West—and
no one better to lead it than Chang Ch'ien. Though shorn of his titles, he had continued to
advise the emperor. One of his suggestions was that China try to divide and weaken the
remaining Hsiung-nu by allying itself with one of the peoples north of the T'ien Shan, the
Wu-sun (possibly the Issedones Herodotus had mentioned), who lived in the Ili River valley
near the Issyk Kul (Warm Lake). "Since the barbarians covet the rich produce of China," he
reasoned, they should bribe these people with "liberal presents and invite them to settle farther
east" in former Hsiung-nu territory. More than that, they might even send a Chinese princess
to cement the alliance. The Chinese would employ such tactics for centuries, attempting to
divide enemies through judicious cultivation of allies, with princesses often sent as hostages to
these political aims.

Chang Ch'ien was restored to favor:

> The Son of Heaven approved of Chang Ch'ien's proposal and appointed him commander
> in the Imperial Bodyguard as well as leader of an expedition consisting of 300 men, each
> with two horses, and thousands of oxen and sheep. He also furnished him with gifts of
> gold and silken stuffs worth millions, and with assistant envoys, holding credentials,
> whom Chang Ch'ien could dispatch to, or leave behind in, other nearby countries.

These oxen and sheep were largely for provisions on the way; the other goods were, in a sense,
gifts in name only. In early times, and throughout much of their history, the Chinese carried
on trade under the guise of exchange of gifts; in truth, they expected to be given equal "gifts" in
return, of items they desired. And they were angered by any lack of respect for these "gifts"
from the "Son of Heaven."

That, indeed, is what Chang Ch'ien found when he met the Wu-sun. He "keenly
resented the humiliation offered to him, the ambassador of China" by the "barbarians," and
threatened to withdraw the gifts if they were not treated with due respect. At that, the Wu-sun
ruler "bowed low before the gifts," somewhat repairing the damage. But the Wu-sun were a
people divided and unwilling to ally themselves firmly with China. Their main contribution
was to provide guides and interpreters for the assistant ambassadors that Chang Ch'ien now

sent on westward, to the countries of Ferghana, Sogdiana, Bactria, Parthia, India, Khotan, and other nearby lands.

★   ★   ★

Chang Ch'ien himself returned home, accompanied by several dozen embassies from the Wu-sun, and many horses "in acknowledgment of the emperor's gift." These were not the Heavenly Horses of Ferghana, but, since warriors and traders of the time depended heavily on horses, steeds of a more ordinary kind were always a welcome "gift." The visiting Wu-sun embassies were able "to see China with their own eyes and thus to realize her extent and greatness"; they returned home with appropriately glowing reports of China's wealth and might. Over a year later, the several assistant envoys returned to China as well, bringing with them foreign representatives. After this, noted Sšu-ma Ch'ien, "the countries of the northwest began to have intercourse with China." Chang Ch'ien was feted as the "Great Traveler," and was promoted to state minister for foreign affairs, one of the top posts in the empire. His reputation was such that "envoys proceeding to the West after him always referred to [Chang Ch'ien] . . . as an introduction in foreign countries, the mention of his name being regarded as a guarantee of good faith."

From the distant lands of the west, China's envoys also returned with samples of new and unknown plants and minerals; as the *Ch'ien Han Shu (Annals of the Former Han Dynasty)* put it, in this period "specimens of strange things began to arrive from every direction." Chang Ch'ien himself is thought to have brought into China the grapevine (though the Chinese apparently did not make wine from the fruit until much later) and alfalfa, the prime fodder for horses and camels. Other new and exotic plants also came to China: fruits like the cucumber, the fig, the pomegranate, and the walnut, and herbs and spices like the sesame, the chive, the coriander, and the safflower.

Tradition ascribes to Chang Ch'ien credit for bringing them all from Persia or Central Asia. Although they are now thought to have been established in later centuries, samples may well have been brought eastward during this early period of contact. Some native Chinese fruits had, despite the barrier of the Tarim, traveled westward, even before Chang Ch'ien's time; from China's western borderlands came the orange, the peach, and the pear. These same frontier regions were also the homeland for some of the flowers that would become staples in modern gardens: roses, azaleas, camellias, chrysanthemums, and peonies among them.

China's envoys also returned with much valuable military and commercial intelligence. They found the western kingdoms warm and hospitable in these early contacts. Although the lands of Central Asia were unknown to China, the reverse was not also true. The Westerners well knew of the Seres and their *serica*. The Chinese found that sericulture was unknown in the West, China having made a thorough success of keeping secret the techniques of manufacturing silk. The Chinese therefore had an eager market for their fine gossamer fabric, as well as for their superior metalwork, especially their weaponry. These prime goods would, they hoped, bring them in return the things they most desired from the West, especially the Heavenly Horses.

★   ★   ★

But the way was difficult. The Hsiung-nu may have been pushed farther north, but roving bands of marauders still remained. And the problem of lack of food and water for large parties crossing the desert regions was unsolved. The Chinese attacked these difficulties with energy. No sooner had they defeated the Hsiung-nu, in 121 B.C., than they founded the western province of Chiu-Ch'an (Fountain of Wine) as a bridgehead for the push along the Kansu Corridor. Following the age-old pattern of empire, the emperor settled the wild frontier region with deported criminals, exiled dissidents, and unemployed laborers, under the watchful eye of military commanders. These and other like peoples gradually brought under Chinese protection the whole Kansu panhandle, as well as the fertile valley of the Etsin Gol which juts north of the corridor. Watchtowers were built all along the way west, and the Great Wall's earthen embankments were stretched out to link the watchtowers and the few fortresses that guarded the way.

Prime among these were the Yang Kuan and Yümen Kuan (Jade Gate), placed to guard the exit gates of the southern and northern Tarim routes of the Silk Road through the Great Wall. Tunhuang, where the two main branches of the emerging Silk Road divided, became China's main western outpost. In the same period, the Chinese led some highly successful raids to the north, into the Hsiung-nu's homeland in what is now Outer Mongolia, at times aided by surprise and by sandstorms blowing into the faces of their opponents. For more lasting accomplishments, they concentrated on taking some of the main oases of the Tarim—in this period small, independent city-states—notably those near Lop Nor and in the Turfan Basin, which would be staging areas for further conquests. Remembering the triumph, the poet Li Shih-min (late Emperor T'ai Tsung) would trumpet:

> *Beyond the frontiers lie the hard winters and the*
> *raging winds . . .*
> *We entered the land of the Huns [Hsiung-nu] and subdued*
> *them in their desert strongholds . . .*

The emperor went to all this trouble, Sšu-ma Ch'ien chronicles, "so as to keep in touch with the lands of the northwest." Not the least of his aims was to obtain some of the highly

Travelers who ventured into the Taklamakan found an ocean
of sand, blown into dunes tens or even hundreds of feet high.
(By Sven Hedin, from his *Through Asia*, 1899)

prized horses of Ferghana, specifically those of Kokand, rumored to be the best of all. Sšu-ma
Ch'ien related:

> . . . the Son of Heaven greatly loved the horses of Kokand, and embassies set out one
> after the other on the road to that country. The largest of them comprised several hundred
> men; the smallest fewer than 100. Some years the Chinese court would send off ten
> embassies or more; in other years the number would be five or six. The ambassadors
> returned from their missions to the most distant lands in 8 or 9 years; it took them but
> two or three years to return from nearer countries.

The length of time necessary for such missions was a part of the problem. Embassies
which were on the road for years had to find food and water at oasis–cities along the way. The

local inhabitants were by no means always happy to provide for such wants; persuasion might take the form of quasi-military action or presentation of "gifts," but both of these greatly enlarged the train an embassy needed for the round trip of 5,000 miles or more. The Chinese attempted to extend their sphere of influence partway along the westward routes, but with limited success in these early times. The *Annals of the Former Han Dynasty* noted, for example, that the inhabitants of Shan-shan on the southern Tarim route were supposed "to provide guides, to carry water and to forward provisions to meet the Chinese envoys." Easier said than done, however, for robbery and killing continued to be common along the Tarim routes, and the good people of Shan-shan "being frequently exposed to the oppressive raids of the soldiery, they at last resolved that it was inconvenient to hold intercourse with China."

Faced with such difficulties, the most qualified people no longer applied for these westward journeys. Rougher, more unscrupulous, and sometimes downright dishonest ambassadors quickly used up the good credit that Chang Ch'ien and his kin had gained for China. Far from home, and dependent on the good graces of others, these ambassadors had little power to carry out their missions. And the western rulers found themselves very much in a "buyer's market;" they had no need to accede to China's wishes and send back the goods they desired. The prosperous far western countries could take vast quantities of Chinese goods, especially silk; but the small mountain countries of the Pamirs, not yet seeing the extraordinary possibilities for trans-Asian trade, could themselves absorb only a limited amount of Chinese crafts, no matter how high the quality of the workmanship. The annals explained the problem:

> . . . as these embassies were excessively numerous, the presents began to pall on foreign rulers and the products of Chinese craftsmanship were not very highly valued.

★   ★   ★

But the Son of Heaven still desired the horses of Kokand. He had heard that the people of Kokand kept hidden "a great number of magnificent horses," and refused to give them to the Chinese ambassador. On hearing this, the Chinese emperor sent a special mission to Kokand:

> He gave them a great quantity of silver and a horse made of solid gold, which they could offer to the ruler of Kokand in exchange for the horses he had.

Unfortunately for the emperor, the court of Kokand "already had many Chinese objects in their possession." The court counselors decided that, however grand the presents offered, they would keep their horses. These particular horses may have had a special religious significance, modern sinologist Arthur Waley suggests, making the ruler of Kokand set against giving up the horses; perhaps, like the Chinese emperor, he thought they would bear him to heaven, to join the immortals. In any case, the Kokand counselors reasoned that they had nothing to fear from refusing the Chinese, noting:

> China is far off and the road is long; travelers lack both fodder and water; in the north they run the risk of being attacked by the Hsiung-nu; in the south there is neither water nor grass. Moreover, as the country along the road is but thinly populated, the travelers themselves are often short of food. The Chinese ambassadors bring with them a suite of several hundred men, and they are always so short of food that about half of them die of starvation. How could an army ever reach us? China can do nothing to harm us. The inestimable horses . . . shall remain the horses of Kokand.

Incensed at this lack of respect for their emperor, one Chinese ambassador insulted the court, battering the golden horse into a shapeless mass, for which outrage he was murdered as he left the borders of Kokand.

At first, it seemed as though the Kokand counselors had been right. Emperor Wu sent an army westward against Kokand, but it greatly overtaxed the resources of oasis-cities en route and weakened itself trying to gain submission from the local rulers; the surviving remnant of the army had no chance of breaching the walls of Kokand. Heading home in ignominy, the Chinese army had even more difficulty, for the cities of the desert, seeing China's weakness, felt no need to provide for its army's needs.

Dismayed and dishonored, the Son of Heaven would not accept defeat, however:

> The Emperor thought that his having sent an unsuccessful expedition against . . . a small country . . . would cause Bactria and other neighboring states to feel contempt for China, and that the . . . horses . . . would never be forthcoming.

So the Emperor assembled a truly astonishing force to send against Kokand:

> . . . 60,000 men not counting those who followed as carriers of extra provisions; 100,000 oxen; more than 30,000 horses, myriads of donkeys, mules and camels, and a commissariat well stocked with supplies besides cross-bows and other arms. All parts of the empire had to bestir themselves in making contributions.

So the problem of food was solved. But the meager and scattered water supplies along the Tarim routes could not provide for such massive numbers of people and animals. The Chinese general solved this problem by dividing the troops into columns, taking different routes. Being thus provided, the army had no need to waste energy extracting submission from cities en route, but went directly toward Kokand.

Even so, the way was hard. Only about half the army survived the journey to take part in the siege of Kokand in 102 B.C. The city was heavily fortified and not easily gained. The Chinese, no doubt drawing on the experience gained in their earlier defeat, had come prepared with siege engineers; their plan—and a good one it was—was to divert the river that provided the city with its only water supply. Even so, it took the Chinese army 40 days to breach the outer defenses of the city. The Kokand court, secure behind the city's inner wall but cut off from provisions, at this point sued for a truce, stating that if granted "honorable terms," they would provide the desired horses, but, if not, they would kill all the horses and themselves die fighting. The Chinese accepted the proposal, possibly influenced by the fact that the Kokand army was about to receive reinforcements, including some well-digging engineers from the western land of Ta-ch'in. (This is apparently the first mention of the Roman Empire recorded in Chinese annals.)

The Chinese had wisely prepared for success, bringing with them experts to select the finest horses for the Chinese court. In the end, the expedition produced a mere 30 "superior" or "Heavenly" horses—presumably those with the most sacred lineage or markings—and 3,000 of "middling or lower quality." Less than half of these survived the return journey, but they were sufficient to provide stock for judicious breeding under the imperial eye. And the king of Kokand sent at least two "Heavenly Horses" a year to China for some time after that.

So Emperor Wu finally had his Heavenly Horses. It is no wonder that hymns were written to celebrate their coming, given the enormous resources that had been mobilized to obtain them. But China had won a good deal more than the Heavenly Horses so dear to its emperor. By the stunning victory at Kokand, it had won effective control over the whole region of the Tarim Basin, which was thereafter called Sinkiang (the New Dominion). On its return from Kokand, the army accepted the usually-ready submission of the main cities along the Tarim routes. And soon after that "China sent more than ten embassies to countries west of Ferghana to collect curiosities and at the same time to impress upon countries the importance of the victory."

Just after the successful Ferghana campaigns, the Chinese chronicle *T'oung-pao* tells us:

> . . . *military posts were established from place to place from Tun-huang westwards to the Salt Marsh [Lop Nor]; there were besides in the region . . . several hundreds of military colonists; an imperial commissioner was placed [there] to direct and protect [these people and the land they cultivated] in order to meet the needs of envoys sent to the foreign countries.*

So the Chinese provided for the travelers who would be heading westward in increasing numbers from now on. Continuing vigilance was necessary, for China was new in the Tarim, and the desert-dwellers were used to responding to the Hsiung-nu's whip. Until Chinese hegemony was fully established, Sšu-ma Ch'ien reported in the *Shih Chi,* ambassadors to the Western territories were often robbed by the people of cities such as Loulan, who "on various occasions acted as the eyes and ears to the Hsiung-nu, causing their troops to intercept the Chinese envoys."

★   ★   ★

With the Chinese established in the Tarim, the eastern half of the Silk Road was now fully open. No longer divided, east and west, this great highway became for the first time a continuous route across the nearly 5,000 miles between the empire of China—now, under the Han dynasty, entering one of its greatest periods—and the Mediterranean lands of Asia, in which another great empire, the Roman, was just beginning to make its mark.

Even before the Chinese had concluded their siege of Kokand, trade had begun on the Silk Road west; the first through caravan from China to Parthia was, so the annals tell us, in 106 B.C. *The Annals of the Former Han Dynasty* tells of a mission around this time to the land the Chinese called An-hsi (Parthia), on the Iranian Plateau. The Chinese ambassador sent there by Emperor Wu was accorded an extraordinary welcome:

> The [Parthian] sovereign ordered his military chiefs to meet the Chinese ambassador at the eastern frontier with 20,000 horsemen—and from the frontier to the capital [at that time, Hecatompylos] there is a distance of several thousand li. The road passed through some dozens of towns. The population covers the land almost without a break.

So the territory along the Silk Road—built up by Iranian tribes, Assyrians, Greeks, and all their predecessors—was in this period a virtually unbroken string of walled cities. The Silk Road soon became even more heavily settled, as East and West came to appreciate what each had to offer. The West was, of course, most interested in silk, which commodity may well have inspired such a magnificent welcome for the Chinese envoy. For their part, the early Chinese were much taken with ostriches—sometimes called "camel birds" for the great, though ungainly, speed of their long legs—which they had never seen before. The ostriches were not native to the Iranian Plateau, but had been imported from the warmer desert lowlands of southwest Asia.

The Chinese were also entranced by the tumblers and jugglers they saw in the Parthian lands. These, too, were not native to the plateau, but had traveled along the Silk Road from their home in the lowlands. As a result, the annals continued:

> When the Chinese mission left, the soverign of An-hsi sent with them an ambassador of his own that he might learn something of China. To the Chinese court he presented an

ostrich egg and some conjurors from Li-Chien [Li-Kan]. The Son of Heaven took great pleasure in these.

From this date, about 105 B.C.—though possibly as early as 115 B.C.—China and the Iranian lands had direct relations, both political and commercial. For over eight centuries, the Chinese and the Iranians would be allies, even with changes of government in their own lands and the intervention of other powers between them on the Silk Road.

In this exchange, China learned more of the lands beyond Parthia. When the emperor asked where the conjurors—a catch-all name for jugglers, dancers, and acrobats—came from,

Modern Chinese acrobats and illusionists trace their traditions back at least to the arrival of Near Eastern conjurors during Han and Roman times. (From *Zeldzaame Reizen...* by Edward Melton, Amsterdam, 1702, reprinted in Yule's *Marco Polo*)

he was told "Li–Kan." The origin of the name "Li–Kan" has occasioned considerable dispute among scholars. To some, it was obvious that Li–Kan was the Chinese version of Alexandria, which was indeed famous for its performers, who were often sent as human exports to foreign lands. Others insist that Li–Kan is the Chinese transliteration of Re–kem, the native name for the town the Greeks called Petra (both meaning "rock"). Whatever its origin, for the Chinese, Li–Kan meant the territory beyond Parthia, which they later came to recognize as a great empire. That China did not know it as the "Roman Empire" is understandable; it was only beginning to make its presence known in Western Asia. More to the point, the Romans themselves called their territory simply *orbis terrarum* (the world), so we should not expect the Chinese name to be some version of "Rome." From this time date Chinese attempts to reach beyond Parthia to the land of Li–Kan.

Throughout the first century B.C., the Chinese continued to strengthen their hold on the Tarim Basin, occupying the important oasis–states of Karashar, on the northern route, and Yarkand, southern gateway to the Pamirs. Perhaps more to the point, they fomented division among the Hsiung–nu. By 51 B.C. the chief of the eastern Hsiung–nu was subjected so thoroughly that he came in person to Ch'ang–an to kowtow—that is, literally to knock his head to the ground—before the Han emperor. The Chinese also captured and decapitated the leader of the western Hsiung–nu, who would not revive for another four centuries (at which point, then known as the Huns and led by Attila, they turned their attention toward Europe).

By these moves, the Han Chinese established relative peace in the Tarim Basin. The Central Asian trade in silk, jade, horses, furs, and camels, which had been hindered by the Hsiung–nu's expansions, could now stretch farther than ever before. The Chinese traded with all comers, including the Hsiung–nu, making trade practically an instrument of foreign policy. The Lord Grand Secretary of the Han Council, for example, put it this way in 81 B.C.:

> *A piece of Chinese plain silk can be exchanged with the Hsiung–nu for articles worth several pieces of gold and thereby reduce the resources of our enemy. Mules, donkeys and camels enter the frontier in unbroken lines; horses, dapples and bays and prancing mounts, come into our possession. The furs of sables, marmots, foxes and badgers, colored rugs and decorated carpets fill the imperial treasury, while jade and auspicious stones, corals and crystals become national treasures.*

⋆   ⋆   ⋆

For the Chinese, of course, the Silk Road was nothing so sordid as a trade route. They staunchly maintained the fiction that they were receiving tribute from lesser countries and dispensing gifts. But the reality is clear, as in the comment that the Han Emperor Wu distributed to foreign visitors "treasures and silks as rewards and gifts and gave them back in richer measure all that they had brought to him in abundance." As in the partly or wholly legendary tales of the early travels of Emperor Mu, the annals carefully record many of these transactions. In 51 B.C., for example, one of the Western "tributaries" was presented with 77 sets of bedcovers, and two years later received a like amount, along with 110 suits of clothes. Once peace was fully established the numbers increased rapidly. One branch of the Hsiung-nu, for example, received 8,000 pieces of embroidered silks and 6,000 pounds of silk floss in 51 B.C.; 50 years later those figures had mushroomed to 84,000 and 78,000, respectively. Items received from the nomads, such as furs, were often dyed or worked into clothing and then sent on the way west.

During this first century B.C., the Chinese were actively exploring contacts with kingdoms of Central Asia. Not all of these were prepared to carry on a long-distance trade—as suggested by the Chinese attempts to trade for the Heavenly Horses of Ferghana. Even after the stunning Chinese victory at Kokand, some of the city-states beyond the Pamirs remained unconvinced of the desirability of substantial trade with the Chinese. Part of the problem was that the plains of Russian Turkestan were at this time hotly disputed by several Scythian groups. In moving into Bactria, the Yüeh-chih had pushed ahead of them the Sakae, who took over the remains of the Indo-Greek kingdom in northwest India. But the Yüeh-chih were themselves being pressed by other nomads from the steppe.

It may be for this reason that the Chinese took the unusual step of attempting to open trading routes through the difficult Karakorum and Hindu Kush Mountains into India, a magnet for both East and West. China, in an expansive mood seldom seen in its history, was very much the wooer in this early period, and not always a successful one. The *Thung Chien Kang Mu* (Mirror of Universal History), a 12th century A.D. distillation of earlier accounts, tells of one Chinese exploratory mission in about 30 B.C. over the rugged mountains toward India. The object of the mission was the state of Chi-Pin, whose precise location is unknown, but was probably in Kashmir or Afghanistan:

> When, under Emperor Wu, communication with the Western countries began, only the kingdom of Chi-Pin refused to submit, considering that the soldiers of Han could never reach there. Its king even put to death several Chinese envoys. In the time of the Emperor Yüan [48-33 B.C.] the King of Chi-Pin sent an embassy to apologize, but the emperor lacked interest in foreign relations and refused to receive it. After the Emperor [Ch'eng, 32-7 B.C.] had ascended the throne, a further embassy was sent, with offerings and apologies, and it was planned [to accept them and] to send a mission to conduct the ambassadors home with all honor.

Some have suggested that Chi-Pin was actually the Indo-Greek kingdom of Kophen, which survived in the region of Kabul. The peoples ruling there at this time were the Sakae, the nomads who had conquered Greek Bactria and then been displaced toward India by the Yüeh-chih. Did the change of heart described above perhaps come about as the Greeks in the region educated the Sakae as to the benefits of trade? It is an intriguing hypothesis.

China, too, had a change of heart, with a change of emperor. It hurt Chinese pride to appear to be soliciting contact, especially when it had the character of mere trade. This is reflected in the Chinese counselors' arguments about whether or not to accede to the requests of the Chi-Pin envoys. A high court official put the case against full-scale trading contacts this way:

> *Friendly intercourse with barbarian nations is advisable only where communications are reasonably easy. The Hsientu [Hindu Kush] passes will always be an obstacle to relations with Chi-Pin. The friendship of that country could not benefit the western cities [those in the Tarim Basin], and even if it should be hostile it could do them no harm. We were first friendly with the Chi-Pin people, then they did us harm, hence we broke off relations with them. Moreover, the so-called ambassadors who have just arrived are neither nobles nor men of mark, but really merchants who want to engage in commerce; their offerings and apologies are only a pretext. To despatch a return embassy would have no meaning; it would only show that we had been deceived.*

City gates, as here in modern Langchow, were natural gathering places for buyers and sellers. (By Sven Hedin, from his *Through Asia*, 1899)

From the Phi-Shan [possibly the mountains above Khotan], our envoys would have to traverse four or five countries, each of which is full of robbers. Then one must cross the Greater and the Lesser Headache Mountains, chains of naked and burning rocks, so named because they cause headache, dizziness and vomiting. Then comes the San-Ch'ih-Phan gorge [possibly the Karakorum Pass], thirty li long, where the path is only 16 or 17 inches wide, on the edge of a precipice, and where the travelers have to be tied together with ropes. From here through Hsientu it is 3000 li and more, on a road full of dangers.

The sage kings of old devoted themselves to the nine provinces and the five concentric zones, caring nothing about what was outside. Yet now it is proposed to order the escort home of these barbarian merchants, thus exposing soldiers and imperial envoys to indescribable fatigues and dangers. Such useless enterprises should not be the policy of an enduring dynasty. If the officers of the escort have already been nominated, let them at any rate accompany the Chi-Pin people no further than the Phi-Shan Mountains.

The prime minister agreed with this view and the record continues: "So they [the envoys from Chi-Pin] were allowed to trade and sent away with presents. And afterwards envoys from Chi-Pin arrived in China every few years." It is tantalizing to speculate whether the envoys from Chi-Pin were Greek traders forced to cross the high Karakorum Mountains, enduring severe altitude sickness, because they were cut off from their old easier route through Bactria.

So the silks of China made their way by tortuous routes across the spine of Asia, there to be picked up by traders on the old routes toward Iran and Mesopotamia. The Parthians, who continued connections with the Chinese, as much as was possible across the turbulent plains of Turkestan, were especially eager for the unique silks of China, for themselves and, soon, for the Western buyers who would make Parthia's fortune. Prime among those would be the Romans.

CHAPTER SIX

THE GREAT CHAIN

Silk was at first rather shocking to the early Romans, a rough farming and fighting people. In a major battle with the Parthians at Carrhae (Harran) in 53 B.C., the Romans, already at a disadvantage against the powerful Parthian archers, were completely disrupted when the Parthians unfurled their brilliantly dyed iridescent silk banners, apparently the first silk ever seen by the Roman troops. The effect was devastating. The Roman attempt to imitate Alexander's triumphs in Asia quickly collapsed, and the Roman eagles—the standards of the defeated legions—were taken up onto the Iranian Plateau to decorate Parthian palaces on the Silk Road.

For the Romans, silk was also a symbol of Eastern decadence. Cleopatra, last ruler of the Ptolemaic line in Egypt, may have owed something of her reputation as a seductress to her penchant for dressing in fine silks. This was, perhaps, a more daring and alluring attire than it might seem at first, for many of the silks of early times were extremely sheer gauzes—the Indians called them "woven wind"—not the later and heavier figured satins, damasks, and brocades, or even the light, but more opaque fabrics of modern times.

Transparent, or nearly transparent, silk was apparently worn in China for many centuries. A later Arab merchant in China related that he noticed a mark on the chest of a fully clothed officer of the imperial household, a mark that was clearly visible through the multiple folds of

. . . the Seres [are] famous for the fleecy product of their forests. This pale floss, which they find growing on the leaves, they wet with waters, and then comb out, furnishing thus a double task to our womenkind in first dressing the threads, and then again of weaving them into silk fabrics. So has toil to be multiplied; so have the ends of the earth to be traversed: and all that a Roman dame may exhibit her charms in transparent gauze.

—Pliny the Elder,
Natural History

no less than five silk robes. This merchant commented that these were "silks of the first quality, such as were never imported in Arabia." But the fabrics worn in Western Asia were apparently sheer enough. Pliny complained in his *Natural History* of the transparency of an inferior wild-silk fabric produced in Western Asia, though he noted of the woman credited with first inventing the process of preparing and weaving these threads: "Let us not cheat her of her glory in having devised a method by which women shall be dressed and yet naked."

Silk was, in the mid-first century B.C., still extremely rare in the West. The Chinese may have driven halfway across Asia to open the eastern half of the Silk Road, but the 5,000-mile-long route was still long and tortuous. With peoples all along the way battling to control a piece of the great trans-Asian highway, only minuscule amounts of the tissue-like fabric reached Western Asia. Apart from a few luminaries like Cleopatra, even the richest and most powerful Romans wore only small pieces—strips, circles, or squares—of silk sewn onto their otherwise all-white wool, cotton, or linen togas or tunics. If these silk fragments were then dyed purple or embroidered with gold and silver threads, their cost might increase forty-fold. It is no wonder, given its expense and rarity, that dyed silk was used to indicate high station. So, purple edging a toga was the mark of a patrician, as stripes of scarlet and purple identified a highly placed court soothsayer.

These bits of silk represented an extraordinary investment, considering the cost and difficulty of bringing goods all the way across Asia. Of course, the Romans themselves were responsible for some of the political turmoil on the Silk Road in this period. They had made a foothold in Asia as early as 190 B.C., when they defeated the Seleucid Greeks at the battle of Magnesia on the western coast of Anatolia. But during much of the second century B.C., the Romans were occupied with their Punic (Phoenician) wars in the western Mediterranean, then the main focus of their empire. Not until late in the century did Rome begin to press eastward from the Mediterranean, as Parthia was pushing westward from the Iranian Plateau.

So it was that, as China was making the eastern half of the Silk Road relatively safe and secure, the western half was becoming a battlefield. Rome and Parthia between them successively squeezed the flaccid remains of the Seleucid Empire until, by about 74 B.C., the Seleucid princes were confined to a few cities near the western end of the Silk Road, and later were submerged altogether. Between the two superpowers various small states would rise and fall, sometimes as pawns for one or the other, notably in Armenia and the Syrian Desert.

The Romans and the Parthians had their first major confrontation in 53 B.C. at Carrhae. The Romans, fresh from their great victories elsewhere around the Mediterranean, had little respect for the people they (like the Greeks before them) considered barbarians. They had a typical farmer's or city-dweller's contempt for these long-haired semi-nomads, dressed in loose trousers and long-sleeved tunics, whose lives centered around their horses. Nor, before that first meeting, did the Romans have much respect for the Parthians' military prowess. They could not conceive that the close-ranked foot soldiers who had won them an empire in

Europe and had defeated the Seleucids might be at a disadvantage against these rough horse soldiers.

But that was before the Romans met the Parthian cavalry—part heavy-armored horse-men like the later European knights and part more lightly mounted but still extremely formidable archers. These Parthian archers used bows so powerful they sometimes skewered two soldiers with a single arrow, actually nailing soldiers to their shields. More than that, they had perfected a technique known as the Parthian shot (in truth, widespread among the Central Asian cavalry), in which archers would wheel away as if in retreat, and then twist their bodies around to fire deadly arrows over their shoulders. The Romans could not even hope that the Parthians would run out of ammunition, for camel caravans laden with arrows attended in the rear. Beyond that were the deafening noise of the great bell-filled leather drums used to spur on the Parthian army and, of course, the dazzling banners of silk.

The combination spelled disaster for the Romans. The Roman general, Crassus, who had dreamed of following in the footsteps of Alexander, was trapped and killed and his head sent to the Parthian king. As many as 20,000 Roman soldiers died in the battle, and another 10,000 were taken prisoner and, it is believed, transported eastward to Antiocheia Margiana (Merv).

The possible fate of these prisoners of war is one of the more curious stories in the history of the Silk Road. Sinologist Homer Dubs pieced together evidence leading to an ingenious and plausible hypothesis about the lot of some of them. In 36 B.C., 17 years after the battle of Carrhae, Chinese forces laid siege to a Hsiung-nu walled camp in Sogdiana, probably on the Talas River. What was remarkable about this, among all the other sieges recorded in the Chinese annals, is that the camp and its surrounding defensive ditch were further guarded by a double wooden palisade, a practice unknown in the East. In addition, the *Annals of the Former Han Dynasty* tells us, "more than a hundred foot-soldiers lined up on either side of the gate, in a fish-scale formation." This, too, is very far from the Central Asian style of warfare, which was more like a massed rush than a disciplined maneuver. Nor do the Chinese annals anywhere else mention this "fish-scale formation." But the Roman formation called the *testudo*, in which soldiers stood side by side in close ranks so their overlapping shields provided a defensive wall, could well seem to an outsider to resemble fish scales.

As the battle went to the Chinese, the Hsiung-nu leader was killed, and the Chinese reported that they took the surrender of more than a thousand men, who were dispersed as slaves, but that they had also taken alive 145 captives, who accompanied them back to the East. Dubs hypothesized that these 145 soldiers were Romans who, having escaped from the Parthians and being unable to make their way back to Roman territory, hired out as mercenaries to the Hsiung-nu and that, once their employer was killed, they ceased fighting (they did not surrender) and chose to follow the Chinese rather than die on the steppe, where they were quite unsuited to make a life.

Like their kin who remained on the steppe, these Parthians wore the trousers and short tunics suited for riders. (Gandhara, from Royal Ontario Museum)

It seems that these soldiers "taken in the storming of the city" were allowed to settle a frontier city (China was always happy to have additional troops guarding its border) in the heart of the Kansu Corridor. What is most interesting about this city is that it was called Li-Kan. This was one of the oldest names that China had for the lands beyond Parthia, for this was the Chinese name for the homeland of the jugglers brought as gifts from the Parthians over six decades earlier, in about 100 B.C. Naming the city after the Romans would suit the Confucian practice of making the name appropriate to the thing; the Chinese did not give cities foreign names, except when they were settled by foreigners.

So it seems possible that Roman soldiers, some of whom had been born in Italy or Gaul and may even have seen Caesar or Pompey ride in triumph through Rome, lived out their days in a city on the frontier of China, marrying local women and gradually merging into the general population. The city of Li-Kan is mentioned as late as the seventh century A.D., and may have survived until 746 A.D., when Tibetans swept in and destroyed most settlements in the region.

Whatever the fate of the Roman prisoners of war from Carrhae, the Roman generals did not learn the lesson that was taught there. Only a decade later, Julius Caesar was planning his own eastern expedition, to regain the standards of the defeated Roman legions (and with them Rome's honor). His assassination ended that plan and plunged Rome into a civil war. In 36 B.C., one of the principals in the battle for control, Mark Antony, himself embarked on an eastern campaign. But he had little more success than Crassus. Driving for Ecbatana, he was defeated not only by the Parthian archers but also by lack of supplies over a bitter winter in the upland country. In the end he returned to Egypt, to find solace in the silk-clad arms of Cleopatra.

Some have wondered if, had he not lost in Asia, Antony might with his powerful army have won control of the empire. Instead, the civil war concluded with the Roman republic transformed into an empire united under Octavian Augustus, after the defeat of Antony and Cleopatra at Actium in 31 B.C. So began the *Pax Romana*—the great era of the Roman Empire.

It was Augustus who retrieved the precious Roman standards, the "lost eagles," from Parthia, and then not by battle but by negotiation. Having captured the Parthian king's son, the Romans exchanged him for the standards in 20 B.C. But beyond that, the peace treaty between the two powers called for four Parthian princes to live in Rome as diplomatic hostages. There they were well-known men-about-town, commonly seen at the theater and wheeling their chariots about the city with their patrician friends, including young Caligula.

For a time Rome and Parthia were at peace. A cold war still existed between them, especially evident in the continuing contention for spheres of influence among the smaller states of the region, notably Armenia and the tiny Arab states of Syria. But through Augustus's long reign and the two following it, peace prevailed on the far western end of the Silk Road. One contemporary observer, Velleius Paterculus, even tells of Roman and Parthian princes picnicking together on the banks of the Euphrates, the border between the two empires:

> On an island in the Euphrates, with an equal retinue on each side Gaius [Augustus's grandson] had a meeting with the king of the Parthians, a young man of distinguished appearance. This spectacle of the Roman army arrayed on the one side, the Parthian on the other, while these two eminent leaders not only of the empires they represented but also of mankind thus met in conference, it was my fortunate lot to see early in my career as a soldier . . . first the Parthian dined with Gaius upon the Roman bank, and later Gaius supped with the king on the soil of the enemy.

This peace brought surcease to war-drained Rome and also an increase in demand for the new luxuries of the East. Less than a decade after the battle at Carrhae, with that first view of the bright silken banners, like banners had flown over Rome itself to honor Julius Caesar back from one of his many triumphs. With peace again returned, the leaders of the now-massive empire wanted their share of the East's silks, spices, and jewels, as the once-simple Romans sought to emulate the opulent Eastern lifestyle.

In the East the Chinese continued to trade across the continent to Parthia. Whether any Chinese merchants or envoys reached beyond Parthia into Roman territory is unclear. Certainly Parthia's profits depended on keeping control of the Silk Road. For many centuries, and possibly starting as early as this, the Parthians would bar others from crossing their territory, retaining the middleman's profits for themselves. And Chinese annals seem to indicate that, until the late first century A.D., no official Han envoy reached beyond Parthia. But some unofficial Chinese or Central Asian envoys, attempting to expand their trade, may have managed to pass through to Roman territory in the early years of the empire's existence. Writing two centuries later, the Roman historian Florus seems to suggest as much in his praise of Augustus's *Pax Romana*:

> *Even the rest of the nations of the world which were not subject to the imperial sway were sensible of its grandeur, and looked with reverence to the Roman people, the great conqueror of nations. Thus even Scythians and Sarmatians sent envoys to seek the friendship of Rome. Nay the Seres came likewise, and the Indians who dwelt beneath the vertical sun, bringing presents of precious stones and pearls and elephants, but thinking all of less moment than the vastness of the journey which they had undertaken, and which they said had occupied four years. In truth it needed but to look at their complexion to see that they were people of another world than ours. The Parthians also, as if repenting for their presumption in defeating the Romans, spontaneously brought back the standards which they had captured in the catastrophe of Crassus. Thus all round the inhabited earth there was an unbroken circle of peace or at least of armistice.*

During this brief era of peace, the Parthians were only too happy to supply Romans with the luxuries they desired. The Greeks, Syrians, Jews, Armenians, and others who had been traders on the Silk Road under the Seleucids continued to be honored citizens under Parthia's rule. The Parthians were also very much aware of the value of their hold on the Silk Road. No comparable alternative route existed in the region and, having a monopoly, they charged heavy duties on the trade goods that passed through their territory, duties that formed a large part of their state revenues.

★   ★   ★

The merchants who plied the Silk Road under the Parthians had apparently continued the old tradition of circulating itineraries, which informed travelers of the main stations or caravanserais where they might find shelter on the way, the distances between them, and any noteworthy sights to be seen on the way. These were not fulsome guidebooks but brief notations for working merchants and officials. By luck, one of these survived, a work called the *Parthian Stations* by one Isidore, from the seaport of Charax. It is he who allows us to trace the outline of the western section of the Silk Road in the age of Augustus Caesar. In this period, the old Seleucid capital of Antioch was the Roman capital of the Western Asian provinces, retaining all its old pomp and splendor.

Isidore's account started at Zeugma, the ancient crossing of the Euphrates, and proceeded thence via numerous small villages—if any such were fortified and had a well with good drinking water, it was worth mentioning—to the crossroads city of Seleucia. (This city would soon be eclipsed by the Parthians' own city, Ctesiphon, established nearby.) Then the route took travelers up through the land of the Medes, passing through Ecbatana, "the metropolis of Media," with a notable temple and a treasury. Beyond that was Rhagae, "the greatest of the cities in Media," and the narrow valley called the Caspian Gates, which lay beneath a high mountain. All along the route, through the fertile plains of Hyrcania and beyond, Isidore noted many villages and cities, tallying with the description of the region given by the first Chinese visitors a century earlier. Farther east, the villages are fewer. At Antiocheia Margiana, for example, where the Roman prisoners of war were supposedly taken after Carrhae, Isidore noted that although the station was well-watered, there were no villages nearby. From here the itinerary described by Isidore diverged from the east-pointing route familiar in both earlier and later times. Instead of heading toward either Bactria or the regions of Ferghana, the route swung down through the more desolate country of eastern Parthia, along the ridge of mountains leading toward India.

Our picture of the lands between the Iranian Plateau and the Tarim Basin is none too clear for this period. While the Romans were fighting their civil war in the West, various groups of Central Asian nomads were contending for this middle portion, apparently making the more direct route to the East both difficult and dangerous. Judging by the angling of Isidore's route, the Parthians seem to have been trading most routinely southeast into India. One interesting sidelight in this connection is that, during the Augustan reign, which bridges into the Christian calendar era, the ruler of an empire in northwest India was a king named Gondopharnes, regarded in Christian legend as one of the "three wise men of the East" who came to visit Jesus at Bethlehem.

Farther east, the Chinese had continued to expand their westward trade. In about 2 A.D. they opened their New Route to the North, shortening the distance between the Jade Gate and the caravan centers in the Turfan region and north.

Unfortunately, as China was extending its reach out across the continent, the Han dynasty became so weak at home that it was overthrown in 9 A.D. by a usurper, Wang Mang. A succession of troubles—drought, famine, and then floods so severe that the Huang River changed its course—hampered his efforts to rule the land. In the end, an army of peasants who called themselves the Red Eyebrows, after the paint they used to identify themselves, brought down Wang Mang's regime in 25 A.D., pillaging the always-vulnerable city of Ch'ang-an in the process. The Han dynasty was restored, dubbed the Later (or Eastern) Han, as opposed to the Former (or Western) Han dynasty, and began rule from the new capital of Loyang.

But in a little over a dozen years, almost all China's work in the Tarim Basin was undone. Sensing the weakness of their old enemy, the Hsiung-nu launched a furious attack on China's northern borders. Many of the Tarim oasis-states revolted, some finding a precarious independence, but most being obliged to pay tribute to the Hsiung-nu in the north, or to the Tibetan raiders who bedeviled much of the Kansu Corridor. With Chinese sufferance some Hsiung-nu peoples even settled inside the Great Wall and in the corridor itself. China maintained a few allies, notably Yarkand, far across the Tarim, but elsewhere all was desolation. Even the Protector General of the Western Territories (a post established in 59 B.C.) was killed in the ensuing revolts. As the Chinese annals put it, "the Western Regions were broken up and scattered like loose tiles." China would not regain control of the Tarim Basin for several decades.

★   ★   ★

Some silks continued to make their way across the continent to the West, especially as the Romans were soon recognized as an eager market for such finery. But the costs of trading were extremely high and the supply that reached across the continent limited. During the disordered period of Wang Mang's rule, for example, one of China's "tributary" trading partners, a Hsiung-nu tribe called the Shan-yu, received just about one-eighth of the embroidered silks and silk floss they had received just a decade or so earlier. In the absence of secure passage, much was lost en route to raiders who had no taste for the longer-term rewards of trading. And in the absence of a central power favorable to merchants, traders had to pay high taxes and duties to every petty state along the way west. The result was a diminution of the flow of silks from the East, just as Rome was developing a powerful appetite for them. And Parthia took advantage of the "buyer's market" to make the highest profits it could.

In this situation, Augustus Caesar set about trying to find alternative routes to the East, to get more silks and other desired goods, and at a lower cost. The route north of or across the Caspian was afflicted by the same ills as the Silk Road, so he turned to the natural alternative, the Spice Route. The Indians had long been sailing the waters south of Asia, exchanging the products of distant lands along the way. By the late second century B.C., Greeks had also begun sailing from Egypt to India to share in the wealth directly. The Romans were well aware of the riches being tapped by the Spice Route, riches which had long flowed up Arabia's Incense Road or on the Red Sea to Petra and other caravan cities, or to Alexandria. Caravans on this route were so large that the Greco-Roman geographer Strabo thought them much like an army.

It was Alexandria that Augustus made the main funnel for sea-borne Eastern luxuries headed for Rome. Greeks continued to sail the Spice Route, now under Roman auspices, and were even celebrated by poets of the south Indian ports. One talked of the "beautiful large ships of the Yavanas [Greeks], bringing gold, [that] come splashing the white foam on the waters . . . and return laden with pepper." Another poet went further:

> . . . sacks of pepper are brought from the houses to the market; the gold received from
> ships, in exchange for articles sold, is brought to shore in barges . . . where the music of

the surging sea never ceases, and where [the king] presents to visitors the rare products of the seas and mountains.

Augustus Caesar, of course, had no desire to share this trade with or to pay a middleman's share to the Arabs. Strabo was quite clear about that:

The Arabs were . . . known from earliest times to be rich, as they traded their spices and precious stones against gold and silver and gave nothing back to strangers of what they received. For this reason he [Augustus] hoped either to exploit them as rich friends or to conquer them as rich enemies.

In truth, he tried both. At first he took a military approach, but the Arabs were able to lead the Romans a merry dance in the desert, until the legions admitted to defeat. Apparently the Romans did, however, sack and raze the prime port of the Incense Road, Arabia Eudaemon, forcing the Spice Route traffic up the Red Sea to Roman-controlled ports, such as Aela, at the head of the Gulf of Aqaba. Gradually they took the caravan cities that stretched northward from Aela, building forts and wells along the old caravan tracks. The highway eventually would stretch from Aela through rockbound Petra, northward through Damascus and the semi-independent Arab city of Palmyra, and all the way across the Anatolian Plateau to Trapezus (Trebizond) on the Black Sea.

With the Silk Road nearly pinched off, silks and spices from China often made their way westward in Indian or Indo-Malayan ships from the ports of Nan-hai (Canton) and Cattigara (probably modern Hanoi), just then coming into prominence. Since the Parthians were still in the market, some of these goods, along with the spices and jewels that India itself had to offer, were shipped overland from various Indian ports to Bactria and then on to Parthia. But much more went by water, as Greek ships sailed from India, landing their cargo at ports along the Red Sea. The short-term destination was generally Alexandria or one of the Phoenician cities, which acted as refining and distribution centers for the whole Mediterranean world.

★   ★   ★

With the trickle that crossed the Silk Road proper and the larger flow that followed the Spice Route, Asian luxuries soon made their mark not only in Rome itself, but also throughout the Roman Empire. Silk that had been spun in China, traded at Malaya or India, woven and dyed in Phoenicia, might be worn by patricians anywhere around the Mediterranean, from Anatolia to Spain. Jewels that had been mined in Afghanistan, cut in India, and shipped to Alexandria, might grace the body of a Roman subject anywhere from the Nile to the Rhine.

The impact on Roman life was enormous, and many were the Cassandras who warned of the dire results that could flow from such indulgence.

All in vain, of course. The taste for exotic luxuries, once whetted, is hard to blunt. The Romans rapidly became entranced by the myriad goods of the East. Pliny, a puritan out of tune with his age, lamented:

> . . . *we have come now to see whole mountains cut down into marble slabs, journeys made to the Seres [Chinese] to get stuffs for clothing, the abysses of the Red Sea explored for pearls, and the depths of the earth in search of emeralds. Nay, more, they have taken up the notion also of piercing the ears, as if it were too small a matter to wear these gems in necklaces and tiaras, unless holes also were made in the body to insert them in.*

Paying no attention to such tirades, more and more Romans spent their patrimony and the fruits of their empire on the gems, spices, and finery of Asia. The result was devastating in sum, and would contribute in some measure to the eventual downfall of the empire itself, as Pliny noted:

> . . . *at the lowest computation, India and the Seres and that [Arabian] Peninsula put together drain our empire of one hundred million of sesterces every year. That is the price that our luxuries and our womankind cost us!*

Above all, this meant silk. It was silk that drained the purses of the Romans and captured the imaginations of all those who came after them. Silk was integral to the Silk Road, and in this period to the Spice Route as well, because China would keep the secret of its manufacture within its borders for another half a millennium. Until around the fifth century A.D., Westerners generally believed—as Pliny did, in the quotation that opened this chapter—that silk was produced by a plant. The mistake is a natural one, for flax and cotton are both vegetable fibers; and no doubt the Chinese encouraged the misapprehension to keep inquirers from tumbling to the truth. In this they were entirely successful. Even when a Westerner learned part of the truth, the resulting story was a jumble of misinformation. Take the story of the Greek Pausanias in the second century A.D.:

> . . . *the filaments from which the Seres make their stuffs are the growth of no plant, but are produced in quite another manner; and thus it is. There exists in their country a certain insect which the Greeks call Ser, but by the Seres it is not called Ser, but something quite different. In size it is twice as big as the biggest of beetles; but, in other respects, it resembles the spiders that spin under trees; and, moreover, it has eight legs as spiders have. The Seres keep these creatures, and make houses for their shelter adapted to*

Many Romans lamented the cost of the luxurious silks, dyes, and spices desired from the East by men and women of their empire. ("House of the Tragic Poet—Sallust," from *Museum of Antiquity* . . . , 1882)

summer and winter respectively. And the substance wrought by these insects is found in the shape of a slender filament entangled about their legs. The people feed them for about four years upon millet, and in the fifth year (for they know that the creatures will not live longer than that) they give them a kind of green reed to eat. This is the food that the insect likes best of all; and it crams itself with it to such an extent that it bursts from repletion. And when it is thus dead, they find the bulk of what it has spun in its inside.

The truth was rather different, though Pausanias did, at least, understand that silk was an animal, not a plant, product.

But the ignorance of the Romans did not matter greatly, for they were in these years more buyers than producers, and they had supplies of silk and other Eastern luxuries flowing to them over land and sea. Silks became so popular in Rome in just these few decades that, by 14 A.D., the Senate was attempting to bar men from wearing silk, saying that they were "dishonored" and made effeminate by it.

The Spice Route had one significant disadvantage: pirates. Many of these were people driven to brigandage by the loss of their former livelihoods. The Alexandrian writer Agatharchides, writing two centuries later, put it quite succinctly, talking of the Arabs the Romans had bypassed with their new sea route:

> Of old, they earned a just livelihood . . . but later, when the kings from Alexandria
> made the gulf navigable to merchants, they attacked shipwrecked persons, and building
> pirate ships plundered seafarers.

All along the route, from China to Egypt, pirates haunted the narrow passages, the island sprays, and other places from which they could easily prey on the vessels that plied the Spice Route. And, as on land, various sea kingdoms rose up to try to control sections of the route, demanding heavy duties in exchange for safe passage through the vital straits along the way. Despite these disadvantages the Spice Route would continue to operate for many centuries, in counterpoint to the Silk Road.

But the Romans were eager for the full reopening of the overland route. The journey might be long and difficult, but the highway could be made safe if strong powers ruled, and the distance was considerably shorter than the roundabout sea route. The restoration of Chinese power in Central Asia was, then, as attractive to the peoples of the West as to those of the East.

★   ★   ★

The reopening of the Tarim Basin was destined to be a long process. The Han, first of all, had to re-establish order at home. Some of the Tarim states, such as Shan-shan, sought Chinese protection, as they chafed under the heavy tribute exacted by the Hsiung-nu, while others resisted Hsiung-nu domination. The king of Yarkand, China's main Central Asian ally, even suggested that he be appointed Protector General of the Western Territories. When that request was refused, he went on his own course of conquest. As a result, a dozen and a half Tarim kingdoms, including Shan-shan and Turfan, implored the Han emperor to appoint a Protector General to come to their defense. But the Han rulers were still focused on their internal affairs, and the desert cities were left to the mercies of the contending powers in the region.

Not until the seventh decade of the West's Christian Calendar did the Han rulers begin to move in force beyond the Great Wall once again. Various expeditions sent northward against the Hsiung-nu brought into the Chinese fold the oases of Hami, Guchen (beyond the low Pei Shan), and Turfan, where the local ruler "came out of the town, removed his headdress, and embracing the hooves of the [Chinese general's] horse, made his submission." In these towns the Chinese set up military garrisons, as bulwarks against Hsiung-nu invasion of the Western Territories.

It was the general Pan Ch'ao who was primarily responsible for regaining China's Western Territories. Pan Ch'ao came from an illustrious family. His father began and his brother finished the *Ch'ien Han Shu*, the *Annals of the Former Han Dynasty*, while his sister was a highly regarded literary writer. Pan Ch'ao himself was a shrewd and daring man of action, who could be extremely ruthless on occasion. When he first ventured westward through the Jade Gate into the Tarim, in about 73 A.D., China's might had little credit among the peoples of the desert. But Pan Ch'ao believed that "only he who penetrates into the tiger's lair can carry off the cubs."

So he and his small party made their way across the parched sands, through the land of the wild camels. In these lands, to them strange and new, they remembered all the old tales told of evil spirits in the desert, of a legendary City of the Dragon beneath the waters of the Lop Nor. They also faced more immediate danger, possible raids by Hsiung-nu and Tibetans, and the lack of water, in a land where they now had few friends. Indeed, at their first destination, the city of Shan-shan, some three to four weeks from the Jade Gate, the local prince planned to hand his Chinese visitors over to the Hsiung-nu, knowing that to do otherwise would be to

On the fringe of the wide Tarim Basin and surrounded on three sides by the Pamirs, Kashgar's site is magnificent. (From *Tartary*, by R. Shaw, reprinted in Yule's *Marco Polo*)

call their wrath down on his head. Pan Ch'ao rightly read the situation and made what modern militarists would call a preventive strike. That night he set fire to the city and, in the ensuing confusion, massacred much of the population. Thereafter, Shan-shan came under the control of the Commander of Western Territories and held a Chinese garrison, serving as an outpost for further conquests to the west. Centainly Shan-shan occupied a strategic position on the way west, but Pan Ch'ao's action was also symbolic, signalling to all that China intended to retake the Western Territories.

For the next 30 years, Pan Ch'ao led Chinese forces throughout the Tarim Basin, taking the key cities all the way to the Pamirs. Khotan and Yarkand in the south, Aksu, Kucha, and Kashgar in the north, all were brought into the Chinese orbit. But each victory in Central Asia was simply part of a long war, for princes brought into submission would waver and turn toward the Hsiung-nu. Many of these cities were, after all, far from China. But Pan Ch'ao, as representative of China's power, used all his cunning and ruthlessness to identify potential defectors and to execute them and their followers. Even when the Chinese were temporarily turned out and recalled home, as at Kashgar in 75 A.D., Pan Ch'ao would sometimes ignore orders and return to retake a vital oasis.

In the end he was honored with the title of Protector of the Western Territories, having virtually the whole of the Tarim Basin under his control. As the Chinese annals put it: "He kept order as far as the Pamirs and the Hanging Passes," the high notches through which the caravans passed to Iran and India. His success was due, in part, to the old imperial policy of using the conquered peoples to extend the conquest. From each newly conquered desert city Pan Ch'ao took troops, adding these to the native Chinese soldiers, who were often adventurers, ex-criminals, or dissidents forced into exile. And with the territory won up to the Pamirs, Pan Ch'ao settled these soldiers in the string of garrisons that would now line the routes to the west, providing both protection and supplies for the caravans that trod the still-fragile routes of the Silk Road. By judicious use of irrigation, these soldiers also extended the farmlands around the garrisons, providing supplies for caravans in the desert, and themselves living largely off the land. Especially around Yarkand and Kashgar, as Pan Ch'ao pointed out to his emperor, the land was so fertile that "the soldiers who are garrisoned there cost the empire nothing."

Pan Ch'ao's conquests were not mere acquisitions of territory, however. They had a point: to open direct and untroubled contact with the peoples of the West. In that they succeeded handsomely. As the *Hou Han Shu (Annals of the Later Han Dynasty)* records:

> . . . *Since the time they [the peoples of the Western Territories] had been compelled to submit by force of arms or had been won over by gifts, all the kingdoms of the Western Regions came to offer the rare products of their lands and to deliver up as hostages those who were dear to them . . . Dispatch bearers and post runners came and went uninter-*

ruptedly in every season and month. Merchants and foreigners engaged in trade knocked
daily at the gates of the Barrier [the Great Wall].

As this excerpt implies, much of the trade, estimated as at least 12 caravans a year, was carried on by peoples of the Western Territories or beyond. Certainly Chinese traders operated in the newly reopened region. Even Pan Ch'ao did some private trading, for we have a letter from his brother, Pan Ku, saying: "I now send 300 pieces of white silk, which I want you to trade for Bactrian horses, storax [an aromatic], and rugs." But increasingly the trade would be carried on by the various Scythian peoples who had long fought each other for control of Western Turkestan.

While Pan Ch'ao was winning the Tarim for China, one of these peoples, a tribe called the Kushans, was coming to the fore. The Kushans and their subject peoples now traded with the Chinese through prime caravan centers like Bactra and Bukhara. Remembering how, as the Yüeh-chih, these people had two centuries earlier occupied the Kansu Corridor, the Chinese would continue to call them the Great Yüeh-chih.

The Kushans and the Chinese seem to have had generally friendly relations, being allied against the Hsiung-nu. True, relations were somewhat strained in about 90 A.D. when the powerful Kushan king suggested a marriage between himself and a Chinese princess. Pan Ch'ao rejected the (to him) presumptuous idea out of hand, arresting the Kushan ambassador and then packing him off back home. At that, the Kushans sent an army of 70,000 men against China's western garrisons. But Pan Ch'ao, with his typical combination of bold bluff and hardness, forestalled a major engagement and restored peace. Thereafter, the annals tell us, the Kushans sent yearly tribute to China, which, in the old-fashioned Chinese euphemism, probably means that the Kushans came to China to trade. In this same period the Tibetans, who laid claim to cities along the southern Tarim, also attempted to throw off Chinese rule, for a time cutting the route, but Pan Ch'ao prevailed against them as well.

In the end, the Kushans saw the overriding benefit of keeping open the long-distance connnections between East and West. So the Silk Road remained open through Chinese and Kushan territory. When, in 97 A.D., Pan Ch'ao sent an emissary, Kan Ying, to explore the western half of the Silk Road, the Kushans apparently made no objection to the Chinese envoy crossing their territory.

The Chinese were still in contact with the Parthians on the Iranian Plateau. Just a few years earlier, the Parthians had sent an ambassador, who made "use of numerous successive interpreters" on the way to Loyang with gifts for the Han court. From such contacts, the Chinese had formed some picture of the West. They knew the Roman lands at the far Western end of the Silk Road as Li-Kan or Ta-ch'in (Great China). The Chinese seem not to have known that the Roman Empire was actually centered much farther west. For them, from the few bits of information they had gleaned across thousands of miles, "Rome" was the Roman lands of Western Asia, Syria, and Phoenicia. It was to these lands, Ta-ch'in, that Kan Ying was dispatched in 97 A.D.

The *Annals of the Later Han Dynasty* record something of the report he made on his return:

> The country of An-hsi [Parthia] has its residence at the city of Ho-tu [Hecatompylos]; it is 25,000 li distant from Loyang . . . The size of the country is several thousand li. There are several hundred small cities with a vast number of inhabitants and soldiers. On its eastern frontier is the city of Mu-lu [probably Antiocheia Margiana], which is called Little An-hsi. It is 20,000 li distant from Loyang.

The cities described here are tentatively identified not simply by their relative positions on the Silk Road, but also because of the distances indicated. If the Roman measure *stadia* is substituted for *li*, the route as outlined seems quite accurate, suggesting that Kan Ying may have collected much of his information from the merchants' itineraries current for the Silk Road.

From the Iranian highlands, Kan Ying, apparently still in the company of the Parthians, went down into the land of T'iao-chih, apparently referring to Mesopotamia. The annals continue:

> The city of the country of T'iao-chih is situated on a hill; its circumference is over forty li and it borders on the western sea [Persian Gulf]. The waters of the sea crookedly surround it. In the south, and northeast, the road is cut off; only in the northwest there is access to it by means of a land road. The country is hot and low. It produces lions, rhinoceros . . . peacocks, and large birds [probably ostriches] whose eggs are like urns. If you turn to the north and then towards the east again go on horseback some sixty days, you come to An-hsi [Parthia], to which afterwards it became subject as a vassal state under a military governor who had control of all the small cities.

What the annals seem to be describing, in a somewhat backwards way, is a route from the Iranian highlands west into the lowlands of Mesopotamia and then south to where the old crossroads cities were clustered together, protected by rivers, canals, and swamps. Which "capital city" Kan Ying referred to is not entirely clear. Elsewhere in the annals comes a slightly different description of the same route:

> From An-hsi you go west 3400 li to the country of A-man [Ecbatana]; from A-man you go west 3600 li to the country of Ssu-pin [Ctesiphon]; from Ssu-pin you go south, crossing a river, and again southwest to the country of Yü-lo, 960 li, to the extreme west frontier of An-hsi.

Though the identification of the cities noted above is generally agreed upon, there is some controversy as to the identity of Yü-lo. Candidates include the now-abandoned site of Hira, southwest of and across the river from Babylon and Ctesiphon, and Charax or Apologos (further downriver), all of which acted as ports for ships heading down to the Persian Gulf to join the Spice Route.

Yü-lo was a seaport, as is clear from the rest of Kan Ying's experiences. The annals describe that he:

> . . . arrived in T'iao-chih, on the coast of the great sea. When about to take his passage across the sea, the sailors of the western frontier of An-hsi told Kan Ying: "The sea is vast and great; with favorable winds it is possible to cross within three months; but if you meet slow winds, it may also take you two years. It is for this reason that those who go to sea take on board a supply of three years' provisions. There is something in the sea which is apt to make man homesick, and several have thus lost their lives." When Kan Ying heard this, he stopped.

This passage has been a continual puzzle to sinologists. How, they ask, could Kan Ying have headed for Roman Syria and ended his mission on the seashore? Why is there no mention of an overland caravan route to Ta-ch'in, the land to which he had been dispatched? The answer seems to lie with the Parthians. As the Chinese deliberately guarded the secrets of sericulture and spread misinformation to confuse intelligence-gatherers, so the Parthians seem to have acted to retain the secrets of their own routes to the West, on which so much of their wealth depended. It seems very likely that, not wishing to offend the Chinese, their valuable trading partners and allies, by forbidding them to cross to Syria, the Parthians chose instead to covertly dissuade the Chinese emissary from continuing on his journeys. Correctly sizing up Kan Ying as a landlubber, they grossly inflated the times and distances involved in a sea voyage. In fact, even the journey on the Spice Route all the way to China did not take half so long as three years, much less the short trip from the head of the Persian Gulf around the Arabian Peninsula and up the Red Sea.

It is possible that such a route was in use at this time, especially because, for a few years at the time of Kan Ying's visit, disturbances in the Syrian Desert may have temporarily closed the overland routes to the Mediterranean. Some portion, perhaps even a considerable portion, of the Eastern goods may have gone by sea from Mesopotamia around Arabia to the Red Sea ports and perhaps then on to Petra, which would tie in with the hypothesis that Petra was the Chinese Li-Kan. Certainly that route would take the goods to ports with easy access to the main refining and distributing centers, Alexandria and the Phoenician cities. This would be especially important for silk, which often had to be dyed and woven before being shipped on to Rome and farther parts of the empire. Some have argued that such a sea route may have been preferable to traders who bought from the Parthians and then shipped goods directly in their

At Petra, tombs, treasuries, and even homes were carved out of the "living rock." ("Eastern End of the Valley," by David Roberts)

own craft to their business partners along the Red Sea, the point being to avoid paying tolls to other middlemen, such as Arab rulers of the Syrian Desert. All that may be true. But, whatever portion of the Silk Road's goods passed by sea along this route, the heart of the matter seems to be that the Parthians simply deceived poor Kan Ying.

The hoax was stunningly successful. It would be centuries before the Chinese learned of a land route to Syria. And the Parthians averted what was, to them, a mortal danger: the possibility of an independent alliance between the Chinese and the Romans. That the land routes were still important—and probably the main avenues for the Silk Road—is amply indicated by the wealth of the caravan cities of the Syrian Desert, as we shall see.

But though the Chinese ambassador did not reach Ta-ch'in, he (and perhaps later envoys to Parthia) built up a picture of the western lands, which was recorded in the *Hou Han Shu*:

> *The country of Ta-ch'in is also called Li-Kan and [is] situated on the western part of the sea. Its territory amounts to several thousand* li; *it contains over four hundred cities, and*

of dependent states there are several times ten. The defences of cities are made of stone. The postal stations and milestones on the roads are covered with plaster. There are pine and cypress trees and all kinds of other trees and plants. The people are much bent on agriculture, and practice the planting of trees and the rearing of silkworms. [Because some silk woven in distinctive Western styles found its way back to the East, some Chinese believed that the Westerners actually knew how to make silk.] They cut the hair of their heads, wear embroidered clothing, and drive in small carriages covered with canopies; when going in or out they beat drums, and hoist flags, banners, and pennants. The precincts of the walled city in which they live measure over a hundred li in circumference. In the city there are five palaces, ten li distant from each other. In the palace buildings they use crystal to make pillars; vessels used in taking meals are also so made . . . The inhabitants of that country are tall and well-proportioned, somewhat like the Chinese, whence they are called Ta-ch'in.

★ ★ ★

The *Hou Han Shu* tells us that no other Chinese embassies reached as far west as T'iao-chih, much less Ta-ch'in. The annals do, however, record some picture of travel in Roman lands, presumably gathered from informants living in Parthian territory:

The country is densely populated; every ten li are marked by a t'ing [shed?]; thirty li by a chih [beacon tower?]. One is not alarmed by robbers, but the road becomes unsafe by fierce tigers and lions who will attack passengers, and unless these be traveling in caravans of a hundred men or more, or be protected by military equipment, they may be devoured by those beasts. They also say there is a "flying bridge" of several hundred li, by which one may cross to the countries north of the sea.

It is unclear what the "flying bridge" is, though perhaps it is a reference to one of the causeways for which the Romans were so famous throughout their empire. For the rest, the picture, though clearly drawn from secondhand information, conforms fairly well with what we know of the character of the roads and of travel in the well-ordered Roman territories.

Pictures like these would be carried in the Chinese annals for many centuries. But China also heard of many beautiful things found in the West, some of which were as desirable to the Chinese as silk was to the Romans. The annals describe the riches of Ta-ch'in:

The country contains much gold, silver, and rare precious stones, especially the "jewel that shines at night," "the moonshine pearl," corals, amber, glass . . . green jadestone, gold-embroidered rugs and thin silk-cloth of various colors. They make gold-colored cloth and asbestos cloth. They further have "fine cloth," also called "down of the water-sheep;" it is made from the cocoons of wild silkworms. They collect all kinds of fragrant substances . . . All the rare gems of other foreign countries come from there.

Here is a litany of items dear to the Chinese heart. Much scholarly work has gone into a not-always-successful attempt to identify the various things mentioned. The "down of the water-sheep" may be a reference to *byssus*, a linen cloth so fine that some Chinese, in their confusion, thought it was made from the cocoons of wild silkworms.

One prime candidate for "the jewel that shines at night" is the diamond. It does not, of course, do any such thing under normal circumstances, but certain kinds of diamonds can be made phosphorescent by rubbing, heating, or exposure to light. Such stones would be particularly attractive to the Chinese who were until then unfamiliar with transparent gems (the highly prized jade being opaque). Some scholars, however, feel that the Chinese had little or no contact with diamonds as gems, but only as "industrial" stones embedded in knives for fine carving or incisions, these special tools being imported from the West. The Chinese were in this period much impressed by some brilliant green stones from the West. In their ignorance they apparently lumped together quite different minerals—including both gem-sized emeralds and other stones in blocks large enough to be used for decorating buildings—simply because of their color and transparency.

China's unfamiliarity with such stones also made them fair game for Western artisans, who sold glass beads and other easily manufactured objects as gems. The "crystal" used in pillars, as noted above in the *Hou Han Shu*, may have been glass. In any case, until the fifth century A.D., when the Chinese learned the secrets of making glass, especially the colored glass they prized most highly, Western traders made a handsome profit on the glass goods they shipped to China. That the Chinese were not entirely taken in, however, is suggested by a side comment in the *Hou Han Shu*, noting that:

> *The articles made of rare precious stones produced in this country [Ta-ch'in] are sham curiosities and mostly not genuine . . .*

After Kan Ying, we know of no other Chinese ambassadors who reached west of the Iranian Plateau. Whether or not the Chinese understood that Kan Ying had been tricked, they certainly recognized that the Parthians were preventing Romans and Chinese from meeting. The *Hou Han Shu* comments that the kings of Ta-ch'in:

> *. . . always desired to send embassies to China, but the Anhsi [Parthia] wished to carry on trade with them in Chinese silks, and it is for this reason that they were cut off from communication.*

It is not to be expected that the Romans would accept this without protest. Apparently, the Romans tried with little or no success to open alternative routes to the East, around or across the Caspian, circumventing Parthian territory.

The only direct contact recorded between Romans and Chinese was made by sea. The *Hou Han Shu* noted that the Romans were blocked from communicating with the Chinese until about 166 A.D.:

> . . . *when the king of Ta-ch'in, An-tun, sent an embassy who, from the frontier of Jih-nan [Indo-China] offered ivory, rhinoceros horns, and tortoise shell.*

Though these Romans apparently presented themselves as envoys from their emperor (until 161 Antoninus Pius, followed by Marcus Aurelius Antoninus) and were accepted as such by the Chinese, they were most likely free-lancing merchants. The gifts they brought were probably bartered for other goods in Indo-China. Unfortunately, these goods, which seemed so exotic to the Romans, were utterly familiar to the Chinese, who pointedly mentioned that the "tribute," as they called it, contained no jewels. Nevertheless, the *Hou Han Shu* notes: "From that time dates the [direct] intercourse with this country [Ta ch'in]." But no such firsthand contact, as far as we can tell, ever took place overland.

Certainly the Romans, or at least merchants operating in Roman territory, tried to contact the Chinese overland. And geographers gamely recorded their efforts. At about the middle of the first century A.D. Pomponius Mela, in his *De Situ Orbis*, tried to put the continent of Asia in some perspective, noting:

> *In the furthest east of Asia are the Indians, Seres, and Scythians. The Indians and Scythians occupy the two extremities, the Seres are in the middle.*

Clearly the Roman view of Asia was at this time quite vague and distorted. He goes on with more striking detail but little more accuracy:

> *That part [of the Caspian Sea coast] which adjoins the Scythian promontory is first of all impassable from snow; then an uncultivated tract occupied by savages. These tribes are the Cannibal Scythians and the Sagae [Sakae], severed from one another by a region where none can dwell because of the number of wild animals. Another vast wilderness follows, occupied also by wild beasts, reaching to a mountain called Thabis which overhangs the sea. A long way from that the ridge of Taurus rises. The Seres come between the two; a race eminent for integrity, and well known for the trade which they allow to be transacted behind their backs, leaving their wares in a desert spot.*

At this point it seems clear that the Romans were still seeing the intermediaries as the "Seres." The trade referred to is the silent barter that had been practiced in Asia for untold centuries. Pliny, writing somewhat later in the century, describes the process more fully, noting that:

> *The Seres are inoffensive in their manners indeed; but, like the beasts of the forest, they eschew the contact of mankind; and, though ready to engage in trade, wait for it to come to them instead of seeking it . . . The [Western traders'] goods . . . are deposited on the further side of a certain river beside what the Seres have for sale, and the latter, if content with the bargain, carry them off; acting, in fact, as if in contempt of the luxury to which they ministered, and just as if they saw in the mind's eye the object and destination and result of this traffic.*

It is highly unlikely that the people engaging in such a primitive kind of trade were Chinese. That idea is reinforced by Pliny's description of the people called the Seres, noting that observers had:

> *. . . described these [Seres] as surpassing the ordinary stature of mankind, as having red hair, blue eyes, hoarse voices, and no common language to communicate by.*

This is clearly not a description of the Chinese, but it fits well the largely Indo-European population of the mountains and steppes between Parthia and China. So it seems that, in the late first century A.D., the Romans still had little idea of who the Chinese even were.

The Chinese, too, heard of the silent trade carried on in Central Asia. The later Chinese annals, the *Chau Ju-Kwa*, speaking of this period note that:

> *The country of Ta-ch'in, also called Li-kan, is the general mart of the natives of the Western Heaven, the place where the foreign merchants . . . assemble.*

But the writer goes on to say:

> *In the Western Sea there is a market where a [silent] agreement exists between buyer and seller that if one comes the other goes. The seller first spreads out his goods; afterwards the [would-be] purchaser spreads out the equivalent, which must lie by the side of the articles for sale till taken by the seller, when the objects purchased may be carried off. This is called the "Devil or Spirit Market."*

Judging by this account, the Chinese, too, seem to have taken the intermediaries for their true partners in this long-distance trade.

In the end, the Romans and the Chinese had to be content to deal through surrogates such as these. We may assume that the silent trade did not last long, at least on the main route, for soon the Romans, Parthians, and Chinese had a full partner on the Silk Road. Early in the second century A.D., shortly after the retirement and death of Pan Ch'ao, the Kushans came under the rule of a remarkable leader named Kanishka, who was to have a profound effect on the character of the Silk Road. In the previous century the Kushans—described as large, pink-faced men who wore long-skirted coats and soft leather boots—had pushed across the lofty mountain passes of the Karakorum range and the Hindu Kush into India, gradually extending their empire from Bactria to include Afghanistan and the Punjab, as far as Benares in northern India. They adopted much from the Indians, most especially their administrative skills and their religion. Kanishka, who came to power in about 120 A.D., warmly embraced the Buddhist religion, itself changing in this period. From a somewhat distant, perhaps even cold teacher, Buddha came to be seen as a savior or god; and, not insignificantly, the Hellenistic artistic styles that had permeated the region centuries before served to humanize Buddha's image, making it more attractive to the general population.

What resulted, then, was a relatively peaceful, well-organized empire eager to spread the word of Buddha. Early in Kanishka's reign, perhaps even before, the Kushans spread over the Pamirs and into the Tarim Basin, taking the key western oases of Yarkand, Kashgar, and Khotan. China's hold on the region had always been precarious; indeed, in 107 A.D. combined attacks by the Tibetans in the Kansu and the Hsiung-nu on the northern Tarim route had cut off communication so completely that the Chinese vacated the post of Protector General and recalled their ambassadors from the Western Territories. In the absence of a leader of Pan Ch'ao's ability, the Chinese had little hope of holding the far Western oases, and soon seem to have accepted the Kushan presence in the area. Perhaps the assurance of a power eager to trade relieved the Chinese somewhat from the difficult chore of defending those far-distant outposts. In any case, the Kushans quickly established themselves as a force on the Silk Road, and for the next five centuries, at least, the Tarim Basin would be under the strong Buddhist influence they introduced.

★   ★   ★

So the Silk Road fell into the rhythm it would have for the next century and, to a lesser extent, for a thousand years or more. Empires could and would rise and fall, but on the road the traders and pilgrims would continue their journeys, carrying their stock of goods and ideas across the 5,000-mile expanse of Asia. While they remained strong, these four powers—the Chinese, the Kushans, the Parthians, and the Romans—formed a great chain stretching across the continent.

From China the silks flowed westward, as skeins of yarn or bolts of cloth woven to specified widths in the imperial workshops. Along with these the Chinese sent to Rome fine ironware. They had learned ironworking late, and from the West, but they developed a technique of making cast iron that would be unknown in the West for centuries, so their iron goods were highly prized by Asian traders. Furs from the Tibetan heights and the Mongolian hills were also gathered for the Western trade, for the Chinese were still carrying on their tribute trade with the peoples on their borders. As Pan Ch'ao's father, Pan Piao, had commented on the trade with the Hsiung-nu to the north: ". . . we may well give them liberal presents—calculated on the value of what they offer us." Loyang remained the Han capital but Ch'ang-an was the main terminus of the Silk Road, where all the goods were gathered for the trip west. From Ch'ang-an, caravans—on this section of the route, sometimes wagon trains—followed the Imperial Highway westward through the Kansu Corridor to Tunhuang. The Chinese controlled this portion of the trade wholly, but they increasingly stayed at home, hiring agents to carry on the actual trading.

Sogdians, Kushan subjects from the region of Samarkand, specialized as caravaneers in the Tarim and the Pamirs, so much so that their language, Sogdian, became the lingua franca on the eastern half of the Silk Road in this period. If not at Ch'ang-an, these camel-driving specialists often took charge of the trade from Tunhuang westward. Great caravans of hundreds of camels, sometimes well over a thousand, would wind across the desert toward the West. When political conditions allowed, they would follow the High Road to Hami, and proceed along the northern curve of the Tarim. If trouble brewed, as when the Hsiung-nu were

Vessels of colored glass, like these from Pompeii, were much desired by the Chinese, who did not know the secrets of their manufacture. (From *Museum of Antiquity* . . . , 1882)

on the move, or if their destination was Bactria or India, they might prefer the drier, but more protected southern route. The Loulan direction was least favored, for the region was rapidly drying out. Like the Chinese, the Kushans built lines of garrisoned outposts to guard the caravans as best they could from marauders.

In this period, as in much of history, soldiers and traders were the main travelers on the Silk Road. The difficulties of the route did not inspire casual private excursions, such as might be taken within the great empires at either end of the highway. But another important type of traveler was emerging on the Silk Road in this period: the religious wayfarer. Even they were not idle sojourners, but people with a purpose, be it their own enlightenment or that of others. Buddhist missionaries were most active in this period.

Word of this new religion had been filtering into China from the West for at least a century; a golden statue of Buddha had been taken as booty from the Hsiung-nu as early as 121 B.C. But in 65 A.D., when the Chinese emperor dreamt of a "golden man" and was told it was the Buddha, missionaries were requested to come from India to the Han court. Two came, bringing with them sacred texts and relics and a white horse, which itself passed into legend. This was the first official recognition of Buddhism in China, but Buddhist missionaries were spreading their religion all along the eastern half of the Silk Road, on the Tarim and in the Pamirs and beyond. Their influence generally stopped short of the Iranian Plateau, though Chinese annals record the visit of a Buddhist from Parthia.

If these were official missionaries, the Sogdian and other Kushan traders were unofficial emissaries of their religion, and it was they who were perhaps most instrumental in spreading the religion so widely and deeply throughout the Tarim and into China itself. They knew the languages, terrain, and customs of the peoples of Central Asia, so were as well suited to converting others to their new-found religion as to handling the trade between China and the Pamirs.

At caravanserais in the Pamirs or in cities on the plains beyond, these caravaneers often relayed their goods to other carriers. Sogdians continued to handle the trade north through Western Turkestan to the Eurasian Steppe, but Bactrians or Kushans generally handled the trade southward on the main route toward India, as Indians handled the trade on the routes that branched through the Karakorum and Kashmir passes.

The Romans, still barred from crossing Parthian territory, tried in vain to get some clear picture of the trade to the East. Ptolemy, the Greco-Roman geographer writing in around 150 A.D., put together the shreds of evidence that had been gathered by mercantile agents sent East for intelligence. Such agents were presumably not Romans or necessarily even Roman subjects, but people who could pass eastward without hindrance. Of one of his sources, a Macedonian named Maës Titianus, "a merchant like his father before him," Ptolemy noted ". . . not that he made the journey himself, but he had sent agents to the Seres." From agents such as these Ptolemy learned of the two great cities of the East: Sera Metropolis (City of Silk), apparently Ch'ang-an, and Sinae Metropolis, most likely Loyang. From them he also heard of a Stone Tower, somewhere in the Pamirs, where merchants from all over Asia met to trade their wares, noting:

> . . . *from [Bactria] northward up the ascent of the hill country of the Comedi, and then*
> *inclining somewhat south through the hill country itself as far as the gorge in which the*
> *plains terminate . . . This Stone Tower stands in the way of those who ascend the gorge,*
> *and from it the mountains extend eastward to join the chain of Imaus [the Pamirs] which*
> *run north to [here from India] . . .*

Hot has been the dispute over where this Stone Tower is. Many have suggested that the description implies a site in the southern Pamirs, near Bactra, somewhere on the headwaters of the Yarkand River. The valleys there are rather precipitous and difficult of access, however, so many others are inclined to agree with Marc Aurel Stein's placement of the Stone Tower in the Alai River valley, between Kashgar and Ferghana. Apart from the fact that Stone Tower (in Turkish, *Tashkurgan*) is a very common name in the region, the identification is complicated by the fact that Ptolemy's information is, at best, thirdhand, as he himself was aware. Commenting on a fellow geographer, who used the same sources and with whom he disagreed on a number of points, he noted:

> *Now Marinus himself has [on other occasions] shown little faith in traders' stories . . .*
> *For such people, he observes, don't take any trouble to search into the truth of things,*
> *being constantly taken up with their business and often exaggerating distances through a*
> *spirit of brag. Just so, as there seems to have been nothing else that they thought worth*
> *remembering or telling about this seven months' journey, they made a wonder about the*
> *length of time it had occupied.*

More precisely, here, Ptolemy is criticizing Marinus for accepting Maës Titianus's report that the journey from the Stone Tower to Sera Metropolis took seven months. Ptolemy considers that an exaggeration, and cuts the figure to four months and fourteen days, though noting "it was not to be supposed that traveling should have gone on without intermission all that time." His guess is surprisingly close for, if we estimate (in round numbers) 2,500 miles at a caravan pace of 20 miles a day, travelers would spend about four-and-one-half months actually on the road. One is led to believe, however, that Maës Titianus's agents never reached beyond the Pamirs, but were themselves reporting mere hearsay, for surely the difficult journey across the Tarim would have been worthy of comment beyond its mere length.

Ptolemy's information is rather more reliable regarding the trip from the Mediterranean across the Iranian Plateau:

> . . . *[the road goes] from the ferry of the Euphrates at Hierapolis through Mesopotamia*
> *to the Tigris, and thence through the territory of the Garamaeans of Assyria, and Media,*

to Ecbatana and the Caspian Gates, and through Parthia to Hecatompylos . . . the road
from Hecatompylos to Hyrcania must decline to the north . . . Then the route runs on
through Aria to Margiana Antiochia, first declining south (for Aria lies in the same
latitude as the Caspian Gates) and then to the north. . . Thence the road proceeds
eastward to Bactra. . . .

The city of Bactra was then as important as it had ever been. It was no longer the
Kushan capital (that had been moved to Peshawar in northwest India), but since the Indian
route was in this period as active as the Silk Road, it retained and even expanded its role as a
prime caravan center. It was in the process of obtaining a new name, however, for the Indians
called the city Balhika, which would in time become Balkh, the city's name in later centuries.

The loss of the old Greek name was a sign of the times all along the western half of the
Silk Road. Though Greek merchants like Maës Titianus were still active in the trade, the Greek
language, customs, and heritage were gradually being submerged along the route. From the
Iranian Plateau down into Mesopotamia and across to Syria, the caravaneers were generally
Greek, Syrian, or Jewish, but increasingly the commercial language was Aramaic, the
language of Babylon and of Jesus—as it had been before Alexander's appearance on the scene.

So the silks, furs, and ironware, supplemented by gems, spices, and cottons from India,
made their way across the Parthian barrier. The walled cities that had given protection to
itinerant merchants for over 2,000 years continued to shelter the Silk Road caravaneers. With
local tribes, and perhaps government camel corps, assigned to guard them from station to
station, Parthian caravans threaded their way through the Iranian uplands and down into
Mesopotamia.

There a new city had come to the fore on the Silk Road: the Parthian city of Ctesiphon,
built as a new winter capital in 129 B.C. Trade that had once been funneled through the old
Greek capital of Seleucia now passed under the great arch at Ctesiphon, which still dominates
the city's ruins 20 miles southeast of Baghdad. As of old, caravans then followed a
northwesterly route along the fringe of the Syrian Desert.

Partway up the Euphrates lay the city of Dura-Europos, founded on the banks of the
river by the Seleucids in 280 B.C. but now, in the first century A.D., a flourishing Parthian
stronghold, guarding the vital trade route. There, from desert lands watered by irrigation
canals from the river, the locals produced vegetables, grapes for wine, olives for oil, wheat for
bread. There caravans bought the last of their provisions for the desert journey, including
beasts of burden, primarily Arabian camels. There the local rulers collected the last of the
Parthian customs duties that would be levied on the Silk Road. Beyond Dura, caravans entered
a buffer zone, tolerated by both the Romans and Parthians, consisting of lands ceded to the
various small Arab states that lay between the borders of the two empires.

From Dura, some caravans might follow the old line of the Great Desert Route
northwest to Antioch. Greco–Roman geographer Strabo described the pattern of life on the

route, over the 25–day journey between Skenae, "a noteworthy city situated on a canal towards the borders of Babylonia," and Hierapolis east of Antioch:

> And on that road are camel-drivers who keep halting-places, which sometimes are well equipped with reservoirs, generally cisterns, though sometimes the camel-drivers use waters brought in from other places. The Scenitae (as the Arab camel-drivers were known) are peaceful, and moderate towards travelers in the exaction of tribute, and on this account merchants avoid the land along the river and risk a journey through the desert, leaving the river on the right for approximately a three days' journey. For the chieftains who live along the river on both sides occupy country which, though not rich in resources, is less resourceless than that of others, and are each invested with their own domains and exact a tribute of no moderate amount. For it is hard among so many peoples, and that too among peoples that are self-willed, for a common standard of tribute to be set that is advantageous to the merchant.

★   ★   ★

Much the same kind of description might apply to what was the main route in this period—the desert route straight west from Dura–Europos to Palmyra to Damascus. The sulphur springs of Palmyra had been visited by desert nomads for at least 2,000 years by

At the height of their power, the Parthians forced practically all of the Silk Road trade to pass through this great arch into Ctesiphon. (Iraq Petroleum Company)

Roman times, acting as a tribal center in the midst of the desert and as a stopping place for swift-riding couriers or small parties crossing the desert. It had not been a main caravan route because, if large caravans were to have sufficient water, wells would have to be dug and maintained all along the route. More to the point, predatory nomads haunted the cross-desert route, which was far from garrisoned forts. Even so, it had gradually developed a modest, if still half-settled prosperity. By 41 B.C. it was large enough to excite the interest of Mark Antony, but not so large that, on being warned of the army's approach, the inhabitants could not pack their belongings and depart (presumably for temporary refuge in Dura-Europos), leaving the questing Roman general with an empty city.

As the Silk Road developed, so did the desire for a shorter route to the Mediterranean refining cities. So Palmyra flowered in the desert. In his *Caravan Cities*, Mikhail Rostovtzeff called it "one of the wealthiest, most luxurious, and most elegant towns in Syria," citing especially its unparalleled broad avenues, lined with hundreds of columns in the Greco-Roman style, leading through the town. He continued: "One would almost imagine that she had sprung from the desert sands at the wave of a magic wand, so rapidly was the old and apparently small and unpretentious . . . village of Tadmor transformed [into Palmyra]."

Palmyra had a rather complicated relationship with Rome. On paper, it was considered part of the Roman Empire; but, in practice, it collected its own customs duties and seems to have largely ruled itself. It maintained an active desert police force of mounted archers, who patrolled the buffer zone between the two superpowers, Rome and Parthia; but from the mid-second century A.D. a Roman garrison was stationed there, ostensibly to back up the desert police. In the territory they directly controlled, the Romans dug wells and built watchtowers, to help guard the way across the desert.

Pliny—who estimated Palmyra's population at 600,000 in the first century A.D.—attests to the city's unique situation, as a semi-autonomous city-state:

> *Palmyra is a city famous for its situation, for the richness of its soil and for its agreeable springs; its fields are surrounded on every side by a vast circuit of sand, and it is as it were isolated by Nature from the world, having a destiny of its own between the two mighty empires of Rome and Parthia, and at the first moment of a quarrel between them always attracting the attention of both sides.*

As more and more caravans trekked across the arid steppe called the Palmyrena, the city's inhabitants, mostly Semitic, but some Greek, grew closer and closer to the Roman Empire. Many of the city's wealthy and powerful inhabitants adopted Roman names (as, centuries before, people had adopted Greek ones) and even became Roman citizens. Some Palmyrene merchants, following the path of the Eastern goods they traded, spread throughout the Roman Empire, to Egypt, to the Danube Valley, and to Rome itself, where they had their own trading centers and temples to their own gods.

Palmyra's whole fortune was based on trade. Its commercial statutes specified tariffs to be paid on all items that merchants might be bearing East or West. Slaves and prostitutes, cloth of all sorts, dry goods, perfumes, oils, salt (vital to health in the desert), even water—the raison d'être for Palmyra's existence—were taxed at specified, sometimes seasonal, rates.

Peace was temporarily disrupted in 114 A.D., when the Roman emperor Trajan, still following the dreams that had inspired Mark Antony and Julius Caesar, attacked Parthia, taking both Dura-Europos and the capital, Ctesiphon. But under his successor, Hadrian, the Parthian lands were restored and trade revived. Hadrian himself visited Palmyra, dubbing it Hadriana Palmyra, and made it a free city within the empire.

Hadrian's lavish reception was paid for not by Rome's coffers but by a prosperous Palmyrene merchant. Such merchants, caravan leaders, and even camel-drivers—the people on whom so much of the city's wealth depended—were often honored with statues. A line of over 200 stretched along one of Palmyra's main avenues. Many of the statues have been destroyed or defaced, victims of idol-smashing campaigns in later Islamic times, but the inscriptions often remain. One honoring the caravan leader Soados Boliadou, for example, noted that "in many and important circumstances" he had "aided with princely generosity merchants, caravans, and . . . his fellow citizens." Those statues that do remain show that Palmyrenes had strong ties to the East as well as to Rome. Their clothing—long tunics, loose trousers, and long riding coats with flared bottoms—was all in Parthian style. Decorations on their silk and other fabrics also followed Eastern styles. In his *Palmyra*, Iain Browning noted that the "intertwining and repetitive designs . . . woven in glowing colours along with bands of stylised flowers and nightmarish animals clawing their way through the silken undergrowth" were quite unlike the current styles west of Palmyra.

As Palmyra's star was rising, Petra's was setting. The very safety of the Asian land under Roman hegemony led to Petra's downfall. The cross-desert route through Palmyra was, by far, the shortest route to Damascus and the coastal cities. No longer was it profitable for any significant portion of the Eastern goods to be sent around Arabia to the inland caravan route. And, in any case, with Roman protection along the route, caravans no longer needed the shelter of Petra's rocky stronghold. By the second century A.D., Petra's Nabataeans had transferred their capital to Bostra on the main Incense Road. Petra was gradually abandoned and even quite forgotten for many centuries.

So the silks from China, the jade from Central Asia, the ivory of India, all the spices, the pearls, the gems, the fine metals, flowed westward, mostly through Palmyra, to the cities of Western Asia, to Damascus, Tyre, Sidon, Beirut (then called Berytus), and Antioch, in particular. Each had its own specialties, its own offerings in the East-West trade.

On the direct route from Palmyra was Damascus. From flax grown on the nearby plains, the justly famed Damascus weavers made fine linen. These expert artisans also developed their own distinctive patterns for weaving silk, the resulting cloth being named after the city: *damask*. So favored were these fabrics that some bolts of the Damascus-woven silk made the return trip all the way across Asia back to China. Shipped in all directions as well were dried fruits, products of Damascus's lush orchards, gardens, and vineyards. The city may also, at this early date, have developed something of a reputation for the fine metalwork (using Indian and Chinese iron and steel) at which it would excel in later Arab times.

Beirut, Tyre, and Sidon, too, had their expert weavers, especially of silks and linens. But they added the still-unique specialty of purple dyeing. Here, too, were the glassmaking centers (the technique of glassblowing seems to have been discovered in Sidon in around the first century B.C.). The glass appears to have been not only beautiful but also strong, for legends of "unbreakable glass" circulated in the region for centuries. Indeed, its strength may be attested to by its survival of the Silk Road crossing to China.

As the prime port cities of Western Asia, shipping to the entire Mediterranean world, these cities were active in a whole range of manufacturing and commercial activities. As one contemporary put it: "Tyre seethes with every kind of business." Sidon had special importance as the port of nearby Damascus, and the Romans set extra garrisons on the road between the two, for gangs of robbers had their strongholds in the mountains separating the two cities.

Above all, there was Antioch, rightly named the "Fair Crown of the Orient." Spread out over the banks of the Orontes River and the surrounding mountain slopes, it was the capital of the Roman Orient. To the Chinese, it was Rome itself. Here, as befitted a commercial as well as political capital, the great merchants made their homes. Here they funded and hired the caravaneers who journeyed from China to Antioch and the sailors who plied the Mediterranean from Antioch (through its port, Seleucia) to Rome and even on to Spain. Not the least of the city's attractions was its salubrious climate, with fresh breezes from the Mediterranean and the Orontes River making this a popular summer resort even for residents of other cities.

Entering the city itself, caravans found themselves on a 30-foot-wide granite-paved roadway, which led them to a massive entryway, guarded by heavy doors. Leading their asses and camels through the doorway—some said "as though they were brides"—they found themselves on a wide thoroughfare lined with great columns, reminiscent of Palmyra's colonnaded avenues. There, between the columns, despite official disapproval, many merchants set up small shops. Large-scale manufacturing—weaving, leatherworking, metalworking, and so on—were carried on elsewhere, each in its own section of the city, though these industries were no match for those in the other prime cities of the region. But the grand merchants, the ones who controlled the whole export-import trade that passed through Syria, were not found on these city streets, however beautiful and even brilliantly lit they might be. Their luxurious mansions were—in a pattern we think of as modern—out in the suburbs, on the cool, shaded slopes surrounding the oval heart of the city. Like their counterparts in Palmyra, traders from Antioch (and other nearby cities) were found throughout the Roman Empire.

Antioch, then, was in a sense the end of the Silk Road, the terminus of the overland route, the city which controlled the trans-Asian trade. But, at least at the height of the Roman Empire, the journey of the silk was far from over when it reached the cities of Western Asia. From the ports of the Roman Orient, the dyed, woven, and embroidered silks were shipped to Rome and on to the most distant parts of the empire, sometimes making a journey all the way from the Pacific to the Atlantic. In return, the Romans sent gold and silver, along with the manufactures of Western Asia, gradually draining their empire of its riches, for the sake of wearing the precious silk. It is no wonder that Pliny lamented: "This is the price that our luxuries . . . cost us!"

CHAPTER SEVEN

PILGRIMS AND PROSELYTIZERS

Simply reciting a *sutra*, a piece of sacred Buddhist writing, was not sufficient to quell all dangers and to waft devout pilgrims across Asia, despite the romances of medieval China. In truth, the terrors and dangers of their journeys are all too evident in the travel writings left by the intrepid Buddhist pilgrims of China, some of whom spent over a decade on their round trip to India, homeland of their beloved Buddha. As merchants and their caravans were the characteristic figures on the Silk Road at its height in the second century A.D., so it is the wandering pilgrims who characterize the troubled centuries that followed. These religious wanderers faced a very different world than that of the well-guarded caravans that had plodded slowly across the desert during the first great flowering of the Silk Road. For the world of strong nations, which had the power and resources to plant garrisons in watchtowers hundreds of miles from home, collapsed in just a few brief decades.

Like a kaleidoscope at the twist of a dial, the whole aspect of the Silk Road changed around 200 A.D. Powers that had once ruled in splendor—Roman, Parthian, Kushan, and Chinese—fell into ignominious decline, each in its own way and for different reasons. The increasing dryness of Asia's steppes and deserts contributed to the upheaval, setting in motion the great hordes of nomads who had always lived a precarious existence, and who now toppled the great civilizations on Asia's perimeter. Activities on the great trans–Asian highway, which had long had a largely

. . . when he recited [the sutra], the mountains and the streams became traversable, and the roads were made plain and passable; tigers and leopards vanished from sight; demons and spirits disappeared. Hsüan-tsang thus reached the land of Buddha.
    —*from* T'ai-p'ing kuang-chi,
        *a late 10th-century
        Chinese anthology*

commercial-political-military cast to them, now came to have an increasingly religious tinge. In truth, there is more than a little truth to the suggestion that the insecurity and fragmentation of Asia in the following centuries caused many people to turn to the relatively new religions that were to change the face of the Silk Road.

Rome did not, of course, fall in the third century A.D.; the great capital city did not surrender to the "barbarians" until 476 A.D. But by about 200 A.D. the empire was already in decline and was being hard pressed by nomads pouring into Europe as if they had been shot out of a cannon from the East. And the Romans, not proof against the principle that weakness often breeds military action, were blustering on all fronts. In Western Asia, it was only too clear that little real strength lay behind the bluster.

In the vacuum that resulted, local states increased in power, among them Palmyra, whose last queen, Zenobia, stretched her influence to Egypt and even, we are told, drank from Cleopatra's goblets. Palmyra paid for its *hubris* with destruction in 273 A.D., though Zenobia herself may have survived to live in wealth and comfort in Rome. The great city that had flowered in the desert would bloom no more, and Rome would be the poorer for it, gaining the short-term riches of Palmyra's coffers but losing the steady flow of luxuries from the East that had followed the route over the Palmyrena.

For a time, trade on the western end of the Silk Road was fractured and uncertain. Tyre, Sidon, Beirut, Antioch, all these were still main dyeing, weaving, and manufacturing centers, but the westward routes to them were in flux—as were their main markets—for the Roman Empire's center of gravity was gradually shifting eastward. Reflecting that shift, Emperor Constantine in 330 A.D. founded an eastern Roman capital at Constantinople, on the site of the older Greek city of Byzantium. Over the next century the Western Roman Empire would go into a steep decline. Such power as remained in the empire—and at times that could be considerable—would increasingly reside in the Eastern Roman Empire, especially at Constantinople.

A change of a different sort was also occurring in the region—the rise of Christianity. Constantine's adoption of this religion gave it, for the first time, official status in the empire, but by then it had been spreading under persecution for three centuries. Many of the cities on the far western end of the Silk Road, notably Antioch and Tarsus, had been important in the early development of the new religion, and would continue to be powerful Christian centers. There was, as yet, however, no central unifying church center recognized by all, so there existed in Western Asia various schools of thought on key theological questions. Some of these schools would have an interesting role to play later in the history of the Silk Road.

At the turn of the third century A.D., the Parthians were weakening. Virtual anarchy prevailed among the numerous supposed vassals of the Parthian king. It is not surprising that, before the first quarter of the century was over, the Parthians had been overthrown—and by the Persians, always one of the Parthians' most powerful subject tribes. With the memory of their past glories very much in mind, the Persians set about to revive their old empire. Within a few years, the Persians were once again masters on the Euphrates and, though it involved difficult battles with the Romans, of two prime Mesopotamian fortresses: Carrhae, scene of Rome's disastrous loss to the Parthians centuries before, and Nisibis, on the Euphrates, destined to be a key city on the Silk Road in the coming centuries.

The resurgent Persians next turned east, where the Kushans offered both a threat to the new nation and a plum ripe for the picking, having grown rich in the silk trade. Like a juggernaut, the Persians rolled along the Indian Grand Road, from the Kushan capital of Peshawar to Bactra and on to Samarkand and Tashkent. All came into the Persian fold, as the Kushans passed into history. The traders of the old Kushan Empire would, however, continue to trek back and forth across the continent with their caravans; the Sogdians, in particular, would have a special influence in Central Asia during the coming chaotic centuries.

As for the Persians, having extended their territory to the "natural" border of the Pamirs, they once again turned westward. Through Roman weakness, the Persian leader, Shapur, quickly possessed himself of Mesopotamia and Armenia. Then, in 260 A.D., at the major Christian town of Edessa, he had the astonishing good fortune to capture the Christian bishop of Antioch, as many as 70,000 soldiers, and the Roman emperor himself. The unfortunate emperor, Valerian, died in captivity but the bishop and the Roman legionnaires were transported to new towns, spread throughout Persian territory, modeled on Roman military camps. Many were settled in the lands east of southern Mesopotamia, notably at a major new city called Gundeshapur (the better Antioch of Shapur). Others were settled in towns, new and old, around the Persian lands, including some along the Silk Road. Among these prisoners-of-war were many skilled people, architects, engineers, technicians, and the like. As Roman soldiers had always been used, in peacetime or war, to build bridges or roads as necessary, so the Persians set them to work on large-scale public works projects around the Persian Empire. A number of Christian communities sprang from among these involuntary exiles and dotted the Persian lands.

Shapur himself was inclined toward a new religion, a blend of Zoroastrianism, Buddhism, and Christianity, put forth by a prophet named Mani. Very much in the Eastern tradition, Mani had left his home near Ctesiphon some years before to live as a wandering ascetic. Rejected by the Zoroastrians as a heretic, he sampled Buddhism on the Grand Road in India, then returned to Ctesiphon when Shapur made it the new Persian capital. There he propounded his new "universal" religion, known as Manichaeism, called himself an apostle of Jesus Christ, though he rejected all of the Old Testament and some of the New. Central to Manichaeism is the duality of good and evil, of light and dark. After Shapur's death, Mani and his followers were persecuted, as Zoroastrianism became the state religion of the highly nationalistic Persian Empire. But Mani's influence spread over the centuries to Europe, sparking some of the sects branded as heretical in the late Middle Ages, and to Asia, where Manichaean communities still existed in China a thousand years after Mani's death.

Over the next few centuries, Persia would occupy a unique position on the Silk Road. With trouble and turbulence all around them, among allies and enemies alike, the Persians were by far the strongest nation on the great trans-Asian highway. And because they occupied the slot through which the silk caravans were forced to pass, they exercised a powerful monopoly over trade on the Silk Road and, through it, a powerful influence over the fate of Asia's peoples on either side.

But more than that, Persia also came to control the Spice Route. This route linked the Mediterranean and China by sea, forming the other half of a great oval that, with the Silk Road, united Asia. The importance of the Spice Route and its relation to the Silk Road was well expressed by the Roman writer Cosmas Indicopleustes in the early sixth century:

> The country of silk, I may mention, is in the furthest part of the Indies, lying to the left as you enter the Indian Sea, but a vast distance further than the Persian Gulf from the island which . . . the Greeks [call] Taprobane [Ceylon, or Sri Lanka]. Tzinista [China] is the name of the country . . . It lies very much to the left, so that loads of silk passing on through several different nations in succession over the land reach Persia in a comparatively short time, but the distance by sea is very much greater. For the voyager to Tzinista has to turn up from Taprobane and the regions beyond [referring to Malaya], and further there is no small distance to be covered in sailing over the whole of the Indian sea from the Persian Gulf to Taprobane and thence to the regions beyond. Thus it is obvious that any one who comes by the overland route from Tzinista to Persia makes a very short cut; which accounts for the fact that such quantities of silk are always to be found in Persia. Further than Tzinista there is neither navigation nor inhabited land.

Though Persia's western border with the Eastern Roman Empire shifted over the centuries, as the two waxed and waned in relative strength, the Persians held firmly the all-important seaports of southern Mesopotamia, opening onto the Spice Route. Over time Persian ships would extend their reach, first to India, then to Malaya, and finally on to China itself, buying silks and spices directly from the Chinese at the port of Canton. Trading by sea with southern China in the troubled times between the fourth and seventh centuries was sometimes easier and more reliable—though a good deal farther—than overland trading, for China, too, had weakened and fragmented after the great days of the Han dynasty.

History records that the Han dynasty lasted until 220 A.D., when the last emperor died; but from 185 A.D. the empire was virtually paralyzed. Floods and famine sparked popular revolts at home, some led by a mystical society known as the Yellow Turbans. Though the rebellions were eventually quelled, the massacre and devastation on all sides shocked the land. Poet Wang Ts'an, who lived through those years, described what it was like:

> The Western Capital lies in sad confusion;
> The wolf and tiger come to plague her people . . .

For thousands of years the Chinese peoples tried to keep out raiders from the steppe with fortifications like this Great Wall. (Adapted from *Peking and the Pekingese* by Dr. Rennie, from Yule's *Marco Polo*)

Whitened bones were strewn across the plain . . .
I turned about to gaze back on Ch'ang-an,
And thought how many had gone to the underworld,
Sighing a heavy sigh and my heart in pain.

When no imperial ruler proved capable of restoring order, military anarchy prevailed, with various generals seizing provinces for themselves. One general, on deciding to make his headquarters at Ch'ang-an in 190, set his soldiers loose in the old capital at Loyang. The imperial palace, the main library where the Han archives were stored, the art treasures that had been collected over the centuries, were set ablaze and almost all destroyed. The general himself did not last far beyond this wanton act of destruction, and when some semblance of order was restored, China was divided into three kingdoms, one centered on Szechuan in the southwest, one on Nanking in the south, and one on Loyang in the north. In 280 the empire was briefly reunited, but that was short-lived, for China, whose weakness was plain for all to see, was about to receive the first of the many invasions that would come over the next three centuries from the northern steppe and the western desert.

First among the invaders were the Hsiung-nu clans that long before had been allowed to settle inside the Great Wall, in the loop of the Huang River. No longer willing to act as allies and buffers for the invasions they knew were coming, the Hsiung-nu fell upon northern

China. They laid waste first the partly rebuilt Loyang, burning the palace, killing as many as 30,000 citizens, and looting imperial tombs. Ch'ang-an, too, they devastated. Chinese annals record: "In the ruins of Ch'ang-an . . . the population had dwindled to less than a hundred families. Weeds and brushwood had sprung up everywhere."

In this period, many of the inhabitants of northern China, not simply the affluent, took refuge in the south. As the Roman Empire's cultural center had shifted to Constantinople from Rome, so China's shifted to Nanking from Ch'ang-an and Loyang. The north was abandoned to successive rulers from the steppe. Fields were left untilled and towns were emptied. The land became so desolate that the remaining inhabitants of the Wei River valley, China's traditional heartland, were prey to wolves and tigers. The rough nomadic rulers, of course, had little interest in either farms or farmers. When people complained about attacks by wild animals, one ruler replied (so the annals record): "These animals are hungry; when once they are replete they won't eat anyone else."

The Hsiung-nu who had lived along the Great Wall were not the worst of these invaders, for many of them had been somewhat sinicized by long contact with the Chinese. Stronger and far more ruthless than they were the Hsiung-nu tribes who had remained on the steppe and the Hsien-pi (ancestors of the Mongols), who drove down into northeastern China from Manchuria. Various tribes of Hsiung-nu and Hsien-pi vied for and took power in northern China over the next three centuries. As one group became somewhat sinicized, another rougher tribe, not yet softened by a more settled life, came thundering in. In much the same way, wave after wave of nomadic invaders—among them the Huns, western counterparts of the Hsiung-nu—were pouring into Europe in the same period, both set in motion, perhaps partly, by unrecorded territorial wars taking place far away on the Eurasian Steppe.

Not surprisingly, under the circumstances, we know less about the history of Central Asia in these tumultuous centuries than at any other time since Ch'ang Ch'ien's westward explorations. The political situation between the Kansu Corridor and the Pamirs can only be described as chaotic, with each city-state attempting to hold some bit of independence and making whatever fragile alliances it could, while being forced to pay tribute—real tribute, not trade by another name—to each new power that arose in the region.

★   ★   ★

For all the political anarchy, many of the peoples along the eastern half of the Silk Road were in this period united by one thing: their religion. It was their shared belief in Buddhism that allowed the passage of pilgrims, in small parties or even completely alone, with relative safety across the now-anarchic lands of Central Asia.

The first Buddhist missionaries in China had established a monastery near Loyang, named the White Horse Temple, after the patient beast who had borne the sacred texts and relics on the long and difficult journey from India. There they began the arduous task of translating the Buddhist writings into Chinese. At first, in Han times, the religion had no wide influence in China, if only because of the staunch opposition of the dominant Confucianists. But in the turbulent period that followed, many Chinese were drawn to the comforting new religion.

The collapse of political order led to tenuous and uncertain communications between China and India, so many devout Chinese Buddhists became concerned that their religious practice had strayed from the true path. That concern spurred some to make pilgrimages over the thousands of miles of desert and mountain to India to seek enlightenment for themselves and their fellow Buddhists. Such journeys began as early as the mid-third century A.D., but the first substantial record of a pilgrimage to India is that of Fa-hsien, who left Ch'ang-an with several other Buddhist companions in 399. As he later recorded, he "regretted the imperfect condition of" the Buddhist writings available to him in Chinese, and went "to India for the purpose of seeking the rules and regulations" of proper Buddhism.

Fa-hsien and his party found the country troubled. The lands west of Ch'ang-an inside the Great Wall were "much disturbed, and the roadways . . . not open." The local prince himself was anxious for their welfare, and "kept them there, himself entertaining them." This was a pattern found by many Buddhist travelers. Local rulers and isolated subjects, not just the local Buddhist monks, delighted in the company of visiting pilgrims and often detained them from journeying rapidly on their way to India. In this case, Fa-hsien reported, "pleased that they were like-minded, they kept the rainy season together." Then after a month, Fa-hsien set out for Tunhuang, where the local prefect "provided them with means to cross the desert [sand-river]."

The desert west of Tunhuang had lost none of its terrors, as Fa-hsien reported:

> In this desert are many evil demons and hot winds; when encountered, then all die without exception. There are no flying birds above, no roaming beasts below, but everywhere gazing as far as the eye can reach in search of the onward route, it would be impossible to know the way but for dead men's decaying bones, which show the direction.

Even in this wasteland, however, the official missionaries and the unofficial missionary-traders had been astonishingly successful in converting the peoples of the Tarim Basin to Buddhism. In the oasis-state of Shan-shan, for example, Fa-hsien found some 4,000 priests, "all of the Little Vehicle belief." (This refers to the long-standing split between the more rigorous Little Vehicle, or Hinayana, branch of Buddhism and the Mahayana, or Greater Vehicle, a more mystical branch that includes worship of several deities; the latter was the form of Buddhism generally adopted in China and many other areas north of India.) Traveling westward on the southern Tarim route, Fa-hsien found 4,000 Buddhist priests in another town as well. Then, after journeying on a "road with no dwellings or people," during which their sufferings "on account of the difficulties of the road" and lack of water "exceeded human power of comparison," he arrived in Khotan.

Befitting its status as a main Tarim center, with close connections to India, Khotan much impressed Fa-hsien:

> This country is prosperous and happy; the people are very wealthy, and all without exception honor the law [of Buddha]. They use religious music for mutual entertainment. The body of priests number even several myriads, principally belonging to the Great Vehicle. They all have food provided for them . . . Before their houses [the people] raise little towers, the least about twenty feet high. There are priests' houses for the entertainment of foreign priests and for providing them with what they need.

One of the historical objections raised against Buddhism in China and elsewhere was that the priests—we would call them monks—were anti-family, being celibate, and a drain on society, for they lived on charity. (That they kept down the population and wasted not on luxuries was not considered by their enemies.) But the people of Khotan and other devout Buddhists demonstrated their feelings on the matter through these elaborate arrangements they made for wandering pilgrims.

Leaving Khotan, perhaps with a merchant caravan, Fa-hsien chose a route across the rugged southern Pamirs, which he called the Tsung-ling (Onion) range. There he came to the country of the Kie-sha (possibly a mountain people Ptolemy called Kossaioi), where he arrived in time for the great assembly of Buddhists held every five years. His report provides a stunning picture of both the prosperity of these mountain caravan centers and the depth of their support for Buddhism:

> At the time of the assembly [the king] asks Sramanas [Buddhist priests] from the four quarters, who come together like clouds. Being assembled, he decorates the priests' session place; he suspends silken flags and spreads out canopies; he makes gold and silver lotus flowers; he spreads silk behind the throne, and arranges the paraphernalia of the priests' seats. The king and the ministers offer their religious presents for one, two, or three months, generally during spring-time. The king-made assembly being over, he further exhorts his ministers to arrange their offerings; they then offer for one day, two days, three days, or five days. The offerings being finished, the king . . . mounts [his horse] and then [taking] white taffeta, jewels of various kinds, and things required by the Sramanas, in union with his ministers, he vows to give them all to the priests; having thus given them, they are redeemed at a price from the priests.

Not only that, but every year the king "induces the priests to make the wheat ripen," that being the main grain that grows in that cold, hilly country, and "after that [the priests] receive their yearly portion." As in many places throughout his journey, Fa-hsien found relics reputed to have belonged to Buddha—an alms-dish or a tooth—housed in shrines built for their veneration, much as Europeans would do with Christian relics in medieval times.

Rather than following the easier main route through Bactra, Fa-hsien seems to have taken instead a mountainous route to northern India. This was a common choice, for Buddha himself was said to have wandered in these towering ranges, and many pilgrims wanted to tread, literally and figuratively, in his footsteps. From the Pamirs he passed into the Snowy Mountains, most likely the high Hindu Kush, of which he has left a vivid, if somewhat fanciful, description:

> . . . there is snow both in winter and summer. Moreover there are poison-dragons, who when evil-purposed spit poisons, winds, rain, snow, drifting sand, and gravel-stones; not one of ten thousand meeting these calamities escapes . . . The road is difficult and broken, with steep crags and precipices in the way. The mountainside is simply a stone wall standing up 10,000 feet. Looking down, the sight is confused, and on going forward there is no sure foothold. Below is a river . . . In old days men bored through the rocks to make a way, and spread out side-ladders, of which there are seven hundred [steps?] in all to pass. Having passed the ladders, we proceed by a hanging rope-bridge and cross the river . . .

All through the mountains, Fa-hsien and his companions visited shrines and monasteries, sometimes staying months at a time, before inching on again over the wintry peaks. Making a mountain crossing in winter, Fa-hsien and his companions met more than theoretical danger:

> The Snowy Mountains, both in summer and winter, are heaped with snow. On the north side of the mountains, in the shade, excessive cold came on suddenly, and all the men were struck mute with dread; one of them, Hwui-king, was unable to proceed onwards. The white froth came from his mouth as he addressed Fa-hsien and said, "I have no power of life left; but while there is opportunity, do you press on, lest you all perish." Thus he died.

So Fa-hsien and the remainder of his party struggled forward across the range, into Afghanistan, and then down along the banks of the Indus River, where their appearance caused some astonishment among the Indians:

> When they saw pilgrims from China arrive, they were much affected and spoke thus, "How is it that men from the frontiers are able to know the religion of family-renunciation and come from far to seek the law of Buddha?" They liberally provided necessary entertainment according to the rules of religion.

Heading down through India, in the path of the Buddha, visiting shrines and monasteries, they were often greeted in that way. At one chapel along the Ganges, the local priests were astounded that the visitors had come from "the land of Han," exclaiming:

> *"Wonderful! to think that men from the frontiers of the earth should come so far as this from a desire to search for the law . . . Our various superiors and brethren, who have succeeded one another in this place from the earliest time till now, have none of them seen men of Han come so far as this before."*

So Fa-hsien traveled for 12 years, learning the ways of Buddha. Like many another long-distance traveler, however, he eventually began to long for home:

> *Fa-hsien had now been absent many years from the land of Han; the manners and customs of the people with whom he had intercourse were entirely strange to him. The towns, people, mountains, valleys, and plants and trees which met his eyes, were unlike those of old times. Moreover, his fellow-travelers were now separated from him—some had remained behind, and some were dead. To consider the shadow [of the past] was all that was left him; and so his heart was continually saddened. All at once, as he was standing by the side of this jasper figure [of Buddha], he beheld a merchant present to it as a religious offering a white taffeta fan of Chinese manufacture. Unwittingly Fa-hsien gave way to his sorrowful feelings, and the tears flowing down filled his eyes.*

So Fa-hsien headed for home—not overland, but by sea. The choice was a reasonable one, and would later be made by many others. The land route was treacherous and difficult, despite the warm welcome accorded the pilgrims on their six-year trek to middle India. But the Spice Route was in this period unplagued by the anarchy prevalent on the eastern half of the Silk Road. Indeed, as the Persians grew stronger, they made the Spice Route an increasingly important trading route. Southern China, too, was a logical destination for travelers, for it was now, for the first time in history, the prime seat of Chinese culture.

So Fa-hsien completed his great circuit of Asia, returning to the southern Chinese capital of Nanking to write his memoirs and inform others of what he had learned about Buddhism. Though the religion remained a minority belief in China, it often had strong royal patronage, inspiring the building of massive and magnificent cave-temples throughout China, such as those near Lung-men and Tunhuang. In northwest China, the region in closest contact with Central Asia and the Silk Road, it is estimated that, by the late fourth century, 90 percent of the people were Buddhists.

The pilgrims who followed in Fa-hsien's footsteps were never very numerous. Few travelers of any kind, traders aside, found their way into Central Asia. Buffeted by repeated invasions, China had little power in the Tarim Basin, and the imperial records tell us little about the "Western Territories" in this period. Silk caravans moved haltingly along the old routes (except for the Loulan route, by the third century so dry it was abandoned), much at hazard and with the burden of heavy tolls, taxes, and "protection money" to the many states along the way. The trade was, however, substantial enough so that Persia and China continued to exchange embassies directly, for at least some of the time between the fourth and seventh centuries.

★   ★   ★

In these centuries Persia's interest in the silk trade was considerable, for the Eastern Roman Empire was developing an insatiable desire for silks. Rulers, aristocrats, clerics, merchants, all desired to dress themselves in silken robes. Abandoning its earlier simple styles, the Christian church began to use elaborate silken hangings, many of them heavily embroidered with gold and silver. Silk was also beginning to be used for winding sheets in the new Christian style of burial for the dead. Even in the early years after Constantinople was founded, the city had five guilds that dealt solely with trading or working with silk.

Nor was the Eastern Roman Empire alone in its hunger for silks. As the Eastern hordes were sinicized by contact with China, so Europe's invaders quickly developed a taste for the luxuries of the East. In 408 A.D., when the Visigoths had Rome under siege, their leader, Alaric, demanded (and got) from the city a ransom of 4,000 tunics of silk, along with 5,000 pounds of gold, 30,000 pounds of silver, 3,000 pounds of pepper, and 3,000 skins dyed a brilliant red. And again like the Chinese in the East, the Romans found that payment of bribes for peace was often preferable to mounting a military defense. As the invaders settled in, the clergy and the royal courts of Europe kept up a steady demand for Eastern goods, however mean life might be for more ordinary people.

As the Persians monopolized the flow of silk overland across the Iranian Plateau, so the Romans were well-placed to be the sole suppliers of Europe. To help ensure that they were, they and the Persians made agreements that sharply restricted the silk trade. So, in 297, the two powers agreed that the only official silk mart in Western Asia would be at the Persian city of Nisibis, in northern Mesopotamia, en route from Ecbatana. In 408, another agreement affirmed the restriction of the silk trade, but added two other cities: Callinicum, a Roman city on the west bank of the Euphrates, on the old Great Desert Route from lower Mesopotamia to Antioch, and Artaxata (Artashat), later replaced by Dubius (Dovin), on the high road through Armenia, an increasingly important route with the rise of the Eastern Roman Empire. The routes across the Syrian Desert were largely abandoned by the silk caravans, in part because the land was drier and more dangerous, in part because neither the Romans nor the Persians wished to share the Eastern trade with the Arabs (some of whom had managed to edge their

Drawing on Syrian weaving traditions, Persian artisans produced fine silk cloths like this one. (10th century, from Musée du Louvre, Paris)

way into the Spice Route). The Roman government also embarked on the thankless and futile policy of price-fixing when Diocletian in 301 set a firm price for raw silk.

As Rome declined and Constantinople became the primary destination of the Chinese silks, so the Syrian and Phoenician cities—home of generations of weavers and dyers—were gradually bypassed. The Syrian industry was hard hit in 360, when the Persians, temporary rulers in Syria, abducted many weavers and dyers for the imperial workshops in Persia, where they wove and dyed much of the silk destined for the Eastern Roman Empire. From the fifth century A.D., the Byzantine Romans operated their own massive imperial workshops, called *gynaecea* because they were staffed entirely by women. These weavers, once accepted and trained in the craft of weaving ornate robes and hangings for their aristocratic clients, were virtual prisoners, not allowed to leave their employment.

Independent merchants and weavers throughout the empire were at an increasing disadvantage because government officials (*commerciarii*) would buy most of the silk available at the designated markets for the *gynaecea*, leaving little for private parties. The use of purple dyes also came to be reserved for imperial dyers at Constantinople, leaving the Tyrian and other Phoenician dyers, who had developed their techniques over many centuries, unable to practice their trade on pain of death. Many Syrian weavers were further cut off from the use of their skills in 369, when the weaving of gold brocades—gold threads woven with silk—was also reserved for imperial workshops, either in Constantinople itself or at just a few honored sites.

Both government and private manufacturers alike were hampered by periodic wars between the Persians and Romans, when silk supplies were cut off altogether, sometimes by disagreements over the proper price of silk. In 540, the Persians went so far as to invade Syria, sacking and burning the city of Antioch. Then, when the so-called "perpetual peace" was restored, the Persians raised the price of raw silk, while the Romans tried to hold the line. The Roman historian Procopius explains what happened:

> *[Emperor] Justinian forbade the sale [purchase] of silk at more than 9 chrysos a*
> *pound—an absurd and impracticable measure, this price being below that which the*
> *[Persian] merchants had to pay. Consequently, they were no longer willing to undertake*
> *this form of trade. They hastened to sell off their remaining stock, secretly, to those who*
> *were known to be fond of dressing themselves in this material and were prepared to satisfy*
> *their desires in spite of all obstacles.*

In an effort to halt the black market that resulted, the Empress Theodora (Justinian's wife) put the silk trade under the control of one of her favorites, who "secured great riches for the emperor—but secretly diverted even greater sums to his own use." He created a royal monopoly on the silk trade, with disastrous effect, as Procopius explained:

> *All who had been engaged in this trade, whether in Byzantium or elsewhere, both*
> *mariners and those who worked on land, were hard hit by these developments. In the*
> *towns, all those who had devoted themselves to the silk trade were reduced to beggary;*
> *craftsmen and laborers finished up in poverty. Many of them emigrated and went to take*
> *refuge among the Persians.*

So ended the ancient dyeing and weaving trades of the Levant. Mariners who had continued to supply silk from the Levantine ports throughout the Mediterranean were ruined and torched their ships in despair.

Persia's own weaving industry was once again much enhanced by the arrival of weavers and dyers from the lowlands. Syrian weavers did work so fine that some observers swore the animals in their textiles looked as if they had been painted. Their skills were especially valued in Persia, whose textile designs (reflecting the people's Central Asian roots) abounded in animals, often in pairs and framed in circles—rams, elephants, lions, birds, and of course, horses (sometimes winged). These sinuous forms, often depicted with a fire altar or a symbolic tree of life, widely influenced textile patterns throughout Eurasia—by way of Constantinople through Europe, and via Central Asia through China and later even Japan.

But the problems of supply across the wastelands of Central Asia still remained. The Persians had improved the routes through their own territory, building more caravanserais and providing more watering-places for merchant caravans, as well as increasing the number of checkpoints at which customs inspectors and tax collectors monitored the trade passing east and west. But trouble loomed in the East.

The Ephthalite (White) Huns, remnants of the once-great Hsiung-nu, were being pushed westward by a new power in Central Asia, the Turks, of whom more would soon be heard. Coming to rest on the west side of the Pamirs, as the Yüeh-chih had done centuries before, the Ephthalite Huns menaced Persian trade lines. Despite being bitter enemies, the Romans and Persians extended their trade cooperation far enough for the Romans to help finance the building of new, stronger fortifications as defences against these Huns, along the Silk Road in the East and also at the Caucasus passes above Armenia.

Of course, the Persians were not dependent solely on the Silk Road for their supply of silk or other Eastern wares. These goods also came to Persia via the Spice Route, either from India by way of the Indian Grand Road, or directly by sea through the Persian Gulf. Though we tend to think of the Persians as landlubbers, in this period they were, or at least they employed, consummate sailors, known to the Chinese as the *Po-sse*, who traded directly at southern Chinese ports. Perhaps they recalled how profitably the Romans had circumvented Parthian control of the land route by use of the sea route. Sometimes, of course, Persians traded nearer to home, at the island mart of Taprobane (later Ceylon or Sri Lanka), off the southern tip of the Indian peninsula. As Cosmos Indicopleustes, a contemporary Roman observer, reported:

> From all India and Persia and Ethiopia many ships come to this island, and it also sends out many of its own, being in a central position. From the further regions, that is Tzinista [China] and other exporting countries, Taprobane imports silk, aloeswood, cloves, sandal-wood and so on, according to the production of the place.

But the Romans always chafed under the Persian monopoly and tried periodically (especially when Persian-Roman relations were strained, as was common) to circumvent the Persians. In what is now Ethiopia, there had arisen, with the decline of western Roman power, a Christian trading nation called Axum. From their kingdom on the Red Sea, Axumites (of mostly Arab descent) sailed to Ceylon, where they specialized in the spice trade as the Persians focused on silk. The Roman Emperor Justinian, appealing to the common religion of their two countries, hoped to make common cause with the Axumites against Persia. More specifically, he obtained an agreement whereby Axumite merchants would buy silk in Ceylon and deliver it to the Romans. In the end, however, no silks were forthcoming, most likely because the Axumites and the Persians had rather amicably divided the Eastern trade between themselves, and the Axumites did not wish to jeopardize these established trade arrangements for the uncertain favor of the Romans.

At this point in the proceedings, another religious group began to figure in the story of the Silk Road, probably contributing to a partial solution of the Byzantine hunger for silks. Though the Roman Empire had officially adopted Christianity as a state religion in the fourth century, there was still no agreement among the followers of Christ as to even the main points of belief. In the second quarter of the fifth century, a Christian leader named Nestorius, bishop of Constantinople but a native of Antioch, was a leading spokesman for the view that Jesus Christ was two persons, both God and man, distinct but inextricably intertwined, and that Mary was the mother of the man, but not the god. In the standardizing church councils of the fifth century, this view was condemned as heretical. Nestorius was exiled, and died in 451, but some of his followers, mostly Syrians from cities like Antioch and Edessa, started a long trek eastward that would eventually take them all the way to China.

Nestorian Christian refugees found shelter under Persian rule, founding a theological school at Nisibis, the Persian silk center, and then spreading their doctrine throughout Persia, whose Christians gradually adopted Nestorian views. Many of these emigrants were highly educated people, among them skilled physicians, for example, who contributed a great deal to the Persian culture. But they led a somewhat precarious existence on the Iranian Plateau. Under some rulers, Christians, Jews, Manichaeans, and others were treated tolerantly, even though the Persian majority strongly favored Zoroastrianism or even a revival of an older Iranian religion, Mazdaism. One Persian king, who himself married a Jewish woman, was so well disposed toward the followers of Jesus that he was called "the Christian king." But at other times, when xenophobia ran strong, minority religions were badly persecuted. Christians were especially mistrusted because the church's center was in the Roman Empire, even though the Christian Church of Iran, also called the Persian Church, had been made independent of Roman connections in the mid-fifth century. Periodic uncertainty as to their status in Persia as well as missionary zeal spurred some of these Nestorian or Persian Christians to head eastward, into Central Asia.

It was most likely from some of these Central Asian Christians that the West finally learned the secret of sericulture. Procopius writes that:

> . . . *certain monks arrived from the [country of the] Indians, and learning that the Emperor Justinian had it much at heart that the Romans should no longer buy silk from the Persians, they came to the king and promised that they would so manage about silk that the Romans should not have to purchase the article either from the Persians or from any other nation; for they had lived, they said, a long time in a country where there were many nations of the Indians and which goes by the name of Serinda. And when there*

they had made themselves thoroughly acquainted with the way in which silk might be
produced in the Roman territory.

Another Roman chronicler, Theophanes, writing at the end of the sixth century relates a similar, but slightly different, story:

Now in the reign of Justinian a certain Persian exhibited in Byzantium the mode in
which [silk] worms were hatched, a thing which the Romans had never known before.
This Persian on coming away from the country of the Seres had taken with him the eggs
of these worms [concealed] in a walking-stick, and succeeded in bringing them safely to
Byzantium. In the beginning of spring he put out the eggs upon the mulberry leaves
which form their food; and the worms feeding upon those leaves developed into winged in-
sects and performed their other operations. Afterwards when the emperor . . . showed the
Turks the manner in which the worms were hatched, and the silk which they produced,
he astonished them greatly.

Serinda, the place where Justinian's benefactors learned the secrets of sericulture, is very likely to have been the city of Khotan, on the southern rim of the Tarim, for it had long been influenced by both China and India—hence, presumably, the name. (Some have suggested, less convincingly, other sites, such as Kashgar, or even sites on the sea route, such as Cambodia.) But, if our supposition is correct, how did the people of Khotan learn how to make silk, when the Chinese had been guarding the secret for over 2,000 years? The answer seems to be in the Chinese annals. According to one story, sericulture security was breached in the West in about 400 A.D. by a Chinese princess sent to marry a Khotan prince, in the old and continuing pattern of marital alliances. (The Japanese had apparently learned the secret in about 200 A.D.)

Hsüan–tsang, a Chinese pilgrim traveling two centuries later in the Tarim, tells how the incident was remembered in Khotan:

In old times this country knew nothing about mulberry trees or silkworms. Hearing that
the eastern country [China] had them, they sent an embassy to seek for them. At that
time the prince of the eastern kingdom kept the secret and would not give the possession of
it to any. He kept guard over his territory and would not permit either the seeds of the
mulberry or the silkworms' eggs to be carried off.
*   The king of Kustana [Khotan] set off to seek a marriage union with a princess of the*
eastern kingdom, in token of his allegiance and submission. The king . . . acceded to his
wish. Then the king of Kustana dispatched a messenger to escort the royal princess and
give the following direction: "Speak thus to the eastern princess: Our country has neither

*silk or silken stuffs. You had better bring with you some mulberry seeds and silkworms,
then you can make robes for yourself."*

*The princess, hearing these words, secretly procured the seed of the mulberry and
silkworms' eggs and concealed them in her head-dress . . . at the barrier, the guard
searched everywhere, but he did not dare to remove the princess' head-dress.*

So the secrets of sericulture reached the Western Territories. The Chinese princess had
protected her home country to this extent, however: she apparently did not tell her new
countrymen that the incipient moth had to be killed before it burst the chrysalis and broke the
filaments. On the contrary, according to the Khotan reporters, she had made quite a point of
not killing the moth:

*. . . the queen wrote on a stone the following decree: "It is not permitted to kill the
silkworm! After the butterfly has gone, then the silk may be twined off [the cocoon].
Whoever offends against this rule may he be deprived of divine protection."*

Theophanes suggested that the silkworms introduced into Byzantium developed into
winged insects. If so, the silk would have been of the much inferior type that results from the
use of broken filaments. The Romans could produce their own silk, but they may not have
known how to unravel the continuous filament necessary for fine silk. In any case, they simply
would not have had the skills that the Chinese had developed over many centuries. So, even
while their own silk industry developed, the Romans still hungered for the delicate Chinese
silks.

★   ★   ★

The Romans then turned their thoughts to the possibility of other overland routes.
With the Iranian Plateau closed off to them, they looked to the Eurasian Steppe, which they
could reach easily from their trading outposts on the Black Sea. There they found others with a
like idea.

Out in Central Asia, the Ephthalite Huns had been pushed into India by the rising
Turks. In the early sixth century, these Turks—the name refers to the helmets they wore,
signifying both strength and skill in metalwork—had still been subject to the Avars (known in
the East as the Jou-jan). Then in 552, the Turks sent the Avars hurtling toward Europe, and set
themselves up as rulers of Mongolia. Rapidly expanding, especially toward the West, by 565
they had established themselves on the Oxus River, with Tashkent, Bukhara, Samarkand, and
the other prime caravan centers of Turkestan—the region that would be named for

them—now in their hands. A Turkish poem dating from 732, almost two centuries later, celebrates these astonishing successes:

> *When the blue sky was created above and the dark earth below, between the two were created the sons of men. Above the sons of men rose up the kaghan [khan] . . . After becoming masters, they governed the institutions and the empire of the Turkish people. In the four corners of the earth they had many enemies, but making expeditions with armies they enslaved and pacified many peoples in the four corners of the earth. They forced them to bow the head and to bend the knee. They enabled us to dwell between the Khingan Mountains in the east and the Iron Gates in the west. All the way between these two outposts stretched the dominion of the Blue Turks!*

These, then, product of a mixture of the ancient Hsuing-nu and the many Indo-European peoples of the Eurasian Steppe, were the people the Eastern Roman Empire now wanted to deal with.

The Turks had temporarily been allied with the Persians in their drive against the Ephthalite Huns. But then the Persians apparently grew to fear the power of their erstwhile ally—and for good reason. The Persians abruptly closed off the overland Silk Road, perhaps because they feared that Sogdian traders might be spies for their new overlords, the Turks. The Sogdians, who had made their living at the silk trade, tried desperately to persuade the Persians to reopen the route. The Roman chronicler Menander, writing at the end of the sixth century, explained:

> *. . . the people of Sogdia . . . besought the king [of the Turks] to send an embassy to the Persians, in order to obtain permission for them to carry silks for sale into Persia.*

The Turkish khan Dizabul agreed to do so and sent as his emissary the chief of the Sogdians, a man called Maniah (brother of Mani), by his name a follower of Manichaeism.

The Persian king Chosroes stalled about responding to the embassy, until an Ephthalite advisor at the Persian court:

> *. . . exhorted the Persian king on no account to let the silk have free passage, but to have a price put upon it, buy it up, and have it burnt in the presence of the ambassadors. It would thus be seen that though he would do no injustice, he would have nothing to do with the silk of the Turks. So the silk was put into the fires and the ambassadors turned homeward, anything but pleased with the result of their journey.*

Still hopeful, the Turks sent another embassy to the Persian court; but, Menander reported:

> . . . the Persian ministers and [the Ephthalite advisor] came to the conclusion that it would be highly inexpedient for the Persians to enter into friendly relations with the Turks, for the whole race of the Scythians was one not to be trusted. So he ordered some of the ambassadors to be taken off by a deadly poison, in order to prevent any more such missions from coming. Most of the Turkish envoys accordingly, in fact all but three or four, were put an end to by a deadly poison which was mixed with their food, while the king [Chosroes] caused it to be whispered about among the Persians that the Turkish ambassadors had died of the suffocating dry heat of the Persian climate; for their own country could not exist except in a cold climate.

But, says Menander, "Dizabulus [was] a sharp and astute person, [who] was not ignorant of the real state of the case."

Felt-covered *yurts*, transported on great wagons during migrations, were home to the steppe peoples for many centuries. (By Quinto Cenni, from Yule's *Marco Polo*)

So, as the Romans themselves were looking for a northerly overland route, the Turks were impelled to do the same. The Sogdian Maniah—after all, the chief of a trading people—suggested to Dizabul that:

> . . . it would be more for the interest of the Turks to cultivate the friendship of the
> Romans, and to transfer the sale of silk to them, seeing also that they consumed it more
> largely than any other people.

Though they were dogged by Persian spies, Maniah's embassy met no hindrance, since the Turks now controlled the northern Eurasian Steppe as far west as the Sea of Azov, atop the Black Sea, with ready access to the Roman outposts on the Crimean Peninsula. "Carrying complimentary salutations, with a present of silk of no small value, and letters to the Roman Emperor," Maniah's party arrived at the Roman court in Constantinople in the year 568.

We may imagine the eagerness with which the Roman emperor heard the promises of peaceful silk trade with the Turks. Having established "amity and alliance" between the two nations, the Romans in turn sent an embassy, Zemarchus, to accompany the Turkish party back to their khan. His account, as chronicled by Menander, gives us a rare picture of the Central Asian peoples of the time. After a "journey of many days," the party arrived in Sogdian territory. There they met some Turks—famous for their ironwork—who offered some iron for sale. Menander continues:

> Some others of the tribe . . . announcing themselves as the conjurors away of evil omens,
> came up to Zemarchus and taking all the baggage of the party set it down in the middle.
> They then began ringing a bell and beating a kind of drum over the baggage, while some
> ran around it carrying leaves of burning incense flaming and crackling, and raged about
> like maniacs, gesticulating as if repelling evil spirits. Carrying on this exorcism of evil as
> they considered it, they made Zemarchus himself also pass through the fire, and in the
> same manner they appeared to perform an act of purification for themselves.

This kind of purification ritual would be undergone by travelers among the Turks for many centuries. After this, the party "proceeded with those who had been set to receive them" to Dizabul's camp, apparently somewhere on the steppe east of the Jaxartes River, perhaps around the Dzungarian Gap.

What Zemarchus found there is striking testimony to the riches brought into these otherwise waste places by the silk trade between the peoples of East and West:

> The party of Zemarchus on their arrival were immediately summoned to an interview
> with Dizabulus. They found him in his tent, seated on a golden chair with two wheels,

which could be drawn by one horse when required . . . Now this tent was furnished with silken hangings of various colors artfully wrought . . . another pavilion [was] adorned in like manner with rich hangings of silk, in which figures of different kinds were wrought. Dizabulus was seated on a couch that was all of gold, and in the middle of the pavilion were drinking vessels and flagons and great jars, all of gold . . . [another] pavilion [was] supported by wooden posts covered with gold, and in [it] was a gilded throne resting on four golden peacocks. In front of the place of meeting there was a great array of wagons, in which there was a huge quantity of silver articles consisting of plates and dishes, besides numerous figures of animals in silver, in no respect inferior to our own. To such a pitch has attained the luxury of the Turkish Sovereign!

So Zemarchus—the first European since Aristeas, as far as we know, to travel into the heart of the Eurasian Steppe and return—completed the diplomatic exchange between the Romans and the Turks. Parts of Menander's chronicle have been lost, but apparently Zemarchus joined the Turks as they broke camp and headed westward to the trading town of Talas. Then, while the Turks headed southwest across the Jaxartes River to attack the Persians, Zemarchus and his companions headed northwest toward home. An express messenger named George, accompanied by a dozen Turks, was sent by the shortest route "to announce to the [Roman] Emperor the return of the party from the Turks." Zemarchus and the rest did not take that route, for it "was without water, and altogether desert." Instead they "traveled for 12 days along the sandy shores of the Lagoon [Aral Sea]," crossing at "some very difficult places," and then cut north of the Caspian Sea, and across the Ural and Volga Rivers (the latter called by them the Attila). Rounding the Caspian Sea, the returning embassy threaded through the Caucasus, where they were warned by allies that "4,000 Persians were stationed in ambuscade [waiting] to lay hands on the party as it passed." Avoiding that danger by a ruse, Zemarchus headed toward the east coast of the Black Sea "and so to Trebizond, whence he rode post to Byzantium."

Following roughly this route, the Romans and Turks traded with each other—surely not without further attempts at interference by the Persians—for a brief 10 years until, at about the time of Dizabul's death, the alliance fell apart in a rush of bad feeling.

But during this brief period, the Romans began to hear tales of a great land to the east of the Turks, a land called Taugas, whose ruler was called the Son of God. There is little doubt that Taugas is China, the name possibly being a Turkish word for "Great Wei" (a Chinese dynasty of the time), and that the "Son of God" is the Chinese emperor, the "Son of Heaven." Oddly, however, geographical knowledge had declined to such a state that the Romans did not connect Taugas with the land of the Seres and the Sinae, even though Taugas was said to be a great country, grown rich in commerce, with consummate skill at keeping silkworms, which "go through many alterations, and are of various colors."

The seventh-century writings of Theophylactus Simocatta show the kind of admixture of factual report and romantic invention that would increasingly characterize medieval writings. So, for example, Theophylactus reported that:

> . . . this city of Taugus they say was founded by Alexander the Macedonian, after he had enslaved the Bactrians and the Sogdianians, and had consumed by fire twelve myriads of barbarians.

Tales of Alexander's exploits would circulate around Asia for centuries. The Romans were only too happy to believe them, since their heritage was actually far more Greek than Roman. To Alexander was even attributed the founding of the city Theophylactus calls Khubdan, a city that "has two great rivers flowing through it, the banks of which are lined with nodding cypresses," which apparently is a reference to Ch'ang-an. But any hope of direct contact between Romans and Chinese, which might have revealed the true identity of Taugas, was dashed when the alliance with the Turks collapsed.

Buddhist temples like this one in Kashmir dotted the routes between China and India. (From *History of Architecture* by Fergusson, reprinted in Yule's *Marco Polo*)

The Persians retained their monopoly on the silk trade, and prospered with it. Through their own industry and the infusion of talented artisans from the lowlands, the Persians had become skilled producers, especially of fine woven goods. But their fortunes still lay in handling the East-West trade, and they mobilized the monetary and banking system to handle it. It was the Persians—assisted by Jewish refugees, some of whom had (like the Nestorians) fled persecution at the hands of the Christians—who developed the use of bills of exchange, the predecessors of our modern checks (a term that also stems from the Persian). Bills had been known on the Silk Road for at least 2,000 years, but only now were they being used on a large scale and in a modern form. Syrian traders, who learned to use these bills of exchange in the silk trade, introduced them to Europe where, centuries later, they would lay the basis for the banking structure so vital to the Italian Renaissance.

But the Persian pre-eminence in the silk trade did not last long. For, if the Romans could not immediately make silk like the finest Chinese goods, they soon learned how to make silk of passable quality. Chinese silks continued to be in demand for decades, even centuries, but China was no longer the sole source of supply. Western sericulture was not, as we might think, established in the capital of Constantinople, but in the traditional textile cities of Syria. Tyre, Sidon, and Beirut revived, growing into great centers for raising silkworms and throwing silk yarn. The weaving industry, too, revived, notably at Damascus. These cities continued to flourish, increasingly supplying the needs of both the Byzantine Empire and Europe over the coming centuries, even when they later passed from Christian to Islamic hands.

★   ★   ★

Perhaps the most astonishing feature of the Silk Road in this period is the continuous flow of silks from China. Though northern China had been subject to successive invasions from the steppe, the silk industry remained and was eagerly annexed by each new government, it being the source of much of the state's revenue.

Intertwined with this, the thread of Buddhism continued to run through Chinese history. As new rulers took over the silk industry, many also took to Buddhism. The Wei dynasty, founded in northern China by Turkish invaders in the early fifth century, first persecuted Buddhists, averring that the religion "did away with the family," and, more seriously, that it allowed men to escape service in the army. But by 471 the Wei ruler had become such a devout Buddhist that he abdicated the throne, although his son and heir was only five years old. "He retired to a pagoda built in the royal park," the annals tell us, "where he lived in the company of contemplative monks, and refused to listen to any news apart from events of exceptional gravity."

Though many of his successors in the Wei dynasty were as bloodthirsty as the most prototypical barbarian, they continued to espouse Buddhist beliefs. In the early sixth century, for example, the dowager Empress Hu was notorious for murdering her former lovers and even her son, yet she urged the creation of the magnificent Buddhist grottoes at Lung-men, near Loyang. Here, as also in the Caves of the Thousand Buddhas near Tunhuang, devout artists carved hundreds of small caves, intended as monks' cells and temples, into loess cliff-faces. (This was not unusual, for many people in northern China, where little wood or stone was available for building, carved their homes out of the loess hillsides. Even in the 20th century, Mao Tse-tung and his followers lived during the years before power in cave-homes in the region.) It was in caves such as these that the fusion of Greek and Indian art, evolved centuries earlier in Afghanistan, reached China in a fully developed form. So the statues of Buddha—some of them huge, perhaps 100 feet high, many of them smaller, tucked away in the tiny monks' cells—showed features reminiscent of a Grecian Apollo, with the modeling of the clothes looking for all the world like the folds of a Greek toga.

The dowager empress Hu showed her devotion by sending a pilgrim named Sung-yun on a mission to India "to obtain Buddhist books," the tradition of such journeys being continued under the Wei dynasty. An account of Sung-yun's journey, though shot through with tales of religious miracles and conversions, appears in the *History of the Temples of Loyang* and gives us some brief glimpses of the Silk Road as it was in about 518. The winter crossing of the "Drifting Sands" was a bitter one:

> Along the road the cold was very severe, while the high winds, and the driving snow, and the pelting sand and gravel were so bad, that it was impossible to raise one's eyes without getting them filled.

The initial destination of Sung-yun and his companion was the land of the Eastern Turks. The Turkish Empire in Central Asia had grown so large that it had split in two, the Western Turks being headquartered near the Issyk Kul (these were the Turks who were briefly allied with the Byzantine Romans and fought the Persians) and the Eastern Turks, centered on the Orkhon River, south of Lake Baikal, heartland of Mongolia. At the mobile camp that the Eastern Turks made their capital, Sung-yun noted clearly the Chinese influence that had continued in Central Asia, even if Chinese power had not. "The written character of this country is nearly the same as that of the Wei," but, he noted sadly, "The customs and regulations observed by these people are mostly barbarous in character (after the rules of the outside barbarians or foreigners)."

Quite naturally, for travelers heading toward India, the pilgrims took the southern route through the Tarim Basin. At Shan-shan, Sung-yun found the Eastern Turks had a garrison of 3,000 men, under a military officer assigned to "pacify" the West. Beyond that lay a town he called Tso-moh, containing perhaps 100 families. There, he noted, "the country is not visited with rain, but they irrigate their crops from the streams of water," though they "know not the use of oxen or ploughs in their husbandry." In the next town, Moh, he found that the "flowers and fruits" were just like those of Loyang, though he noted that the buildings and the "foreign officials" are different in appearance.

Beyond that, in the city of Han-mo, he found a large temple, housing about 300 priests and an 18-foot-high statue of Buddha. The local tradition had it that the statue "originally came from the south transporting itself through the air." The king of Khotan himself coveted it and garnered it for his own temple, "but in the middle of the route, when they halted at night the figure suddenly disappeared." The statue, according to the locals, "had returned to its old place." In token of this miracle:

> Men in after ages built towers around this image . . . all of which are ornamented with many thousand flags and streamers of variegated silk . . . perhaps as many as 10,000 of these, and more than half of them belonging to the Wei country.

Sung-yun has little to say about Khotan, focusing mostly on tales of the early king's conversion, except that the kingdom stretched about 3,000 li from east to west.

From there Sung-yun and his companion passed into the mountains, where "the customs and spoken language are like those of Khotan, but the written character in use is that of the Brahmans." That he refers to the Indians as "Brahmans" is a recognition of a change that was beginning to take place in India. The very homeland of Buddha, to which these devout pilgrims were tending, was turning away from Buddhism and back to the earlier Hindu religion, of which the Brahmans were the highest caste. (Buddha's own vision had been to reform Hinduism, doing away with the caste structure.)

Sung-yun's route through the Tsung-ling Mountains (Pamirs) and the "Untrustworthy Mountains" beyond is unclear, but his description of the region is uncompromising, if occasionally a bit fanciful:

> This spot is extremely cold. The snow accumulates both by winter and summer. In the midst of the mountain is a lake in which dwells a mischievous dragon . . . From this spot westward the road is one continuous ascent of the most precipitous character; for a thousand li there are overhanging crags, 10,000 fathoms high, towering up to the very heavens. Compared with this road, the ruggedness of the great pass known as the Mang-men is as nothing, and the eminences of the celebrated Hian Mountains [both places are in northern China] are like level country. After entering the Tsung-ling Mountains, step by step, we crept upwards for four days, and then reached the highest part of the range. From this point as a center, looking downwards, it seems just as though one was poised in mid-air . . . Men say that this is the middle point of heaven and earth.

The time was the eighth month of the year 519, the party having started from China in the eleventh month of the previous year. Even so, Sung-yun found, "the air is icy cold, and the north wind carries along with it the drifting snow for a thousand *li*." The high lands of these mountains "do not produce trees or shrubs," but people farm using river water for irrigation. When told that the people in the "middle country" (China) farmed fields that were watered by the rain, "they laughed and said, 'How could heaven provide enough for all?'" Since these people apparently lived on a tributary of a river flowing toward Kashgar, Sung-yun was presumably somewhere in the rugged southern Pamirs. This is supported by his comment that the people in the next kingdom, where "the mountains . . . are as lofty and the gorges deep as ever" live north of the "great Snowy Mountains [the Hindu Kush], which, in the morning and evening vapors, rise up like gem-spires."

By the tenth month, Sung-yun and his companion had reached the country of the Ephthalite Huns, apparently still in the Pamirs. Non–Buddhist interlopers, the Ephthalites were apparently still living at least a semi-nomadic life for, in this region that had known fortified towns for many centuries, Sung-yun noted: "They have no walled towns, but they keep order by means of a standing army that constantly moves here and there." There is some suggestion, however, that the Ephthalites were enriched by participation in the silk trade. Sung-yun noted that "they receive tribute from all surrounding nations . . . more than forty countries in all." Might this not be the old Chinese euphemism for trade, applied to "ambassadors" from as far east as Khotan and as far west as Persia? It seems likely. But, apart from describing the state robes, carpets, and hangings used by the royal family (clearly obtained through trade with weaving nations east or west, for the general population of the land wore felt garments), Sung-yun helps us little on that point.

Beyond Ephthalite lands lay some other territories of a different character, quite impoverished and ill-favored, nominally under Persian control. In this "very contracted" region, "the rugged narrow road is dangerous—a traveler and his horse can hardly pass along it one at a time." Where Fa-hsien, over a century earlier, had noted rope bridges used in these mountains and the rugged foothills beyond, Sung-yun noted that:

> . . . they use iron chains for bridges. These are suspended in the air for the purposes of crossing [over the mountain chasms]. On looking downwards one can perceive no bottom; there is nothing on the side to grasp at in case of a slip, but in a moment the body is hurled down 10,000 fathoms. On this account travelers will not cross over in case of high winds.

What a contrast he found on the far side of the mountains, that paradise often called the Babylonia of the East:

> The climate is agreeably warm . . . The people and productions are very abundant. The fertility of the soil is equal to that of [Shantung] in China and the climate more equable .

*. . At the proper time they let the streams overflow the land, by which the soil is
rendered loamy and fertile. All provisions necessary for man are very abundant, cereals of
every kind flourish, and the different fruits ripen in great numbers. In the evening the
sound of [temple] bells may be heard on every side, filling the air; the earth is covered
with flowers of different hues, which succeed each other winter and summer, and are
gathered by clergy and laity alike as offerings for Buddha.*

From this favored land, the pilgrims passed on into India itself, pausing here and there
to erect a pagoda with part of their traveling funds, to leave servants to keep a shrine neat and
tidy "in perpetuity," or to employ an artist to depict a Chinese offering. Sung-yun's
companion had been given by the Empress "a thousand streamers of a hundred feet in length
and of the five colors, and five hundred variegated silk [mats?] of scented grass." These and the
2,000 flags given him by the princes, dukes, and nobility—a graphic indication of royal
support for Buddhism—he distributed before they had even reached the Indus River. Alas, the
travel chronicles tell us little more of the trip, and nothing about their return—though there are
disquieting notes (to the devout) of many people in the region who "did not believe the law of
Buddha, but loved to worship demons."

Sung-yun returned to China in the year 521, but the dowager Empress Hu survived for
less than a decade more, being drowned during a revolt, after a vain attempt to take refuge in a
Buddhist nunnery. Just a few years later, the Wei dynasty itself broke apart, but in 581 one of
the successor states succeeded in uniting all of China for the first time in over 250 years, under
the new Sui dynasty.

★　　★　　★

The Sui emperors quickly made it their business to foment dissension between the two
branches of the Turks—with considerable success, such civil wars being very much the pattern
of life on the steppe. By the early seventh century, the Turks were so involved in their internecine affairs that China was able to recover some of its tattered prestige in Central Asia. By
608, the Sui emperor was sufficiently secure to tour the Kansu Corridor, where he received
embassies from several western oases, notably from Turfan, always exposed to depredations
from Mongolia. He even, on occasion, acted as mediator between different Turkish factions.

In keeping with their clear interest in regaining China's long-lost Western Territories,
the Sui emperors rebuilt Ch'ang-an, making it the key to the Silk Road, once again the capital
of a united China. Loyang they made a second capital, linked with river routes by canals. The
description of Loyang at the time of Emperor Yang (605-616) shows how much northern
China was recovering from the devastations of the previous centuries:

*He [Emperor Yang] embellished its surroundings with a park 120 kilometers in
circumference, where he made a lake nine kilometers long, out of which rose three Islands*

of the Immortals, adorned with magnificent pavilions. Along the banks of a waterway
which opened into the lake he constructed sixteen villas for his favorites, and these houses
were reached by boat. All the known refinements of luxury were displayed in these
dwellings and in the gardens which surrounded them. In autumn, when the leaves had
fallen from the maples, the trees and bushes were decked with leaves and flowers made of
glistening fabrics. In addition to real lotuses, the lake was adorned with artificial lotus
blossoms which were continually renewed. The emperor enjoyed sailing on the lake or rid-
ing in the park on moonlight nights, with a band of beautiful girls who improvised verses
or sang songs.

But China was not yet to return to the full greatness of the past. The life of pleasure so graphically described here led to the downfall of the Sui dynasty and a return to anarchy, with generals battling for control of the provinces. After 618, Loyang became the haunt of rioters and robbers, its streets marked not by silken flowers but by rotting corpses. For a time it seemed as if both Confucius and Buddha had been forgotten, and the only arts were the arts of war.

In the northwest, the young Count of T'ang declared himself emperor and was accepted as such by the city of Ch'ang-an. His way was far from clear, however. Other generals, including one at Loyang, rivaled him for the title. Not only that, but the Turks, always alert to weakness in their neighbors, took the offensive, and were only beaten back by the T'ang cavalry's surprise attack after a rare torrential rain. The Turks retreated to the Mongolian steppe, while the self-proclaimed T'ang emperor went about expanding and consolidating his rule in China.

It was in this turbulent period that the most famous of all the Chinese Buddhist pilgrims made his entrance into history, giving us a unique view of the Silk Road in a time of transition. Hsüan-tsang, a devoutly religious young man, was "a tall, handsome man with beautiful eyes, who had a serious but gentle expression and a sedate, rather stately manner," his biographer tells us. Years before he had come to join his brother at the Pure Land Monastery in Loyang. But in the chaotic times following the fall of the Sui dynasty, he said to his brother, "I have heard that the prince of T'ang has established himself at Ch'ang-an, his new capital. The empire relies on him as on father and mother. Let my brother go there with me." So they went.

But, though some order reigned in Ch'ang-an, still the study of Buddhism languished, and Hsüan-tsang despaired of knowing the truth. Chang Yueh, author of the *T'ang Records of the Western World*, which described Hsüan-tsang's pilgrimage, explained the problem:

. . . [the Buddhist] religion having spread eastwards, the sounds of the words translated
have been often mistaken, the phrases of the different regions have been misunderstood on
account of the wrong sounds, and thus the sense has been lost.

Hsüan-tsang, on realizing this, was "afflicted at heart, and fearing lest he should be unable to find out completely the errors of translations, he proposed to examine thoroughly the literature . . ." To this end, he decided to journey to India.

Easier said than done, however, for with trouble at home, the T'ang ruler had forbidden foreign travel. Undeterred, Hsüan-tsang journeyed first to Langchow (Wuwei) on the upper Huang River, near the start of the Kansu Corridor, where he met and talked with the many Central Asian merchants and traders who frequented the city. Their praise of his religious devotion reached the local governor, who reiterated the imperial ban on travel; but, with the help of local Buddhist monks, Hsüan-tsang stole away westward, traveling under cover of darkness and hiding during the day, until he reached An-hsi, the provisioning city for the northern route to Hami.

Here Hsüan-tsang faced some formidable obstacles. The Sulo River, a steep-sided, narrow torrent, had to be crossed, but the only proper crossing was guarded by a Chinese fortress. And beyond this barrier lay five more Chinese watchtowers, which were on the alert, since the governor of Langchow had sent mounted deputies to arrest him. To complete the gloomy picture, Hsüan-tsang's horse had died, and the two monks assigned as his guides had left him to make his way alone.

By luck, or so it seemed, Hsüan-tsang found a young "barbarian," a fellow Buddhist, who agreed to guide him past these obstacles. By agreement, the two met the next day at sunset, and the new-found friend, Bandha, introduced him to an old man, also a Westerner, explaining that: "He has gone to and come back from Hami more than thirty times." The old man took quite a jaundiced view of Hsüan-tsang's intentions, warning:

> "The western routes are bad and dangerous. At times streams of drift sand bar the traveler's way, at other times demons and burning winds. If they are met, no man can escape their fury. Often large caravans are lost and perish utterly. How much worse for you, sir, going alone! I pray you consider this seriously and do not trifle with your life."

But Hsüan-tsang was hardly to be dissuaded now. He did accept the old man's aged red horse, an experienced mount which had been to and from Hami 15 times, exchanging it for his own newly purchased horse. It was a providential decision, as we shall see.

So Hsüan-tsang and Bandha set out toward the west. Bandha improvised a wooden footbridge across the Sulo River, at a point less than a dozen feet wide. But as they slept on the far side of the river, Hsüan-tsang awoke to find Bandha approaching him stealthily with a drawn knife; only a few steps away, the young man hesitated and returned to his sleeping mat. By the next morning, Bandha was talking of the perils of the journey and of his unwillingness to break the laws of the land. He wanted not only to return himself, but to take Hsüan-tsang with him, for he feared that, if caught, Hsüan-tsang would reveal his part in the escape. Only when Hsüan-tsang swore "that though my body be cut up as small as the very dust I will never turn back" was Bandha satisfied to let the pilgrim proceed.

So Hsüan-tsang headed westward alone, guided only by the ancient signposts of the desert, piles of bleaching bones and droppings left by passing camels. Almost immediately he fell prey to one of the mirages that haunt the desert. On the horizon he saw a vast army "now marching, now at the halt," dressed in the felts and furs of the steppe peoples:

> *Here were camels and horses with splendid harnesses, there glittering lances and gleaming standards. Soon these became new shapes, new figures; each instant it changed, this teeming scene, offering one by one a thousand metamorphoses.*

He heard voices, too, shouting, "Do not fear!"; but as soon as he approached the desert host, they disappeared.

In this confused state he came to the first watchtower and, while attempting to fill his water bottle under cover of night, was spotted immediately by archers who took him to the garrison commander. But Hsüan-tsang's luck held, for here was another fellow Buddhist. After attempting in vain to dissuade the pilgrim, the commander provided Hsüan-tsang with water and provisions—and, more important, with a letter to a relative of his at the next tower. Hsüan-tsang proceeded, being passed from tower to tower, but was warned not to approach the last watchtower, for the commander there had no sympathy with Buddhists. Instead he was advised to head straight across the desert toward the Spring of the Wild Horses, 100 *li* away.

Along with his aged horse, Hsüan-tsang embarked on the "River of Sand," where "there are to be found neither birds nor four-footed animals nor water nor grazing." Mirages and visions of demons again assailed him; and after traveling 100 *li* he found he had lost his way. In a panic he dropped his waterbag, watching in desperation as the last of his vital supply drained away in the sand. This one time Hsüan-tsang thought of returning to China, but he remembered his oath never to take a step back toward China, even if he should die on the road to the West.

> *Whereupon he reined his horse round and, uttering fervent prayers . . . set off toward the northwest. Looking around him in every direction he could see only a limitless plain with no trace of either men or horses. During the night evil spirits shone torches as numerous as the stars; during the day terrible winds lifted the sand and scattered it like torrents of rain. Amidst all these cruel assaults his heart remained a stranger to fear, but he suffered greatly from lack of water and at last was so tortured with thirst that he could not take another step. For four nights and five days not one drop of water had passed his lips. A devouring fire was burning at his entrails and he was almost expiring. Unable to continue, he lay down in the sand where he was, and . . . prayed.*

Mirages and illusory sound led many Silk Road travelers to their deaths in the Taklamakan. (By Aurel Stein, Royal Geographic Society)

In the middle of the fifth night, he and his horse both were revived by a cool breeze and set out on their way again. Then, the barter with the old man proved its true value:

> When he had gone about four miles his horse suddenly changed direction and nothing he could do would hold it back or keep it on the original path.

After only a few miles, his horse found a swath of green pasture, and beyond it a clear pond of fresh water. Both lives were saved, and the two came unscathed to the most welcome oasis of Hami.

Here they were beyond direct Chinese power, but not Chinese influence. While Hsüan-tsang was being entertained by the local Buddhist king, there arrived from the larger and richer oasis of Turfan (which had been ruled by a Chinese-descended dynasty since the early sixth century) a mounted escort to bring the pilgrim to the Turfan court. Hsüan-tsang had had another itinerary in mind, for he had planned to visit a shrine at the Turkish city of Beshbalik, but the king would be obeyed, so to Turfan he went. There he received a royal welcome and urgent pleas—so urgent that he was able to continue his journey only by instituting a hunger strike—that he stay to head the Buddhist community in Turfan.

Once convinced of Hsüan-tsang's determination, however, the king of Turfan made bounteous provision for his journey, providing face masks, boots, gloves, and all necessary warm clothing for the planned crossing of the T'ien Shan and the Pamirs; 30 horses and 24 servants, plus a high official bearing silks and fruits to escort the pilgrim to the neighboring kingdoms; 100 ounces of gold, 30,000 pieces of silver, and 500 rolls of silk, all for Hsüan-tsang's own use; and beyond that letters of introduction to the kings of 24 countries en route, each accompanied by a large roll of satin as a gift. To the Grand Khan of the Turks alone, the king sent, on Hsüan-tsang's behalf, "two wagons loaded with 500 pieces of satin." Such was the measure of the Turfan king's devotion—and of the luxury to be found in these apparently isolated oasis-states. The friendship and munificence of the king of Turfan, and his influence with the Turkish khan (to whom he was, in effect, a vassal), took Hsüan-tsang in safety and even relative comfort to the very borders of India.

Not that the journey was necessarily safe, as was immediately clear. En route to the next oasis-center, Karashahr, Hsüan-tsang's caravan—he now had quite an entourage—found the corpses of traders who, instead of waiting, had left just ahead of them and had the ill-fortune to meet a band of robbers.

Hsüan-tsang found Karashahr to be an oasis "on all sides . . . girt with hills," and with "roads . . . precipitous and easy of defense." A rather pleasant place, noted for its many fruits, Karashahr showed affinities with India in its writing as well as its religion. Fifty miles away, but separated by a mountain spur of the T'ien Shan, Kucha was also famed for its fruits—grapes, pomegranates, plums, pears—as well as for the many precious metals found in the ground. Kucha's women, their charms enhanced with perfumes and cosmetics brought from Persia, were a great attraction to the traveling merchants of the desert, as were the musicians who, Hsüan-tsang reported, "were at that time so skillful that they could, after a little practice, reproduce an air which they had heard only once." Many of the inhabitants of these towns were descendants of the Indo-Europeans who had once dominated Central Asia. Their languages were still Indo-European, though written in an Indian script, adopted along with Buddhism.

Proceeding westward on the northern course of the Silk Road, the party would have traveled next to Aksu, if they had been following the normal route. But the power of the Turkish khan and the necessity of visiting him before proceeding to India forced Hsüan-tsang into the bitter T'ien Shan. En route he and his caravan met twin dangers. Two days out of Kucha they met a horde of 200 Turkish bandits, who let the pilgrim party pass only because they were so busy arguing about the division of the spoils from a trading caravan they had just pillaged. Then Hsüan-tsang passed into the glacier-covered face of the T'ien Shan:

This mountain of ice . . . is extremely dangerous and its peak reaches to the sky. Ever since the world began snow has collected there and has changed into ice which melts neither in spring nor in summer. Sheets of this ice, hard and gleaming, stretch as far as the eye can see and mingle with the clouds. Looking at them one is blinded by their brightness. The road is strewn with cliffs and pinnacles of ice some of which are up to a hundred feet high and others several tens of feet across. One cannot cross the latter without great peril. Added to this the traveler is constantly assailed by blasts of wind and by snowstorms so that, even with shoes and garments lined and trimmed with fur, he cannot help shivering in the cold. When it comes to eating or sleeping he can find no dry place to lie down. He has no alternative but to hang up the cooking-pot to prepare his food and lay out his mat upon the ice.

So severe was this passage that 14 men died from hunger and exposure—and, perhaps, by avalanche—and an even greater number of oxen and horses were frozen to death. On the far side, Hsüan-tsang arrived at the Issyk Kul, the Warm Lake. Nearby, in this relatively clement

Against the imperial ban, Buddhist pilgrim Hsüan-tsang set out alone for India. (From *Toyō Bijutsu Taikan*, early 9th century, British Museum)

country, lay the winter camp of the Turks. Hsüan-tsang arrived there in 630, just over 50 years after Zemarchus had made his journey to the region from the Eastern Roman Empire.

From Hsüan-tsang's description, the khan's court had lost none of its magnificence. The Turks, he tells us, had a great many horses. The troops were "riders mounted on camels or horses, dressed in furs and fine woolen cloth and carrying long lances, banners, and straight bows." The khan himself, in a green satin coat, with his long loose hair bound around the forehead by a long trailing piece of silk, was attended by some 200 officers in brocade coats. The whole multitude assembled on the Kirghiz Steppe "stretched for so far that the eye could not tell where it ended."

Hsüan-tsang's view of this great nomadic assembly has a special interest for us in retrospect, because, following the pattern of steppe empires, the Turks were about to lose the always-fragile unity of the steppe peoples, fragmenting into several main branches that would make their separate names in the world.

Like other rulers on the way, we are told, the khan delighted in hearing Hsüan-tsang expound the Law of Buddha (though he was himself no Buddhist) and tried to dissuade him from continuing to India, which he thought "too hot." But when Hsüan-tsang persisted, the khan provided him with an interpreter who would serve him as far as Afghanistan, as well as gifts of silk and satin. He even joined Hsüan-tsang partway on the road toward India. The region through which they traveled was called the Land of the Thousand Springs. North of the T'ien Shan, the "level tableland" of the Kirghiz Steppe was attractive enough to be the khan's favorite summer camp, as:

> The soil is well-watered, the trees afford a grateful shade, and the flowers in the spring months are varied and like tapestry. There are a thousand springs of water and lakes here, and hence the name . . . There are a number of deer here, many of which are ornamented with bells and rings . . .

Continuing to curve around the outer rim of the T'ien Shan, Hsüan-tsang's caravan came to the town of Talas, on the river of the same name, where "merchants from all parts assemble and live with the natives." Beyond that lay the then-modest town we know as Tashkent and the Jaxartes River. The well-watered land ended abruptly at the Kizil Kum (Red Sand Desert), which lies between the Jaxartes (the Syr) and the Oxus (Amu). It was a fearsome obstacle, and one of the main defects of this otherwise pleasant route north of the T'ien Shan:

> . . . we enter on a great sandy desert, where there is neither water nor grass. The road is lost in the waste, which appears boundless, and only by looking in the direction of some great mountain, and following the guidance of the bones which lie scattered about, can we know the way in which we ought to go.

Only after crossing many tens of miles of desert did the pilgrim party once again emerge in hospitable land, at the city of Samarkand, near the head of the mountain spur that forms one side of the wide valley of Ferghana. Hsüan-tsang was duly impressed by this city, on the west side of the Pamirs, center of the Sogdian trading network:

> The capital . . . is 20 li or so in circuit. It is completely enclosed by rugged land and very populous. The precious merchandise of many foreign countries is stored up here. The soil is rich and productive, and yields abundant harvests. The forest trees afford a thick vegetation, and flowers and fruits are plentiful. The shen [the most favored type, always] horses are bred here. The inhabitants are skillful in the arts and trades beyond those of other countries.

The *T'ang Shu* (*Annals of the T'ang Dynasty*) agreed:

> The peoples of this country excel at trade and adore profit. As soon as a man reaches the age of twenty he departs for the neighboring kingdoms . . . Everywhere where profit is to be had, they have been there.

Modern archaeology has confirmed this assessment, locating Sogdian trading colonies on the very borders of China, near the Lop Nor. Though subject to the Turks, the Sogdians had close ties of language, culture, and ethnic heritage with the Persians—even their alphabet was derived from Western Asia, via Persia, and many professed to the Zoroastrian belief. But, perhaps recognizing the unique importance of China to their trading fortunes, in 631, just a few years after this visit by Hsüan-tsang, a Sogdian delegation traveled all the way to China to request that the T'ang dynasty take over their land as overlords. The T'ang emperor, T'ai-tsung, declined, noting that it was very far away:

> "I am averse to adorning myself with vain titles at the expense of the people. If I took Sogdiana into subjection I would have to send troops to defend it and those troops, in order to reach it, would have to travel 10,000 li."

It was, of course, the old problem faced by the rulers of the early Han dynasty. But although T'ai-tsung declined this request, it is possible that the Sogdian proposal played a role in his later decision to expand Chinese hegemony once more into Central Asia.

From Samarkand on toward India, Hsüan-tsang found a succession of melancholy scenes spread out before him. The Samarkand king and most of his people were "fire-worshippers"—that is, Zoroastrians—a reflection of their ever-closer ties with Persia. The two Buddhist temples there—and, remember, these Sogdian traders had been among the most successful Buddhist missionaries in Central Asia—were empty, and visiting pilgrims were driven off by local Zoroastrians with burning torches. Hsüan-tsang was temporarily able to reverse the trend away from Buddhism; the king rescued him from the mob with their firebrands, and his missionary zeal turned many of the citizens back to Buddhism. Even the abandoned monasteries were restored and peopled with monks ordained by Hsüan-tsang. But the defection of the Sogdians from Buddhism was only a foretaste of what he would find in India itself, where the pilgrim in all his zeal would possess no power to change the course of history.

On finally leaving Samarkand, Hsüan-tsang threaded his way through the westernmost mountain tongue of the Pamirs on the way to the land of Bactria:

> . . . we enter the mountain; the mountain road is steep and precipitous, and the passage along the defiles dangerous and difficult. There are no people or villages, and little water or vegetation. Going along the mountains 300 li or so southeast, we enter the Iron Gates [Buzgala Defile]. The pass so called is bordered in the right and left by mountains. These mountains are of prodigious height. The road is narrow, which adds to the difficulty and danger. On both sides there is a rocky wall of an iron color. Here there are set up double wooden doors, strengthened with iron and furnished with many bells hung up. Because of the protection afforded to the pass by these doors, when closed, the name Iron Gates is given.

Whatever semblance of safety and security the famous Iron Gates offered, Turkish power had not been deterred, but had established itself firmly in Bactria. After a detour to visit the local Turkish prince, Hsüan-tsang headed toward the religious and trading center of Balkh (once Bactra). In this beautiful city, "full of flowers too many to enumerate," Hsüan-tsang found "about 100 convents and 3,000 monks." The impact of successive attacks by the Huns, the Zoroastrian Persians, and the non-believing Turks had greatly impaired local Buddhist practices, however. Hsüan-tsang noticed that "so irregular are they morning and night in their duties, that it is hard to tell saints from sinners."

He now passed southward through the formidable Snowy Mountains (Hindu Kush) toward India:

> These mountains are high and the valleys deep; the precipices and crevasses are very dangerous. The wind and snow keep on without intermission; the ice remains through the full summer; the snowdrifts fall into the valleys and block the roads. The mountain spirits and demons send, in their rage, all sorts of calamities; robbers crossing the path of travelers kill them . . . The road is twice as difficult and dangerous as in the desert regions and among the glaciers. The sky is continually overcast with frozen clouds and

*whirling snowstorms. If occasionally one comes across a more favorable spot it is at most a
few dozen feet of even terrain.*

Threading his way through these desolate mountain valleys, Hsüan-tsang emerged at
the city of Bamiyan, long famous for its many rockhewn statues of Buddha, some over 100
feet high, with "precious ornaments [that] dazzle the eyes by their brightness." Here he was
following one of the old caravan and pilgrimage routes across the Hindu Kush down into the
Kabul River valley. Though he found the inhabitants of this Afghan tableland—he called it the
"black ridge"—rough and fierce, he admired their devotion to Buddha, even if it was not
always what he would consider orthodox. He would treasure their religious fervor, and the
memory of those great statues, showing some of the finest examples of Greco-Indian Buddhist
art, as he passed on into India itself.

Detouring from the main route to visit cities on either side that had strong Buddhist
associations, he found much desolation. At Gandhara, generally considered the homeland of
the Greco-Indian Buddhist art that had already reached China's borders, he found the towns
and villages with but a few inhabitants:

*There are about 1,000 sangharamas [monasteries], which are deserted and in ruins. They
are filled with wild shrubs, and solitary to the last degree. The stupas are mostly decayed.
The heretical temples, to the number of about 100, are occupied pell-mell by heretics
[non-Buddhists].*

At Peshawar, once the winter capital of the Buddhist devotee Kanishka, king of the Kushans,
he found:

*A thousand Buddhist monasteries lie deserted and in ruins; they are overgrown with weeds
and offer only a melancholy solitude.*

The story would be repeated time after time, as Hsüan-tsang descended from the bleak
and bitter mountains down onto the torpid plains of India. There, though the villages were not
deserted, the Buddhist temples had been abandoned by a people that now favored Hinduism.
Like his pilgrim predecessors, Hsüan-tsang spent the following years traveling around India,
visiting Buddhist shrines, even though he sometimes had to take off alone into overgrown
jungles to do so. Often he joined in widely attended debates with fellow Buddhists (of various
persuasions) and representatives of other religions as well.

But after some years of travel, he turned toward home, having gathered hundreds of
Buddhist records, the very things he had sought in making this long journey. As Hsüan-tsang

himself said to those who urged him to remain in India: "Why does the sun traverse the world? To dispel the shadows. Precisely for that very reason do I wish to return to my own country."

Fortunately for our picture of that period, Hsüan-tsang returned overland by a different route through the mountains beyond the Kabul River valley, then onto the southern branch of the Silk Road to China. At one point on his journeys, he had reached so far east in India that, natives told him, the Chinese province of Szechuan was only two months away. But luckily for him, he did not attempt the route through mountainous jungle, teeming with malaria and wild elephants.

As on his journey to India, Hsüan-tsang had the protection of princes on his homeward trek. The Buddhist king Harsha, whose capital was Kanauj, on the Ganges in eastern India, had sponsored one of the greatest of the religious assemblies that Hsüan-tsang attended. In early 643, thousands of celebrated visitors, kings and monks, Buddhist, Hindu, and Jain, gathered at Kanauj, some on elephants, some in chariots, some carried in palanquins, all displaying brilliantly colored standards and parasols. But though Hsüan-tsang's biographer tells us that he made mass conversions to his form of Buddhism, elsewhere we learn that disputes were so heated that some rival Buddhists even "hatched a plot against his life." A tower built to house a statue of Buddha was the target of arson, and Harsha himself was subject to an assassination attempt. Out of his own religious feeling and a desire to protect a Chinese visitor, albeit an unofficial one, Harsha proclaimed openly his protection of Hsüan-tsang, and made it tangible as well:

> He gave the Master of the Law 10,000 gold pieces, 30,000 silver pieces, and 100 garments of fine cotton. He ordered one of his officers to caparison a large elephant with a rich adornment of costly materials and invited the Master of the Law to ride upon it. Finally he ordered the highest dignitaries of the land to form his escort and thus make a tour of the assembled multitude . . .

Harsha was the last of the great Buddhist princes in India; after failing in his attempt to keep the Chinese pilgrim as a missionary among his Indian subjects, he sent Hsüan-tsang on his way in safety. Harsha's swift couriers traveled ahead of Hsüan-tsang bearing letters "written on pieces of white cotton and sealed with red wax" to ensure a welcome on the way. The books and statues that Hsüan-tsang was taking back to China were entrusted to a raja, who shipped them by horse and wagon. So sad was Harsha at Hsüan-tsang's departure that, three days after the pilgrim had left for home, the king and a fellow Buddhist prince, along with some hundreds of mounted soldiers, raced after the slow-moving caravan and rode with it for some leagues more. The date was April 643 A.D.

Northern India was, in this period, much infested with bands of robbers, but Hsüan-tsang sent monks ahead of his caravan to say: "We are religious who have come from afar to obtain instructions in the Law. What we carry with us are sacred books, relics and statues. Men of generous heart, we ask your help and protection." His appeal seems to have had some effect, for they were not bothered by robbers across the Punjab. Would that he could have made such an appeal to the Indus River, which posed a real danger to the precious cargo of the pilgrims:

> The books and statues and the travelers were embarked upon a large boat and the Master of the Law crossed the river on the back of an elephant. He had instructed one of his men to keep an eye on the books and the seeds of the rare Indian flowers on the boat. But as they arrived in mid-stream the boat was violently shaken by an eddy and almost swamped. The guardian of the books was filled with terror and fell into the water. He was pulled out by his companions but he lost fifty manuscripts and the flower seeds and it was only with great difficulty that they were able to save the rest.

But, as a tribute to the honor in which he was held, the kings of Kapisa and Kashmir came to greet Hsüan-tsang on the Indus, and the former sent for copies of the books swallowed up by the river. Their motives were not entirely religious, of course. The nomad hordes of Central Asia always threatened to sweep down the northwest Indian frontier, and some Indian kings were thinking of China as a future ally.

So Hsüan-tsang headed out on the tortuous route over the Hindu Kush to Kashgar, in by far the worst country he had yet traversed, buffeted by snowstorms and icy winds as they climbed from peak to peak:

> . . . when bitter cold had crusted the snow, they advanced up the ridge guided by a native riding a mountain camel. They floundered in deep snowdrifts and crossed crevasses trusting to snow bridges. Anyone who did not follow in the guide's footsteps would have fallen and perished. The entire party of seven monks, twenty porters, one elephant, ten asses and four horses struggled up the pass . . . There was not a trace of vegetation, only a mass of crazily piled rock on rock and everywhere slender stone pinnacles looking like a forest of trees without leaves.

The pilgrim's party heard of a caravan caught in a particularly violent blizzard in which every one of the several thousand traders and camels was frozen to death. Yet this stark region, swept by snowstorms even in mid-summer, was sacred land to the pilgrims, for here Buddha was said to have wandered and by these passes Buddhism came to Central Asia.

As the pilgrims passed from the Hindu Kush through the Pamirs to Kashgar they met danger of a different sort: a gang of robbers. When the bandits attacked, several pack animals fell to their deaths in the crevasses below, and some merchants who had joined the party fled into the mountains. But Hsüan-tsang somehow was able to wait out the danger and then pick his way, with the remnants of his caravan, over the Pamirs to Kashgar. Interestingly, in one of the mountain kingdoms he passed on the way, the local people had a legend that a king of

Pilgrims and traders on the mountain routes traversed
gorges by rope bridges or trestle roads, like this one
on the Sino-Tibetan border. (From *Travels of a Pioneer
of Commerce*, by Cooper, reprinted in Yule's *Marco Polo*)

Persia had been promised a wife from the Han country; meeting trouble on the road to Persia,
the Han princess stopped in the mountain kingdom, first temporarily and then permanently.
One wonders if this is some survival of the ancient connections between Persia and China, or
relates to the fate of one of the many later Chinese princesses sent as hostages to their country's
political ambitions.

Passing through jade country, Hsüan-tsang finally came to Kashgar, a bountiful
region. There, he was happy to find, Buddhism flourished, for Kashgar had several hundred
monasteries with some 10,000 followers. Now down in the Tarim Basin, but still following

the rim of mountains, Hsüan–tsang turned southward toward Yarkand, a city he estimated at 10 *li* around:

> *It is hemmed in by crags and mountain fastnesses. The residences are numerous. Mountains and hills succeed each other in a continuous line. Cold and winds prevail throughout the year.*

In both cities, regardless of their "honest faith," Hsüan–tsang had little liking for the people, noting: "Their politeness is very scant, and their knowledge of literature and the arts equally so." Though trading caravans had, clearly, been threading their way through the mountains all this time, these kingdoms had been rather out of touch with the great civilizations of Asia.

From the foothills of the Pamirs, it was out along the desert to Khotan, a land mostly made up of "sand and gravel," afflicted with periodic "tornadoes, which bring with them clouds of flying gravel." Still, the small arable part of the land Hsüan–tsang found attractive and agreeable, with its abundance of fruits. Khotan also had an active industry for manufacturing carpets, taffetas, felts, and fine silks, as well as mining the finest white and green jade. Here he found the people more urbane and cultivated, with a conspicuous love of music and dance, and still with a strong devotion to Buddhism. They remembered well how a Chinese princess had brought them the secret of sericulture.

Here Hsüan–tsang found clear evidence of how the Tarim Basin was drying up—as streams and rivers disappeared. Towns once bustling he found ruined and uninhabited, in country long "deserted and wild," no longer able to survive with the lack of water. In some places, the "city walls still stand lofty, but the inhabitants are dispersed and scattered." In others the sites of former towns were marked simply by great mounds of sand. Of one such, he reported:

> *The kings of the neighboring countries and persons in power from distant spots have many times wished to excavate the mound and take away the precious things buried there; but as soon as they have arrived at the borders of the place, a furious wind has sprung up, dark clouds have gathered together from the four quarters of heaven, and they have become lost to find their way.*

Superstitions such as these would be passed on for centuries, so many old sites were left untouched until the arrival of modern archaeologists.

Hsüan–tsang spent several months in the region, waiting for arrival of the manuscripts to replace those lost in the Indus River crossing. The local population welcomed him not only as a Buddhist teacher, but also as a Chinese subject, for in Hsüan–tsang's absence, China's empire had once more been gathering its strength. He was much impressed with the religious fervor of the people, and with the many caves, monasteries, statues, and paintings related to Buddhism. The king of Khotan himself lived in a fine "house decorated with paintings."

Despite the comfort of being surrounded by enthusiastic fellow Buddhists at Khotan, Shan-shan, and Tunhuang, Hsüan-tsang must have been extremely anxious about what kind of reception he would receive. He had, after all, left 16 years earlier against the direct orders of the emperor. In past (and future) centuries, Chinese citizens might be castrated or beheaded for offenses far less grievous than his. So he paused at the border outpost of Tunhuang, there to wait for a reply from the emperor to his request to re-enter China without prejudice.

What he could not know was how the world had changed in those 16 years. He had seen the end of one era and was to see the beginning of the other. The gathering he had seen on the Kirghiz Steppe was the last great assembly of the Turks. His friend, King Harsha, survived only four years after Hsüan-tsang's departure, and Buddhism in India declined even more sharply after his passing. In Central Asia and China, a new day was dawning with the rise of the T'ang dynasty. It was this new world that he now entered.

CHAPTER EIGHT

A SECOND FLOWERING

If Persia was the greatest power on the Silk Road in the fifth and sixth centuries, T'ang China would be without doubt the dominant nation in the centuries to come. Just a year after Hsüan-tsang had left China, then a country in disarray, the first T'ang emperor, T'ai-tsung, faced down the Eastern Turks at the gates of Ch'ang-an with a bluff, then chased them all the way to their home grounds in Outer Mongolia, on the Orkhon River. For the next half-century, their lands would be part of the Chinese empire. A Turkish record of the result tells us:

> *The sons of the Turkish nobility became slaves of the Chinese people and their virgin daughters became bondmaids. The Turkish nobles abandoned their Turkish titles and received Chinese ones in their place. They submitted to the Chinese kaghan, and for fifty years worked and strove on his behalf. For him they undertook expeditions towards the rising sun, and to the west as far as the Iron Gates [in Turkestan]. But to the Chinese kaghan they surrendered their empire and their institutions.*

Using the Turkish forces as vassal armies, the T'ang emperor, now proclaimed as ruler of all China, swiftly brought much of Central Asia under Chinese control.

Some of the Tarim oases correctly read the signs of emerging Chinese power, and offered tribute to the T'ang emperor, among them Kucha in 630, Khotan and Kashgar in 632, and Yarkand in 635. The king of Turfan, who was

Ever since the Western horsemen began raising smut and dust,
Fur and fleece, rank and rancid, have filled Hsien [Ch'ang-an] and Lo [Loyang].
Women make themselves Western matrons by the study of Western makeup;
Entertainers present Western tunes, in their devotion to Western music.

—Yüan Chen,
eighth century T'ang poet

himself partly of Chinese extraction, a product of one of Central Asia's innumerable marital alliances, traveled to China to show his support for the new T'ang ruler. But the Tarim oases did not fall to China like ripe apples. In 640 the king of Turfan changed his mind, allying himself instead with some Western Turkish tribes, who had fragmented at their khan's death in 630, a few months after Hsüan-tsang saw their glorious assembly. Perhaps the Turfan ruler thought, as so many had before him, that the desert would deter the Chinese army. If so, he had not learned the lesson of the Chinese annals. When a Chinese army abruptly appeared out of the Gobi Desert, the king of Turfan, we are told, died of shock.

One cannot blame the kings of these petty states if, after centuries of disorder and weakness in both China and Central Asia, they continued their pattern of shifting alliances. Who was to say that T'ai-tsung would be different? The king of Karashahr, who aided the Chinese army at Turfan, later allied himself with the king of Kucha and some of the Western Turks. By surprise and brilliant strategy, the Chinese again won stunning victories, emphasizing their displeasure with massive executions afterwards. The Chinese annals rightly say: "The Western Territories were stricken with terror." By 640, the Chinese army, including troops from the Eastern Turks and other Tarim states, had overcome the Western Turks, annihilating some tribes who resisted. To hold their gains in the Tarim, the Chinese stationed troops in the ancient pattern at what they called the Four Garrisons: Karashahr, Kucha (headquarters of the Western Territories), Kashgar, and Khotan. The former Turkish lands north of the T'ien Shan were administered from Chinese headquarters at Beshbalik (Five Towns).

In the south, too, the T'ang emperor imposed his will. The mountain tribes who had long been raiding northwest China from the wild regions near the Koko Nor, were in this period largely united under a powerful king in the newly founded city of Lhasa, high on the Tibetan Plateau. Recognizing the benefits of an alliance with the great empire of the East, the king asked for and received a Chinese princess as his wife. Tibet would become a strongly Buddhist kingdom, and there would gradually develop, under the Chinese princess's sponsorship, a new pilgrim's route over the Tibetan Plateau and down into Nepal and thence to India. If this route did not have the ancient associations with Buddha's own travels and with shrines honoring various Buddhist relics, it had the considerable virtue of being much shorter.

The T'ang emperor also looked farther afield. In 643, before Hsüan-tsang had even returned from his pilgrimage, T'ai-tsung had dispatched an envoy to the Buddhist king Harsha in India. When, only four years later, a Chinese ambassador was attacked en route to India, T'ai-tsung was able to call upon Tibetan and Nepalese troops to seek out and capture the culprits, who were brought in chains to Ch'ang-an. Princes from as far away as Samarkand, Bukhara, and Kapisa, in the Kabul River valley, sent tribute to the new T'ang dynasty. T'ai-tsung was justly proud of his achievements, saying (according to his biographer):

> *In olden times the only rulers who subdued the barbarians were Ch'in Shih-huang-ti and Han Wu-ti. But taking my three-foot sword in hand, I have subjugated the two hundred*

*kingdoms and made quiet all within the four seas, while the far-off barbarians have come
one after another to make their submission.*

So it was that, in 645, when Hsüan-tsang returned from his forbidden mission, T'ai-tsung could afford to be magnanimous and overlook a 16-year-old direct challenge to his authority. From his newly gained position of power, T'ai-tsung could see that Hsüan-tsang had made many friends around Asia, winning great honor for himself and China, and that his direct experience of distant lands could be a considerable asset.

There was a great swell of popular interest in the travels of the redoubtable pilgrim. On the spring day when Hsüan-tsang finally approached Ch'ang-an, he found that:

. . . the rumor of his arrival spread like lightning and the streets were filled with an immense multitude of people eager to set eyes upon him. Disembarking, he attempted in vain to make his way through the crowd, and decided to spend the night on the canal.

T'ai-tsung himself was temporarily away from the city, but he had ordered a lavish welcome. Buddhist followers were assembled in the streets to bear the manuscripts, statues, and sacred objects to their prepared places of honor in the Monastery of Supreme Happiness. From the Street of the Red Bird, where the monks and nuns gathered in their religious robes, the procession wound its way through the city. "The inhabitants of the capital, scholars and magistrates lined both sides of the street, standing in postures redolent of both love and wonder."

A few days later, Hsüan-tsang was received by the emperor himself at Loyang. They agreed to put the pilgrim's contravention of the imperial decree down to religious zeal. The emperor questioned him closely about the people and places he had seen on his journey; the detailed descriptions that we find in his travel writings and in the annals of the time probably had their origin in these careful debriefings. T'ai-tsung found the pilgrim's information so useful that he wished him to take office as an imperial advisor, an honor which was respectfully declined. With the emperor's reluctant blessing, Hsüan-tsang spent the rest of his life in a monastery translating from Sanskrit into Chinese the hundreds of Buddhist works brought from India. But the monastery was close enough to the imperial palace at Ch'ang-an so that he could also go to court and give advice when called upon by the emperor, as he often was. Hsüan-tsang's visit to India did not, of course, resolve all questions regarding Buddhist beliefs, but the writings, art, and relics he brought from India set the general pattern for Buddhism in China for as long as the religion retained its power there. By luck, even after Buddhism fell from favor in China, many of Hsüan-tsang's translations survived in the desert, there to be rediscovered in the 20th century.

If the states of Central Asia in the end fairly rushed to pay tribute to the Chinese Empire, it was not simply because the Chinese had forced them to do so. Rather, independence being a luxury small states could seldom afford, many felt the need of a new and strong protector, for the signs of weakness in Western Asia were many and ominous.

Persia, like Parthia before it, was increasingly afflicted by factional disputes. These reached such a pass that, around the turn of the seventh century, a general took the Persian throne in a *coup d'état*, and the rightful heir, Chosroes, had to seek refuge with, of all people, the Romans. The Roman emperor provided the Persian king with the army he needed to regain the throne, though at the cost of ceding Armenia. But by 610 the Persians were on the move again. They reclaimed Armenia, sacked the prime Syrian cities of Antioch, Damascus, and Jerusalem (in the process executing over 50,000 Christians and carting the "true cross" off to Ctesiphon), swept out to Egypt, where Persians had not ruled since before Alexander, captured the Anatolian crossroads of Ankara, and besieged Constantinople itself.

In this time of grave danger, the Romans in Asia Minor were fortunate to have the aid of a new ally, the kingdom of Khazaria. The Khazars are a fascinating, largely unsung people, who played a little-acknowledged key role in events on the Silk Road in these centuries. Their name may come from the Turkish word for *nomads*, which they were, or from another root, meaning "on the north side of the mountain," also an apt possibility, for they were often called the "people of the north" or "the kingdom of the north," beyond the Caucasus.

Who the Khazars were is something of a mystery. Some suggest that they came from Hunnish (Hsiung-nu) stock, while others believe that they were actually the K'o-sa tribe of the Uighur Turks, some of whom had been pushed westward. Some of these mystery people, a group called the Black Khazars, are described as "being dusky like the Indians." Others seem to have been fair. A ninth-century Arab description reads: " . . . their complexions are white, their eyes blue, their hair flowing and predominantly reddish, their bodies large and their natures cold. Their general aspect is wild." Still others are alleged to be fair-skinned and blue-eyed, but with dark hair, while some may have had slanted eyes. In short, these Khazars were a people of widely diverse racial stock (like most Central Asian peoples), and destined to become even more so as they expanded and brought other tribes under their rule.

But, at the time of which we are speaking, the Khazars were subject to the still-united Western Turks and had been so for long enough to have adopted their language and many of their social and political forms. It is possible that these Khazars, who occupied the important pocket along the Caspian Sea between the Caucasus and the Atil (Volga) River, were the un-named allies who had, some decades earlier, warned the Roman envoy Zemarchus of the Persian ambush awaiting him as he crossed the mountains. The Khazars did control the Derbend Pass, the main, though not the only, pathway through the Caucasus range.

In any case, the Khazars now provided much-needed assistance to the Eastern Roman Empire. As Heraclius, the Roman emperor, swept Persian forces out of Anatolia and Armenia, the Khazars poured through the Caucasus to join the attack on Mesopotamia.

The Derbend Pass, a narrow passageway through the
Caucasus Mountains near the shore of the Caspian
Sea, was the main route between Russia and Armenia.
(From Yule's *Marco Polo*, after *Tour du Monde*, drawing
by M. Moynet)

Within a few years, the Persian King Chosroes was cornered in Ctesiphon and, when he
refused to make peace, was killed by his own followers, among them his son (whose mother
had been a Roman princess). In what had become something of a holy war, the Romans
restored the "true cross" to Jerusalem. So the two Western powers made an uneasy peace.

The Eastern Roman Empire recovered its Asian lands and even gained a toehold on the
Silk Road at the Caspian Sea. Though they were apparently unsuccessful in making direct
contact with the Chinese, some of their trade goods seem to have crossed the continent. In the

620s, Chinese annals record that the king of Turfan twice presented the Son of Heaven with a lap dog from Fu-lin. Fu-lin was the name by which the Chinese would from then on know the Eastern Roman Empire. References to Li-kan or Ta-Ch'in, the great Roman Empire, gradually ceased, recognizing the shift of power from Rome—for the Chinese, from Antioch—to Constantinople.

The Eastern Roman Empire itself was reorganized in this period. Though many of the people still thought of themselves as Rome's heirs, and called their language *Rom*, in truth the empire was now largely Greek-speaking. In a sense, it was the last of Alexander's successor states. In token of this, the state is generally referred to after this period as the Byzantine Empire, Byzantium being the name of the old Greek city Constantinople had replaced.

Still a major market for Eastern goods and supplier of Europe, the Byzantine Empire seems to have traded primarily north of the Black Sea, through the now-prosperous Khazars, and the network of Central Asian traders who operated in the Turkish cities north of the T'ien Shan, notably Almalik and Beshbalik, once China had them under control. As always, when peace prevailed, this was by far the preferred route. Despite their modest presence on the Silk Road proper, the Byzantine Greeks probably did not rely on it for their main supply of Eastern goods, for Persia was still very much troubled.

★   ★   ★

The peace with the Byzantine Empire may have left the Persians in possession of their eastern territories, but the crowning of a dozen kings in the next 14 years showed only too clearly the desperate pass to which Persia had come. By 632, when the last Persian king, Yazdagird, took the throne, all hope of saving the empire was lost, for in that year died the prophet Mohammed (himself a trader and caravan leader on the Incense Road between Arabia and Syria, before he received his revelation).

Within the year, Moslem armies were on the road, taking Mohammed's faith by force into the heartland of Western Asia. In just two short decades, they overpowered Syria, Mesopotamia, Egypt, much of Armenia, and most of Persia. Only in the mountainous slot where the Silk Road passed south of the Caspian Sea were the Iranian tribes strong enough to hold their independence for a time, in the kingdom called Tabaristan. As Darius before Alexander, so Yazdagird fled before the Arabs to the East, reaching as far as Merv, where he, too, was killed by his own followers. His desperate letters to other Asian kings pleading for help were unavailing. So ended the Persian Empire, in 651 A.D.

Yazdagird's son, Peroz, took refuge in Bactria (then called Tokhara) and urgently called for help from the T'ang emperor. This was not altogether surprising, for China and Persia had kept in contact over the centuries. Chinese annals record the arrival of Persian embassies in the years 461, 518, and 528, with another in the second quarter of the sixth century and another in the second decade of the seventh century—most likely only a sampling of the contacts between

China and Persia. That much is suggested by a Chinese gift to the Persian king Chosroes at some time before his death in 579, described as:

> . . . a silk robe on which was represented a king in the same costume as the king of Persia, wearing his royal garments, with a crown on his head and surrounded by his serving-men, each of whom held a robe of material brocaded in gold to represent a similar personage. The ground of this robe was of sky-blue silk; it was enclosed in a golden box.

With Chinese aid, Peroz in 661 re-entered Persia and pushed as far as Ctesiphon, on the Tigris. But he did not long retain his throne. Within seven years, he was again in exile, in Ch'ang-an. In 674 the Chinese offered him a ceremonial office at the palace at the silk city, but he left China within the year to try once more to regain his throne. This attempt was even less successful than the last. After a final, crushing defeat by the Arabs at Balkh (formerly Bactra) in 707, Peroz and his son, Narseh, returned to Ch'ang-an to live and die as landless exiles.

They were not without compatriots in China, however. Many people from Persia and Turkestan fled before the Arab onslaught, and the Silk Road became, to some extent, a highway for refugees. The move had actually begun some time earlier. During their final wars with the Byzantine Empire, Persians had harshly persecuted Christians in their territory, regarding them as potential traitors. Many accepted the shelter of Constantinople and helped to set the tone of the reformed Byzantine Empire. But many Western Asian Christians—being Nestorians, and therefore considered heretics by the orthodox church of Byzantium—headed not west but east along the Silk Road into Central Asia, proselytizing all the way to China. The arrival in China of one Christian from Persia in 635 was recorded 150 years later on a stele in Ch'ang-an (rediscovered in the 17th century). It reads:

> At the time when T'ai-tsung, the brilliant emperor, was gloriously and splendidly beginning his prosperous reign, governing the people with far-sighted wisdom, there was in the land of Ta-Ch'in a man of high virtue named A-lo-pen, who, upon the augury of blue clouds, brought hither the true writings. After studying the harmony of the winds, he hastened to confront the dangers and difficulties and arrived in Ch'ang-an . . .

Though renowned primarily for his military prowess, T'ai-tsung was a remarkably tolerant ruler in many respects. Three years later (and seven years before he would provide Hsüan-tsang with such a magnificent homecoming reception) he proclaimed:

> The way has more than one name, and wise men have more than one method. Knowledge is such that it may suit all countries, so that all creatures may be saved. The

virtuous A-lo-pen came from afar, bringing books and pictures to our capital . . . It is the salvation of living creatures, the riches of mankind, and it is right that this teaching should spread freely through the world . . . Let the local officials, therefore, build a monastery of Ta-Ch'in in the I-ning quarter of the capital for 21 regular monks.

So people whose faith tied them to Jerusalem found a home in Ch'ang-an.

In the face of Arab armies, many other Persians also headed eastward, especially toward the thriving caravan cities of Sogdiana, and some as far east as China. Among them were Manichaeans, who had survived as a minority within the Persian Empire and had also been spreading eastward. Unlike the Nestorians, who did not settle in large numbers along the Silk Road, and therefore had relatively few converts along the Tarim routes, the Manichaean missionaries worked slowly along the northern route of the Tarim, establishing their influence in oasis after oasis. As the Buddhists had a chain of oases along the southern Tarim route, so the Manichaeans soon were powers on the northern route, battling the Buddhists for religous

This fresco from Bezeklik, near Turfan, honors elaborately dressed Persian emigrants who worshipped at the temple. (From *Chotscho*, by Albert von le Coq, Berlin)

dominance. The Manichaean religion seems to have reached China in the late sixth century, though the first Manichaean missionary direct from the West apparently arrived only in 694.

Sogdians, too, fled eastward before the Arabs. Sogdian merchants had over the previous centuries been establishing colonies throughout the Tarim, not only on China's doorstep but also in Loyang, the eastern capital. In their wake others, apparently seeking more land, had emigrated to found fortified towns on streams and at oases from Samarkand to the Lop Nor. The collapse of the Persians and the arrival of the Arabs merely spurred this ongoing process. These newcomers made some striking contributions to the culture of East-Central Asia.

It was also the Sogdians who brought to East Asia the use of *qanats* (also called *kariz*), underground irrigation tunnels that allowed growers to bring life-giving water sometimes tens of miles to desert fields, without losing all the moisture to the dry air. Widely used in the arid parts of the Persian Empire (though they were later allowed to fall into decay and disrepair), these *qanats* allowed the Sogdians to create lush orchards and fields where there had been only wasteland. Succulent melons and fruits of all kinds became popular products of the northern oases, including exotic peaches from Sogdiana, large ("the size of a goose's egg"), yellow, and tasty. Gifts of these "Golden Peaches of Samarkand" so pleased the Chinese emperor that some of the special fruit trees were brought along the Silk Road and planted in the imperial orchards of Ch'ang-an.

But most of all the Sogdians loved grapes and the fine wines made from the fruit. One of their cities in the Lop Nor was even known to the Chinese as "the wine-lover's city." The Chinese had known and grown grapes since Chang Ch'ien's first visit to the West, seven centuries before, but they had not used them for making wine—perhaps because the vines they had imported grew small grapes little suited for winemaking. But the Sogdian "mare's teat" grapes were so large and juicy that the Chinese actually wrote poems praising these "grapes of the Royal Mother [of the West]." From T'ang times on, the Chinese made wine from grapes, though it never supplanted the native wines, such as those made from rice.

The Sogdians were also superb metalworkers. During their long sojourn under Turkish rule, they had learned all the skills possessed by these famous ironworkers. To this they had added their own special touches, drawing as well on Western Asian techniques that had reached them through the Persians. The result was all their own. Sogdian armor, the specialty of these metalsmiths, was famous throughout Asia. Samarkand armorers supplied Asian warriors with pliable coats of mail for centuries; during the T'ang period, this type of mail replaced the scale armor used in China since Han times.

The Sogdians also brought eastward the glassmaking techniques they had used in the great glass-houses near Samarkand. The Chinese had long wished to know how to make the high-quality glass, especially the colored glass, they so desired—and had continued to import—from the West. They finally learned the secret techniques from the Sogdians in the fifth century. The Chinese never became well known for their glassworking, however, perhaps because in the seventh century they developed the techniques for making the true porcelain for which they are so noted throughout the world.

The Sogdians brought other skills, such as wood-carving and weaving; whether or not they brought along the Silk Road a new method of weaving, as some have suggested, is unclear. But certainly the designs and styles imported by Sogdians and other Western immigrants much influenced Chinese artists and artisans in the centuries of T'ang, as when Persian motifs like repeated pairs of peacocks and winged horses began to appear in Chinese art and design—as a little later they influenced design in medieval Europe.

★   ★   ★

China as a whole was much more affected by its contact with Westerners in T'ang times than at any previous time in its history. Buddhist writings and relics continued to flow along the pilgrimage routes from India to China, via both Tibet and Khotan. With Indian influence at its height, Sanskrit works on medicine, astronomy, mathematics, and music also found their way to China. Their influence was magnified when T'ang artisans in the early eighth century developed the techniques of block printing. Whole pages of text or art were carved on wooden blocks, from which multiple copies could be printed, either single sheets or, using successive blocks, whole books—not in leaves, as with modern Western books, but on rolled scrolls. The Chinese had centuries earlier learned to make paper from rags, a far cheaper medium for printing than silk, or parchment or papyrus, as in the West. The combination of block printing and paper meant that Western, as well as Chinese, works could easily be disseminated to a much wider public. The Chinese also printed paper playing cards and money, both of which much astonished and intrigued generations of Western visitors.

With all these influences from the West, the great cities at the end of the Silk Road, Ch'ang-an and Loyang, were truly cosmopolitan. Loyang, with over a million inhabitants, was at the crossroads of the Silk Road and the Ambassador's Road, which ran south to the seaport of Canton (Nan Hai). The Persians had continued an active sea trade on the Spice Route to southern China; after a brief hiatus, this was inherited and expanded by the conquering Arabs, who became consummate sailors. Native officials, foreign ambassadors, and merchants of every description found their way from the south to Loyang, discovering there gracious palaces and parks, a great complex of bazaars called the Southern Market, and temples for their alien religions, be they Zoroastrian, Christian, Buddhist, Manichaean, or, later, Moslem.

Ch'ang-an, the terminus of the Silk Road itself and the main destination for most Western travelers, was almost twice as large as Loyang, with nearly two million inhabitants. Sogdians, Turks, Persians, Indians, Arabs, and all the peoples of Central Asia crowded into the great Western Market, where foreign merchants generally sold their goods. (The Eastern

Market was tonier and less roisterous, purveying primarily to the rich and well-placed native Chinese in nearby mansions.) Following the Asian pattern, the markets were divided into innumerable bazaars, each for a different commodity, such as iron, silk, drugs, the newly popular tea, or saddles. Here, too, were found the moneylenders, most of them Uighur Turks, who reaped for themselves the ill-feeling generally engendered in borrowers by lenders. So many foreign merchants gathered in Ch'ang-an that the T'ang rulers even appointed a special "official to the Sārthavāk" (the Indian word for caravan leader) to oversee their activities in China.

The Chinese government placed foreigners under many restrictions. They were generally obliged to live in segregated quarters within the city. Casual fraternization with the natives was not encouraged, especially because the government knew that merchants were likely to form attachments and then leave China. To protect the victims of such temporary arrangements, the emperor decreed in 628 that if a foreign man took a Chinese wife or mistress, he had to remain in China. The Chinese mate could not join him in the West, nor could he return alone. (This despite the fact that Chinese princesses had, for centuries, been sent around Asia to cement short-lived political alliances.)

Foreign merchants were also hampered by government monopolies on many key items. In 714, for example, it was made illegal for individual Chinese citizens to sell or export to foreigners yak tails, pearls, iron, gold, or fine silks, including tapestries, damasks, gauzes, and elaborately embroidered fabrics. The Chinese government also strictly controlled materials brought into the country. Goods thought unhealthy for the public, morally or materially, were confiscated; those thought to be counterfeit or adulterated brought the same result, and possibly a prison sentence for the importer. Even allowed imports could only be sold in special markets under strict government supervision, where officials often took a hefty share for "custom duties."

For all this, foreign merchants continued to come to China, and some profited handsomely. They made their foreign quarters as lively and alluring as any such quarter in a modern port. Buddhists from India or Central Asia could find in the northern Chinese cities religious dances and entertainments at many temples. Visitors from afar could find in the taverns Western performers who both entertained them and reminded them of the delights of home. Many a Western barmaid or courtesan was employed in these taverns to attract lonely merchants and help divest them of their money.

But, as in many modern cities, the foreign quarters were also magnets for native citizens seeking the frisson of the exotic. So, affluent Chinese were drawn to the Westernized taverns of Ch'ang-an and other cities, and the poets among them immortalized the exotic performers—beautiful women and young boys from Kucha, Kashgar, Samarkand, Persia—in the literature of the time. One wrote of the "Western houri [who] beckons with her white hand, inviting the stranger to intoxicate himself with a golden beaker." Some of these glamorous creatures seem to live and breathe in the words of over 1,200 years ago, as does this Western woman described by the poet Li Po:

> That Western houri with features like a flower—
> She stands by the wine-warmer, and laughs with the breath
>   of spring
> Laughs with the breath of spring,
> Dances in a dress of gauze!

Men-about-town who wandered into the foreign quarter were not the only ones to be influenced by the exotic. The Chinese court itself attracted innumerable Westerners. Many of these were, of course, emissaries of foreign nations. But many were, in effect, "human tribute" sent by Western rulers hoping to ingratiate themselves with the Chinese emperor. China's rulers had long been fascinated by the odd and unusual, in humans as well as things. So Western kings sent to Ch'ang-an people unusual in themselves, such as a dwarf from Samarkand or a woman whose mottled skin was said to resemble Buddhist statues and temples. Others sent as "human tribute" had special skills, such as wise men from the West, orchestras from defeated lands (whose music the Chinese considered part of their booty), gifted performers of all sorts—singers, dancers, instrumentalists, tightrope walkers, fire-eaters, acrobats, contortionists, illusionists.

Many of these came eastward of their own free will, for Western dance, music, and conjuring found a wide and enthusiastic audience within China. Appreciation of these Western delights was not limited to the rich and wellborn, for the early T'ang victories had brought into China thousands of Central Asian prisoners-of-war, some of whom had married Chinese war widows. Among the most popular players were the musicians and dancers of Kucha and Samarkand, such as the Sogdian "twirling girls," dressed in scarlet brocade robes and loose trousers of bright green damask, who danced atop a series of rolling balls.

Nor were the Chinese content with simply being spectators. From the earliest decades of T'ang rule, they increasingly adopted Western styles. Court ladies learned to dance like the Sogdian twirling girls. Chinese singers and musicians learned to play in Western modes using unfamiliar instruments. Poets and other writers enshrined the most popular performers in adoring word portraits. "Geisha of Chāch," by poet Po Chü'i, for example, describes two young women dancers from Chāch (near Tashkent) dressed in bare-shouldered gauze dresses with silver sashes, crimson brocade shoes, and bell-tipped peaked hats:

> Matched pair spread flat—the brocaded mats unroll;
> Linked beats of triple sounds—the painted drums drive on.
> Red wax candles are taken away, peach petals rise;

Purple net shirts are set in motion—the Chāch [dancers] come!
Girdles droop from gilded thighs, flowered waists are heavy,
Hats revolve with golden bells, snowy faces turn.

The art of the time, too, reflected the passion for things Western. Painters and sculptors often depicted people of Western ethnic stock, in Central Asian costumes and in foreign styles, notably Greco-Indian and Persian. The literati of the time followed suit by writing exotic

Central Asian paintings on silk often had religious themes, like this one from the Caves of the Thousand Buddhas near Tunhuang. (Ninth century, from Musée Guimet)

travel romances, among them many based on the travels of pilgrims like Hsüan-tsang, often merging them with references to earlier mythical figures such as the Royal Mother of the West.

Western influence did not stop even there. In China's northwestern cities, especially Ch'ang-an and Loyang, many Chinese citizens adopted Central Asian styles of dress. Veiled headdresses, designed to protect against the Central Asian dust, were worn by highborn men and women as they rode about town on horseback in the early seventh century. Later on, women who should by tradition have been riding in screened carriages, rode out alone, with veils traded in for open-faced hoods, Turkish caps, or even no hats at all. The boldest among them adopted the desert fashion of trousers and riding boots. Hats, blouses, trousers, skirts, hairstyles, all of these bore the stamp of Turkish or Persian styles in the T'ang period.

Nor were men immune to Western fashions in dress or life-style. The poet Po Chu-i, who immortalized the dancers of Chāch, was so taken by Central Asian styles that he forsook his fine city house for life in two light blue Turkish felt tents set up in his courtyard. (Archaeologist Marc Aurel Stein would do much the same in northern India over a thousand years later.) Even the son of the renowned emperor-general, T'ai-tsung, was so taken with Western exotica that he spoke only Turkish and lived in a Turk-like camp set up outside the palace.

It was during the early T'ang, when the Silk Road to the West was wide open, that China was most under the influence of Central Asian culture. The arts and religions brought from the West, and then infused with Chinese spirit, were passed on to others even farther east. For under the T'ang, the Silk Road stretched not only to Korea, which had been brought under Chinese rule, but also to Japan. These two countries, which embraced Buddhism with fervor, sent many students to China to study both religion and the arts. So it was that, long after Buddhism had died in India and been transformed in China, and after Central Asian dancers had come under the more austere bans of the Islamic religion, Buddhist rituals and Central Asian dances would still be performed in Japan—where today at Sho-sho-in is one of the finest surviving repositories of T'ang art, including many Buddhist images painted on fine silk.

★   ★   ★

The Silk Road, which had been the main avenue for this massive cultural invasion from the West, also brought China closer to the Mediterranean countries than ever before. The Chinese had been unable to establish direct contact with Fu-lin, the Byzantine Empire. But in 643, with the accession of the T'ang, the annals record that Fu-lin sent Emperor T'ai-tsung an embassy bearing an expensive present. Whether the ambassador traveled via the Iranian Plateau, during those few decades when Persian weakness allowed the Romans an opening onto the Silk Road at the Caspian Sea, or whether (as seems more likely) the ambassador circled northward around the Caspian Sea through Khazaria on the way east, is unclear. But this seems to have been the first direct contact between China and the Roman, now Byzantine, Empire.

It was followed by other Fu-lin embassies in 667, 711, and 719, so the annals tell us. Byzantine sources do not allow us to confirm this, and the ambassadors may in any case have come from provincial governors or even have been private merchant adventurers, in the ancient Asian tradition. The Chinese annals were, at least, accurate enough to record the siege of the capital of Fu-lin—Constantinople—by the Arabs in the 670s. The eighth century Fu-lin embassies could not have come via the Iranian Plateau, for the Arabs had by then taken all of it except the mountain fastnesses of Tabaristan; more likely they came to China via Khazaria, following a route well north of Moslem incursions. The Khazars themselves sent ambassadors to China. This is not surprising for they had, by the early eighth century, established a considerable trading empire.

In the middle of the seventh century—in the years when Hsüan-tsang had just returned to China and T'ai-tsung was consolidating his power in the East—the Khazars rapidly expanded from their small corner of the Caspian. The better to defend themselves against the Arabs, they established a new capital atop the Caspian Sea at Atil, near the mouth of the river of the same name, which we know as the Volga. Trade, not agriculture or other natural resources, always being the mainstay of the Khazar Empire, it is no coincidence that the rapid growth of the empire occurred when trade from the East was mainly following a northern route: from the Turkish steppe cities dipping south to Transoxiana and then north around the Caspian and westward across the steppe to the Crimea, and then by ship to Constantinople, still the main market for Eastern goods.

The Khazar expansion indeed followed the outline of this trans-Asian trade. By 650, the Khazars had extended their power to the east, down between the Caspian and Aral Seas to where the Sogdian trading cities operated in a kind of limbo, not at that time directly in the power of either the Arabs or the Chinese, but rightly watchful of both. To the north the Khazars pushed up the Atil, the Dnieper, and the Don, bringing under their rule such disparate peoples as the Bulgars, the Alans, and the Magyars. But most important, they pushed westward along the Black Sea's north coast, eventually controlling the swath from the Caucasus almost to the Danube, except for the Byzantine outposts on the southern tip of the Crimea. They became the lords of the fertile region we now know as the Ukraine, and the Caspian Sea was known as the Sea of the Khazars.

The Khazars throughout this period and the centuries to come maintained a close, though not always untroubled, alliance with the Byzantine Empire. The Byzantine Greeks were far weaker than their luxurious capital might suggest, and the partnership was by no means always in their favor. Constantinople was under siege by the Arabs from 674 to 678, and gained its deliverance only through the development and use of the deadly chemical called Greek fire, which was rained down on the heads of the besiegers. (Greek fire would be Constantinople's secret weapon for centuries, until the city fell in 1453, when the formula was lost, along with the method of making Phoenician purple and other such secrets of the ancient world.) The empire as a whole was badly drained by the continuing defensive wars against the

Moslems. Nor was the leadership all that could have been desired. In 695, the population became so disaffected with the Emperor Justinian II that he was forced into exile, taking refuge first in the Byzantine port of Cherson, in the southern Crimea, and then seeking the protection of the Khazars, where he married the sister of the Khazar khagan. Not receiving the wholehearted support he sought, however, Justinian turned to the still-independent western Bulgars, who helped him regain his throne—though he made an ignominious re-entry into Constantinople by crawling through a water pipe.

In the end the Khazars helped bring about Justinian's final downfall, and virtually hand-picked his successor on the Byzantine throne, in 711. Two decades later, another Byzantine prince married a Khazar princess, who was given the Greek name of Irene; her son later ruled in Constantinople as Leo the Khazar. Considering the closeness of these two empires, and their complementary desires regarding the luxuries of the East—one to receive and the other to supply—it would not be surprising if they sent ambassadors to China, to attempt to ease trade along the Silk Road. That no Western records survive of such embassies is equally unsurprising, for Western Asia continued to be troubled terrain.

In the full flush of their successes, the Khazars surged across the Caucasus in the 680s to plunder Armenia, taking booty and prisoners and then retiring across the Caucasus. Other incursions followed. The Khazars and the Islamic army met directly in 723 when a Khazar force of 30,000 soldiers routed the Moslems; in 730 the Khazars even reached as far as Mosul on the northern Tigris River. From their capital at Damascus, the Moslems felt seriously threatened and, gathering their reserves, launched a counterattack, pushing the Khazars back across the Caucasus and—in what was immortalized as the "Raid of the Courser"—pursuing them all the way back to their capital at Atil. There the Moslem generals gave the Khazars a choice: conversion to Islam or death. The Khazar kaghan chose to live and was sent two religious teachers to show the way to Islam.

Once out on the open steppe, with the Khazars defeated, the Moslem armies had out-flanked the Byzantine Empire and all Europe was open to them. That Constantinople did not fall and Europe become Moslem (if only for a time and by force) may be one of the great quirks of history. For, without even leaving an occupying force, the Moslem general returned across the Caucasus, perhaps fearing that his supply line might be cut. (His fear was proper, since the Umayyad caliphs ruling the Moslem world from Damascus were beset by revolt and would fall just a dozen years later, in 750.) The Khazars quickly shook off any pretense of being a Moslem nation and, regaining their strength and power in the region, barred future Moslem armies from attempting to cross the Caucasus.

★   ★   ★

The effect of religious conflict in the region was not anticipated. In about 720, the Byzantine Emperor Leo the Isuarian decreed that all Jews in the empire should be forcibly converted to Christianity. Erstwhile religious tolerance in the Moslem world was also ending. Mohammed himself had had close ties to both Christianity and Judaism, to which his own religion is closely related; even his personal physician was a Jew. Under the Umayyad caliphs who ruled for most of the century following his death, Jews and Christians were more tolerated than persecuted, thought they were, at best, third-class citizens, paying heavy taxes from which Moslems were exempt.

Even converted Moslems were no better than second-class citizens, for only Arab Moslems were allowed into the ruling aristocracy. The disaffection engendered by this discrimination against non-Arab Moslems partly contributed to the overthrow of the Umayyads and their replacement by the Abbasid caliphs. These were (at the start) Moslem fundamentalists, no longer purely Arab but aspiring to establish a theocracy, a world in which religion was inseparable from government.

The growing religious intolerance in both the Byzantine and Moslem empires led to a new wave of emigrations; Jews, Christians, and even Moslems fled to countries on the fringes of these rigid lands. A goodly number found their way across the Caucasus to Khazaria, where their arrival had a marked effect. Both the Byzantine Christians and the Arab Moslems had tried to win Khazaria to their own religion, with no great success, even though the land included believers of both persuasions. But the new emigration seems to have brought to Khazaria a substantial number of believers in another religion: Judaism. And it is in this period—about 20 years after Leo's edict against Byzantine Jews and about three years after the Moslems' abortive attempt at converting them—that the Khazars apparently adopted Judaism, the only country in history known to do so. Arab chronicler Dimashqi, writing in about 1327, noted that in the days of the Abbasids, the Moslem emperor Harun al-Rashid:

> . . . forced the Jews to emigrate. They came to the Khazar country, where they found an intelligent but untutored race and offered them their religion. The inhabitants found it better than their own and accepted it.

The whole of Khazaria was not converted, nor was the population forced to adopt Judaism, but many of the ruling aristocrats and merchants apparently became "proselytes." (So they were called in the records of Spanish Jews, who became much interested in this Jewish state and in later centuries attempted to learn more about it, as a possible refuge for Jews from other persecuted lands.)

In truth, Khazaria became a multi-religious state. Arab geographer Mas'udi, writing in the 940s, explained:

> In this city [Atil] are Moslems, Christians, Jews and pagans. The Jews are the king, his attendants and the Khazars of his kind. The king had already become a Jew in the

Open mosques like this one were once a common sight along the central portions of the Silk Road. (By Sven Hedin, from his *Through Asia*, 1899)

Caliphate of Harun al-Rashid, and there joined him Jews from all the lands of Islam and from the country of the Greeks. Indeed the king of the Greeks at the present time . . . has converted the Jews in his kingdom to Christianity and has coerced them . . . Many Jews took flight from the country of the Greeks to Khazaria.

Multi-ethnic and multi-religious it would remain. Writing in about 932, the Moslem chronicler Istākhrī noted that most of Khazaria's people were Moslems, Christians, or "idolators"—which could mean Buddhist, Zoroastrian, Manichaean, or even animist—but that the smallest group, Jews, included the king and his court. Indeed, in later centuries, Khazaria's army was made up largely of Moslems.

The capital city, Atil, reflected this multi-faceted society. According to Istākhrī:

The eastern half of [Atil] . . . contains most of the merchants, the Moslems, and the merchandise. The western [bank of the river] is reserved for the king, his attendants, his army and the pure-bred Khazars.

This was no classical city, leaving behind ruins to dazzle travelers and archaeologists of modern times. Rather Atil was more fitted to its people, semi-nomadic in origin and itinerant traders in main industry. Even as late as 932, two centuries after the Khazars had driven all the way into Mesopotamia, their city still reflected their Central Asian origins, as Istākhrī describes:

> Atil is in two parts, one west of the river called Atil, which is the larger, and the other east of it. The king lives in the western part . . . It is surrounded by a wall, though the buildings spread beyond. Their houses are felt tents except a small number built of clay. They have markets and baths. In the town are people of the Moslems, more than 10,000 it is said. They have about thirty mosques. The king's castle is at a distance from the river-bank and is of brick. No one else owns a brick building, the king not permitting anyone to build with brick. The wall already mentioned has four gates, one of which opens on the river and another on the steppe at the back of the city. The other two also open on the steppe.

Others reported that the king's palace was on an island in the river, and that there was a bridge of ships from it to one of the banks.

Khazar caravans curved around the Caspian and down toward the Oxus River to the region then coming to be known as Khwarizm. From there Sogdian and other Central Asian caraveneers still handled the trade eastward to China. This trade seems to have been at its height early in the eighth century, when the Arabs were still entangled with civil wars and the Chinese held the Tarim. That would change, making Khazaria a less vital link in the trans-Asian trade, though the Khazar trading state continued in strength for another two centuries, protecting Europe from incursions out of the Near East and Central Asia.

★   ★   ★

The changes, when they came, were sudden and dramatic. Throughout the first few decades of the eighth century, the small kingdoms of the Pamirs and beyond had looked to the Chinese to protect them. As the Moslems—like many conquerors, drawing strength from those they conquered—crossed the steppe and pushed toward the Pamirs, princes from cities like Bukhara, Samarkand, Tashkent, and Balkh pledged their loyalty to the Chinese emperor and begged for assistance. To their aid China sometimes sent subject Western Turkish tribes, and on rare occasions an army of Chinese soldiers. China's influence and aid went even farther afield in these decades, as forces were sent to the aid of small countries on the main Buddhist pilgrim routes, which were being cut by rebel bands from the Tibetan Plateau. As late as 750, Chinese forces were acting on behalf of allies in Kashmir and Kabul, attempting also to prevent the Tibetans and Arabs from joining forces, as they threatened to do. This seemed the high-water mark of Chinese influence.

Then, suddenly, China's empire collapsed. A leading Chinese general, inspired by personal greed to execute the king of Tashkent, precipitated a fearful battle. The Tashkent heir appealed to the Arabs at Bukhara and Samarkand for aid in avenging his family's honor against the Chinese. The result was a face-to-face confrontation between the Chinese army, war-weary and stretched thin, and the Arabs, young, powerful, and riding on the new wave of Abbasid successes. Allied with the Arabs were the Tibetans (the name itself was given them by the Arabs), who were ever more determined to burst out of the confines of their arid plateau wasteland and break Chinese power in Central Asia. These were joined by some of the Western Turks who, after the Tashkent incident, had revolted against the Chinese army.

In the summer of 751, the two sides met on the banks of the Talas River in northern Turkestan. There, in one of the most devastating defeats it had ever suffered, the Chinese army was broken. Thousands of Chinese prisoners-of-war—soldiers and artisan-colonists—were taken, many of them to Samarkand. Their capture had a particular significance in the history of Western civilization, for among the many skilled artisans captured were papermakers, who taught the West their manufacturing techniques. Paper would gradually replace the expensive and cumbersome parchment and papyrus used in the West until then, laying the practical basis for the later explosion of learning and dissemination that culminated in the European Renaissance.

Of less importance in human history, perhaps, but more to our story, many Chinese silkworkers were captured after Talas and transported into Moslem lands. The peoples of the Near East had continued to supply some of their own needs and Europe's with homegrown silk, but the quality of the silk never equaled that of China, which had continued to supply the finer silks desired by the West. We are not even sure when or if the Western silkworkers learned to keep the silk moth from bursting the bonds of its chrysalis. But such questions were now moot, for China's expert silkworkers passed on their millennia-old techniques of sericulture to the Moslems, whose domain included many expert Syrian and Persian weavers.

All along the Silk Road, wherever the temperature range was suitable, as up in Tabaristan and in some oasis cities of Transoxiana, silk was produced. Merv even made a specialty of producing silkworm eggs for export to other Moslem provinces. From this time on the Moslems produced most of the silk for their own lands and for Western Europe. (Byzantium's silk industry stagnated.) And it was through the Moslems that sericulture and fine silkweaving were brought to Western Europe, first in Moslem Spain and Sicily. China's silk more often went to supply Central Asia's desires. For a time, however, all the producers would co-exist—and how far their silk traveled! A French religious manuscript from the time of Charlemagne has survived with leaves of silk inserted to protect the parchment. Modern analysts have concluded that four of the silk leaves are Chinese, six Moslem, and at least three Byzantine.

For the Moslems, the main impact of the Talas River battle was technological. They pushed over the Pamirs to take Kashgar, but did not seriously attempt to penetrate the Tarim Basin. But for the Chinese the Talas River defeat was devastating; suddenly the great empire of the East had become impotent. Once this power vacuum had been created, the Tibetan tribes overran the Tarim Basin and the Kansu Corridor. The city of Tunhuang, taken in around 766, came so much under their influence that for many centuries thereafter it was named "Little Tibet." As the Tibetans moved across the Tarim to the oases on the northern route, they brought with them their own Lamaist version of Buddhism, which now became widespread in Central Asia. At one point Tibetans even advanced as far as Ch'ang-an, being pushed back beyond the Jade Gate only with some difficulty. The pilgrim routes to India were cut; trade, on the southern route especially, was much diminished in these unsettled times.

Nor was this all. In the same year as the Talas debacle, a Chinese army in the north was routed by a people known as the Khitan. Foreshadowing things to come, this was a tribe of Mongols, some of the earliest to push out of the north and bedevil the Chinese. They are perhaps best known to us today through the Turkish version of their name: Khitai. Long after they had themselves been pushed on by other invaders, this name remained attached to the region, being transformed much later by Marco Polo into "Cathay," the name by which romantics for centuries knew northern China.

Court poet Li Po depicted the devastation to be found in these times along China's once-flourishing borders:

> *The Great Wall, which separates China from the desert,*
> *Winds on into infinity.*
> *On all stretches of the frontier*
> *No towns have been left standing.*
> *Here and there a few scattered human bones*
> *Seem to express their everlasting hatred.*

The country very much felt the drain resulting from years of war and the loss of the riches once brought to them by the Central Asian territories. When the Sogdian-Turkish general who had led the Chinese army to defeat against the Khitai openly revolted against the emperor, he found so much support among the population that a civil war raged in China from 755 to 763. The T'ang emperor was forced to abandon Ch'ang-an and Loyang to the rebels without a fight and flee southwest to the mountain fastnesses of Szechuan.

In the end, his successor succeeded in retaking and holding Ch'ang-an and Loyang only with the help of forces from Central Asia, among them Uighur Turks and—in one of those lightning changes of alliance characteristic to the region—even some Arabs, just seven years after the Talas River battle. Some of the Arabs stayed on in China to form the nucleus of a small Moslem community. The Uighur Turks, recently from Outer Mongolia, partly abandoned their nomadic life and more or less settled in the region north of the Kansu Corridor.

In the course of these moves, the Uighur kaghan was converted to the Manichaean faith; and through the Uighurs this religion, a blend of various Western religions with a special

Persian twist, which had slowly moved along the Silk Road over several centuries, now spread as far as the Mongolian Steppe. And, as the Chinese had adopted Greco-Indian art along with Buddhism, the Uighurs adopted Persian art styles with the Persian-derived religion. So cities like Turfan, once the home of avid Buddhists, like the prince who tried to keep Hsüan-tsung from his pilgrimage, now sported Manichaean frescoes in the Persian style.

The Uighurs had long played a role in China, as the main moneylenders in the international markets. Now, having restored the T'ang princes to their throne, they were even more favored. They were allowed to build Manichaean temples in several major cities, helping to spread their newly adopted religion among the Chinese. And, in the ancient tradition, Chinese princesses were sometimes wed to Uighur princes. The Uighurs became increasingly sinicized and, long after their formal ties with China were broken, would preserve in their art, literature, and life-style traces of this close tie with the great civilization of the East. Because few nomadic peoples could read or write, the Uighurs also became scribes and administrators to most of Central Asia.

The T'ang dynasty may have been restored to the throne in northern China in 763, but it would never recover its power, though it survived for a century and a half more. After the arrival of the Tibetans, the southern Tarim route was largely abandoned by long-distance trade. With the help of the Uighur Turks, the Chinese held onto the northern territories for somewhat longer. But in 790 Beshbalik, administrative center for the Chinese lands north of the T'ien Shan, was lost. Chinese forces retreated toward Turfan, only to have their leader killed by Uighurs en route "to save themselves further complications," the annals tell us. Chinese chronicler Tzu chih T'ung chien wrote of the events of 790:

> After this An-hsi [Kucha, the headquarters of the Four Garrisons] was completely isolated and no one knew what became of it. But the district of Hsi-chou [Turfan] continued to hold out bravely in order to remain faithful to the T'ang.

So the Chinese were increasingly forced to huddle behind their Great Wall, which was not always effective at barring invasion. In about 840, the Uighur Turks, defeated and pushed south by the Kirghiz Turks, forced the Tibetans out of the Kansu marches and ruled there on China's border until the 11th century. Trade continued to struggle on over the northern Tarim route of the Silk Road and over the steppe route of the T'ien Shan. But, after China's loss of hegemony, it was never the same and dwindled, with more and more of the east-west trade traveling by the Spice Route.

★   ★   ★

As so often with people under attack, the Chinese gradually grew from one of the most tolerant and open societies to a sometimes violently xenophobic one. Not that the Chinese lost so quickly their interest in the exotic; actually, with the road to the West being largely cut, they first entered a period of nostalgia for things that could no longer be. In *The Golden Peaches of Samarkand*, Edward Schafer put it this way:

> . . . the thirst for wonderful things from beyond the sea and across the
> mountains—whether for Buddhist manuscripts and medical books, or for costly brocades
> and rare wines, or perhaps just for the sight of an itinerant juggler from Turkestan—could
> no longer be readily satisfied, [so] the ancient wonder tale gained new and vigorous life,
> and furnished to the nostalgic imagination what could not be granted the senses.

The result was an extraordinary outpouring of fictional travel fantasies. Long-dead pilgrims and half-legendary traveling kings were not the sole inspirations for these tales. Even the humblest of the traders who had once gathered in Ch'ang-an's markets now inspired awe, for they had actually seen and done things that the ninth-century Chinese could only dream about. In the gray days that had followed the downfall of the Han, centuries before, China's power had still been recognized and its aid sought by many Central Asian states. But now, for the first time since Chang Ch'ien had opened the way west, China was largely cut off from intercourse with the Western Territories.

The defeats in war and the loss of trade were disastrous for the country's economy. In the 780s, the T'ang rulers appropriated a portion of every merchant's stock, to help rebuild the treasury. As a result, as René Grousset described it, Ch'ang-an "was as devastated as if it had been attacked by the barbarians."

Not all parts of China felt the loss of the overland trade equally. The southern regions, around Canton, were actually flourishing, for the Moslems had taken over Persia's trade on the Spice Route. Each year thousands of traders came from the Mediterranean world to Canton to trade. As in Ch'ang-an at the height of T'ang power, foreigners of all faiths and nationalities found their way to Canton.

Perhaps it was the very starkness of the contrast between the blasted north and the flourishing south that sparked revolutionaries in 874 to turn their attention toward the southern ports. They successfully laid siege to Canton, massacring its inhabitants, including (according to one Chinese estimate) 120,000 foreign traders—a number probably grossly inflated, but still indicative of the importance of the foreign merchant community. Warehouses were looted. In addition, the annals tell us, the rebels "cut down the mulberry trees throughout the region, so that for a long time there was no silk to send to the Arabian Empire." Returning north, the revolutionaries wreaked similar devastation on Ch'ang-an and Loyang and their citizens. The T'ang emperor was, once again, restored, and the rebels put down, only with the help of Turkish allies. But the damage remained, as the chroniclers reported: "Grass and bushes were growing in the deserted streets of the capital, which had become the home of foxes and hares."

The xenophobia of the rebels was a reflection of a more widespread temper in the country. In the 840s, with the resurgence of the old Confucian and Taoist ideas, China turned against foreign religions. Buddhism, always criticized by the Confucianists, came under an imperial ban in 845; over 4,600 temples and monasteries were shut and their devotees barred from the religious life. Nestorian Christianity and Manichaeism, whose believers were mainly of Persian or Turkish extraction, fell under the same ban. Though two decades later a new emperor, himself a Buddhist, rescinded the ban, Buddhism never revived in quite the same form. Cut off from its roots in India (where Buddhism fared badly, in any case) and from Central Asia, Buddhism developed a peculiarly Chinese cast, merging with other popular religions in the land.

China's unity would also soon be a thing of the past. Even the emperor's Turkish allies could not forestall the breakdown of order, as the land gradually fragmented into a jigsaw puzzle of provinces, each under a self-proclaimed ruler. One of these leaders, a former bandit named Chou Wen, systematically assassinated the remaining members of the T'ang royal family, in 907 announcing the end of the T'ang dynasty and the beginning of his own rule. But

The Diamond Sutra, found at the Caves of the Thousand Buddhas, is the oldest dated book—actually a scroll—in the world, printed in 868 A.D. (British Museum)

neither this bloodthirsty leader nor any of his rivals was able to reunite China, which lapsed into a feudal order much like that across the globe in contemporary medieval Europe.

Within 20 years, northern China had passed from Chinese rule into the hands of various Mongol peoples, and there it remained for another four centuries. It was one of the rival Chinese contenders who actually brought the Khitan within the Great Wall. While that contender established a new "dynasty" at Kaifeng, the Khitan settled in the northeastern lands, around the area of modern Peking. Later, when the new Chinese dynasty wished to be rid of the Khitan, the sword cut against them. The Khitan sacked Kaifeng, and temporarily established themselves there as rulers.

In 960, a new Chinese dynasty, the Sung, took the throne in Kaifeng. At this point, it was just one of several independent Chinese states, but under pressure from the various Mongol tribes over the coming centuries, the Sung dynasty moved ever farther south, eventually absorbing the other states to form a Chinese empire based far from the ancient heartland around the Wei and Huang Rivers. The ancient capitals of Ch'ang-an and Loyang never recovered their former dominance within the empire. When the Silk Road was once again opened to the West, under the Mongols, the Eastern terminus was shifted to the newly important region of Peking.

It was at some point in these turbulent centuries, probably around 1015, that some forward-thinking monks made a momentous decision. At the Caves of the Thousand Buddhas, near Tunhuang, they stored in a sealed room well over 10,000 manuscripts and silk paintings, many of which were Hsüan-tsang's own translations of Buddhist texts, patiently copied and preserved by Buddhist monks. In the centuries that followed, all memory of this vast storehouse seems to have been lost, but the precious artifacts survived in safety until the 20th century, when they were rediscovered by an appreciating world. Among the manuscripts was perhaps the oldest printed book—actually a scroll—in existence, the Diamond Sutra, dated 868. That only fragments from this period survive elsewhere, such as a printed charm from Korea dated around 770, is testimony to the importance of the monks' decision to protect their invaluable cache.

★　　★　　★

But if the eastern half of the Silk Road collapsed except for local tribe-to-tribe trade, the western half presented a very different picture. Like the two buckets of Shakespeare's *Richard II*, while that of the Chinese world sank, that of the Moslem world rose. It was no longer properly an Arab empire in Western Asia, certainly not since the rise of the Abbasid rulers in 750. In truth, it was more of a neo-Persian empire, though with an all-pervasive new state religion. The earliest Arabs to bring their faith to the cities of Mesopotamia, Iran, and Turkestan had been ill-equipped to rule the great and ancient lands they conquered. But they did find in place an administrative network of long standing, one that had been developed over successive empires, from Darius through Alexander all the way to the unfortunate Yazdagird and Peroz. This Mesopotamian and Persian infrastructure was extended under Moslem rule to the cities of Western Turkestan as well. As a result, although all Moslems had to learn at least some Arabic (translations of the Koran were not allowed), Persian increasingly became the court and literary language of the eastern Islamic world. In Turkestan itself, this was supplemented by the Turkish language, the speech of much of the local population.

The Moslems in Western Asia were also heirs to the intellectual and scientific traditions of the Persians. In addition to their own considerable traditions, the Persians were guardians of the many incomparably valuable written works brought to the Iranian Plateau by refugee Nestorian Christians. It was through these writings that ideas and techniques from Classical times reached across the Silk Road to China and, more strongly, down the Grand Road into India. The Moslems now took charge of this priceless heritage, cherishing and preserving what would later be the intellectual inspiration of Europe's Renaissance.

The Moslems of this period were not simply guardians. Quite the contrary. They made their own substantial contributions in science and literature, and in the variety of their pursuits many Moslem intellectuals fit the later European image of the "Renaissance man." The Moslem poet Omar Khayyam, for example, was also known in his own time as a mathematician and astronomer who helped reform the Moslem calendar.

What resulted was a Moslem world of considerable cultural unity. In the seventh century, tens of thousands of Arabs had followed their successful early armies to settle in Persia and Western Turkestan, in cities like Merv and Balkh. Many Persians, Turks, Sogdians, and others in these regions—once they had become reconciled to Moslem rule and no longer sought help from the Chinese—took Arabic names and converted to Islam, if only because converts paid considerably less in taxes. The Persians, playing key roles as administrators and scribes, came to have considerable importance at court, and laid the basis for the flowering of Persianized Islam.

Under the Abbasids, the center of the Moslem world was the city of Baghdad (Gift of God), founded by Caliph al-Mansur in 762 on the west bank of the Tigris (though a village named Baghdadu had existed on the site since Babylonian times, as early as 2000 B.C.). Following the pattern of great conquerors before them, these Moslems had founded their new capital at the waist of Mesopotamia, near Babylon, Seleucia, and Ctesiphon, astride the Silk Road. In a plan followed by many other new or rebuilt Moslem cities in this period, the city was built in concentric circles, with the limits defined by a wall pierced with four gates toward the four points of the compass. The roads passing through these gates crossed in the center; here were found the mosque, the palace, and the main markets—in many cities the actual crossroads was covered. But, like many another fast-growing Moslem city, Baghdad soon spread beyond its original walls, flowing over into suburbs on the east bank of the river (where the modern city is centered). At its height in the early ninth century, Baghdad was said to have a population of 2,000,000. Mesopotamia having little wood or building stone, the city was largely built of brick and tiles, in the brightly colored geometric patterns favored by the Moslems (whose religion forbids depiction of living creatures).

Baghdad was in every sense the capital of Islam. It was, in the early days when the Abbasids held sway over all Moslem lands, the political capital. It was also, secular and sacred authority being intertwined, the religious capital of Islam, as important to Moslems as Rome to the Christians. Even the Jews who still lived under Moslem rule in the Near East for a time made Baghdad their administrative center. The city was also the commercial hub of the Moslem world, as its neighboring predecessors had been for earlier empires. The site was not chosen by inadvertence, for the Moslems had taken over the existing long-distance networks that had operated in the East for centuries. To be sure, these had been disrupted by years of war, but the Moslems soon set them right again. By 720 they had organized a postal service that ran into Transoxiana. Caravanserais and staging posts for horses were refurbished along the routes, and many new ones were added.

These facilities, in truth, served both commercial and religious purposes, for every Moslem was obliged to visit the sacred city of Mecca, in southwest Arabia, once in a lifetime. Each year, around the time of Ramadan (the ninth month of Islam's shifting lunar calendar), pilgrims from throughout Moslem lands gathered to make the required journey, the *hajj*. As itinerant traders had been doing for centuries, they grouped together in large caravans for safety and took to the main roads. So it was that the Silk Road became in this period a pilgrim road once again, this time for Moslems, as *hajji* from Central Asia and Persia funneled westward, over the plateau and down to Baghdad; as earlier traders, especially in Roman times, had opened new routes across the Syrian Desert, so the Moslems dug new wells and built supply stations in the wasteland, to which sufficient water and food were carried during the pilgrimage season to provide for the religious caravans. On the far side of the Syrian Desert, the *hajji* joined the old Incense Road, now more often called the Pilgrimage Road, down the west side of the Arabian Peninsula to Mecca.

But if the pilgrimage caravans made only one round trip a year in the prescribed season, it was the traders who, as always, kept the Silk Road active all the year round. By the ninth century, some Arab traders had pushed overland to China, but the halting and troubled trade across the Tarim, though it enriched the resident Uighur Turks, was very far from what it had been in the great early days of the T'ang dynasty. As a result, the main activity on the Silk Road in this period was within the Moslem world itself, as the cities of Western Turkestan sent their wares over the Iranian Plateau and down into Mesopotamia, and some of it on by sea to India, receiving in return precious articles brought on the Spice Route from India and China.

Although the cities of Moslem Western Asia were united by culture and trade, they were not long united politically. By the ninth century the Abbasid empire had already begun to break up into a series of petty principalities. Not surprisingly, given the traditional independence of the peoples of eastern Persia, one of the first regions to break away was the stretch eastward from Rayy (formerly Rhogae, near Teheran), with its capital at Nishapur, one of the Persians' now-old "new" cities on the Silk Road. Another breakaway principality, established by the Samanids, who originated around Balkh, was centered on Bukhara and Samarkand.

These and other local capitals vied with each other, with the court in each small province or state pressing its claims in learning and literature, architecture and technology. An example of this decentralization and dissemination of culture in the Moslem Asia of this period is the city of Kath, in the state of Khwarizm, which lay along the Amu (formerly Oxus) River. Not a great city, though at that time larger than Bukhara, Kath lay off the Silk Road proper, but on the spur that fed northward toward Khazaria. In his description of Kath, the Moslem geographer Maqdisi gives us a sense of what other such cities in the region might have been like:

> The town lies to the east of the river, and contains a cathedral mosque in the midst of bazaars . . . The palace of the amir is in the centre of town; the citadel has already been destroyed by the river [erosion was to erase all trace of the old city by the end of the 10th century]; there are ariqs [canals] flowing through the midst of the town. The town is magnificent; it contains many learned men and men of letters, many wealthy persons, and many fine commodities and merchandise. The architects are distinguished for their skill; the readers of the Koran have no equals in Iraq for beauty of voice, expressiveness in recitation, deportment, and learning.

We should not think this or any such city too grand, however, for the standards of sanitation even in a magnificent city with abundant flowing water left a great deal to be desired, even by medieval standards, as Maqdisi attests:

> The town is [dirty] and contains many refuse drains, which everywhere overflow the high road. The inhabitants use the streets as latrines, and collect the filth in pits, whence it is subsequently carried out to the fields in sacks. On account of the enormous quantity of filth strangers can walk about the town only by daylight; the inhabitants kick the dirt into heaps [simply] with their feet.

★   ★   ★

Like many other religions, Islam was afflicted by sectarianism. By far the largest number of Moslems are the Sunni (literally, "orthodox"), who accept the historical succession following Mohammed's death; but a significant minority (today about 15 percent) of Moslems, the Shi'ites—meaning "sectarians"—believe that the rightful successor to Mohammed should have been his nephew Ali. Around the question of whether religious—and, in these theocratic societies, political—rule should follow within a single line

Irrigation canals like this one in a small modern town near Khotan for centuries carried water to houses and fields in Asia's desert oases. (By Sven Hedin, from his *Through Asia*, 1899)

from Mohammed or whether caliphs (literally, "successors") should be drawn from among the Moslem community, there have developed whole bodies of religious theory. The Shi'ites were, after the downfall of the Umayyad caliphate, based in the western Moslem territories, especially in Egypt. But some of their followers were also found in the eastern Sunni lands. It was some of these Shi'ite extremists, awash in a sea of rival believers, who developed a deadly approach to proselytizing and dealing with their enemies. This particular sect, which went under many names, notably the Isma'ilis, is best known to the West as the Assassins.

In the late 11th century, a Moslem named Hasan Sabah returned from a visit to the Egyptian court as an accredited Isma'ili missionary to Persia. He apparently preached with some success in Iraq and Persia, making a fair number of converts and committing what seems to have been his group's first assassination—the killing of a *muezzin* (caller to prayer) who had failed to join the sect. Soon Hasan Sabah and his followers began to seize a series of fortresses in the rugged mountains of Tabaristan along the Caspian section of the Silk Road. The best known of these fortresses was Alamut, perched on a craggy rock northwest of modern Teheran, where the leader of the sect, the Old Man of the Mountain—perhaps more properly, the Master of the Mountain—held sway.

Among the several classes of the sect's disciples was a group called the *fida'i* (devotees ready for sacrifice), who were pledged to kill anyone the Old Man of the Mountain marked for death. Some centuries later, Marco Polo reported that these *fida'i* took the drug *hashish* as part of their religious observance, hence the Western name *hashishins*, or *assassins*. Whatever role drugs actually played in the lives of these faithful, they were not simple killers. They were given elaborate training in the language, rites, and rituals of other courts and religions, for their mission was to ingratiate themselves with and win the confidence of their intended victims; established as a victim's favorite, the Assassin might maintain the disguise for months or even years before striking. If caught and forced to confess, the Assassins often named their assigned victims or worst enemies as fellow conspirators; in the atmosphere of suspicion they bred, they were then still able to succeed in their missions.

Assassins were not found only in Persia; the sect spread later into India, and was also found in many parts of Syria, notably in Aleppo and Damascus, though it is not clear whether these were under the control of the Old Man of the Mountain. In one ironic twist, in the late 12th century, a Syrian Assassin named Rashid ad-Din was sent to the fortress of Alamut; there he gained the special favor of the ruling Old Man of the Mountain, who only on his deathbed realized that Rashid ad-Din had been sent to replace him.

The Assassins at one point held at least 10 fortresses on the Iranian Plateau, and some territory in Syria as well. Though they never ruled a wide area, their presence struck proper terror in the hearts of those who ruled the land around them. And terror alone was sometimes all that was necessary to gain their will. When an 11th-century Persian ruler embarked on a mission against the Assassins, he returned to his supposedly secure tent to find pinned to the ground by a dagger a note reading: "The dagger that has opened the hard earth might well have penetrated thy softer breast. Beware!" The campaign was ended. The Assassins were rightly feared by Moslem rulers all along the Silk Road, from the Pamirs to the Mediterranean, and the terror they practiced survived the rise and fall of many a dynasty in these regions, including that of a new wave of Turks who made their mark on the region beginning in the early 11th century: the Seljuks.

Just before their striking appearance on the Silk Road, the Seljuk Turks seem to have been in some close relation to the Khazars. One tale suggests that Seljuk, leader of the people, had been orphaned and reared at the Khazar court. Another chronicle, written by 'Amid-al-Mulk in about 1045, records how the later Seljuks viewed the matter:

> As to the lineage of the Sultan—may God make him greatly victorious—it is a sufficient proof of his nobility that it ends not like the lineage of others in some unknown and obscure slave. Among his ancestors was Sarjuq [Seljuk], who struck the king of the Khazars with his sword and beat him with a mace which he had in his hand, till his horse foundered and he fell on his face. Such a deed is not done save by a free soul and a spirit that aspires above the star Capella. From him began the empire . . .

Whatever the truth of their origins, the Seljuk Turks swiftly rolled westward. Appearing in the late 10th century on the lower Syr (formerly Jaxartes) River, they took Western Turkestan by 1040 and then began their march across the Iranian Plateau. Within decades they had moved down into Mesopotamia. In 1071 they crushed the Byzantine army at Manzikert, in Asia Minor; the Byzantine Empire eventually lost Anatolia and survived primarily because of the capital's impregnable site across the sea channel of the Bosporus. Soon the Seljuk Turks had wrested the Levant and the west coast of Arabia from the Fatimid caliphs based in Egypt. The Seljuks now ruled the Silk Road from Kashgar to the Mediterranean. In this period—and partly in response to the Seljuk irruption—the Silk Road also saw the arrival of a group of a very different persuasion, small in number but powerful in influence: the Crusaders.

Since the rise of the Abbasid caliphs in the mid-eighth century, the Moslems and the Byzantine Christians had had a general accommodation in the Levant. In spite of strains and occasional outbreaks of war, still the two traded together, often through a route across the Armenian hills to Trebizond, from whence goods were taken via the Black Sea to and from Constantinople, still a major market for Eastern goods and supplier of much of Western Europe. Christian pilgrims had also begun to make the trek to the Holy Land in great numbers and were allowed by the ruling caliphs to visit Jerusalem and nearby sacred sights. But the arrival of the Seljuk Turks in the region ruptured these agreements; Byzantium was placed in jeopardy and the pilgrimage routes were cut.

Following a Byzantine appeal for help, European Christians responded with a Crusade, in the closing years of the 11th century, by which they established a number of small Christian states on the Mediterranean shore. These states centered on Antioch (long eclipsed by the Arab preference for Aleppo), Tripoli on the Lebanon shore, Edessa on the northern Euphrates, and Jerusalem. Once there, established in their new-built crusader's castles, they faced not only the Seljuk Turks but also the Assassins. The Count of Tripoli and the self-styled King of Jerusalem were both apparently killed by Assassins (probably disguised as monks) in the 12th century, though whether by order of the Old Man of the Mountain is unclear. The Knights Templar from Tripoli responded by invading Assassin territory in Syria and extracting tribute. The Assassins remained a threat, however; indeed, in later years Western as well as Eastern rulers, among them Byzantine emperors, would employ Assassins for their own nefarious purposes.

The arrival of the Crusaders in the Levant had a far wider impact, of course. The Byzantine Empire had shrunk to little more than two knobby projections—Greece and Asia Minor—reaching out toward each other like hands across the sea. But now Europeans were back on the Silk Road, as they had not been for centuries, and in place to once again make contact with the riches of the East. Not the least of these riches was Europe's own Classical heritage, preserved through the centuries by Islamic scribes, scientists, and scholars, which would now begin to flow back across the Mediterranean, through Italy, to enrich Europe. And, though religious differences were strong and feelings sometimes ran high, trade gradually resumed across the Moslem-Christian frontier. As Syrians, Greeks, Armenians, and Jews had continued to operate as merchants and caravaneers on the Silk Road under the Moslems, so they now (many having adopted Islam) acted as go-betweens in trade with the newly arrived Christians. The Europeans then were established on the western end of the Silk Road, in place for the astonishing opening to the East that would take place under—of all people—the dreaded Mongols.

CHAPTER NINE

THE AGE OF THE GREAT KHANS

In 1162, the year when the man we know as Genghis Khan was born, there was little to suggest that he would be the greatest conqueror Asia had ever known. In the course of things, it is true, the time was perhaps ripe for the rise of another of the transitory nomadic empires Central Asia had seen over the centuries. In the East, while the Sung dynasty was flowering in southern China, northern China had seen a succession of overlords, most of Mongol descent. In Central Asia, the Tibetans had fragmented in the southern Tarim and the Uighur Turks held the northern Tarim routes, while other Turkish and Tibetan tribes warred over the rest. In Western Asia, the Moslem lands were increasingly decentralized, with regional states achieving brief independence and fleeting brilliance.

The young boy Temujin was an unlikely hero (despite his name, meaning blacksmith and signifying strength). His father and grandfather may have ruled as khans, but their following had shrunk to only a few small Mongol tribes. Made fatherless at the age of nine, he fled to the very fringes of Mongol lands with his mother, brothers, a few old retainers, and some mangy herd animals. A few years later, he was taken prisoner by a local khan, who feared him as a potential rival. But through shrewdness, skillful cultivation of allies, and sheer force of will, Temujin over the next decade gathered under his rule so many

The almond groves of Samarqand
Bokhara, where red lilies blow.
And Oxus, by whose yellow sand
The grave white-turbaned
merchants go.

—Oscar Wilde

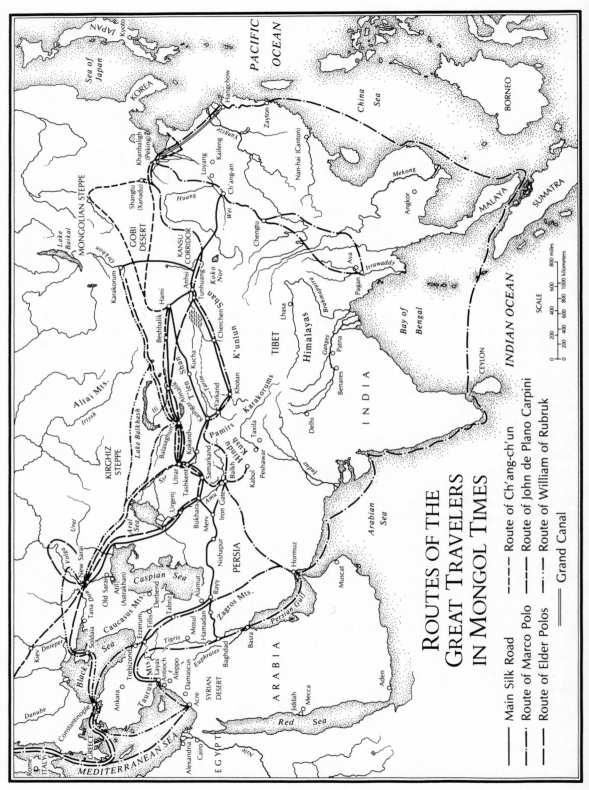

ROUTES OF THE GREAT TRAVELERS IN MONGOL TIMES

Legend	
—— Main Silk Road	--- Route of Ch'ang-ch'un
-··- Route of Marco Polo	-·-· Route of John de Plano Carpini
—— Route of Elder Polos	——— Route of William of Rubruk
	════ Grand Canal

SCALE

0 200 400 600 800 miles

0 200 400 600 800 1000 kilometers

diverse tribes that in 1196 he was proclaimed Genghis Khan, supreme, all-conquering ruler of the peoples of Mongolia.

So far Genghis Khan's rule was confined to the region around the Orkhon River, tributary of Lake Baikal. His main camp was at Karakorum, near where the Hsiung-nu and the Eastern Turks had once had their headquarters. But in the early years of the 13th century, the Mongols would subject northern China from the Pacific to the Kansu Corridor. Taking technological specialists captured in early raids and turning them on their former rulers, the Mongols pierced the Great Wall, drove the Ch'in rulers south to Kaifeng, and finally took the northern capital of Peking in 1215. With their newly acquired expertise, Genghis Khan's armies then moved westward to take most of Asia, including much of the Silk Road and the Eurasian Steppe Route as well.

Some of the Mongol's early successes in eastern Central Asia might have resulted from the fragmentation of power, for no strong, united front was willing or able to stand against them. Beyond the Pamirs in Turkestan, however, it seemed as though the Mongols must face stronger opponents.

Some of the Khitans, who had once occupied China's trading corridor in the Kansu, had been pushed westward; perhaps drawn by their experience with the Silk Road trade, they had established themselves in Eastern Turkestan. There, in the lands between Kashgar and the Issyk Kul, these Kara Khitai (Black Cathayans) had set up a kingdom on the Chinese model. In the mid-12th century they had become so powerful that they even pushed back the Moslems, taking the prime caravan cities of Bukhara and Samarkand, and setting up the first non-Moslem kingdom in Transoxiana for four centuries. The ruler of the Kara Khitai, being a partly sinicized Buddhist, transformed mosques into Buddhist temples, while granting freedom of worship to Nestorian Christians.

This was an astonishing defeat for the Moslem Seljuk Turks; the European Crusaders, who were battling for their very existence in their Euphrates castle of Edessa, near the western end of the Silk Road, were much heartened to hear of it. And—as rumors often convert fact to fancy—the hopeful Crusaders, in their own minds, apparently transformed the Kara Khitai leader Gur-khan into a great Christian prince of Central Asia named Prester (for *Presbyter*, meaning *elder* or *priest*) John (a transliteration of Gur-khan).

Fed by New Testament references to "John the Elder" and by memories of Nestorian Christians driven eastward beyond Persia and Armenia, legends of Prester John would circulate among Europeans for centuries, acting as siren songs to explorers. Even as late as 1487, when Bartholomeu Dias was attempting to reach Asia by sailing around Africa's Cape of Good Hope, he released "agents" (actually formerly captured African slaves) along the coast so that they might alert Prester John of their impending arrival. The Crusaders' hopes of help from this mythical patriarch soon collapsed, however. The Seljuk Turks drove them from Edessa in 1144, confining the Europeans to the Mediterranean coastal strip.

The Kara Khitai themselves were soon overcome by a stronger power, the prosperous trading kingdom of Khwarizm, centered on the lower Amu (Oxus) River, with Samarkand and Bukhara the jewels in its setting. Khwarizm's ruler signaled his pretensions by assuming the Persian title of "Shah." He wanted nothing less than to restore Moslem power to Transoxiana and, in the end, to rule the whole Moslem world from Baghdad. As the 12th century drew to a close, the Khwarizm shah quickly reduced the Kara Khitai to vassalage, turned toward the Iranian Plateau, where he killed the last Seljuk ruler at Rayy in 1194, and threatened the Baghdad caliph himself. The shah's son and successor, after taking Balkh from another Moslem ruler in 1204, actually marched toward Baghdad, which was saved when a winter storm pinned down the Khwarizm forces, making them easy targets for local Kurdish hill soldiers. So it seemed as if the kingdom of Khwarizm should give Genghis Khan some formidable opposition in his advance westward along the Silk Road.

Genghis Khan had considerable skill, intelligence, and ferocity on his side, however. Some of these skills were new to the Mongols. Before their early successes, the Mongols were a simple people, living with their mounts and herds, subsisting on yogurt, *kumiss* (fermented mare's milk), and millet. But though the Mongols were illiterate and unsophisticated, it was a key of Genghis Khan's success that he recognized the importance of people of skill and learning and sought them out in the cities he conquered. People with special skills—whether goldsmiths and scribes, or siege engineers and armorers—were spared the normal blood bath and brought to serve the imperial court. So the great mobile camps of the Mongols became, to some extent, like Alexander's moving capital of almost 1,500 years before. Of particular importance to the Mongol advance westward was the acquisition of Eastern specialists who could mount sieges on the great cities of Central Asia, for the techniques were quite new to the Mongols, who had lived their lives on the steppe.

Genghis Khan also brought to his campaigns considerable intelligence, perhaps fine-honed by his years in the wilderness, and the careful observation developed by climbing to power with little but his own brains and will. As ruler of most of the Mongol and Turkic peoples of the Mongolian Steppe and the Tarim Basin, this remarkable man employed others to provide him with the vital information he needed for planning and executing his campaigns. In the small merchant caravans that still plied the old routes of the Silk Road, he planted spies to bring him information. By the time he turned his attentions to Western Turkestan, such strategems were widely known. So it was that, in 1218, when a mission of Mongol merchants, which included a diplomatic envoy, arrived at the city of Utrar on the Syr (Jaxartes) River, the local Khwarizm governor killed them all, precipitating a war that was, in any case, clearly in the cards.

And it was here that Genghis Khan's ferocity showed itself, even more fully than in his earlier campaigns on the Eurasian Steppe and in northern China. It is true that the capital city of Peking had been devastated, and much of its population massacred. But as Genghis Khan gained in strength, many of the peoples of Central Asia chose to join rather than fight him, among them the Uighur Turks centered on Beshbalik. Some of Genghis Khan's old enemies found temporary refuge in more westerly cities, such as Khotan, Kashgar, and Balasaghun, west of the Issyk Kul, capital of the Kara Khitai remnants. But these interlopers made themselves so unpopular that the local citizens rose against them, especially the persecuted Moslems, who welcomed the Mongols as liberators.

But now the Mongols were facing the heavily fortified cities of Turkestan, built and defended with all the skill that could be mustered by the Moslem world. Not trusting simply to borrowed techniques in dealing with these formidable Moslem opponents, Genghis Khan unleashed a reign of terror such as had never before been seen in the region, even at the hands of the Assassins, who by comparison seemed almost delicate in their handiwork. The beginning was deceptive. With an army estimated at 200,000 men, Genghis Khan headed toward Khwarizm in early 1219, the year after the Mongol mission had been killed at Utrar. He sent

In the 13th century, Mongol archers were the scourge of Eurasia. (Victoria and Albert Museum)

divisions under his sons to Khojend and Utrar (where molten gold was poured down the governor's throat in punishment for his act).

Genghis Khan himself headed toward the prime city of the region—Bukhara. After some looting and burning of the city, he took to the pulpit at the main mosque to announce that he was "the flail of God" sent as a punishment for their sins. So far the campaign had seen the usual ferocity of war, but no general massacres. Matters worsened with the attack on Samarkand in early 1220. The Turkish garrison, defeated after a five-day siege, was executed, as was a very large proportion of the population, though the clergy were spared and some 30,000 skilled artisans excepted and sent to the Mongol headquarters in Mongolia.

In the face of these terrible losses, the Khwarizm shah fled along the Silk Road into Persia seeking aid. Mongol cavalry divisions pursued him all the way across the Iranian Plateau through Rayy to Hamadan (formerly Ecbatana). The desolate shah finally met his end on an island in the Caspian, where he had taken refuge. While Genghis Khan remained in Turkestan, these Mongol divisions continued an astonishing and bloody string of successes. Curving around the Caspian through the region now called Azerbaijan, they headed toward the Caucasus, defeating the Christian kingdom of Georgia at Tiflis in 1221. A revolt in their rear caused them to return, where they leveled rebellious Hamadan and executed its citizens. Then they resumed their tour around the Caspian, cutting through the once heavily defended Derbend Pass.

The Khazars no longer ruled supreme beyond the Caucasus. In the late 10th century, the Rus (Swedish Vikings centered on Kiev) and the Byzantines, perhaps jealous of Khazaria's success, had combined to destroy the kingdom, sacking its capital at Atil. Though Khazar traders remained active in the area (and may be the ancestors of many of the Russian Jews of modern times), no strong state occupied the vital region north of the Caucasus, to protect against an invasion such as this from the south, or from the East, out of the Eurasian Steppe. So the Mongol wings continued their swing around the Caspian, handily defeating all armies thrown up against them and finally returning triumphant to Western Turkestan.

Genghis Khan, meanwhile, was completing the conquest and devastation of Khwarizm. The city of Gurganj, on the Amu River held out for a desperate seven months, inflicting heavy casualties on the Mongols. The Mongol revenge was total. Apart from craftsmen deported to Mongolia, perhaps as many as 100,000, the rest of the population was either enslaved or killed. Dams above the city were smashed, flooding the town and destroying it utterly; so great was the disruption that the Amu apparently was diverted to flow into the Caspian, resuming its course toward the Ural only three centuries later. The city never recovered, though a new trading city named Urgenj was later built at the site.

The motive for such destruction was partly revenge and partly a campaign of terror designed to induce other cities to surrender without a fight. That tactic apparently worked on some occasions, but blood and devastation were the norm. Balkh, Merv, Nishapur, Herat in southwest Persia, Kabul toward India—all were razed and their citizens massacred, even though some were spared for a time after their surrender. At Merv, one chronicler estimated that 700,000 people were killed; at Nishapur, pyramids were made of the victim's heads, with men, women, and children in separate piles. Even dogs and cats were massacred. Moslem historian Juvaini lamented: "rose gardens became furnaces." Only some dozens of artisans—80 from Merv, so the chronicler reported—were left alive, carefully culled by Genghis Khan's troops as being of potential use to the empire. The Mongols in this fashion pushed as far as the Indus River, but no farther, the torpid plains proving inhospitable for both the Mongols and their cold-bred ponies.

★   ★   ★

While Genghis Khan was subjecting the heart of the Silk Road to the bloodiest destruction it had yet seen, he was also beginning to think seriously about how to properly rule the great empire he had now created. Though unlettered, he clearly recognized the power of ideas, the value of people who carried them, and the need to build a body of statecraft with which to rule a continent. So he summoned to his camp sages of the various religions and philosophies now to be found in his ever-growing empire. Some of these, luckily for us, left records of their journeys, and furnish us with rare glimpses of travel on the Central Asian highways in early Mongol times. One of these sages, a Taoist named Ch'ang-ch'un, even recorded the summons he received, which gives us some sense of the man who sent it. Expressing his master's intention, Genghis Khan's Chinese private secretary wrote:

> In the space of seven years I have succeeded in accomplishing a great work—uniting the whole world in one empire. I have not myself distinguished qualities. But as my calling is high, the obligations incumbent on me are also heavy; and I fear that in my ruling there may be something wanting. To cross a river we make boats and rudders. Likewise we invite sage men, and choose assistants for keeping the empire in good order.

Ch'ang-ch'un could hardly refuse the invitation, though he was an elderly man. So he set out in the year 1220, with 19 disciples and an escort of 20 Mongols, toward the Mongol lands. He was immediately disheartened to learn at Peking, where he was given a warm welcome, that the khan was not in the heartland of Mongolia, which was distant enough, but on a campaign in Khwarizm, far to the west. There was nothing for it but to follow him. This meant a route across the Mongolian and Dzungarian Steppes, north of the T'ien Shan. As always, when powerful rulers afforded the necessary security, this was the preferable route, even more so when a northern people ruled.

Traveling across the northern steppe, Ch'ang-ch'un found abundant evidence of the changes in the region over the previous centuries. North and east of Turfan and Hami, he saw his first Moslem, the religion having percolated that far. Farther on, a transplanted colony of

Chinese artisans, notable silk and wool weavers, gave Ch'ang-ch'un a joyful greeting, escorting him into their city with colorful, sweet-smelling bouquets of flowers and bright pennants flying. Leaving nine of his disciples there, Ch'ang-ch'un proceeded on the trail of Genghis Khan, crossing through a ridge of hills by a precipitous mountain route, over which the party's two wagons had to be lowered by ropes.

As he headed toward the still-important town of Beshbalik, Ch'ang-ch'un passed into the territory of the Uighur Turks, who now ruled under Genghis Khan's auspices. Here, too, many people came far out of the city to greet the renowned visitor, among them Confucians and many Buddhist and Taoist monks (though, from his comment that the Taoists wore different headdresses from those in China, the latter may actually have been Manichaean priests). The party pitched their traveling tents in the vineyards of the city, and were showered with fruits and plied with grape wines. Ch'ang-ch'un was treated as well to a pocket history of the city, learning that in T'ang times Beshbalik had been the residence of the Chinese governor of the northern regions, and that some of the frontier towns the dynasty had established still existed.

The pattern was followed in other cities on the route west. Honored both in his own right and as a wise man under Genghis Khan's protection, and therefore one to be treated with great care, Ch'ang-ch'un would be greeted by an escort from each city and presented with fruits, especially luscious melons and grapes, as well as wine. In cities beyond Beshbalik he found Zoroastrians and Nestorian Christians, along with Buddhists still, for, as he noted, all that land had belonged to China in the time of the T'ang dynasty. But once past the city of Chambalik, he found that: "West of this place there are neither Buddhists or Taoists, only Moslems, people who worship the west [that is, pray toward Mecca, in western Arabia]."

Then as Ch'ang-ch'un proceeded along the north slope of the T'ien Shan, he came to a desert:

> . . . where the loose sand, tossed by the wind, now was swept up into the hillocks and now was leveled, seemingly rather like ocean waves. It was utterly without any vegetation. The wagons sank deep into the sand and even the horses plodded through it . . .

This was a desert of which Ch'ang-ch'un had been warned. It was called the Field of White Bones, after the many soldiers who had fallen here, either in battle or by heat and thirst, for it was said to be death to attempt a daytime crossing of the desert. Not in this season, apparently, for Ch'ang-ch'un's party crossed during the day and found that when they stopped to rest "the night was bitterly cold and we found no water." Ch'ang-ch'un and his disciples were much touched by the unconsecrated array of bones and, on their return trip, would conduct a special funeral service for the dead.

Passing through a better-watered but rugged mountainous region in which one of Genghis Khan's sons had carved a road, the party emerged finally at the city of Almalik, with its many fruit orchards. But Ch'ang-ch'un and his party were less interested in the fruits than in something quite unknown to them: cotton.

The Chinese had long coveted and imported cotton goods from India. Indeed, silk being so common and cotton so rare in China, cotton gauzes were sometimes favored by Chinese buyers over all but the finest silks. Distance, uncertain communication, and traditions of commercial obfuscation being what they were, it is not surprising to find that the Chinese knew as little about cotton as the early Romans had known about silk. As the Romans found it hard to believe that silk was an animal product, so the Chinese could not credit that cotton came from a plant. As early as the sixth century, the Chinese had developed a myth of the "vegetable lamb," a strange creature that was planted in the ground to sprout more lambs, from which the cotton was supposedly taken. This curious invention circulated in Asia for centuries, and would be picked up and transported to the West by later credulous European travelers. For the moment, however, Ch'ang-ch'un had more practical needs in mind, especially since the winter was approaching:

We obtained seven pieces of this cloth to be made into winter clothes. The hair of this stuff resembles the down in which willow seeds are wrapped; it is very clean, fine, and soft, and it is used to make thread, ropes, cloth, and wadding.

The myth of a "vegetable lamb," an animal-plant that produced cotton, spread across Eurasia during and after the *Pax Mongolica.* (Authors' archives)

Once across the Ili River, Ch'ang-ch'un found himself in mulberry country. He had already noted that the people in oasis cities used irrigation canals to make wasteland arable. Here he noted as well that many farmers specialized in raising mulberry trees for the growing of silkworms. He learned that this had once been the domain of the Kara Khitai, former rulers of northern China who had been pushed across the continent, but after the spread of Islam the empire of Khwarizm had grown up around the Amu and Syr Rivers. It was in this region that Ch'ang-ch'un expected to find Genghis Khan. But a fast messenger sent ahead to the imperial encampment to announce the party's impending arrival found that Genghis Khan had left following the retreating shah of Khwarizm.

Abandoning one of their two carts, which was broken, the little party pushed on along the well-watered foothills of the T'ien Shan "until they turned sharply to the south." There they found the city of Talas, near the site of China's mid-eighth-century devastating defeat at the hands of the Arabs, where still could be seen the red stone traces of an old military camp. Now, as they proceeded southward, it was Moslem escorts who came out of the cities to greet

Years past its peak and partly in ruins, Samarkand in the 19th century still showed its magnificence. (By D. Ivanoff, reprinted in Yule's *Marco Polo*)

Ch'ang-ch'un's party and direct them to guest quarters. Past Tashkent they crossed the Syr River on a pontoon bridge and then followed the line of the mountains toward Samarkand. At one city en route, they found a "splendid mulberry tree whose branches could shelter a hundred men." Wine was still very much a part of the entertainment of the visitors (the strict Moslem prohibition was circumvented by boiling it) and performers such as sword dancers and acrobats were produced for their delight.

Finally in December 1221, the party reached the great city of Samarkand, where Ch'ang-ch'un was greeted by Genghis Khan's chief minister, Yëh-lu Ch'u-ts'ai, who had written the letter summoning him. He immediately sent word to Genghis Khan of Ch'ang-ch'un's arrival, but suggested that the party spend a few months in Samarkand, since winter was upon them and "bandits" had apparently destroyed both the pontoon bridge and the boats necessary for crossing the Amu River. The reluctant pilgrim agreed and entered the "city of canals." There he found ample evidence of Samarkand's change of fortunes. Noting that the city had once held over 100,000 families, he estimated that only a quarter of that remained after the coming of the Mongols. The Moslems owned most of the fields and gardens, which were tilled by Chinese, Khitai, and Tangut (Tibetan) workers.

But even before Genghis Khan's arrival, the city had seen dissension and trouble. The Khwarizm shah had built himself a new palace on a 100-foot-high hill within the city limits; but that section of the town was so terrorized by robbers that he had abandoned the palace for another residence in a safer quarter. (In truth his religious zeal made him unpopular even with the Moslems supposedly "liberated" from the unbelieving Kara Khitai.) It was this empty palace that Ch'ang-ch'un made his winter residence, trusting his reputation as a wise man to protect him from the robbers. Streams of visitors came, not only politicians required to care for him and Chinese workers bound by ethnic ties, but also scholars from the region. A local astronomer compared notes with him on a solar eclipse he had witnessed a few months before in Mongolia.

As winter passed and spring came on, Ch'ang-ch'un found out why Samarkand was reputed to be the loveliest city in the Moslem Empire, as his biographer tells us:

> In the first month [mid-February to mid-March] almond trees blossomed. Their fruit is as small as peaches and tastes like walnuts; it is gathered and eaten in the fall. On the second day of the second month, the time of the equinox, the blossoms of the apricot trees began to fall. The astronomer and others invited the master to take a little excursion to the west of the city . . . The day was fine and the air delicious, the flowers and trees were fresh and full; everywhere we looked there were delightful views of lakes and orchards, pagodas, terraces, and tents.

On another walk, two weeks later, they found "nothing but gardens and shaded groves for more than a hundred *li*. Even Chinese gardens do not compare with them . . . "

Spring brought a renewed summons from Genghis Khan, and Ch'ang-ch'un obeyed. Escorted by a thousand soldiers, he was led through the Iron Gates (the Buzgala Defile), a narrow canyon through the tongue of mountains separating Ferghana from Bactria, where (as Hsüan-tsang had reported centuries before) once an actual iron gate had been affixed. Ferried by boat across the Amu and other lesser rivers, all in spring fullness, Ch'ang-ch'un finally came to the camp of Genghis Khan. But the khan was still on campaign, and rather than wait, the Taoist sage returned once again to Samarkand, this time by a different mountain route where at one bridge over a raging stream:

> Several pack asses fell and were drowned as they were being driven across the [stone slab] bridge and on the banks below were carcasses of other animals killed while trying to cross.

Even in this difficult and seemingly inaccessible region, Ch'ang-ch'un and his party met a trading caravan returning "from the West with a big load of coral," some foot-long pieces of which the escorting soldiers bought in exchange for two-pound bars of silver. After a time in Samarkand, where he delighted in the harvest of fruits and vegetables such as delectable eggplants, Ch'ang-ch'un once again headed south toward Genghis Khan's camp, this time in the Snowy Mountains (Hindu Kush). On the way they passed the city of Balkh, whose inhabitants had been massacred by the Mongols only weeks before. Of this once-great city, our Taoist observer has to say only that, as they passed by in the dark, they heard dogs barking in the city streets.

Later, having instructed Genghis Khan in the word of Tao, the indomitable Ch'ang-ch'un returned again toward China. He followed roughly the same route to about the latitude of Hami, but then, instead of swinging on a northerly arc through Mongolia, as he had come, he decided to cut more directly southeast. He was advised against it:

> The southern route is barren, very stony, and grass and water are exceedingly scarce. Our party is too large; the horses will soon get exhausted from insufficient water and fodder; they might slow us down and any delay can prove fatal.

But as the Chinese had done centuries before, in the campaign for the Heavenly Horses of Ferghana, Ch'ang-ch'un dealt with short supplies by breaking the party into groups and sending them off a week apart, so they would not overtax the slender resources of the desert.

Yet even in these inhospitable regions, there were stations where Ch'ang-ch'un could change horses along the way. Later, as they approached closer to China itself, post stations were even more frequent. Once they put the sandy waste behind them, they "began to find huts and tents and had no trouble getting fresh horses." Clearly, although Genghis Khan was still extending the boundaries of his empire, the well-tended post stations that would mark the height of the Mongol period were already in existence. Indeed, no sooner had the Taoist teacher arrived back in China than a letter came from Genghis Khan inquiring if he had been "properly supplied with provisions and remounts" en route and if the officials had made "satisfactory provision for [his] board and lodging."

★   ★   ★

It was the communication system set up by Genghis Khan in this period that would unite the empire after his death, preventing it from immediately collapsing, as had so many other nomadic empires of the past. And this communication system was partly a result of Genghis Khan's recognition and use of skilled advisors, in particular Yëh-lu Ch'u-ts'ai, a young scholar from the last royal line (the Khitan or Liao dynasty) to rule northern China before the Mongols. He had been taken into the Mongol's service in 1215, accompanying the great khan on his Western campaigns and beginning the slow process of civilizing the wild steppe nomads. It was no doubt he who had convinced Genghis Khan to talk with the Taoist Ch'ang-ch'un, to better learn about how to rule. Genghis Khan himself had recognized the importance of writing, very early in his career employing a Uighur scribe to put the Mongol language in written form and teach the script to the royal family. (Whether Genghis Khan himself ever learned how to read and write is unclear; probably not.)

Building on this rudimentary appreciation, Yëh-lu Ch'u-ts'ai gradually convinced Genghis Khan of the value of a civil service, such as that which had served China so successfully for centuries. Once a Mongol general proposed to massacre all the peasants in a newly conquered Chinese province, since they would be no good as soldiers and their land might, to the Mongol way of thinking, better be turned into pasture for the horses that Mongols valued above all else. Yeh-lu Ch'uts'ai avoided this tragedy by pointing out to Genghis Khan that, if the old Chinese administrative system was kept in place, the province would yield to the khan each year half a million ounces of silver, 400,000 sacks of grain, and 80,000 pieces of silk. If the promise impressed Genghis Khan, the reality was even more impressive, and thereafter his ministers were encouraged to apply the same methods to other parts of the empire.

It is therefore to Yëh-lu Ch'u-ts'ai that we primarily owe the existence of the travel and communications network that later visiting Europeans, such as Marco Polo, were surprised to find in place. From China to the western borders of the Mongol empire, post-stations were established, both for the service of imperial couriers—for Genghis Khan well understood the vital need for communications across his vast empire—and for merchants and envoys. Never a trading people themselves, the Mongols now supplied merchants with capital needed for long-distance trade, and received substantial profits in return, such profits that they exempted these valuable merchants from normal taxes. It was in their own interest to keep the routes safe and clear of robbers, and local rulers in each region were expected to guarantee the safety of legitimate travelers, merchants, and envoys. Where once the Mongols had simply wasted, most notably in the cities of Turkestan and Persia, they later rebuilt and fostered trade. Never before or since had the Silk Road and the Eurasian Steppe Route seen a peace such as this. Up to the western limits of their control in Persia, as Henry Yule put it, "scarcely a dog might bark without Mongol leave."

The international trade that, after the worst depredations of the Mongols, once again began to flow along the Silk Road worked to unite the newly formed empire and helped it survive the death of Genghis Khan in 1227. For two years, until all the powers in the empire could be assembled near Karakorum, where the traditional great assembly called a *kuriltai* would elect a new leader (someone from the royal family, but not necessarily the oldest son), the empire had no supreme khan.

During Genghis Khan's lifetime, his sons had ruled as khans over vast regions under their father. The eldest, Jochi, ruled the vast Russian Steppe from the Altai Mountains west to Europe. When he died a few months before his father, his patrimony was divided between his sons, Orda and Batu, founders of the White Horde and the Golden Horde, respectively. The second son, Chagatai, ruled in the prime khanate that stretched roughly from Turfan to the Oxus, including the Silk Road highways on either side of the T'ien Shan and the rebuilt caravan cities of Transoxiana. He would remain a sage counselor and interpreter of the Mongol law. Following the Mongol pattern, the youngest son, Tolui, held the imperial homeland just south of Lake Baikal and acted as regent until a new supreme khan was elected. Since many of Genghis Khan's early allies were non–Mongols, it is not surprising that Tolui's wife was a Nestorian Christian. Two of their sons, Möngke and Kubilai, would later rule as supreme khan of the Mongols, and a third, Hülegü, would found a new khanate in Western Asia. But it was the third son, Ögedei, ruler of the lands east of Lake Balkhash, who had been Genghis Khan's choice as successor. The *kuriltai* honored their great leader's wish.

Ögedei showed the continuing influence of Chinese advisors, including the still-powerful Yëh-lu Ch'u-ts'ai, by transforming Karakorum from the seasonal site of a nomadic camp to a permanent city, surrounded by a wall, in 1235. And, though without the ability of his father, he carried forward a kind of master plan laid down by Genghis Khan. This plan called for completing the conquest of northern China, which would end, in other reigns, in the taking of Sung China in the south, as well; rooting out the remains of Khwarizm power in Western Asia; and expanding westward into Europe, onto the wide plains of Hungary and Poland. The latter two actions would form a giant pincers, once again enclosing the Caspian Sea and the lands that surrounded it.

The Mongol generals on the swing through Persia and Armenia were remarkably evenhanded, attacking Moslems and Christians alike. As before, when cities resisted, the Mongols would often put virtually the whole population to the sword. In the face of this, some Christian states in the Armenian and Caucasian highlands resolved to save themselves by submitting without a fight. They were encouraged to ally themselves with the Mongols by the existence of honored and highly placed Nestorian Christians among the imperial nomads and by the pronouncemnets of religious toleration in the Mongol code called the *Yasa*, promulgated under Genghis Khan and continued by his successors. Indeed, in 1240, when Christians in the Caucasian state of Georgia felt themselves to be treated unjustly, they sent an embassy to Ögedei in Karakorum, appealing for relief. In response Ögedei sent a Nestorian emissary to instruct Mongol generals to spare Christian churches from destruction. For many Christians it was just a step from this evidence of toleration to a dream of a Christian–Mongol alliance against the Moslems, a dream born of the increasing influence of Nestorians in Ögedei's court and fed on persistent rumors of Prester John, a potential ally and savior.

Such dreams were rudely shattered when the Mongols began their devastating push into Europe in 1236. Ögedei and his court in the East may have become increasingly civilized by contact with the Chinese and with Nestorian Christians, but the Mongol khans and generals in the West, especially in Russia, had been subject to few such moderating influences. With remarkable military skills but an unbridled taste for destruction, these Mongols inflicted on Europe an offensive unmatched even by their best-known predecessor, Attila the Hun. Thousands were slaughtered, cities were leveled, land was laid waste. A chronicler at one city spoke for many, saying: "No eye remained open to weep for the dead." Crossing the Volga, the Don, the Dnieper, the Danube, preferably in winter when ice turned rivers into roads, they destroyed the Russian state of Kiev, and then Hungary and Poland.

In 1241, all Europe lay open before them. The Christian states were too concerned with their own internecine battles to mount a common defense. Europe was saved, but not by its own efforts. The Mongol supply lines were stretched thin, a problem all the more acute because their armies could draw little support from the lands they had wasted. Also the Mongols were torn by their own jealousies and dissensions. Whether, with the coming of another winter, the Mongols would have pushed farther westward is unclear. The question was made moot by the death of Ögedei in 1241. Genghis Khan's grandsons pulled back to the Ukraine—the name, meaning "borderland," dates from this time—and ruled their Russian lands from a newly-founded camp city at Sarai on the lower Volga, near where the Khazars had once had their capital, Atil. This was the center of the Golden Horde. The White Horde would lie farther to the east, on the Kirghiz Steppe.

★   ★   ★

For four years after Ögedei's death, the Mongols had no supreme khan. His widow acted as regent while forces from throughout the empire withdrew from the borders and assembled for a *kuriltai* to choose a new leader. Joining them were envoys from all over Eurasia, each with vital interests in the outcome, among them a grand duke from Russia, a sultan from Asia Minor representing the Seljuk nation of Rum (Rome, in Turkish), the high constable of Armenia, two pretenders to the throne of Georgia, a prince from Korea, and an envoy from the caliph of Baghdad. The pope of Rome, Innocent IV, himself newly elected, sent his own emissary, Friar John de Plano Carpini, joined on his mission by another friar, Benedict the Pole.

Those travelers coming from Europe took the Eurasian Steppe Route to the Mongol assembly. On their way through the blasted Russian lands they saw ruined cities and piles of bleaching bones. When they came into Mongol lands, "the Tartars [Mongols] rushed in upon us hideously armed, inquiring what manner of men we were," as John de Plano Carpini reported, but once their credentials were shown, they were passed along from tribe to tribe toward the site of the *kuriltai*. Few, if any, of the travelers ever saw Karakorum itself, for Ögedei's widow had set up a special camp some miles away, especially for the great assembly, which included (so Friar John reported) 4,000 envoys. On their arrival, the Christians did not find much comfort. Yĕh-lu Ch'u-ts'ai, long a force for toleration, had been dismissed and died soon afterward. His replacement, a Moslem merchant named Abd al-Rahman, was primarily concerned with doubling the tax revenues of the Mongols.

In late August of 1246, when the steppe was still blooming with flowers and high grasses, the Mongols elected a new leader, Ögedei's son Küyük. Not at all disposed toward Christianity, he believed that the Mongol successes were proof of the superiority of the Mongol god, Tengri, the Eternal Heaven. Nor did the pope's envoys do anything to change his mind. Quite the contrary. When all the other ambassadors from Eurasia prostrated themselves, Chinese-style, before Küyük's throne, only friars John and Benedict demurred. And while Küyük's tents bulged with gifts of gold, silver, silks, jewels, and furs—500 wagonloads—along with 50 camels with richly decorated saddles, the poor friars had none to offer, having given away what little they had—mostly a few furs—on their 3,000-mile journey from Sarai, to purchase the good offices of tribes along the way and to buy a little food. Indeed, protesting that no man could rule such vast lands unless it were the will of God, Küyük suggested that, if the pope wanted him to be baptized as a Christian, he should "come in person to serve us. At that time I shall make known all the commands of the Yasa."

A disappointed Friar John made his way back to Europe, traveling part of the way with the ambassador from the sultan of Egypt and returning to Lyon, France, two and a half years after setting out on his journey. So rare and difficult was such a trip that, on his appearance at Kiev, his party was greeted "as if we had come back from the dead." Some reports indicate that Küyük may have been baptized, perhaps at his mother's behest, but Friar John could bring no comfort to European Christians, except perhaps that he saw signs of rifts among the Mongol camps that might reduce their strength and blunt their drive toward the West. He was prescient. In the coming years, the Mongols would have several supreme khans, none reigning for long, as the heirs of Genghis Khan battled each other for dominance. In these uncertain times, the Christians still hoped to convert the Mongols, encouraged by the continued importance of Nestorians at the Mongol courts.

★   ★   ★

In 1253, another European friar, William of Rubruk, set out on a mission similar to Friar John's. After visiting the French King Louis IX, then in the Crusader states on the Mediterranean, he crossed by sea from Constantinople to the Crimea. On arriving at the plains north of the Black Sea, he reported, it "seemed as if I were stepping into another world." At the Volga he found the Mongol's great camp, Sarai, which "seemed like a great city stretching out a long way and crowded round on every side." But with dissension in the land, travel was not so easy. His party's supposed guides robbed and abused them. For all that, Friar William and his little mission did reach Karakorum the following year and were escorted into the city by a jubilant procession of Nestorian Christians. It is he who provides us with our first Western view of the Mongol capital:

> Of the city of Karakorum, you must know that exclusive of the palace of the Khan it
> is not as big as the village of St. Denis [today part of Paris], and the monastery of St.
> Denis is ten times larger than the palace . . . There are two districts there: the Saracens'
> [Moslems'] quarter where the markets are, and many merchants flock thither on account
> of the court which is always near it and on account of the number of envoys. The other
> district is that of the Cathayans who are all craftsmen. Apart from these districts there are
> the large palaces of the court scribes. There are twelve pagan temples belonging to the
> different nations, two mosques in which the law of Mahomet [Mohammed] is proclaimed,
> and one church for the Christians at the far end of the town. The town is surrounded by a
> mud wall and has four gates. At the east gate are sold millet and other grain, which is
> however seldom bought there; at the west sheep and goats are sold; at the south oxen and
> carts; at the north horses.

The city is striking testimony to Genghis Khan's policy of assembling captured artisans and deporting them to Mongolia. On his visit to Karakorum, Friar William met and talked with, among many others, a master goldsmith from Paris captured in the Mongol raids on Hungary. It was the goldsmith, William Buchier, who built the famous fountain at Karakorum, which Friar William described:

> At the entrance to [the khan's] palace, seeing it would have been unseemly to put skins
> of milk and other drinks there, Master William of Paris has made for him a large silver
> tree, at the foot of which are four silver lions having a pipe and all belching forth white
> mare's milk. Inside the trunk four pipes lead up to the top of the tree and the ends of the

pipe are bent downwards and over each of them is a gilded serpent, the tail of which
twines round the trunk of the tree. One of these pipes pours out wine, another
caracosmos [kumiss], *that is the refined milk of mares, another* boal, *which is a honey*
drink, and another rice mead, which is called terracina. *Each of these has its silver basin*
ready to receive it at the foot of the tree between the other four pipes. At the very top he
fashioned an angel holding a trumpet; underneath the tree he made a crypt in which a
man can be secreted, and a pipe goes up to the angel through the middle of the heart of
the tree . . . Outside the palace there is a chamber in which the drinks are stored, and
servants stand there ready to pour them out when they hear the angel sounding the
trumpet. The tree has branches, leaves and fruit of silver.
  And so when the drinks are getting low the chief butler calls out to the angel to sound
his trumpet. Then, hearing this, the man who is hidden in the crypt blows the pipe going
up to the angel with all his strength, and the angel, placing the trumpet to his mouth,
sounds it very loudly. When the servants in the chamber hear this each one of them pours
out his drink into its proper pipe, and the pipes pour them out from above and below into
the basins prepared for this, and then the cup-bearers draw the drinks and carry them
round the palace to the men and women.

Master William, the inventor of this marvelous device, greeted his countryman from
Europe with "great joy," as we may imagine. Friar William was invited to supper, where he
met Master William's wife, who had been born in Hungary of a French father. Joining the
bittersweet party was an Englishman named Basil who had also been born in Hungary. They
were only a few of the many skilled artisans who had begun their lives on the Danube or the
Huang or the Syr and now found themselves employed in the Mongols' head camp, or
sometimes roaming around the face of Asia as part of the great khan's military train.

Friar William stayed in Karkorum for some time, but he had no more success in converting Mongols to Christianity than had Friar John. A companion friar, unable to face the
terrible return journey, lived the rest of his days in Karakorum. But Friar William returned to
Europe with a melancholy report. (Some suggested that he brought with him the formula for
gunpowder and passed it on in private to his fellow scholar, Roger Bacon; but if so, it was not
in his official report, perhaps because he had seen firsthand the destructive potential of this
explosive mixture of saltpeter, sulfur, and charcoal.) Friar William's fellow Europeans were in
need of an assurance he was unable to give. They desperately feared a renewed assault on
Europe itself. Friar William had seen, as he started his homeward journey, a great army under
Genghis Khan's grandson, Hülegü, sweeping westward. But rather than heading for Europe,
through lands held by other of the great khan's heirs, Hülegü's army chose to strike along the
Silk Road in Persia. His successes would change the face of Western Asia.

In 1256, Hülegü's army reached the stronghold of the Assassins. That insidious order,
which had withstood all charges against it for 200 years, finally fell to the overwhelming
numbers of the Mongols and to the skill of their Chinese siege engineers. One by one the
fortresses surrendered, though the last and strongest, Alamut, held out for three years. The

inhabitants were all executed, and their library, except for some scholarly works and copies of the Koran, was burned as heretical. So, said the historian Juvaini, "the world was cleansed." This portion of the Silk Road was freed of the pernicious influence of the Assassins; others of their faith existed elsewhere, as in Syria, and operated for many centuries more in the region, but never again with the same aura of invincibility.

Proceeding westward, Hülegü made his headquarters at the rebuilt Hamadan (once Ecbatana, the old Median capital), but his real target was Baghdad. The decline of this once great and powerful city is an indication not only of the weakness of the last, ailing Abbasid caliph ruling there, but also of the decline of the Silk Road trade in far Western Asia. All along the Tigris stood empty warehouses and bazaars. But Baghdad was still the center of Islam, and as such was a proper target for the Mongols. Not for the first time, war made strange bedfellows. The Mongols were, in this attack, aided by Christian soldiers from Georgia and Armenia, and by Shi'ite citizens who resented the Sunni caliph's rule. In the end, after a week of bombardment, using rocks brought by caravan from three days' march away, the great city surrendered. Baghdad's palaces and houses were plundered, and its treasures packed on caravans, mostly bound for Karakorum. The city itself was burnt and never recovered its former glory. Though many Christian citizens and some foreign visitors were spared, most of the Moslem population was massacred, the resulting stench from the corpses being so noxious that the Mongols were forced to decamp. The center of Islam shifted to Cairo, never to return.

Moving on along the Silk Road, the Mongols next took Aleppo, in 1260. The city, which had flourished under the Moslems, was razed and its population either slaughtered or enslaved. After that, nothing seemed likely to stop the Mongols. With the Moslems and Christians of Western Asia unable to unite, and with factions within each religion fighting among themselves, it seemed a foregone conclusion that the Mongols would shortly take both the remaining Crusader states and the Moslem lands now controlled by Egypt. But once again, the Western lands may have been saved by a death on the other side of the globe. For Hülegü, learning that the great khan Möngke had died, abandoned his planned assault on Damascus and prepared for another *kuriltai*. The sub-empire he founded continued as the Il-Khan (subordinate ruler) empire, with its capital at Hülegü's winter quarters at Tabriz, and stretched from the Oxus to Aleppo, and from the Black Sea to the Persian Gulf and Indian Ocean. The unity imposed by Hülegü's rule would be important for the revival of the Silk Road that was now to come.

CHAPTER TEN

PAX MONGOLICA

The Mongols had to elect a new great khan. That was not so easy, for family tensions, exacerbated in some instances by differing religious allegiances, had rival heirs warring with each other for four years. Finally the winner emerged: Kubilai Khan, ruler of Mongol China, where he had established the Yüan dynasty. It was under him that the Silk Road was so frequented by Europeans that travel became almost routine. So began the *Pax Mongolica*—the Mongol Peace—which would last for a crucial century, from 1260 to 1368.

Given the West's long and continuing tradition of trading for much-desired Eastern goods, it is not surprising that the promise of a peaceful union of the Mongol Empire under one ruler tempted Western merchants to venture into Central Asia. There may have been others, but it is our good fortune to know a great deal about one group of itinerant traders, Nicolo Polo, his son Marco, and his brother Maffeo, all from Venice. In the 1250s, before Marco was even born or Kubilai Khan crowned, the brothers Polo set sail from Venice to Constantinople. The destination was normal for Venetian merchants of the time.

As it happened, merchants from the Italian trading states, especially Venice, were well placed to make a push to the East. Since the First Crusade in the late 11th century, Mediterranean city-states such as Venice, Genoa, and Pisa had developed a prosperous trade in Eastern goods. Once the Crusader states were established, it was they who ferried

In Xanadu did Kubla Khan
A stately pleasure-dome decree . . .
So twice five miles of fertile ground
With walls and towers were girdled
* round;*
And there were gardens bright with
* sinuous rills*
Where blossomed many an incense-
* bearing tree;*
And there were forests ancient as the
* hills,*
Enfolding sunny spots of greenery.

—Samuel Taylor Coleridge

pilgrims and knights to the Holy Land. These pilgrims and knights had, through peaceful trade and successful plunder, developed a taste for Eastern goods. As a result, a modest commerce had spread from the Crusader states across the Mediterranean to Italy and, to some extent, to Spain. But the continual wars between Christians and Moslems, not to mention Mongols, made this a somewhat unreliable route, so the Mediterranean merchants also opened routes to the East via the Black Sea, where they set up trading posts. Among the places the Mongols plundered, when they swept into Eastern Europe, were Italian trading posts in the Crimea.

By the beginning of the 13th century, Venice had become so powerful that it was able to turn the soldiers of the Fourth Crusade away from their Moslem enemies and toward their erstwhile allies, the Byzantine Christians. In 1204 the Venetians took Constantinople, plundering the once-great city and shipping countless artifacts to Venice (including the famous horses of St. Mark's). The Latin Empire they founded on Constantinople would last until 1261, when the Byzantine Greeks, who had been pushed into the hinterland, regained the centerpiece of their empire.

So, in the 1250s, when Nicolas and Maffeo Polo set out on what was to be a monumental journey, they went first to Constantinople "with their merchants' wares." From the tale later related by Marco Polo, it appears that, like many wandering merchants, they had no specific itinerary or destination in mind. At Constantinople they "took counsel together" to cross the Black Sea and, laying in a store of jewels, sailed to Soldaia, in the Crimea, a city still held by Byzantine Greeks. There they "considered the matter" once more and proceeded to Sarai, the Mongol camp-city on the Volga. They stayed a year, having presented the jewels to the local khan but receiving "at least twice its value" in return; clearly the trading was profitable. But then war broke out and the local khan was defeated. The result was:

> . . . by reason of this war no one could travel without peril of being taken; thus it was at least on the road by which the Brothers had come, though there was no obstacle to their traveling forward.

Willy-nilly, after a detour upriver, the Polos set out eastward, crossing the Volga and traversing a desert for 17 days, "wherein they found neither town nor village, falling in only with the tents of Tartars occupied with their cattle at pasture." They had not, in fact, traveled straight eastward, but curved down on the more normal trading route that took them to Bukhara, a city they found "the best in all Persia." Once again, they found themselves boxed in and were forced to abide there for three years. As it happened, envoys from the western Mongol territories were passing through Bukhara. Noting that "great honor and profit shall come thereof," they suggested that the Polo brothers travel with them to the court of the Great

This 14th-century miniature showed the Great Khan giving his Golden Tablet to Nicolo and Maffeo Polo. (From *Livre des Merveilles du Monde*, reprinted in Yule's *Marco Polo*)

Khan, who "hath never seen any Latins, and he hath a great desire so to do." By this time—the year would be about 1265—Kubilai Khan had ruled supreme for about five years.

Kubilai Khan was, indeed, most pleased to see these European visitors and asked numerous close questions about their homeland and the rulers there. In the end, he enlisted them as his ambassadors to the pope in Rome, accompanied by one of his barons (who became ill on the way and did not complete the journey). In particular:

> *He begged that the Pope would send as many as an hundred persons of our Christian faith; intelligent men acquainted with the Seven Arts, well qualified to enter into controversy, and able clearly to prove by force of argument to idolators and other kinds of folk, that the Law of Christ was best, and that all other religions were false and naught; and that if they would prove this, he and all under him would become Christians . . .*

He gave the Polo brothers a golden tablet, on which was inscribed the command that they should be given "everything needful in all the countries through which they should pass," including horses and escorts. So they set out for Italy, with the additional charge that they bring back to Kubilai Khan "some Oil of the Lamp which burns on the Sepulchre of our Lord at Jerusalem."

Marco Polo's later record does not tell us exactly what route they took, but it was most likely the northern Tarim route across Central Asia and the old Silk Road across the Iranian Plateau. The overland journey was a difficult one, taking three years:

> *. . . because they could not always proceed, being stopped sometimes by snow, or by heavy rains falling, or by great torrents which they found in an impassable state.*

Rather than follow the old road down into the lowlands toward Baghdad, which would have led to something of a dead end at the Syrian Desert, still in hostile Moslem hands, they stayed on the main travel routes in friendly territory, curving around the Caspian, through Azerbaijan and Armenia to the Il-khan capital at Tabriz, then arcing north and west to the mountain crossroad of Erzerum, in this period becoming a great caravan center. From there it was a relatively short distance, perhaps 120 miles, to Trebizond on the Black Sea, an independent trading state at its zenith in Mongol times.

But the Polos took an alternate route from Erzerum, curving south and west over the Anatolian Plateau to emerge on the plains near the Gulf of Issus, where Alexander had once defeated Darius. The main port here was Layas, serving both Antioch and the new country of Lesser Armenia, so-named for the large number of people who had emigrated there from their highland home, now generally called Greater Armenia. The Armenians having allied themselves with the Mongols both in self-protection and in reaction against Moslems, this was the logical route for overland traders such as the Polos to take. As Marco Polo would later report, at Layas:

> *. . . there is a great trade. For you must know that all the spicery, and the cloths of silk and gold, and the other valuable wares that come from the interior [of Asia], are brought to that city. And the merchants of Venice and Genoa, and other countries, come thither to sell their goods, and to buy what they lack. And whatsoever persons would travel to the interior, merchants or others, they take their way by this city of Layas.*

The year was now 1269. Proceeding to the Crusader stronghold at Acre, the Polos learned that the pope was dead, and that they would have to wait to fulfill the Great Khan's request until the European Christians had solved their own problem of succession. In the meantime, they judged that "while the Pope is a-making" they should visit their homes in Venice. There they found that Nicolo's wife was dead and that he had a son whom he had never seen, a teenager named Marco. The Polos remained in Venice for two years until, feeling they could wait no longer for a papal election, they set out for Acre, this time accompanied by

Nicolo's son Marco. The papal legate there gave them a pass to Jerusalem, for they could at least bring the oil Kubilai Khan had requested. Returning to Acre, they checked once more with the papal legate and, finding that no pope seemed to be in the offing, set off with his blessing back to Kubilai Khan.

They had barely reached Layas when they were recalled to Acre; the papal legate, to his surprise, had himself been elected pope of Christendom, taking the name of Gregory X. He made appropriate replies to Kubilai Khan's letters and dispatched two friars to accompany the Polos back to Karakorum. These were very far from the 100 requested, but Christians in Europe, much less in the Crusader states, had few skilled people to spare. Given the previous ambassadorial contacts with the Mongols, the Christian hierarchy may have known that the khans preferred to make use of the skilled people, and did not appear particularly susceptible to conversion. Many have argued—in a "for the want of a shoe" vein—that the Christians here lost their chance to win the Mongols, and thereby Asia, to Christianity. Whatever might have been, only two friars were sent—and turned back at the first sign of trouble. That came in Lesser Armenia, where the Moslems had launched an attack; it was only the first difficulty on a three-and-one-half year trip back to Karakorum.

So the Polos journeyed on alone, toward Greater Armenia, through Erzincan, famous for its weaving of buckram, a cloth of cotton or linen, perhaps quilted and probably deriving

For much of its history, the Silk Road led to the Mediterranean's Gulf of Issus, here at the port of Layas used by the Polo family. (From Yule's *Marco Polo*, after *Voyage en Cilicie*, by Langlois)

its name originally from Bukhara. Here they were apparently dissuaded from following a more easterly route by reports of troublesome mountain peoples, who were described as "an evil generation, whose delight it is to plunder merchants." As Marco later reported:

> There are numerous towns and villages [in Georgia], and silk is produced in great abundance. They also weave cloths of gold, and all kinds of very fine silk stuffs. The country produces the best goshawks in the world. It has indeed no lack of anything, and the people live by trade and handicraft. 'Tis a very mountainous region, and full of strait defiles and of fortresses, insomuch that the Tartars [Mongols] have never been able to subdue it out and out.

In those areas where the Mongols had not fully secured their rule, trade was still hazardous. This was true in many parts of Persia, where Marco noted:

> Unless merchants be well armed they run the risk of being murdered, or at least robbed of everything; and it sometimes happens that a whole party perishes in this way when not on guard.

As a result, the Polos apparently cut down from the Anatolian Plateau to the caravan center of Mosul (near ancient Nineveh), on the upper Tigris. "All the cloths of gold and silk that are called *Mosolins*," he reported, "are made in this country; and those great Merchants called *Mosolins*, who carry for sale such quantities of spicery and pearls and cloths of silk and gold, are also from this kingdom."

They then passed downriver to the city of Baghdad, which "used to be the seat of the Calif of all the Saracens [Moslems] in the world, just as Rome is the seat of the Pope of all the Christians." Since its sack by the Mongols, Baghdad had not recovered its former eminence, but it was still known as "the noblest and greatest city in all these regions," where there is "a great traffic of merchants with their goods." Marco heard special praise of Baghdad's silk stuffs and gold brocades, and "many other beautiful tissue richly wrought with figures of beasts and birds." Following the Tigris down to the Persian Gulf, then sailing to the port of Hormuz, the party headed overland to pick up the line of the Silk Road in eastern Persia.

Even so, the journey was dangerous. As they passed through the Mongol-ravaged land, they found many walled villages and towns, once made rich by trade, that now housed bandits. Of one such bandit group, Marco noted:

> . . . when these . . . wish to make a plundering incursion, they have certain devilish enchantments whereby they do bring darkness over the face of day, insomuch that you can

*scarcely discern your comrade riding beside you; and this darkness they will cause to ex-
tend over a space of seven days' journey. They know the country thoroughly, and ride
abreast, keeping near one another, sometimes to the number of 10,000, at other times
more or fewer. In this way they extend across the whole plain that they are going to
harry, and catch every living thing that is found outside of the towns and villages; man,
woman, or beast, nothing can escape them! The old men whom they take in this way
they butcher; the young men and the women they sell for slaves in other countries; thus
the whole land is ruined, and has become well-nigh a desert.*

The dangers he spoke of were not just hearsay, either, as Rustichello, the scribe to
whom Marco later related his tale in a Genoese prison, described:

*. . . Messer Marco himself was all but caught by their bands in such a darkness as that I
have told you of; but, as it pleased God, he got off and threw himself into a village hard
by . . . Howbeit he lost his whole company except seven persons who escaped along with
him. The rest were caught, and some of them sold, some put to death.*

Despite the fanciful references to "darkness" and other robbers' enchantments, we should
remember that, if history is written by the winners, travel books are written by the survivors.
For every Marco Polo or Ch'ang-ch'un, how many travelers died unrecorded deaths on the
great Silk Road?

★   ★   ★

Crossing through a "desert of surpassing aridity," the Polos linked up with the Silk
Road in eastern Persia, where they found "a good many towns and villages" with a "great
abundance of everything good, for the climate is extremely temperate." There they heard tell
of the Old Man of the Mountains and his Assassins, and how they met their defeat at the hands
of the Mongols. That was in Tabaristan behind them to the west, however. The Polos were
now headed east across Western Turkestan toward Balkh:

*. . . you ride over fine plains and beautiful valleys, and pretty hill-sides producing ex-
cellent grass pasture, and abundance of fruits, and all other products. Armies are glad to
take up their quarters here on account of the plenty that exists. This kind of country ex-
tends for six days' journey, with a goodly number of towns and villages, in which the
people are worshippers of Mahommet. Sometimes also you meet with a tract of desert extending for 50 or 60 miles, or somewhat less, and in these deserts you find no water, but
have to carry it with you. The beasts do without drink until you have got across the
desert tract and come to watering places.*

So after travelling for six days as I have told you, you come to a city called Sapurgan [west of Balkh]. It has great plenty of everything, but especially of the very best melons in the world. They preserve them by paring them round and round into strips, and drying them in the sun. When dry they are sweeter than honey, and are carried off for sale all over the country. There is also abundance of game here, both of birds and beasts.

Balkh itself he found a city that had known greater days, before the Mongols "ravaged and destroyed it." Of the "many fine palaces and buildings of marble," only the ruins remained. Another visitor, the great Moslem traveler Ibn Battuta, who saw the city 60 years later, would add that within the lifeless city: "The remains of its mosques and colleges are still to be seen, and the painted walls traced with azure." Even the villages and countryside beyond Balkh showed the effects of the recent devastation, Marco found:

. . . you ride some 12 days between northeast and east, without finding any human habitation, for the people have all taken refuge in fastnesses among the mountains, on account of the Banditti and armies that harassed them. There is plenty of water on the road, and abundance of game; there are lions too. You can get no provisions on the road, and must carry with you all that you require for these 12 days.

Winding into the Pamirs, they passed through the province of Badakshan (where some place the origin of the "Westerners" who were credited with bringing agriculture and weaving to China in the mid–third millennium B.C.) and marveled at tales of the fine and valuable rubies and azure mined there. Marco noted that this cold country produced excellent horses, which "go at a great pace even down steep descents, where other horses neither would nor could do the like," a trait of particular importance because the mountain roads were very bad. As at Balkh Marco had heard of Alexander's marrying Roxane, so here he heard that some of the Badakshan horses had been bred from "the strain of Alexander's horse Bucephalus."

While travelers over the centuries had complained about the difficulties and dangers of the Pamirs, Marco Polo grew quite eloquent in his praise of the mountains—perhaps because he spent some time there recuperating from an illness and so became accustomed to the thin air of the heights:

Those mountains are so lofty that 'tis a hard day's work, from morning till evening, to get to the top of them. On getting up, you find an extensive plain, with great abundance of grass and trees, and copious springs of pure water running down through rocks and ravines. In those brooks are found trout and many other fish of dainty kinds; and the air in those regions is so pure, and residence so healthful, that when the men who dwell below in the towns, and in the valleys and plains, find themselves attacked by any kind of fever or other ailment that may hap, they lose no time in going to the hills; and after abiding there two or three days, they quite recover their health through the excellence of the air.

Through "many strait and perilous passes, so difficult to force that the people have no fear of invasion," the Polos came to the high plateaus from which the Pamirs take their name:

The plain is called Pamier, and you ride across it twelve days together, finding nothing but a desert without habitations or any living thing, so that travelers are obliged to carry with them whatever they have need of. The region is so lofty and cold that you do not even see any birds flying. [Numerous naturalists have pointed out that the Polos must have passed in winter, for in warmer months the region is teeming with birds.] And I must notice also that because of the great cold [actually the thin air at the heights], fire does not burn so brightly, nor give out so much heat as usual, nor does it cook food so effectually.

Carving a difficult course through the mountains north and northeast, they traveled a good 40 days:

. . . continually passing over mountains and hills, or through valleys, and crossing many rivers and tracts of wilderness. And in all this way you find neither habitation of man, nor any green thing, but must carry with you whatever you require.

The region through which they passed, along the upper reaches of the Yarkand River, is one of the candidates for the site of Tashkurgan, where Indian, Chinese, and Parthian traders met in Roman times. Not all the country is so bleak and lifeless as here described, but, again, a crossing late in the year would partly explain the description.

Finally the Polos emerged on the east side of the Pamirs at Kashgar, which Marco found a country with "beautiful gardens and vineyards, and fine estates," from which "many merchants go forth about the world on trading journeys." And, after having noted in most cities on the way that the inhabitants were predominantly Moslem, he was perhaps pleased to be able to report that at Kashgar were "many Nestorian Christians, who have churches of their own." He noted that Samarkand (which he did not visit but his elders had, on their previous journey) also was inhabited by "both Christians and Saracens."

Ibn Battuta, who traveled through Turkestan some 60 years after Marco Polo crossed Asia, marked the ruination of the once-great city of Samarkand, though he was well aware that the Mongols were not the sole or even the main cause of it. Though it was still, to his mind, "one of the greatest and finest cities, and most perfect of them in beauty"—no small praise from a man who had traveled throughout the Moslem and Mongol world—he nevertheless lamented:

> There were formerly great palaces on its bank, and constructions which bear witness to the lofty aspirations of the townsfolk, but most of this is obliterated, and most of the city has also fallen into ruins. It has no city wall [after the Mongol devastation they presumably had not been rebuilt] and gates, and there are gardens [probably meaning market rather than pleasure gardens] inside it . . .

At Yarkand, the next major city on their route, the Polos found Christians, too, noting also what modern observers can still find: a large proportion of people with goiters (enlarged thyroid glands). These he suggested arose "from some quality in their drinking water," but we know today that they are caused by lack of iodine in the diet. Now descending into the Tarim Basin and following its southern rim, the Polos came to Khotan. There, though they found that "the people have vineyards and gardens and estates" and "live by commerce and manufactures," they reported one major change since the days when this was the favored route of Buddhist pilgrims to India: Now, Marco reported, "all [are] worshippers of Mahommet."

Some have questioned whether Marco might have confounded idol-worship (as Westerners saw Buddhism) with Islam, the Moslem words for the two being similar in sound. Whether or no, Marco's description was at least an accurate prediction of the future, for Khotan was well on its way to becoming a major Moslem center in Central Asia.

Here and to the east were found the rivers where divers had fished for jade for thousands of years. At Cherchen (Shan-shan), where the people also "worship Mahommet," he reported:

> The Province contains rivers which bring Jasper and Chalcedony [jade], and these are carried for sale into Cathay, where they fetch great prices.

Beyond there, the Polos found:

> The whole of the Province is sandy, and so is the road all the way from Pein, and much of the water that you find is bitter and bad . . . Quitting Charchan, you ride some five days through the sands, finding none but bad and bitter water, and then you come to a place where the water is sweet. And there is a city . . . called Lop . . . It is at the

entrance of the great [Lop] Desert, and it is here that travellers repose before entering on the Desert.

★   ★   ★

So the Polos were brought to the edge of the salt desert that had been the bane of travelers for thousands of years. They treated this formidable desert with caution and care, and made special preparations for the journey:

. . . such persons as propose to cross the Desert take a week's rest in this town to refresh themselves and their cattle; and then they make ready for the journey, taking with them a month's supply for man and beast.

On the far side of the desert was the city of Sachiu (Sand City), which we know better as Tunhuang. Here the Polos found "for the most part idolators, but there are also some Nestorian Christians and some Saracens." The idolators speak "a peculiar language," he reported, probably a mark of the Tibetans who had poured into this region with the decline of the T'ang dynasty. But, more oddly, he noted, they "are no traders." Perhaps he was simply reporting that the Tibetan Buddhists left the trading to others, but the comment also reflects the darker days that had fallen on this portion of the Silk Road.

For the Polos were now at Tunhuang, at the head of the Kansu Corridor, the very entranceway to China itself. Even if the Polos were, as ambassadors of the khan, obliged to seek his court first, we would expect them to have some words of wonder about the great cities of silk. That they are silent is a sad reflection on the declined fortunes of Ch'ang-an and Loyang—Sera Metropolis and Sinae Metropolis. In truth, with the successive nomadic dynasties, they had been devastated and then bypassed. Though they would be rebuilt, neither would regain its eminence.

The northern dynasties had set their capitals elsewhere, to the east, where they could be better protected, or to the north, closer to their homelands on the steppe. Betokening the shift of focus, the name Peking (Beijing) means "Northern Capital"; its alternative name over the centuries, Peiping (Beibing), means "Northern Peace." (The Mongols called it Khanbaligh, "City of the Khan.") These were Chinese capitals, however. The Mongols held their main courts elsewhere, at Karakorum in the winter and in the summer at Shangtu (Upper Court), immortalized by Coleridge as Xanadu, north of Peking and east of Karakorum. It was toward these northern cities that the Polos went to complete their mission.

Their route is not entirely clear, since Marco Polo mentions in geographical order a number of cities visited not on this journey, but only later during their many years' residence in

Seen from low hills to the northwest, Khanbaligh—the city that became Peking—lay on a distant, wide, and flat plain. (Adapted from *Peking and The Pekingese*, by Dr. Rennie, reprinted in Yule's *Marco Polo*)

the Mongol East. They may have left the Kansu Corridor via the elongated river-oasis called the Etsin Gol. There, probably at a military post named Etzina established by Kubilai Khan, they would once again have prepared for a desert journey:

> At this city you must needs lay in victuals for forty days, because when you quit Etzina, you enter on a desert which extends forty days' journey to the north, and on which you meet with no habitation . . .

This was the fearsome Gobi, a major portion of which had to be crossed to reach the Mongol cities. Of Karakorum itself, Marco Polo has little to say, beyond that it is a city "three miles in compass . . . surrounded by a strong earthen rampart," and contains a great citadel and a fine palace for the governor.

It is Shangtu that captured his imagination, and his description of it clearly inspired Coleridge's poem about Kubilai Khan's "stately pleasure-dome":

> There is at this place [Shangtu] a very fine marble Palace, the rooms of which are all gilt and painted with figures of men and beasts and birds, and with a variety of trees and

flowers, all executed with such exquisite art that you regard them with delight and astonishment.

Round the Palace a wall is built, inclosing a compass of 16 miles, and inside the Park there are fountains and rivers and brooks, and beautiful meadows, with all kinds of wild animals (excluding such as are of ferocious nature), which the Emperor has procured and placed there to supply food for his gerfalcons and hawks, which he keeps there in mew. Of these there are more than 200 gerfalcons alone, without reckoning the other hawks. The Kaan himself goes every week to see his birds sitting in mew, and sometimes he rides through the park with a leopard behind him on his horse's croup; and then if he sees any animal that takes his fancy, he slips his leopard at it, and the game when taken is made over to feed the hawks in mew. This he does for diversion.

Moreover at a spot in the Park where there is a charming wood he has another Palace built of cane . . . It is gilt all over, and most elaborately finished inside. It [has] gilt and lackered columns, on each of which is a dragon all gilt, the tail of which is attached to the column whilst the head supports the architrave, and the claws likewise are stretched out right and left to support the architrave. The roof, like the rest, is formed of canes, covered with a varnish so strong and excellent that no amount of rain will rot them. These canes are a good 3 palms in girth, and from 10 to 15 paces in length. They are cut across at each knot, and then the pieces are split so as to form from each two hollow tiles, and with these the house is roofed . . . In short, the whole Palace is built of these canes, which . . . . serve also for a great variety of other useful purposes. The construction of the Palace is so devised that it can be taken down and put up again with great celerity; and it can all be taken to pieces and removed whithersoever the Emperor may command. When erected, it is braced against mishaps from the wind by more than 200 cords of silk.

The Lord abides at this Park of his, dwelling sometimes in the Marble Palace and sometimes in the Cane Palace for three months of the year, to wit, June, July, and August; preferring this residence because it is by no means hot; in fact it is a very cool place. When the 28th day of August arrives he takes his departure, and the Cane Palace is taken to pieces.

The Polos stayed in China (the northern part of which was called Cathay, the southern Manzi) for about 16 years, traveling in the khan's service all over China. Having only recently taken over the alien land, Kubilai Khan and his successors were wary of Chinese advisors and employed foreigners in the administration by choice, when possible. If the Christian pope had sent 100 friars, they might well, regardless of the khan's love of religious disputation, have ended up employed primarily as cogs in his civil service. The Polos themselves were only able to obtain permission to leave by undertaking to escort a Mongol princess to her promised husband in Il-khan Persia. That they returned, not overland, but by sea around India is acknowledgment of the sheer physical difficulty of the journey on the Silk Road; the khan's advisors warned of the "great fatigue of that long land journey for a lady."

After a journey on the Spice Route, they disembarked at the Persian Gulf port of Hormuz and crossed southwestern Persia until they reached Tabriz, then effectively the capital of Il-khan Persia, where they safely delivered the princess, who "wept for sorrow at the part–

ing." The Polos found that, despite troubles on the Persian leg of the Silk Road, Tabriz and the region around it were flourishing:

> *The men of Tauris [Tabriz] get their living by trade and handicrafts, for they weave many kinds of beautiful and valuable stuffs of silk and gold. The city has such a good position that merchandize [sic] is brought thither from India, Baudas [Baghdad], Cremesor [in Persia], and many other regions; and that attracts many Latin merchants, especially Genoese, to buy goods and transact other business there; the more as it is also a great market for precious stones. It is a city in fact where merchants make large profits.*

Marco also mentioned that Genoese were active on the Caspian Sea, which he incorrectly suggested was fed by the Euphrates, an indication of the very tenuous geographical knowledge these pioneering travelers had. Genoese merchants, he reported, have "of late . . . begun to navigate the sea, carrying ships across and launching them thereon." This kind of sea trade (which had begun some centuries before as sea raiding, when the Russians had managed to get past the Khazars to the Caspian) is an indication of the increased role of Genoa in the Eastern trade at the time. When, in 1261, the Byzantine Greeks retook Constantinople, it was with the help of Genoese, who benefited by preferential trading agreements as a result. Italian trading communities, especially the Genoese, were to be found throughout the region.

So the Polos journeyed on through Greater Armenia, to Erzerum (whose name means "Roman country," in honor of the long centuries of Byzantine rule there, before the arrival of the Seljuk Turks). In passing, Marco mentioned the well-known oil springs of Georgia, explaining:

> *This oil is not good to use with food, but 'tis good to burn, and is also used to anoint camels that have the mange.*

These are, in modern times, vastly rich oil lands serving Russia, centered on the Caspian port of Baku. The party emerged from the hills at Trebizond, the Black Sea port from which they sailed to Constantinople, Negroponte (a Venetian island protectorate in the Aegean Sea), and then home to Venice.

★   ★   ★

So the Polos completed their unprecedented journey from Europe overland to China and back—for Nicolo and Maffeo, indeed, it was the second such extraordinary round trip. But if the Polos were the first to make such a journey, they were far from the last. Whether others had set out on the same course as they during the years of their stay in the East, we do not know. But once they had brought back word of the riches of the East, many other European, especially Italian, traders set out to follow in the Polos' footsteps.

Nor were they alone on the Silk Road, for in the relative peace brought to Asia by the Mongols the heirs of the hereditary trading professions could safely wind their way through desert and mountains. The khans continued to support merchants in plying their long-distance trade, for there were great profits to be made. Many of the traders, whatever their ethnic backgrounds, were now Moslems; Islam encouraged traders and accorded them higher social status than did other religions. People of other faiths continued to operate on the Silk Road, however. Indeed, as Kubilai Khan had relied on foreign advisors in his distrust of his Chinese subjects, so the early Il-khans of Persia chose to employ Christians and Jews whenever possible, fearing betrayal by their Moslem subjects—especially in Tabaristan, still affected by the ideas that had given rise to the cult of the Assassins.

As the trade was profitable to them, the khans attempted to provide security for merchants and other travelers along the road. The general populace of Persia, for example, was obliged to work at forced labor on the roads and on the fortresses that guarded them. They also had to maintain the horses and asses required by the elaborate communications network of the Mongol Empire. The postal service operated at its fullest extension and refinement in the Chinese territories under Mongol rule. Marco Polo, for example, described in some detail the post system that ran from the Mongol capital of Khanbaligh (Peking) to nearby provinces:

> Now you must know that from this city of Cambaluc [Khanbaligh] proceed many roads and highways leading to a variety of provinces, one to one province, another to another; and each road receives the name of the province to which it leads; and it is a very sensible plan. And the messengers of the Emperor in travelling from Cambaluc, be the road whichsoever they will, find at every twenty-five miles of the journey a station which they call Yamb, or, as we should say, the "Horse-Post-House." And at each of those stations used by the messengers, there is a large and handsome building for them to put up at, in which they find all the rooms furnished with fine beds and all other necessary articles in rich silk, and where they are provided with everything they can want. If even a king were to arrive at one of these, he would find himself well lodged.
>
> At some of these stations, moreover, there shall be posted some four hundred horses standing ready for the use of the messengers; at others there shall be two hundred, according to the requirements, and to what the Emperor has established in each case. At every twenty-five miles, as I said, or anyhow at every thirty miles, you find one of these stations, on all the principal highways leading to the different provincial governments; and the same is the case throughout all the chief provinces subject to the Great Kaan. Even when the messengers have to pass through a roadless tract where neither house nor hostel exists, still there the station-houses have been established just the same, excepting that the intervals are somewhat greater, and the day's journey is fixed at thirty-five to forty-five miles, instead of twenty-five to thirty. But they are provided with horses and all the other

necessaries just like those we have described, so that the Emperor's messengers, come they from what region they may, find everything ready for them.

And in sooth this is a thing done on the greatest scale of magnificence that ever was seen. Never had emperor, king, or lord, such wealth as this manifests! For it is a fact that on all these posts taken together there are more than 300,000 horses kept up, specially for the use of the messengers. And the great buildings that I have mentioned are more than 10,000 in number, all richly furnished, as I told you. The thing is on a scale so wonderful and costly that it is hard to bring oneself to describe it . . .

You must know that by the Great Kaan's orders there has been established between those post-houses, at every interval of three miles, a little fort with some forty houses round about it, in which dwell the people who act as the Emperor's foot-runners. Every one of those runners wears a great wide belt, set all over with bells, so that as they run the three miles from post to post their bells are heard jingling a long way off. And thus on reaching the post the runner finds another man similarly equipt, and all ready to take his place, who instantly takes over whatsoever he has in charge, and with it receives a slip of paper from the clerk, who is always at hand for the purpose; and so the new man sets off and runs his three miles. At the next station he finds his relief ready in like manner; and so the post proceeds, with a change at every three miles. And in this way the Emperor, who has an immense number of these runners, receives despatches with news from places ten days' journey off in one day and night; or, if need be, news from a hundred days off in ten days and nights; and that is no small matter! (In fact in the fruit season many a time fruit shall be gathered one morning in Cambaluc, and the evening of the next day it shall reach the Great Kaan at Chandu [Shangtu], a distance of ten days' journey. The clerk at each of the posts notes the time of each courier's arrival and departure; and there are often other officers whose business it is to make monthly visitations of all the posts, and to punish those runners who have been slack in their work.) The Emperor exempts these men from all tribute, and pays them besides.

Moreover, there are also at those stations other men equipt similarly with girdles hung with bells, who are employed for expresses when there is a call for great haste in sending despatches to any governor of a province, or to give news when any Baron has revolted, or in other such emergencies; and these men travel a good two hundred or two hundred and fifty miles in the day, and as much in the night. I'll tell you how it stands. They take a horse from those at the station which are standing ready saddled, all fresh and in wind, and mount and go at full speed, as hard as they can ride in fact. And when those at the next post hear the bells they get ready another horse and a man equipt in the same way, and he takes over the letter or whatever it be, and is off full-speed to the third station, where again a fresh horse is found all ready, and so the despatch speeds along from post to post, always at full gallop, with regular change of horses. And the speed at which they go is marvellous. (By night, however, they cannot go so fast as by day, because they have to be accompanied by footmen with torches, who could not keep up with them at full speed.)

Those men are highly prized; and they could never do it, did they not bind hard the stomach, chest and head with strong bands. And each of them carries with him a gerfalcon tablet, in sign that he is bound on an urgent express; so that if perchance his horse break down, or he meet with other mishap, whomsoever he may fall in with on the road, he is empowered to make him dismount and give up his horse. Nobody dares refuse in such a *case; so that the courier hath always a good fresh nag to carry him. Now all these numbers of post-horses cost the Emperor nothing at all; and I will tell you the how and the why. Every city, or village, or hamlet, that stands near one of those post-stations, has a fixed demand made on it for as many horses as it can supply, and these it must furnish to the post. And in this way are provided all the posts of the cities, as well as the towns and villages round about them; only in uninhabited tracts the horses are furnished at the expense of the Emperor himself.*

(Nor do the cities maintain the full number, say of 400 horses, always at their station, but month by month 200 shall be kept at the station, and the other 200 at grass, coming in turn to relieve the first 200. And if there chance to be some river or lake to be passed by the runners and horse-posts, the neighbouring cities are bound to keep three or four boats in constant readiness for the purpose.)

Though post stations out on the steppe or desert were surely not so fine as those in China, the principle operated much the same way in far Western Asia. This was true even though the Il-khans of Persia adopted Islam in about 1295 and, at the same time, threw off all semblance of subservience to the Great Khan at Khanbaligh. In some times and places,

On small rivers, like this southern tributary of the Tarim River, modest ferries often existed for trans–Asian travelers. (By Sven Hedin, from his *Through Asia*, 1899)

however, the whole system got out of hand. As one Moslem chronicler reported, in Il-khan Persia:

> There came a time when princesses, princes, courtiers, emirs of ten thousand, of a thousand and of a hundred men, the commanders of provinces, the falcon keepers, panther keepers, equerries, armorers, superintendents of the imperial kitchens and other groups of persons, sent ilchis [state messengers] about any matter large or small to the provinces and—for any reason—even to the Mongol nomadic settlements . . .
>
> Their numbers increased to such an extent, that even if fifty thousand mounts had been stationed at each mail stage, they would not have been enough. All the herds of the Mongols were used for mounts. Then the messengers began quarreling among themselves; thieves exploited the situation for their own purposes, posing as messengers themselves, and waylaying those who were smaller, taking their horses and yarlighs and paizas [insignia of office] from them, and once they had these, cheerfully plundered caravans. The state messengers not only required horses and food, they also robbed the people of turbans, clothes, and other possessions. While on their travels they sold the excess from the food they had requisitioned with such skill and craftiness that they even outshone the Chinese and Indian merchants. They tormented, flogged, hanged, and tortured people in every way so that it was small wonder that cultivation declined and the peasants became preoccupied with protecting their possessions against robbery. The pretentious messengers brought themselves into disrepute with the postmasters and governors, and consequently, if, once in a while, a messenger traveled on important and secret state business, he was considered to be on a par with those rascals, and therefore held in ill repute. In consequence his journey took two or three times as long as expected, since he was given thin horses or no horses at all at the stage posts etc. Even if there were as many as fifty horses assigned to a stage post, there would still not be found two well-fed ones among them for the express messenger to mount. The money intended for the posthouses was largely kept by the governors for their own purposes, and the customs and excise which are the most free flowing sources of revenue to the state were largely used in covering the expenses of the state messengers. Even then it was insufficient. The governors made out drafts, and then made their escape. If this was still not enough the customs and excise officials went into hiding, the messengers started fighting among themselves and the strongest of them pocketed the tax yield. The riffraff attaching themselves to the messengers numbered up to two hundred or even three hundred men on horseback, in the case of messengers traveling with simple orders; some of the more renowned ones had up to five hundred or a a thousand men on horseback with them. At the end of the year all these messengers returned to court without having achieved anything but the squandering of enormous amounts in expenses.

Such messengers were housed at the expense of the local population, settling in sometimes for months at a stretch, and destroying local life in the process, as the same chronicler commented:

> . . . doors that had been particularly delightful had been used for firewood. Gardens that through many years of toil had been made to flourish were destroyed in one day by the

> *messengers allowing their animals to graze there . . . The attendants of the state*
> *messengers tore down the garden walls, and in winter burnt the fruit trees for firewood. If*
> *such a tree was particularly straight, the governors or potentates demanded that it be felled*
> *in order that lances be made from it.*

Things came to such a pass that some people "altered the way into their homes, putting them underground and making them as twisted as possible, in order to deter the state messengers from billeting themselves on them." In some villages, the local people had a compact that "if anybody approached from afar, at some sign they would without exception hide in the irrigation ditch or in the sand" until the interlopers had left.

In such a situation, bandits flourished. (*Bandit*, in fact, derives from an Arab word meaning "one who cuts the road.") The melancholy chronicler continued:

> *At one time there were vast numbers of robbers about, Mongols [and Persians], as well as*
> *escaped slaves and ruffians from the cities. Occasionally peasants and individual settlers*
> *combined with them and acted as their guides. They had spies in all the cities so that they*
> *knew in good time about any caravan due to depart. Some of these robbers were famous*
> *for their bravery, and if they fell into the hands of any tribe, they were spared in view of*
> *their bravery and courageousness. In the event of an ambush it used to be the rule for*
> *caravans, messengers and individual travelers to combine instantly to fight against the*
> *robbers; but now this was no longer the case. The robbers made it their principle to rob*
> *only people above a certain degree of wealth; in this way the poorer people were separated*
> *from the others who now became easy prey. In many villages the robbers had friends*
> *among the notables, and in the cities among the merchants who sold the stolen cloths for*
> *them; occasionally the robbers stayed a month with them and together they ran through*
> *the stolen money with reckless abandon.*
> *. . . generally travelers were less afraid of the robbers than of the protectors of the*
> *highways, since the former robbed them only occasionally, but the latter did so constantly,*
> *wherever they rested.*

Such a situation could not be allowed to continue—the trade was too profitable to all the khans—and they gradually put the situation to rights once again.

★ ★ ★

Travel on the Silk Road again became relatively comfortable and safe. Bandits were less likely to simply murder and plunder, fearing imperial wrath. More generally, they contended themselves with collecting "protection money" for "escorting" the party to the limit of their territory. Such payments became rather formalized; a few decades after the Polos' visit to Armenia, for example, a fellow Italian wrote that on the road between Layas and Tabriz, "for extortions made along the way by Mongolians, that is, Tatar rangers, you may reckon about 50 *aspri* per packload."

The writer here is one Francesco di Balduccio Pegolotti, writing in Florence, Italy, a few decades after the Polos' return to Venice in 1295. Travel to the East had become so common in these years that Pegolotti published *The Practice of Commerce*, a book of advice for merchants contemplating a journey to China; Pegolotti himself may never have taken such a trip, but apparently—like a good reporter—he compiled his information from those who had.

Pegolotti favored a northern route. During the Pax Mongolica, many merchants apparently approached the central portion of the Silk Road from the Eurasian Steppe, prefer- ring its wide flat expanses, and the ability to use wagons, to the long, hard slog over the Anatolian, Armenian, and Iranian heights. What is most striking in Pegolotti's "Advice about the journey to Cathay by the road through Tana" (a city near the mouth of the Don, on the Sea of Azov north of the Black Sea) for merchants "going and returning with wares," is that he made it all seem almost routine:

> First, from Tana to Astrakhan [formerly Atil] it is twenty-five days by ox wagon, and from ten to twelve days by horse wagon. Along the road you meet many Mongolians, that is, armed men.
>
> And from Astrakhan to Sarai it is one day by water on a river, and from Sarai to Saraichuk it is eight days by water on a river. And you can travel [both] by land and water, but people travel by water to spend less [on transportation] of wares.
>
> And from Saraichuk to Urjench [on the Amu] it is twenty days by camel wagon—and for those who are carrying wares it is convenient to go through Urjench, because that is a good market for wares—and from Urjench to Utrar [on the Syr] it is thirty-five to forty days by camel wagon. And should you leave Saraichuk and travel straight to Utrar, you would travel fifty days; and for one who has no wares it would be a better way than traveling through Urjench.
>
> And from Utrar to Almaligh [Almalik] it is forty-five days by pack asses. And you meet Mongolians every day.
>
> And from Almaligh to Kan-chow [in China] it is seventy days by asses.
>
> And from Kan-chow to a river called [the Yangtze?] it is forty-five days by horses.
>
> And from the river you can travel to Quinsay [Hang-chow] and sell there any silver sommi [ingots] you have, because that is a good market for wares. And from Quinsay on you travel with the money you get for the silver sommi you have sold there, that is, with paper money. And said money is called balisci, four of these are worth one silver sommo throughout the country of Cathay.
>
> And from Quinsay to Khanbaligh [Peking], which is the master city in the country of Cathay, it is thirty days . . .
>
> Cathay is a province where there are many towns and many villages. Among others there is one which is the master city, where merchants convene and where is the bulk of trade. And this city is called Khanbaligh. And said city has a circuit of one hundred miles and is all full of people and houses, and of dwellers in the said city.

The route described by Pegolotti took merchants from the Sea of Azov, atop the Black Sea, across the Russian Steppe to Astrakhan on the Caspian, in the region once ruled by the Khazars. Some traders apparently chose to take the shorter land route to the regional Mongol capital of Sarai, farther upstream on the Volga, perhaps doing some trading there (as the Polos had done) and then shipping their goods down by water, before resuming their land journey from Astrakhan. Trading along the way was clearly important for those merchants, for they did not take the easier, more direct route across the steppe to Karakorum (though messengers and envoys might do so). Instead, they arced down between the Caspian and Aral Seas to market cities like Urgenj and often farther south to Bukhara and Samarkand, before looping north again to Utrar and then eastward along the route north of the T'ien Shan. In China, too, they detoured around the country—which foreign traders had not been able to do so readily in previous centuries—to the great port city of Hangchow on the east coast of China, a city Marco Polo and knowledgeable observers called the equal or better of any other European port of the time, perhaps the greatest port in the world. The northern capital, Khanbaligh, was just one of the many destinations for merchants.

Pegolotti also told his readers how they should arrange their affairs for a journey to Cathay. First, he advised, they should not shave, but let their beards grow long. Second, they should at Tana hire *dragomans*, interpreters and guides who would make the necessary arrangements along the way; he gave the sound advice that it was worth the money to hire a good one, since a poor one would be greedy. In addition, he recommended that merchants hire menservants who spoke the Cumanic tongue, the Cumans being the dominant Mongol tribe in the region at the time, and that they would be "regarded as a man of a higher condition" if they also took with them a woman from Tana. As Marco Polo and others noted, there were in many caravan towns women who made themselves available on a long-term basis as "temporary wives," who after their "husbands" had been gone for a certain number of days, say 20, were then free to "marry" again. In some towns, they reported, local citizens occasionally hired out their wives and homes, which itinerant merchants made their own for the duration of their stay. Food also was to be taken on at Tana, enough flour and salt-fish to last 25 days, "for you find meat in sufficiency in every locality along the road"; similar preparations were to be made at every major provisioning town along the way.

As for safety, Pegolotti reported:

> The road leading from Tana to Cathay is quite safe both by day and by night, according to what the merchants report who have used it—except that if the merchant should die along the road, when going or returning, everything would go to the lord of the country where the merchant dies, and the officers of the lord would take everything—and in like manner if he should die in Cathay. Actually if he had a brother or a close associate who could say that he is a brother, the property of the dead man would be given to him, and in this manner the property would be rescued. And there is still another danger; that is,

should the lord die, until the new lord who is to rule has been sent for, in that interval sometimes a disorder occurs against the Franks and other foreigners—they call "Franks" all Christians of the Byzantine Empire westwards—and the road is not safe until the new lord is sent for who is to reign after the one who died.

It is reckoned that from Tana to Sarai the road is less safe than all the rest of the journey. But should there be sixty men [in the caravan], [even] when the road is in its worst condition you would travel as safely as [if you were] in your own home.

Disorder during a succession was, of course, a perennial problem, and one faced by the elder Polos themselves on their first journey into Mongol territory. There were also occasional disorders along the way, too, when the local population chafed under the heavy burden of maintaining roads and mounts for imperial messengers and merchants. Sometimes a region could be temporarily depopulated, as when one Persian khan, repenting that he had remitted taxes for three years, charged four years' worth of taxes all at once, and inflicted terrible mutilations on any who failed to pay; in such a case, it is not surprising that much of the population fled to the hills.

Noting that "merchants on their way may ride a horse or donkey or whatever animal they like," Pegolotti went on to itemize expenses, including salaries for menservants and differential costs depending on whether oxen, camels, or horses were used to carry the loaded wagons. As for what to buy and sell, Pegolotti had some very specific advice:

Anyone wishing to leave from Genoa or from Venice in order to travel to the said places and journey to Cathay would do well to carry linen and go to Urjench, and to buy sommi in Urjench and proceed with these without investing [them] in any other merchandise, unless he has a few bales of the very finest linens, which are not bulky and require no greater expense [for carriage] than would any coarser linens.

From Pegolotti's comments on weights and costs, it appears that, whatever goods merchants brought with them to Turkestan, they brought to China primarily precious metals in the form of money, which they then traded for silk and gold-threaded cloth. The trade was not direct, however, for the Chinese government had for a long time used a system of paper money, as Pegolotti described:

All silver which the merchants carry [with them] when going to Cathay, the lord of Cathay causes to be withdrawn and placed in his treasury; and to the merchants who bring it in he gives paper money, that is, yellow paper struck with the seal of the said lord, that money being called balisci. *And with said money you may and can purchase silk and any other merchandise or goods you may wish to buy. And all the people of the country are bound to accept it, and yet people do not pay more for merchandise although it is paper money. And of the said paper money there are three kinds, one being worth more than another according as the lord orders them to be worth.*

The most popular fabrics for European merchants to buy were heavy patterned silks, like damasks and brocades, quite unlike the wispy gauzes traded westward from China in Roman times.

Pegolotti referred to the paper money as being "struck," since he was familiar only with metal coins. In fact, it was printed using a block printing method employed in China for many centuries. Through such items as paper money and playing cards, including tarot cards, all of which fascinated Europeans, the basic concepts of block printing passed westward to Europe in Mongol times. Oddly, though, the technique that had been used to print whole books for at least seven centuries in China was not apparently put to the same purpose in Europe, which remained entranced with its more modest uses.

Traders like those Pegolotti was addressing continued to traverse the Silk Road and its cousin, the Eurasian Steppe Route, for some decades in that remarkable 14th century. But when in 1368 the Mongols were expelled from China, the open highway of the past 100 years was no more. The Eurasian Steppe Route fell first, victim of the fragmentation that once more befell the steppe. The old line of the Silk Road continued in modest use, being relatively sheltered. But Europeans no longer dared to attempt the dangerous journey through the un-settled lands of Central Asia. They did, for a time, cross through Il-khan Persia to India; that allowed them to circumvent the Egyptians, who otherwise supplied Europe with Eastern goods at a markup of 300 percent or more. But this, too, was barred to Europeans when the Il-khan Persians (in their new devotion to Islam) no longer allowed non-Moslems to pass through their lands unmolested.

So ended Christian Europe's dreams of winning Asia to its faith. Though the Asian Christians had included some influential court advisors and even members of the royal family, they did not have behind them the great numbers of adherents fielded by Islam and Buddhism. Nor was Christianity's attraction increased by association with a highly cultured advanced civilization, unlike Islam, which drew on the golden age of Persian culture, and Buddhism, linked with the ancient Indian and Chinese traditions. Europe at the time was crude and un-lettered; worse, its relatively few representatives—Latins, Greeks, and Nestorians—blunted their proselytizing message by quarreling over heresies among themselves. So as the western khanates gradually adopted Islam and the eastern ones became more uniformly Buddhist, bishops' sees that had once been established from Sarai through Almalik to Peking became vacant, and the Christian faithful, who had carried their religion across Asia into China centuries before, gradually disappeared.

★   ★   ★

But if Christians and Jews were now seldom found on the heart of the Silk Road, the conversion of the western Mongol peoples to Islam brought to the fore other travelers: pilgrims to Mecca. The *Pax Mongolica* had made the *hajj* possible for many during that remarkable century. Some became so enamored of traveling in those golden years that they roamed the world for the joy of it. Just how widely traveled some of these Moslems were is indicated by the fact that Ibn Battuta, a native of Tunisia, met on the borders of China, the brother of a man he had known in North Africa!

But even after the Asian peace and unity were shattered, the common belief in Islam made the way relatively safe for *hajji* traveling on the Silk Road—the more so because, with more converts, there was additional safety in numbers. So, once each year, following the rolling Islamic calendar, Moslems set aside their sectarian differences and gathered in cities along the main westward route to form caravans, which wound over the Iranian saddle and down to Baghdad, where they were joined by fellow Moslems from the Armenian, Georgian, and Anatolian highlands. Barring brief interruptions, *hajji* would continue such long-distance travel, making the Silk Road once again something of a pilgrim's highway until the 17th century, when Persia began to close its borders to outsiders and when it became easier to travel by water from the Persian Gulf or Arabian Sea to reach Mecca's port of Jiddah.

After the break-up of the Mongol Empire, one more Central Asian leader tried to take and hold the Silk Road: the Turco–Mongol warrior called Timur Lang (Timur the Lame, after an old leg wound), a name converted in the West to Tamerlane. Son of a local governor south

The tomb of Mohammed's nephew Ali, at Najaf or Meshed Ali, was a popular stopping place for caravans on the Great Desert Route. (From *The Desert Route to India*, by Douglas Carruthers)

of Samarkand, Timur was well placed from his youth to see the value in the trans–Asian trade that passed his way. By 1369, a year after the Mongols' expulsion from China, he had made himself master of Balkh. In the coming decades he gathered under his mantle the regions of Khwarizm and Transoxiana. In an apparent attempt to force all trans–Asian trade to pass his way, along the old line of the Silk Road, he attacked and razed the cities that had served the more northerly route described by Pegolotti, among them Astrakhan, Sarai, and Urgenj. By the 1380s, Timur was driving with his army along the Silk Road through Persia, destroying the land, transporting most things of value to enrich his homeland, and leaving ghastly pyramids of skulls and bodies reminiscent of those raised by the Mongols a century before. He sacked Tabriz and, like Genghis Khan, transported skilled artisans and artists east to Samarkand. Turning his attention to India for some years, he wreaked a similar devastation there and at the turn of the 15th century in Baghdad.

Samarkand for a time benefited from the men and material poured into it. The city was, in Timur's day, the centerpiece of the Silk Road. An observer in 1404 (a year before Timur's death at the age of 70) noted the arrival in Samarkand of an 800-camel caravan from China, bearing many fine silks and satins, along with jewels, musk, and rhubarb (collected wild and sold widely throughout Eurasia); also in the caravan were Siberian envoys bearing gifts of sables, marten–skins, and falcons, as well as Russian traders carrying linens and other skins.

But such order as Timur had imposed on the Silk Road with his scorched earth policy collapsed at his death. With his passing went the last semblance of order on the great highway. Trade continued, of course; once started, it is hard to stop. But it was and would remain in the hands of local traders, who patched together connections along what had once been a major international thoroughfare. Some scholars suggest that the idea of metal-type printing, which was developed and came into wide use in the early 15th century in Korea, might have reached Europe by some such tenuous network, possibly inspiring the inventive genius of Johann Gutenberg and his lesser-known fellow innovators.

In any case, the great days of the Silk Road were done. The fall of Constantinople to the Ottoman Turks in 1453 only confirmed to the world the death of the 5,000-mile highway. Constantinople had never recovered after its sacking by the Venetians in the early 13th century; it was long past being either the main market for Eastern goods or the main supplier of Europe, though it had continued to serve as a major merchants' marketplace. By the time the Turks finally took the city, it was but a shell; even in the 14th century, the Moslem geographer Abulfeda had noted: "There are sown fields within its walls and a great many ruined houses." The solid line of Moslem countries that now barred Europeans from reaching into Asia was united in one thing: it charged the Europeans heavily for their luxuries. In the end that, plus the Europeans' newly developed skill at ocean sailing, ended any hope of reviving the Silk Road. For, drawn by tales like Marco Polo's, Europeans tried to reach the East by sea. Less than a century after Timur's death, Portuguese sailors were in India; a few decades later, in 1514, they had reached China.

China itself, under the Ming dynasty that followed the Mongols, once more withdrew behind its defensive ramparts, now more definitely than ever before, building the modern version of its Great Wall, the "great stone serpent" that still stands with imposing magnificence today. China not only closed its western frontier but also changed its orientation, so that—quite often involuntarily—its main contacts with the outside world were by sea. The long centuries when the Silk Road had been the main avenue of communication between China and the Mediterranean world, between East and West, had come to an end.

CHAPTER ELEVEN

CITIES IN THE SAND

Afterward, the great caravan cities of the Levant became huge, barely inhabited ruins, and the abandoned oasis cities of the Taklamakan became forbidden places, buried in the sand of the encroaching desert. They were not forgotten, not completely. No matter how desolate the lost cities seemed, the local people knew they existed. The empty husk of cliff-cut Petra still saw the passage of a handful of nomad-traders, and the ruins of Palmyra remained home to a few families of shepherds. Cities like Aleppo and Baghdad retained some importance, but as simple crossroads, and no longer as the termini of a transcontinental highway. The cities on the Iranian Plateau primarily served a poor, self-isolated culture. The damage done by the Mongols to the irrigation systems that had once made Persia something of a garden had never been fully repaired; and the land was no longer enriched by the international trade that had flowed through it for thousands of years.

Farther east, the jewels of Moslem Central Asia, cities like Samarkand and Bukhara, had lost their luster. Though beautifully decorated mosques remained to tell of former majesty, and the great older ruins beyond the city walls told the same tale more quietly, the cities themselves were "an intricate labyrinth of narrow winding streets, bordered by dirty courtyards and miserable houses," as Prince Peter Alexeivitch Kropotkin later described Samarkand. The Tarim cities that had been overwhelmed

Match me such a marvel save in Eastern clime,
A rose-red city half as old as Time.

—*John William Burgon,* Petra

263

Ruins like these told modern explorers of the existence of cities buried in the sands of Central Asia. (By Sven Hedin, from his *Through Asia*, 1899)

by sand, forcing their inhabitants to settle nearer the mountains, were remembered by local people, who certainly knew the ruins were there, but who were impeded by taboos from exploring them.

What the people of the desert and of the wider world had forgotten was the significance of many of the abandoned oasis cities, especially those in the Taklamakan, and the importance they had once had in world affairs. As Voltaire succinctly put it, "The people who at present inhabit those deserts know only that their ancestors have formerly conquered the world." So it was that the Silk Road came to be "rediscovered" by the Europeans—not simply the physical remains, which were there for all who wished to see, but the story those remains had to tell.

For the Europeans, the Silk Road and its great places were history, romance, legend—and more, a locus where all the peoples of Eurasia had met, traded, fought, carried ideas, and intertwined to form the largest single portion of the infinitely diverse human family. Only this can account for the continuing enormous interest in the Silk Road displayed all over the world. The nomads no longer pour out of Asia, wave after wave conquering and transmuting the more fully developed civilizations around them. The nomads are here. We are they, looking back at our own people, our own history.

That is the best way to understand the rediscovery of the Silk Road by the Europeans, late in the great age of European exploration and worldwide expansion. There were imperialist motives, certainly, as the Russians moved east toward the Pacific and the British moved north out of India, with the body of Central Asia as their intended prize. But territorial goals do not fully explain European motives, not nearly well enough. Marc Aurel Stein, Sven Hedin, Nicolai Prejalevsky, Albert Von Le Coq, Paul Pelliot, Albert Grunwedel, and the rest of the explorers, archaeologists, and historians who began to move through Central Asia a century ago were impelled by a wider set of motives, including the simple desire to know, the desire to be first, to be famous for being first, and last but far from least, the desire for treasure. Indeed, these Europeans became looters on a grand scale, and the stolen treasures of Central Asia now grace major museum collections all over the world.

Imperialist rivalries did, however, supply the context within which the European rediscovery of the Silk Road proceeded. Along the route of the Silk Road, from the Mediterranean and Mesopotamia out to Xi'an, the modern successor to nearby Ch'ang-an, 18th- and 19th-century empires met, as they had for some thousands of years—indeed, as they do today. In the west lay the empire of the Ottoman Turks, gradually declining from the powerful conqueror of Constantinople to the "sick man of Europe," with a score of subject peoples developing revolutionary national movements and the independent European nations quarreling over the spoils. To the north, the Russians, pressing south and east after a quick sweep through Siberia to the Pacific in the 17th century. To the south, the British, pushing east through the Arab world and north in the Indian subcontinent. The British-Russian contention in Asia was what the British called the "Great Game," and was itself only a part of the considerably greater imperialist game that culminated in World War I and the Russian Revolution.

To the east, China played a much older game—with whoever controlled the northern marches and whoever came at China from the west, out of Central Asia. That, after all, is the geography and history of it, for the Chinese. Until the modern period, none of China's great adversaries and conquerors had come from the sea, or from the Indian subcontinent. Hsiungnu, Turks, Arabs, Mongols, Manchus—all came from the north and west. And so, too, the Russians in the 18th and 19th centuries, to play the wider "Great Game," for control of Asian desert and steppe.

The Chinese were not passive players in the game, with their territories shrinking under constant European pressure. Far from it. While the Russians were sweeping eastward to the Pacific and then across to North America in the mid-17th century, the Manchus were taking power in China. During the next century, the new ruling dynasty very nearly tripled the amount of territory under its direct control, taking large territories in Sinkiang to the north and west, making it once again the "New Dominion." The name still fit, for China had not held this huge portion of Central Asia for a thousand years, not since the end of the T'ang dominion there. (It was the Mongols who had held Central Asia and China in the 13th and 14th centuries, not the Chinese.)

Although it was Sinkiang that the main drama of the Silk Road's rediscovery was to unfold, it was in the Near East that Europeans first began to understand the history of Eurasia and the great route to China.

On the western half of the Silk Road, traders still plied the routes between the Mediterranean and the old caravan cities of Samarkand and Bukhara. But this local trade, carried on by peoples of many nationalities, including Arabs, Jews, Greeks, and especially

Armenians, was far less lucrative than the long–distance trade in luxury goods that had once flowed over the land. The trading cities along the way had lost much of their wealth and importance. This was not simply because the routes to the East were blocked. More to the point, the power and markets in Europe had shifted west and north with the great age of European exploration. And the main long-range trade of the emerging nation-states of western and northern Europe was carried by ocean routes, west to the Americas and on across the Pacific to the East, or south around Africa and then east to India and China. The Mediterranean was, for a time, something of a backwater.

But it was the length of the sea routes to the East and the continuing search for new markets that compelled the Europeans to once again turn to the Near East. By the early 17th century, the British had established the royally chartered Levant Company, to pursue trade in the Near East, and consulates at the old seaports of Smyrna and Tripoli, as well as in Constantinople (now more commonly called Istanbul, or Stamboul) and Aleppo (known to the Arabs as Haleb). They were, in addition to tapping into the Eastern trade, very much interested in a shorter route to India. Somewhat earlier, the Portuguese (with their own strong interests in India and farther east) and the Venetians (who were attempting in vain to revive their Asian trade) had set up courier routes from Aleppo to Baghdad. But the British favored the course of the old Great Desert Route from Aleppo to Basra, the port on the southern Tigris where couriers and other travelers could embark on boats for the east. Using this shortcut, British couriers could greatly cut the time needed between the dispatch of a question from India and the receipt of a reply from London. Some merchants also hazarded this route, traveling with the caravans that crossed from Aleppo to Basra in April and September, so timed because the ships took advantage of seasonal trade winds in the Indian Ocean.

The Ottoman Turks who ruled the region were, however, ill-disposed to European trading inland. Like the worst of parasites, they virtually killed their host by exacting too punishing a tribute—officially and unofficially—in the form of bribes. But despite the heavy bribes extorted, the Ottomans were unable to guarantee safety on the route; for the Arabs of the Near East—not only desert nomads but also the pashas of cities like Aleppo, Baghdad, and Basra—were periodically rebelling and disrupting the route toward India. The British acknowledged this by sending mail on the Great Desert Route in duplicate, by two separate couriers, attempting to ensure that at least one copy arrived safely at its destination. Travel had become so dangerous by the 1660s that Europeans virtually abandoned the overland routes for nearly a century, until about 1745.

It was in this period that a few inquisitive European merchants stationed in Aleppo set out to see some ruins in the Syrian Desert, of which they had heard from the local Arabs. Their experience in 1678 did not encourage further exploration:

> *These Gentlemen were no sooner arrived there, at Tadmor [Palmyra], but they fell unhappily into ye hands of a Company of Arabian Robbers . . . to satisfy whom they were*

*constrained to part with their very clothes; which great loss & ye fright together so palled
their curiosity that they staied not to take more exact survey of ye ancient ruines, but immediately returned home glad to escape so.*

They were not the first, and far from the last, Europeans to be stripped of their "very clothes";
some returned clothed only in old newspapers. Such treatment so discouraged others from
attempting to reach Palmyra that no Europeans seem to have visited the place for a closer look
until 13 years later, in 1691, when a party found 30 or 40 shepherding families living in "little
huts made of dirt within ye walls of a spacious court, which enclosed a most magnificent
heathen Temple." Dr. William Halifax, who headed this expedition (protected by a pass
bought from a local sheikh), was astounded by the "multitude of marble pillars," many of
them lying broken on the ground. Even so, he felt:

*You have ye prospect of such magnificent ruines, yet if it be lawful to frame a conjecture
of ye original beauty of ye place by what is still remaining I question whether any city in
ye world could have challenged precedence of this in its glory.*

The local Arabs, Dr. Halifax reported, had a bemused and somewhat jaundiced view of
European intentions. When the party visited the sheikh who had given them safe passage, he
asked:

*. . . how we liked Tadmor? & whether we had found a treasure there? for this notion
stickes in ye heads of all these people, that the Frankes [still the local term for all
Europeans at the time] goe to see old Ruines only because there they meet with Inscriptions which direct them to some hid treasure, & therefore tis no unusual thing with
them, when they find a stone with an inscription on one side to turn it down to ye
ground, that it might not be seen or read by any: But we assured him that we went with
no such Expectation, but only out of a desire to see ye place; neither had we brought
anything away with us but a piece of porphyry stone which upon his request we shewed
him . . .*

In this Halifax was rare among Europeans. The fears expressed by the Arabs would be justified
in earnest across Asia, though the treasure that explorers would garner was not necessarily the
kind the Arabs had in mind.

A true survey of the site of Palmyra was not carried out until 1751, with the visit of
Englishmen Robert Wood and James Dawkins. The region was still troubled. Even the pasha
of Damascus, who had nominal control over the region, admitted as much to Wood and
Dawkins:

*The Bashaw [Pasha] of this city told us, he could not promise that his name, or power,
would be any security to us in the place we were going.*

At his suggestion, they hired guards from a local Bedouin leader, and set out in a caravan of about 200 people and a like number of animals toward Palmyra:

> . . . with an escort of the . . . best Arab horsemen, armed with guns and long pikes . . . [on the most dangerous part of the journey, the guide] desired we might submit ourselves entirely to his direction, which was, that the servants should keep with the baggage immediately behind our Arab guard; from which one, two or more of their body were frequently dispatched, for discovery, to what ever eminences they could see, where they remained until we came up. Those horsemen always rode off from the caravan at full speed, in the Tartar and Husiar manner. We doubted whether all this precaution was owing to their being really apprehensive of danger, or whether they only affected to make us think highly of their use and vigilance.

We may imagine how strange it must have seemed to them, coming out of the desert in such a fashion, to find before them a Greco-Roman city that might not have been out of place if transported to the plains of Italy:

> . . . when the hills opening discovered to us, all at once, the greatest quantity of ruins we had ever seen, all of white marble, and beyond them towards the Euphrates a flat waste, as far as the eye could reach, without any object which showed either life or motion. It is scarce possible to imagine anything more striking than this view: So great a number of Corinthian pillars, mixed with so little wall or solid building, afforded a most romantic variety of prospect.

It was the romance that captured the imagination of Europe. Wood and Dawkin's *The Ruins of Palmyra* was a sensation from London to St. Petersburg. Catherine the Great of Russia delighted at being compared to Zenobia, the Palmyrene queen whose name and fame were mentioned in inscriptions on the ruined pillars of the lost city. That a city of such magnificence existed in the middle of a desert gave credence to the great Asian trade that Marco Polo and others had spoken of—often to disbelieving ears.

★   ★   ★

Europeans had long been interested in biblical antiquities (Tadmor itself was mentioned in the Bible); now, they began to be interested in the lost cities of Asia for themselves, as the ruins left by a score of civilizations in the cradle of human history. Travelers found deserts, old cities, new peoples, and invested them all with romance. Men—and women, too—came to see, to write about, and to paint the astonishing views they found along the ancient roads of the Near East. All, of course, saw what they wished to see; thus, Edward Lear's cook commented

These ruins, standing silent on the desert, still testify to the greatness that once was Palmyra. (Iraq Petroleum Company)

on first seeing the rock-cut cliff monuments of Petra: "Oh, Signore, we have come into a world where everything is made of chocolate, ham, curry-powder and salmon." Others, no less romantic but of a more scientific bent, found an archaeological paradise.

Rose-red Petra was only "discovered" by Europeans in 1812. John Burckhardt had disguised himself as a Moslem trader from India (a common device among European travelers) in order to travel in the Near East without attracting hostile attention. Until then the site had been a little Arab settlement known locally as Wadi Mousa and inhabited by half a dozen impoverished families. In these years and those that followed, travelers and then archaeologists were discovering and excavating in Greece, Persia, Mesopotamia, Egypt, and dozens of other places in the ancient world, gradually piecing together the story of the Mediterranean world—and in the process learning about the great highway to the East. The picture is far from complete, even now. It was not until the British occupation of the Near East after World War I, for example, that archaeologists properly identified and began to excavate the Parthian city of

Dura-Europos, on the border of Palmyra's lands. Until then, it had been merely a local town called Salahiya.

While archaeologists continued their work in the Near East, some began to venture eastward to learn the story of the Silk Road. As in every other populated place, Europeans exploring the "trackless wilderness" were guided by local people, to whom the area was simply home. Just how much at home the local people were in the Taklamakan was recalled by English officer Francis Younghusband, traveling back to India from Manchuria, in part via the Gobi and the Taklamakan in the 1880s, long before Sven Hedin and Marc Aurel Stein had begun their explorations. He spoke of his guide:

> *The guide was a doubled-up little man, whose eyes were not generally visible, though they sometimes beamed out from behind his wrinkles and pierced one like a gimlet . . . The way which he remembered where the wells were, at each march in the desert, was simply marvelous. He would be fast asleep on the back of a camel, leaning right over with his head either resting on the camel's hump, or dangling about beside it, when he would suddenly wake up, look first at the stars, by which he could tell time to a quarter of an hour, and then at as much of the country as he could see in the dark. After a time he would turn the camel off the track a little, and sure enough we would find ourselves at a well . . . As a rule no track at all could be seen, especially in the sandy districts, but he used to lead us somehow or other, generally by the droppings of the camels of previous caravans, and often by tracks which they had made, which were so faint that I could not distinguish them myself even when pointed out to me. A camel does not leave much of an impression upon gravel, like a beaten-down path in a garden; but the guide, from indications here and there, managed to make out their tracks even in the dark.*

Not all guides had such finely tuned skills, however. In the early days of this European penetration, some locals, drawn by the promise of easy money to be made from the Europeans, inflated their knowledge, which on the Taklamakan was a recipe for disaster. European explorer Sven Hedin learned this lesson the hard way in 1895. His guide assured him that he was well acquainted with the desert and put in only four days' supply of water, instead of 10 or more. The guide himself was one of the first of the party to die on the attempted crossing of the Taklamakan. Those who survived struggled on, hoping to discover water, until they were reduced to drinking the blood of the few chickens they had left and eating the blood of the sheep they had sacrificed for the purpose (the fluid having coagulated almost immediately into a gelatinous mass). One man even gnawed on the gory lungs of the slaughtered sheep. "I understand now," Hedin commented later, "how thirst can make a man half insane." Some of the party also gathered camel's urine, added vinegar and sugar, and drank it; all were soon prostrate with violent vomiting. Only Hedin and one other man, both of whom had abstained from the noxious mixture, remained fit to travel on in search of water.

Leaving behind a tent pitched on a sand dune, to serve as a signpost for their intended return, they set out toward the east, looking for the life-saving Khotan River. Hedin dressed all in white: "If I was doomed to die in the sand, I wanted to be properly attired; I wanted my burial clothes to be both white and clean." During these desperate days, Hedin thought much about the possibility of his being lost forever, and of the effect on those he would leave behind:

> . . . my soul was harrowed when I pictured the uneasiness, the anxiety which would sieze upon those who were near and dear to me when we never came back and nothing was heard of us. They would wait expectantly year after year, and they would wait in vain; no information would ever reach them . . . Mr. Petrovsky [the Russian counsel at Kashgar] would, of course, send out messengers to inquire about us. They would go to Merket, and would there learn that we left that place on April 10th, intending to steer our course due east. But by then our trail would be long obliterated in the sand; and it would be absolutely impossible to know in which direction we had gone. By the time a systematic and thoroughly exhaustive search could be set on foot, our bodies would probably have been buried several months under the unresting, devouring billows of sand.

Sven Hedin (left) and Marc Aurel Stein are two of the extraordinary explorers and treasure-seekers who opened the Silk Road to the modern world. (From *Through Asia*, by Sven Hedin; India Office Library and Records)

The two men struggled eastward for a few days more, seeking the bed of the Khotan River. In the end Hedin's companion was too weak to go on, and Hedin, now alone, just by chance came on one of the widely spaced pools in the riverbed, now drying with the coming of summer. Having dropped other gear in his weakness, Hedin had no proper vessel in which to carry water to save his companion—until he thought of his waterproof boots, as he later said, the only boots he ever knew that "not only saved a man's life but also travelled right across Asia and back again." This was on the night of May 5, 1895. A few days later the pair met along the slight river with shepherds, who fed and sheltered them while they recovered from their ordeal. All the rest of their party perished. The following winter, when a hunting party came upon the abandoned supplies and the tent Hedin had left as a signpost, the tent (and presumably the bodies of those who had remained behind) was already buried under six feet of drifted sand.

Even on the main line of the Silk Road, the Tarim Basin held dangers for explorers, however expert their guides. In a heavy wind, as so often blows up in moments, wind-blown sand or gravel can kill the unwary today, just as they could 2,000 years ago. Younghusband described the coming of sudden dust storms:

> . . . just as we were preparing to start, we saw a great dark cloud away in the distance over the plain. It was a dust storm coming toward us. Where we were it was quite still, and the sky was bright overhead, and perfectly clear, but away to the west we saw the dark clouds—as black as night. Gradually they overspread the whole sky, and as the storm came nearer we heard a rumbling sound, and then it burst upon us with terrific force, so that we were obliged to lie at full length behind our baggage . . .

In all, he found the gravel plains interspersed with sand dunes:

> . . . the most desolate country I have ever seen. Nothing we have passed hitherto can compare with it—a succession of gravel ranges without any sign of life, animal, or vegetable, and not a drop of water . . .

In spite of the hardships, many of these 19th- and early 20th-century Europeans on the eastern reaches of the Silk Road were still romantics. Two weeks after the dust storm, and after very hard going along the Taklamakan, Younghusband observed that:

> The sunset was wonderful. Even in the Indian hills during the rains I have never seen such a peculiar red tinge as the clouds had tonight. It was not red, it was not purple, but a mixture between the two—very deep, and at the same time shining very brightly . . .

when it was nearly dark, a very light, phosphorescent-looking cloud hung over the place of sunset.

Although Sven Hedin and Aurel Stein were the first of the Europeans to literally dig into the buried oasis cities of the Taklamakan, there had been a fair number of European travelers in that part of Asia a little earlier in the 19th century. Their travels and written work had served to introduce modern Europeans to the area. Most, though not all of them, were traversing and mapping Central Asia in the service of the Russian and British governments. These included both Younghusband and the greatest of the Russian 19th-century traveler-explorers, Nicolai Prejalevsky, who made four major trips through Central Asia between 1870 and 1885, covering in all about 20,000 miles, in the process mapping the Lop Nor, until then unknown to modern Europeans, and sighting, but not digging in, some of the buried oasis cities that were later to be reached by Hedin, Stein, and other European explorer-archaeologists.

★   ★   ★

Even before Younghusband and Prejalevsky, Europeans had begun to travel the eastern portions of the old Silk Road. Indeed, the great German geographer and traveler, Baron Ferdinand Von Richtofen (uncle of the World War I flying ace, the Red Baron, Manfred Von Richtofen), in the mid-19th century coined the modern name *Seidenstrasse*, or Silk Road. Surveyor William Johnson, exploring north out of India into the Taklamakan, reported a visit to old sand-buried ruins in 1865. The visit was a direct result of the Great Game, for Johnson was acting upon information supplied by Indian spies hired by the British to go north and gather information in areas from which the British were effectively debarred.

In 1890, the young Swedish explorer and geographer, Sven Hedin, began half a century of journeying into eastern Central Asia. That year, at the age of 25, he went to Kashgar, and there met both the Russian and British representatives, Nicolai Petrovsky and George McCartney, as well as Francis Younghusband and others of the small international community there. These people were to become vitally important for Hedin, Stein, and many of the explorers who came after them, because Kashgar was the key jumping-off place for the exploration of Chinese Central Asia, the place at which indispensable clearances were to be obtained from Chinese officials—and a place for rest and, if necessary, treatment. It was in Kashgar, for example, that Hedin spent 50 days recuperating under the care of Petrovsky after a near-disastrous mountain-climbing attempt and a related eye inflammation that left him temporarily blind.

Petrovsky and McCartney were bitter rivals, each representing his government in one of the most remote and sensitive areas in Central Asia. Yet between them they provided succor to Western explorers of Chinese Central Asia for half a century. It should also be said that, from the Chinese point of view, they provided a base for those who looted some of China's most precious treasures in those years.

Hedin spent the years 1894–1897 in Central Asia. On January 9, 1896, he made his first visit to one of the old oasis towns of the Taklamakan, Yotkan, by then the small village of Borasan near Khotan. Petrovsky and Hedin had become aware of the place, as Khotanese traders had been bringing antiquities to Kashgar from Borasan since Petrovsky and other Europeans had begun to provide a market for their finds. As soon as it became clear that the Europeans coveted certain kinds of artifacts from the ruins, local excavators—and forgers, too—appeared on the scene, as they have all over the world in similar circumstances. In Borasan, Hedin bought some antiquities, found a few terra-cotta pieces, and employed local people to search for more while he proceeded on his journey into the Taklamakan. The result was the acquisition of 523 pieces, which were to form the basis of the major collection of Stockholm's Sven Hedin Foundation. This marked the start of the great race for the spoils of exploration that was to characterize the next three decades of European exploration and archaeological excavation in Chinese Central Asia, especially on the route of the old Silk Road. Hedin also observed at Borasan that the antiquities he had collected clearly showed their joint Hellenic and several Asian origins, an idea that Aurel Stein later developed very fully in several major works, notably *Serindia*.

Later that year, Hedin found his first sand-buried city, Dandan-Uilik, which the local people called Taklamakan. On a subsequent trip, in 1889–1900, he discovered and took antiquities from Loulan, on the northeast edge of the Taklamakan. The old Chinese garrison city had been abandoned after Han times, perhaps 1,600 years earlier, and had long since been overwhelmed by the desert sand. At Loulan, regarded in the West as his greatest early discovery and in China as his most costly, he took many antiquities, including a considerable cache of early manuscripts.

Sven Hedin was an explorer and a geographer, rather than an archaeologist or historian. And a romantic, too, just as much as Younghusband or any other European discovering ancient civilizations in what was for them a vast and nearly trackless waste. His first sand-buried city, Taklamakan (Dandan-Uilik), yielded these musings:

> *At what period was this mysterious city inhabited? When did its last crop of russet apricots ripen in the sun? . . . When did its despairing people finally abandon their dwellings to the ravenous maw of the desert king? Who were the people who lived here? What was the tongue they spoke? Whence came the unknown inhabitants of this Tadmor [Palmyra] in the wilderness? . . . This city of Takla-makan . . . this city, of whose existence no European had hitherto any inkling, was one of the most unexpected discoveries that I made throughout the whole of my travels in Asia. Who could have imagined that in the interior of the dread Desert of Gobi [at that time referring also to the*

*Taklamakan], and precisely in that part of it which in dreariness and desolation exceeds
all other deserts on the face of the earth, actual cities slumbered under the sand, cities
wind-driven for thousands of years, the ruined survivals of a once flourishing civilization?
And yet there stood I amid the wreck and devastation of an ancient people, within whose
dwellings none had ever entered save the sand-storm in its days of maddest revelry; there
stood I like the prince in the enchanted wood, having awakened to new life the city which
had slumbered for a thousand years, or at any rate rescued the memory of its existence
from oblivion.*

Hedin continued to be active in Central Asia into the late 1930s, as camels gave way to
motor vehicles and expedition size grew enormously. He had first gone into the desert with
four others, all local; by the late 1920s, he was leading hundreds of people into Central Asia. He
was for almost two decades one of the most popular and romantic figures of his time, although
that ended for him in some countries after he espoused the German side in World War I. And
after he made it clear that his sympathies were with the Nazis in World War II, the rest of the
world turned away from him. He died in 1952, at the age of 87, almost forgotten save by a few
specialists. Even so, he was the first, east or west, to travel to, explore, realize the significance
of, and write about the lost cities of the Tarim Basin, the buried oasis cities of the old Silk Road.

After 1900, there was a major new European presence on the Silk Road. In that year,
British historian and archaeologist Marc Aurel Stein crossed the Pamirs to Kashgar to begin
over four decades of work in the deserts and mountains of Central Asia and the Near East. His
work ended only with his death in Kabul, in 1943, at the age of 80, on the verge of yet another
expedition into Central Asia.

Aurel Stein, later Sir Aurel Stein, was the pre-eminent early European historian and
explorer of the Silk Road and of the cultures that met and interpenetrated along that highway
for some thousands of years. He came to Central Asia and the Near East with hypotheses to
test: about the route of Alexander, the role of Dura-Europos and Palmyra, the Greek influences on the art of northern India, the extension of Han power 2,000 years ago, and the
fusion of Chinese, Indian, Persian, Greek, and other cultures into a single Buddhist culture
along the Silk Road a thousand years ago and more, in T'ang times. This was no Sven Hedin,
climbing a mountain or crossing a desert essentially because it was there, as explorers and
adventurers will. Aurel Stein was different, and much more; it was he who first fully brought
the old civilizations along the Silk Road in Central Asia to the attention of an astonished 20th-
century world. And that was unquestionably a massive contribution to world history and to
the developing science and art of archaeology.

He was also unquestionably an antiquities-taker on a grand scale, as were all the major
European archaeologists working in Asia and the Near East in his time. From Sven Hedin's
time on, archaeologists engaged in three decades of "taking" along the Silk Road. Some were
far more destructive than others; the German expeditions, under Von Le Coq and Grunwedel,

This fresco of Chinese Buddhist monks near Turfan
survived for centuries, until Western treasure-hunters
sawed it into sections and carried it off to Berlin,
where it was destroyed in World War II bombings.
(From *Chotscho*, by Albert von le Coq, Berlin)

were notably careless about their excavation and removal methods, irretrievably damaging
many extraordinarily important sites and artworks. Stein did not do that; he was careful to dig
well, though sometimes too fast, as many other archaeologists have since noted.

Aurel Stein made three remarkably successful major expeditions into the Tarim Basin,
the first in 1900-1901, the second in 1906-1908, and the third in 1913-1916. A Hungarian who
went to England as a post–doctoral student in Oriental languages and archaeology, Stein met
and was befriended by several of the most advanced orientalists of the time, including Sir
Henry Yule and Sir Henry Rawlinson. In 1888, they found him a post as registrar of Punjab
University and principal of the new Oriental College in Lahore, a job at which he spent 10 very

impatient years, going north into Kashmir to pursue his real vocation at every opportunity. In 1898, he proposed to the Indian government an archaeological exploration beyond the Pamirs, and with strong sponsorship he eventually gained approval. In this, he was much helped by Sven Hedin's account of his 1894–1897 journey, which had opened the question of Central Asian exploration as never before. He also used the Great Game, for in his proposal he cannily suggested that the Russians were preparing an expedition into the Taklamakan and that Hedin, who was much closer to the Russians than to the British, could be counted on to go back into the Tarim.

Stein's first expedition into the Taklamakan was an enormous success. It brought him fame as soon as his findings were made known and his antiquities shown. He had gone north over the Pamirs, secured the necessary Chinese government permissions in Kashgar, with McCartney's help, and gone directly to Hedin's buried city of Taklamakan. He spent three weeks there and found enough to completely validate his main cross-cultural Buddhist civilization thesis—and to come away with many treasures. He then did much the same at Niya, Yotkan, and several other Tarim sites, in the process creating doors through which many Western archaeologists and treasure-seekers would pass for the next three decades.

By the time of Stein's second Central Asian expedition, in 1906, a race was on between rival European treasure-seekers in the Tarim Basin, a mirror of the great power rivalries that were soon to tear European society apart. On this trip, Stein raced the length of the southern branch of the Silk Road around the Taklamakan, to get to Hedin's second major find, at Loulan, before his rivals. He stopped and worked swiftly at a succession of sites, including Rawak, Khadalik, Niya again, Endere, and Miran. Everywhere he took antiquities: at Khadalik, "six large boxes" of "stucco, frescoes, etc."; at Niya, "an archive of documents"; at Miran, "frescoes, as brittle as pastry."

He was still a working archaeologist and historian, but he was also, and very clearly, a highly competitive treasure-hunter intent on finding and taking all he could—for his government, not for himself. That was never a question for him, Hedin, Grunwedel, Von Le Coq, Pelliot, or almost all of those engaged in this arduous competition. Those expeditions were on behalf of national governments and institutional sponsors, most of whom hold these Asian antiquities to this day.

Stein's greatest haul followed. Two years earlier, at the Caves of the Thousand Buddhas, a Buddhist holy place near Tunhuang, a local monk, Abbot Wang, had unearthed a huge treasure trove of very old manuscripts and artwork, walled up for many centuries. Hearing of the trove, Stein bribed Wang into letting him take away over 500 works of art, including many painted silks, 3,000 complete or nearly complete rolls of printed materials, and 6,000 other pieces of documentary material. Many of the painted silks were folded into small, creased packets; when painstakingly unfolded by scientists at the British Museum, they revealed themselves as large, superb paintings on very fine silken gauze. One of the rolls was the Diamond Sutra, block-printed in 868 A.D., the oldest dated printed book known. (Older printed fragments exist.) This alone is a treasure beyond price. This—and the rest of Stein's takings from the Caves of the Thousand Buddhas—is one of the greatest collections in world history. And as a scholarly resource, it is worth still more, much more.

To add injury to injury, Paul Pelliot went to Tunhuang in 1908, and bribed Wang to let him take away additional thousands of complete manuscripts and documentary fragments. And Aurel Stein was not finished; on a return visit to Tunhuang in 1914, he took 600 more Buddhist manuscript rolls. Similarly, Von Le Coq, Grunwedel, and others sawed many large frescoes off the walls of temples along the Silk Road, notably at Bezeklik and Kyzil, and took them back to Berlin, where most were destroyed by Allied bombings during World War II.

A considerable modern dispute exists today over the activities of these European explorers of the eastern portion of the Silk Road. China wants back what was taken from Sinkiang in those years, arguing that any permissions granted then by a weak, hard-pressed Chinese government should now be regarded as invalid—that whatever was taken was simply stolen. This position is similar to that taken by Greece regarding the Elgin Marbles, where it is argued that Turkish permission to take Greek national treasures should be considered invalid. The significance of the Asian treasures is certainly comparable.

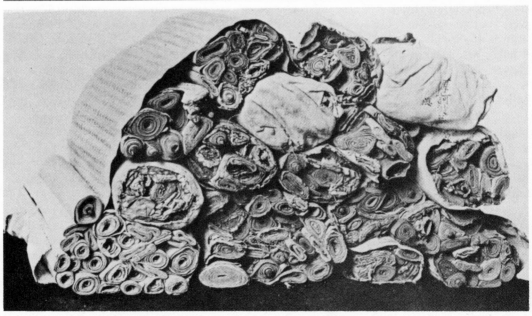

This was just one bundle of the thousands of manuscripts taken by modern explorers from the walled-up room in the Caves of the Thousand Buddhas. (By Aurel Stein, from his *Ruins of Desert Cathay*)

The Chinese argument is powerful, as is the Greek. Those who hold the treasures can respond that, if they had not taken them, they might easily have been destroyed by local excavators seeking to sell them piecemeal, by factional and national warfare in the century of conflict that has wracked Central Asia, or by the Red Guards. And there is some truth in this response—but only some, for whatever has gone before, the works do exist and will sooner or later go home.

Ultimately, the "taking" came to an end, in China and on the whole length of the old Silk Road, all the way to the Mediterranean. Now, archaeologists the world over can dig, and can make great contributions to the study of the history of humanity by digging, but they cannot take their trophies away with them.

As the 20th century wore on, the Silk Road began to take on a more modern aspect. In Western Asia, automobiles began to be used in the Syrian Desert around the time of World War I; they traveled easily on the gravel-covered wasteland and allowed travelers to take advantage of desert shortcuts, with little worry about shortages of water. Farther east, motor vehicles began to be used by European explorers, often in conjunction with camels, which carried the extra supplies of gasoline. Modern technology began to change the character of travel on the great trans-Asian highway.

Automobiles offered little enough comfort in those early days, but even so they were markedly preferable to long days of riding in the saddle across steppe and desert. So, for the first time in the history of the Silk Road, the distances across Eurasia began to shrink. Once the region was in the physical reach of everyone, the Silk Road, theoretically, became open to all. As Roy Chapman Andrews once put it, "the sanctity of the desert was gone forever."

European explorers—even after the advent of the automobile—were certainly not proof against the bandits and raiders who had plied their trade on the route for millennia. Indeed, explorers and scientists in East Asia found that brigandage had adopted a somewhat ritualized form, just as it had in West Asia. Andrews reported that:

> . . . our caravan met five thousand camels just down from Urga [then the Mongolian capital]. Accompanying them was a bandit "liaison officer." A few years before he had been a respectable landlord of one of the motor inns on the Urga trail. I knew him well and knew that now he was a head brigand. What is more, he knew that I knew it. He posed as a "general" who could arrange protection for our caravan through his "soldiers." Half an hour of tea-drinking and extraneous conversation ensued before we got around to business. He suggested the customary fee of five dollars a camel. I offered one dollar. He knew that our boxes contained nothing that his brigands could use or sell, and eventually we settled on half the usual amount.

Modern travelers on the Silk Road are often quite dislocated from the experience of past travelers. Sped along in motor vehicles—even the slowest of which is far faster than the caravan's usual crawl of perhaps two miles an hour—or on trains, or even divorced from the ground altogether, as they are wafted across Asian expanses in modern aircraft, they must have a powerful will to even begin to imagine the way of life on the Silk Road when all were tied to the fragile thread of the caravan trails.

But still they come, drawn by the romance of the old Silk Road.

In the wake of archaeologist and explorer there came a new type of traveler on the Silk Road: the tourist. Like those in whose footsteps they walked, early tourists were drawn first to the Near East, where they hired dragomans to shepherd them to the ancient sites of Western Asia, often as part of a tour that included India and, if politics allowed, perhaps Iran, Turkestan, or China. Twentieth-century package tours of necessity had the same sort of itinerary for many decades.

But as usual during most of its history, the Silk Road in modern times has seldom been open to all or for its full length. The Russian revolution and civil war, the Chinese revolution and civil war, Soviet-Chinese border tensions, the presence of military and atomic power installations (like those in the Lop Nor), the Iran-Iraq war, the decades-long Israeli–Arab-Lebanese clashes in the Middle East, the Afghan–Soviet conflict, and scores of other major and minor dislocations and confrontations have made it impossible for travelers to take the long, long journey across the face of Eurasia that marks the true, full compass of the Silk Road.

On the other hand, it has been possible to traverse many portions of the Silk Road at several times during the last few decades. For some, like Fitzroy Maclean, that has meant a trip through Soviet Central Asia, to some of the great old caravan cities. For others, it has meant a trip to China, culminating in a trek out of the now-bustling industrial city of Xi'an into Sinkiang to the successors of the old oasis cities ringing the Taklamakan. Some have managed to travel north out of India on the Karakorum Highway, generally following pilgrim and archaeologist routes into Central Asia. When the political conditions have been favorable, others have journeyed in Western Asia and Mesopotamia, and to many of the old Silk Road and Incense road sites.

However they go, whenever they go, fortunate and hardy travelers will feel the pulse of history all along the Silk Road. No matter how remote, how seemingly uncharted, wild, and desolate the country, they may be sure that others have passed this way and left their mark. Though much has changed, the memory of the Silk Road remains, the memory of one of the world's oldest highways, a great river, with a score of tributaries, that flowed between humanity's oldest civilizations for thousands of years.

Even when fragmented by political realities, the road remains, the road that saw Chinese silk and Roman gold, and all the treasures, ideas, religions, inventions, products, and skills of the peoples across Eurasia. It is right that the Silk Road should live in our memory and imagination as one of the greatest of all human pathways.

BIBLIOGRAPHY

Allchin, Bridget, and Raymond Allchin. *The Birth of Indian Civilization: India and Pakistan Before 500 B.C.* Harmondsworth: Penguin, 1968.

Ashtor, Eliahu. *A Social and Economic History of the Near East in the Middle Ages.* Berkeley: University of California Press, 1976.

Basham, A.L. *The Wonder That Was India: A Survey of the Culture of the Indian Sub-Continent Before the Coming of the Muslims.* New York: Grove Press, 1959.

Barthold, Vasili V. *Turkestan Down to the Mongol Invasion*, 2nd edition. London: Luzac & Co., 1928. Translated from the Russian by the author with the assistance of H.A.R. Gibb. Original title: *Turkestan at the Time of the Mongol Invasion.*

Bausani, Alessandro. *The Persians.* New York: St. Martin's, 1962. Translated from the Italian by J.B. Donne.

Beal, Samuel. *Buddhist Records of the Western World.* New York: Paragon, 1968. Reprint of 1906 edition.

Bell, M.S. "The Great Central Asian Trade Route from Peking to Kashgaria." *Proceedings of the Royal Geographic Society*, Vol. 12 (1890), pp. 57 ff.

Benveniste, Emile. *Indo-European Language and Society.* Coral Gables, Florida: University of Miami Press, 1973. Miami Linguistic Series No. 12. Translated from the French edition of 1969.

Boulger, G.S. "The History of Silk." *Asiatic Review*, Vol. 16 (1920), pp. 662-77.

Bourlière, Françoise. *The Land and Wildlife of Eurasia.* New York: Time, 1964.

Blunt, Wilfrid. *The Golden Road to Samarkand.* New York: Viking, 1973.

Braudel, Fernand. *Civilization and Capitalism, 15th-18th Century*, 3 volumes. New York: Harper and Row. Volume 1, *The Structures of Everyday Life: The Limits of the Possible*, 1981; originally translated as *Capitalism and Material Life, 1400-1800* by Miriam Kochan, revised by Siân Reynolds. Volume 2, *The Wheels of Commerce*, 1982, and Volume 3, *The Perspective of the World*, 1984, both translated by Siân Reynolds.

Brent, Peter. *Genghis Khan: The Rise, Authority and Decline of Mongol Power*. New York: McGraw-Hill, 1976.

Boulnois, L. *The Silk Road*. London: George Allen & Unwin, 1966. Translated by Dennis Chamberlin.

Bretschneider, Emil. *Medieval Researches from Eastern Asiatic Sources: Fragments Towards the Knowledge of the Geography and History of Central and Western Asia from the 13th to the 17th Century*, 2 volumes. London: Kegan Paul, Trench, Trubner & Co., n.d. (c. 1888).

Brown, Slater. *World of the Desert*. Indianapolis: Bobbs-Merrill, 1963.

Browning, Iain. *Palmyra*. Park Ridge, New Jersey: Noyes Press, 1979.
———. *Petra*, new and revised edition. London: Chatto & Windus, 1982.

Buchanan, Keith, Charles R. Fitzgerald, and Colin A. Ronan. Foreword by Joseph Needham. *China: The Land and the People*. New York: Crown, 1980.

Burnaby, Fred. *A Ride to Khiva*. London: Century, 1983. Reprint of 1877 edition.

Byron, Robert. *The Road to Oxiana*. New York: Oxford University Press, 1982. Reprint of 1937 edition.

Cable, Mildred, and Francesca French. *Through the Jade Gate and Central Asia*. Boston: Houghton Mifflin, 1927.

Carpenter, Rhys. *Beyond the Pillars of Heracles*. New York: Delacorte, 1966. Part of the Great Explorers series.

Cameron, Nigel. *Barbarians and Mandarins: Thirteen Centuries of Western Travelers in China*. Chicago and London: University of Chicago Press, 1976.

Carruthers, Douglas, ed. *The Desert Route to India: Being the Journals of Four Travellers by the Great Desert Caravan Route Between Aleppo and Basra, 1745-1751*. London: Hakluyt Society, 1929.

Chambers, James. *The Devil's Horsemen: The Mongol Invasion of Europe*. New York: Atheneum, 1979.

Chandra, Moti. *Trade and Trade Routes in Ancient India*. New Delhi: Abhinav Publishers, 1977.

Chard, Chester S. *Northeast Asia in Prehistory*. Madison: The University of Wisconsin Press, 1974.

Charlesworth, Martin Percival. *Trade Routes and Commerce of the Roman Empire*. London: Cambridge University Press, 1924.

Chêng Tê-K'un. "Travels of the Emperor Mu." *Journal of the Royal Asiatic Society, North China Branch*, Vol. 64 (1933), pp. 124 ff; Vol. 65 (1934), pp. 128 ff.

Childe, V.G. *The Aryans: A Study of Indo-European Origins*. Port Washington, New York: Kennikat Press, 1970. Reprint of 1926 edition.

College, Malcolm A.R. *The Parthians*. New York: Praeger, 1967. Part of the Ancient Peoples and Places series.

Collins, Robert J. *East to Cathay: The Silk Road*. New York: McGraw-Hill, 1968.

Coon, Carleton S. *Caravan: The Story of the Middle East*. New York: Henry Holt, 1951.

Coyajee, J.C. *Cults and Legends of Ancient Iran and China*. Bombay: Karami, 1936.

Culican, William. *The First Merchant Ventures: The Ancient Levant in History and Commerce*. London: Thames and Hudson, 1966. From the Library of Ancient Civilizations.

Curzon, Robert. *Armenia: A Year at Erzeroom, and on the Frontiers of Russia, Turkey, and Persia*. New York: Harper and Brothers, 1854.

de Gaury, Gerald, and H.V.F. Winstone. *The Road to Kabul: An Anthology*. London: Quartet, 1981.

Dilke, O.A.W. *Greek and Roman Maps*. Ithaca, New York: Cornell University Press, 1985. Part of the Aspects of Greek and Roman Life series.

Downey, Glanville. *Antioch in the Age of Theodosius the Great*. Norman: University of Oklahoma, 1962. Part of the Centers of Civilization series.

Dubs, Homer. *A Roman City in Ancient China*. London: The China Society, 1957. No. 5 in the China Society Sinological series.

Dunlop, D.M. *History of the Jewish Khazars*. New York: Schocken, 1967.

East, Gordon. *The Geography Behind History*, revised and enlarged edition. New York: Norton, 1967.

Edwardes, Michael. *East-West Passage: The Travel of Ideas, Arts and Inventions Between Asia and the Western World*. New York: Taplinger, 1971.

Etherton, Percy Thomas. *In the Heart of Asia*. London: Constable, 1925.

Fairbank, John K., Edwin O. Reischauer, and Albert M. Craig. *East Asia: The Modern Transformation*. Boston: Houghton Mifflin, 1965. Volume Two of *A History of East Asian Civilization*; see Reischauer.

Fairley, Jean. *The Lion River: The Indus*. New York: John Day, 1975.

Fleming, Peter. *News From Tartary: A Journey From Peking to Kashmir*. Los Angeles: J.P. Tarcher, n.d. Reprint of 1936 edition. Part of the Library of Travel Classics.

Fox, Ralph. *Genghis Khan*. New York: Harcourt, Brace & Co., 1936.

Franck, Irene M., and David M. Brownstone. *To the Ends of the Earth: The Great Travel and Trade Routes of Human History*. New York: Facts On File, 1984.

Frye, Richard Nelson. *Bukhara: The Medieval Achievement*. Norman: University of Oklahoma Press, 1965. Part of the Centers of Civilization series.
———. *The Heritage of Persia*. Cleveland and New York: World, 1963.

Gernet, Jacques. *Daily Life in China: On the Eve of the Mongol Invasion, 1250-1276*. New York: Macmillan, 1962. Translated from the French by H.M. Wright.
———. *A History of Chinese Civilization*. Cambridge: Cambridge University Press, 1982. Translated by J.R. Foster.

Ghirshman, Roman. *Iran from the Earliest Times to the Islamic Conquest*. Harmondsworth: Penguin, 1954.

Gibb, Hamilton Alexander Rosskeen. *The Arab Conquests of Central Asia*. London: Royal Asiatic Society, 1925.

Giles, H.A., translator and editor. *The Travels of Fa-Hsien (391-414 A.D.) or Record of the Buddhist Kingdoms*. Cambridge: Cambridge University Press, 1923.

Giles, L. *Six Centuries at Tunhuang*. London: China Society, 1944.

Glover, T.R. *The Ancient World: A Beginning*. Baltimore: Penguin, 1964.

Grant, Michael. *From Alexander to Cleopatra: The Hellenistic World*. New York: Scribner, 1982.

Grant, Christina Phelps. *The Syrian Desert: Caravans, Travel and Exploration*. New York: Macmillan, 1938.

Grousset, René. *Chinese Art and Culture*. New York: Grove Press, 1961. Translated from the French by Haakon Chevalier.
———. *The Civilization of India*. New York: Tudor, 1939. Translated from the French by Catherine Alison Phillips.

———. *Conqueror of the World: The Life of Chingis-Khan*. New York: Orion, 1966. Translated from the French by Marian McKellar and Denis Sinor.

———. *The Empire of the Steppes: A History of Central Asia*. New Brunswick, New Jersey: Rutgers University Press, 1970. Translated from the French by Naomi Walford.

———. *In the Footsteps of the Buddha*. New York: Grossman, 1971. Translated from the French by J.A. Underwood.

———. *The Rise and Splendour of the Chinese Empire*. Berkeley: University of California Press, 1953. Translated by Anthony Watson-Gaudy and Terence Gordon.

Hambly, Gavin, et al. *Central Asia*. London: Weidenfeld and Nicolson, 1969.

Hart, John. *Herodotus and Greek History*. Berkenham: Croom Helm, 1983.

Hayashi, Ryoichi. *The Silk Road and the Shoso-in*. New York: Weatherhill, 1975. Volume 6 of the Heibonsha Survey of Japanese Art.

Hedin, Sven. *The Silk Road*. New York: Dutton, 1938. Translated from the Swedish by F.H. Lyon.

———. *Through Asia*, 2 volumes. London and New York: Harper & Brothers, 1899.

Heichelheim, Fritz Moritz. *An Ancient Economic History, from the Paleolithic Age to the Migrations of the Germanic, Slavic, and Arabic Nations*, 3 volumes. Revised and complete English edition. Leiden: A.W. Sijthoff, 1958.

Hirth, F. *China and the Roman Orient: Researches into Their Ancient and Medieval Relations as Represented in Old Chinese Records*. New York: Paragon, 1966. Reprint of original, 1885 Shanghai edition.

Hitti, Philip K. *The Near East in History: A 5000 Year Story*. Princeton, New Jersey: D. Van Nostrand, 1961.

Hopkirk, Peter. *Foreign Devils on the Silk Road: The Search for the Lost Cities and Treasures of Chinese Central Asia*. London: John Murray, 1980.

Hudson, G.F. *Europe and China: A Survey of Their Relations from the Earliest Times to 1800*. London: Edward Arnold, 1931; reprint, Boston: Beacon Press, 1961.

Humble, Richard. *Marco Polo*. New York: Putnam, 1975.

Huzzayin, S.A. *Arabia and the Far East: Their Commercial and Cultural Relations in Graeco-Roman and Irano-Arabian Times*. Cairo: Publications de la Société Royale Géographie D'Egypte, 1943.

Ibn Battuta. *Travels, A.D. 1325-1354*, 3 volumes. Cambridge: Cambridge University Press, 1958-71. Hakluyt Society Publications, 2nd Series, No. 110. Translated by H.A.R. Gibb.

Irving, Clive. *Crossroads of Civilization: 3000 Years of Persian History*. New York: Barnes & Noble, 1979.

Isidore of Charax. *Parthian Stations: An Account of the Overland Trade Between the Levant and India in the First Century B.C.* Chicago: Ares, 1976. Reprint of 1914 London edition. Translated by Wilfred H. Schoff.

Kirchner, Walther. *Commercial Relations Between Russia and Europe 1400 to 1800*. Bloomington: Indiana University Press, 1946. Volume 33 in the Russian and East European series.

Klimburg-Salter, Deborah E. *The Silk Route and the Diamond Path: Esoteric Buddhist Art on the Trans-Himalayan Trade Routes*. Los Angeles: University of California, Los Angeles, Art Council, 1982.

Koestler, Arthur. *The Thirteenth Tribe: The Khazar Empire and Its Heritage*. London: Pan, 1977.

Krader, Lawrence. *Peoples of Central Asia*, 3rd edition. Bloomington: Indiana University Press, 1971. Volume 26 in the Uralic and Altaic series.

Kuhn, Delia, and Ferdinand Kuhn. *Borderlands*. New York: Knopf, 1962.

Kwanten, Luc. *Imperial Nomads: A History of Central Asia, 500-1500*. Philadelphia: University of Pennsylvania Press, 1979.

de Lacoupérie, Terrien. *Western Origins of Early Chinese Civilization: From 2300 B.C. to 200 A.D. or Chapters on the Elements Derived from Old Civilizations of West Asia, in the Formation of the Ancient Chinese Culture*. London: Asher, 1894.

Larsen, M.T. *Old Assyrian Caravan Procedures*. Istanbul: Nederlands Historisch-Archaeologisch Institut in Het Nabije OØsten, 1967.

Latourette, Kenneth Scott. *The Chinese: Their History and Culture*, 4th edition, two volumes in one. New York: Macmillan, 1967.

Lattimore, Owen. "Caravan Routes of Inner Asia." *Geographical Journal*, Vol. 72 (December 1928), pp. 497-531.
————. *Inner Asian Frontiers of China*. Boston: Little, Brown, 1962.
————. "Origins of the Great Wall of China." *Geographical Review*, Vol. 27, (October 1937), pp. 529-49.
————. "A Ruined Nestorian City in Inner Mongolia." *Geographical Journal*, Vol. 84 (December 1934), pp. 481-97.
————. *Studies in Frontier History: Collected Papers 1929-58*. London: Oxford University Press, 1962.
————. *The Desert Road to Turkestan*. Boston: Little, Brown, 1929.

Lattimore, Owen, and Eleanor Lattimore, eds. *Silks, Spices and Empire: Asia Seen Through the Eyes of Its Discoverers*. New York: Delacorte, 1968. Part of the Great Explorers series.

Laufer, Berthold. *Jade: A Study in Chinese Archaelogy and Religion.* Chicago: Field Museum of Natural History, 1912. Publication 154, Anthropological Series, Volume 10. Reprint, New York: Dover, 1974.

——. *Sino-Iranica: Chinese Contributions to the History of Civilization in Ancient Iran: With Special Reference to the History of Cultural Plants and Products.* Chicago: Field Museum of Natural History, 1919. Publication 207, Anthropological Series, Number 3.

Leemans, W.F. *Foreign Trade in the Old Babylonian Period as Revealed by Texts from Southern Mesopotamia.* Leiden: E.J. Brill, 1960.

Legg, Stuart. *The Heartland.* New York: Farrar, Straus & Giroux, 1971.

Lewis, Bernard. *The Arabs in History.* New York: Harper, 1960.

——, editor. *Islam and the Arab World: Faith, People, Culture.* New York: Knopf, with American Heritage, 1976.

Lewis, Richard Percival. *Genghis Khan.* New York: Stein and Day, 1969.

Lloyd, Seton. *Early Highland Peoples of Anatolia.* London: Thames and Hudson, 1967. Part of the Library of the Early Civilizations.

Lopez, Robert S., and Irving W. Raymond, translators and editors. *Medieval Trade in the Mediterranean World.* New York: Norton, n.d. Part of the Records of Civilization, Sources and Studies series.

McGovern, W.M. *The Early Empires of Central Asia: A Study of the Scythians and the Huns and the Part They Played in World History.* Chapel Hill: University of North Carolina Press, 1939.

Menen, Aubrey. *Cities in the Sand.* New York: Dial, 1973.

Micheli, Silvio. *Mongolia: In Search of Marco Polo and Other Adventurers.* New York: Harcourt, Brace & World, 1967.

Miller, James Innes. *Spice Trade of the Roman Empire, 29 B.C. to A.D. 641.* Oxford: Clarendon Press, 1969.

Mirsky, Jeanette, editor. *The Great Chinese Travelers.* New York: Random House, 1964.

——. *Sir Aurel Stein: Archaeological Explorer.* Chicago and London: University of Chicago Press, 1977.

Morton, W. Scott. *China: Its History and Culture.* New York: Lippincott and Crowell, 1980.

Moscati, Sabatino. *The Face of the Ancient Orient: A Panorama of Near Eastern Civilization in Pre-Classical times.* Garden City, New York: Doubleday, 1962.

Munro, Eleanor C. *Through the Vermilion Gates: A Journey Into China's Past.* New York: Pantheon, 1971.

Myrdal, Jan. *The Silk Road: A Journey From the High Pamirs and Ili Through Sinkiang and Kansu.* New York: Pantheon, 1979. Translated from the Swedish by Ann Henning.

Needham, Joseph. *Science and Civilization in China*, Volume 1- . London: Cambridge University Press, 1954–

Nöldeke, Theodore. *Sketches from Eastern History.* Beirut: Khayats, 1963. Reprint of 1892 London edition. English translation by John Sutherland.

Obolensky, Dimitri. *The Byzantine Commonwealth: Eastern Europe, 500-1453.* New York: Praeger, 1971. Part of the Praeger History of Civilization series.

Pan Ku. *The History of the Former Han Dynasty*, 2 volumes. New York: American Council of Learned Societies, 1944. Translated by H. Dubs.

Panikkar, K.M. *A Survey of Indian History*, 3rd edition. Bombay: Asia Publishing House, 1956.

Pareti, Luigi, et al. *The Ancient World 1200 B.C. to A.D. 500.* New York: Harper & Row, 1965. Volume II of UNESCO's *History of Mankind: Cultural and Scientific Development.*

Parker, E.H. *A Thousand Years of the Tartars*, 2nd edition. New York: Knopf, 1926. Part of the History of Civilization series.

Parker, W.H. *An Historical Geography of Russia.* Chicago: Aldine, 1969.

Penkala, Maria. *A Correlated History of the Far East: China, Korea, Japan.* The Hague and Paris: Mouton, 1966.

Penrose, Boies. *Travel and Discovery in the Renaissance, 1420-1620.* New York: Atheneum, 1972. Reprint of Harvard University Press, 1952 edition.

Perkins, John, with the American Museum of Natural History. *To the Ends of the Earth: Four Expeditions to the Arctic, the Congo, the Gobi, and Siberia.* New York: Pantheon, 1981.

Phillips, E.D. *The Royal Hordes: Nomad Peoples of the Steppes.* London: Thames and Hudson, 1965. Part of the Library of the Early Civilizations.
———. *The Mongols.* New York: Praeger, 1969. Part of the Ancient Peoples and Places series.

Piggott, Stuart. *Prehistoric India: To 1000 B.C.* Harmondsworth: Penguin, 1950.

Plinius Secundus, C. (Pliny The Elder). *Natural History*, 10 volumes. Cambridge, Massachusetts: Harvard University Press, Loeb Classical Library, 1938. Translated by H. Rackham.

Polo, Marco. *The Travels of Marco Polo.* Harmondsworth: Penguin, 1979. Translated by Ronald Latham.

————. *The Book of Ser Marco Polo, the Venetian...* New York: Scribner, 1926. Translated and edited by Col. Sir Henry Yule, 3rd edition revised by Henri Cordier.

Pulleybank, E.G. "Han China in Central Asia." *International Historical Review*, Vol. 3, pp. 278-86.

Rawlley, Ratan C. *Silk Industry and Trade: A Study in the Economic Organizations of the Export Trade of Kashmir and Indian Silk with Special Reference to Their Utilization in the British and French Markets.* London: P.S. King & Son, 1919.

Reischauer, Edwin O., and John K. Fairbank. *East Asia: The Great Tradition.* Boston: Houghton Mifflin, 1960. Volume One of *A History of East Asian Civilization*; see Fairbank.

Roberts, Frances Markley. *Western Travellers to China.* Shanghai: Kelley and Walsh, 1932.

Robinson, Stuart. *History of Dyed Textiles.* Cambridge, Massachusetts: MIT Press, 1969.

Roerich, George Nicholas. *Trails to Inmost Asia: Five Years of Exploration With the Roerich Central Asian Expedition.* New Haven, Connecticut: Yale University Press, 1931.

Rostovzeff, Mikhail Ivanovich. *Caravan Cities.* Oxford: Clarendon Press, 1932. Translated by E. And T. Talbot Rice.
————. *Social and Economic History of the Roman Empire*, 2 volumes, 2nd edition. Oxford: Clarendon Press, 1957.
————. *Iranians and Greeks in South Russia.* New York: Russell and Russell, 1969. Reprint of 1922 Clarendon edition.
————. *Social and Economic History of the Hellenistic World*, 3 volumes. Oxford: Clarendon Press, 1941.

Sabloff, Jeremy A., and C.C. Lamberg-Karlovsky, editors. *Ancient Civilization and Trade.* Albuquerque: University of New Mexico Press, 1975.

Salisbury, Charlotte Y. *Tibetan Diary.* New York: Walker, 1981.

Saunders, J.J. *The History of the Mongol Conquests.* New York: Barnes & Noble, 1971.

Schafer, Edward H. "The Camel in China Down to the Mongol Dynasty." *Sinologica*, Vol. 2 (1950), pp. 165-94, 263-90.
————. *The Golden Peaches of Samarkand: A Study of T'ang Exotics.* Berkeley and Los Angeles: University of California Press, 1963.

Schober, Joseph. *Silk and Silk Industry.* New York: Richard R. Smith, 1930. Translated by R. Cuthill.

Schoff, W.H. *Early Communication Between China and the Mediterranean.* Philadelphia: no publisher listed, 1925.

Schreiber, Hermann. *The History of Roads: From Amber Route to Motorway*. London: Barrie and Rockliff, 1961. Translated by Stewart Thomson.

Seligman, C.G. "The Roman Orient and the Far East," *Antiquity*, Vol. 11 (1937), pp. 5ff. Also Annual Reports of the Smithsonian Institution 1938, pp. 547ff.
———. "Some Aspects of the Overland Oriental Trade at the Christian Era." *Journal of the American Oriental Society*, Vol. 35 (1915), pp. 31ff.

Severin, Timothy. *The Oriental Adventure: Explorers of the East*. Boston: Little, Brown, 1976.

Sherwood, Merriam, and Elmer Mantz. *The Road to Cathay*. New York: Macmillan, 1928.

Simkin, C.G.F. *The Traditional Trade of Asia*. London: Oxford University Press, 1968.

Skrine, C.P. *Chinese Central Asia*. New York: Barnes & Noble, 1971. Reprint of 1926 edition.

Skrine, Francis Henry, and Edward Denison Ross. *The Heart of Asia: A History of Russian Turkestan and the Central Asian Khanates from the Earliest Times*. London: Methuen, 1899.

Spuler, Bertold. *History of the Mongols: Based on Eastern and Western Accounts of the 13th and 14th Centuries*. Berkeley and Los Angeles: University of California Press, 1972. English translation by Helga and Stuart Drummond.

Stark, Freya. *Rome on the Euphrates: The Story of a Frontier*. New York: Harcourt, Brace & World, 1966.
———. *The Valley of the Assassins: and Other Persian Travels*. Los Angeles: J.P. Tarcher, n.d. Reprint of 1936 edition. Part of the Library of Travel Classics.

Stein, Aurel. *Innermost Asia: Detailed Report of Explorations in Central Asia, Kan-su and Eastern Iran*, 5 volumes. Oxford: Clarendon Press, 1928.
———, edited by Jeannette Mirsky. *On Ancient Central-Asian Tracks: Brief Narrative of Three Expeditions in Innermost Asia and Northwestern China*. New York: Pantheon, 1964.

Sullivan, Michael. *A Short History of Chinese Art*. Berkeley and Los Angeles: University of California Press, 1967.

Teggart, Frederick John. *Rome and China: A Study of Correlations in Historical Events*. Berkeley: University of California Press, 1939.

Toynbee, A., editor. *Cities of Destiny*. New York: McGraw-Hill, 1967.

Trippett, Frank, and editors of Time-Life Books. *The First Horsemen*. New York: Time-Life Books, 1974. Part of the Emergence of Man series.

Vlahos, Olivia. *Far Eastern Beginnings*. New York: Viking, 1976.

Vollmer, John E., et al. *Silk Roads—China Ships*. Toronto: Royal Ontario Museum, 1983.

Von Grunebaum, Gustave E. *Medieval Islam: A Study in Cultural Orientation*, 2nd edition. Chicago: University of Chicago Press, 1961.

Von Hagen, Victor Wolfgang. *The Roads That Led to Rome*. Cleveland and New York: World, 1967.

Waley, Arthur. *Ballads and Stories from Tun Huang*. New York: Macmillan, 1960.
———. "The Heavenly Horses of Ferghana: A New View." *History Today*, Vol. 5 (1955), pp. 95-103.
———. *The Secret History of the Mongols and Other Pieces*. London: George Allen and Unwin, 1963.

Warmington, Eric Herbert. *The Commerce Between the Roman Empire and India*. New York: Octagon Books, 1974. Reprint of Cambridge University Press edition of 1928.

Watson, Burton, translator and editor. *Records of the Historian: Chapters from the SHIH CHI of Ssu-ma Ch'ien*. New York: Columbia University Press, 1969.

Wheeler, Mortimer. *Civilizations of the Indus Valley and Beyond*. London: Thames and Hudson, 1966. Part of the Library of Ancient Civilizations.
———. *Rome Beyond the Imperial Frontiers*. London: G. Bell, 1954.

Wintle, Justin. *The Dragon's Almanac: Chinese, Japanese and Other Far Eastern Proverbs*. London: Routledge and Kegan Paul, 1983.

Wu, K.C. *The Chinese Heritage*. New York: Crown, 1982.

Yu, Anthony C., translator and editor. *The Journey to the West*, 4 volumes. Chicago: University of Chicago Press, 1977.

Yule, Henry. *Cathay and the Way Thither*, 2nd edition, 2 volumes. Taipei: Ch'eng-Wen, 1966. Revised by Henri Cordier; based on original 1866 edition.

Zewen, Luo, et al. *The Great Wall*. New York: McGraw-Hill, 1981.

INDEX